CREATING A HOMELAND

A True Story of Dedication, Sacrifice,
and Pioneering Spirit in the Creation of the
Modern State of Israel

DAN GIELAN

NEGEV BOOKS   SANTA MONICA, CA

Published by Negev Books
A subsidiary of Solaray LLC
1223 Wilshire Blvd.
Suite 755
Santa Monica, CA 90403

First printing August, 2018
Second edition March 2021

Printed in the United States of America

Edited by Janis Leibs Dworkis

Cover designed by David Gielan

When ordinary people rise to the occasion
and perform extraordinary feats.

To
Michelle, David, Ron, Adam, and Gil

Know your heritage.

Part I

SAM

Chapter 1

Sam hurried down the deserted city street, stepping on the pavement as softly as he could. He was anxious and concerned. He was anxious because he was getting awfully late and needed to hasten his pace, yet he was concerned about the sounds of his footsteps being echoed loudly by the buildings on both sides. He wished he could have chosen a different pair of shoes, possibly with rubber soles, but sadly this was the only pair of shoes he had, and it would have to do, noise and all.

Every so often he would look over his shoulder, not too conspicuously but long enough to see that the street behind him was empty. Several times he even ducked into an entranceway of an apartment building, stopped, and waited quietly to make sure that he was not being followed.

He glanced at his watch and realized he was getting dangerously late. His orders were to reach his destination between 6:15 and 6:18 a.m. yet he still had some distance to cover. Following his original plan, he would have arrived there by now, but part way his trusted Norton motorcycle ran out of gas and he was forced to abandon it and proceed on foot.

The large scruffy brown leather suitcase circa 1920s was weighing heavily on his right arm, but he barely felt it, so intent was he on making sure that he would not be intercepted by anyone on his way. He was alert to any extraneous sound or movement in front of him, or anywhere within his "safety zone." Meeting anyone on the street at this point, be it friend or foe, would most certainly jeopardize his mission, and possibly endanger his, or others', lives. The suitcase he was carrying contained some extremely precious cargo, and it was vitally important that it be delivered intact at the designated location by the specified time.

The sun had just come up over the horizon and thank God the weather was exceptionally cool for this November morning of 1939. Despite moving quite rapidly and carrying a heavy suitcase, he barely broke a sweat. He, who while being fit and trim, sweat profusely at every opportunity, this morning he was managing this trek perfectly, and that was of paramount importance to him.

Sam reached the corner of the street. He slowed down for a split second, long enough to scan the cross street on his right to make sure that it was clear. He made a right turn and traveled the short block to the next corner. Mid-block he crossed to the other side and hugged the brick fence surrounding the last building on the left. At that corner he crouched some, and peered over the fence to scan the street. It was deserted, so he straightened up and turned left following the curvature of the fence.

As he reached the middle of the building, two British paratroopers with their red berets and their Sten submachine guns slung over their shoulders, stepped out of the entranceway to the building two doors down.

They heard his footsteps and turned, facing him. Within a split second Sam realized that it was too late—were he to turn and run, he would be dead before reaching the corner. His mind was racing, and the adrenalin rushed through his body. He tried to calm himself and restore his clear thinking, all the while continuing to walk toward them, and possibly toward death. If they followed orders and searched his suitcase they would discover the two pistols, 100 rounds of ammunition, the Lee Enfield rifle, and two hand grenades he was carrying. The penalty for a Jew carrying a weapon of any kind was death, either by hanging or by firing squad. No mercy.

He himself was unarmed and the weapons in the suitcase were all disassembled. A shootout with these two British soldiers was not an option, and despite the military training he had undergone every week he was no killer, so he took the only course of action that he could.

Without missing a beat, he continued walking confidently toward the two soldiers who, for some reason, remained calm and at ease seeing him approach them. Maybe it was his non-hesitant body language, or his light complexion, or his deep blue eyes, for whatever reason, they did not react as they should have and go on the alert. Sten submachine guns remained slung over their shoulders.

He approached and addressed them in perfect English with the most British accent he could muster; very matter of fact, nothing out of the ordinary, his internal terror suppressed.

"Pardon me, gentlemen, could you please point me in the direction of Maaze Street?"

"Certainly, sir," one of the soldiers replied. Oh, the polite British, always so courteous, gentlemanly, and willing to assist! "Make a right turn at the next corner, proceed for three city blocks, and then make a left turn. That would be Maaze Street."

"Thank you very much. Have a good day," Sam said with a polite smile as he passed between them.

The two soldiers watched him walk away, suitcase in hand. Probably his calm disposition and his incredible British accent, doubly incredible for a person who had never been to England, had mentally disarmed these two soldiers to the point that they permitted him to proceed on his way without question.

He did not run. He walked the remainder of the block and made the turn to the right as they had directed him to do. As he rounded the corner they must have realized their mistake in letting him go unsearched, and he could hear them calling after him "Halt!" "Halt!" but by then it was too late—he sprang into a superfast sprint.

He could hear them giving him chase, and he ran as fast as he could. At 5'7" and 140 lbs. he was in excellent shape, and were it not for the heavy suitcase, they would not have had a chance of catching up with him. He had another advantage: Having lived in the city for the past five years he knew every nook and cranny in this neighborhood, let alone the locations of the secret passages which he was taught as part of his training.

He quickly passed the first two buildings on his right and ducked into the third entrance. He had been taught that the third element in a series is the one most overlooked. In sharpshooter training, when you have a five round sequence it is invariably the third bullet that goes wild, so he figured they would search the first two buildings, and ignore the third.

He ran up the stairs to the roof of the four-story structure, but despite his theory about them missing the third, he could hear them coming up the stairs behind him. Maybe they had caught a glimpse of him as he entered the building?

He ran toward the back wall of the roof. There, exactly as it was supposed to be, was the plank over the ledge, connecting this building with the one next door. Nothing more than a foot-wide piece of construction lumber, and now he was going to trust his life to it. With one leap he hopped, suitcase and all, onto the wooden plank. He dashed across the void between the buildings, not looking down to not lose his balance, and landed on the other side. With no time to waste he put the suitcase down, lifted the board from the top of the ledge, and let it drop to the yard below hitting the ground with a very loud thud—let the British soldiers think that he fell with the plank, that would slow them down some. He then quickly picked up the suitcase and ducked into the rooftop doorway entrance and into the stairwell.

In no time at all he was at the bottom of the staircase, having taken the three flights of stairs two steps at a time. He dashed toward the back of the small lobby, pulled out his pocket knife, and inserted it into a slot in between two bricks in the wall. He heard the latch release and saw the trap door pop up from the floor, wide enough for him to grab the edge and lift it up. The gaping void underneath was in total darkness but he jumped into the unknown and disappeared into the tunnel under the floor. He stopped and before proceeding made sure that the trap door was secured and shut tight above him. Using his cigarette lighter he followed the long tunnel under several buildings, and emerged at its end three streets away from where he had started.

He reached the front of the address on Geula Street, his true destination, precisely at 6:18 a.m. and saw no one waiting for him. As he was instructed to do, he stopped at the entrance to number 13, knelt down on his right knee and fiddled with his left shoe lace. Without a sound, out of nowhere two young men appeared carrying a burlap sack each, and one of them uttered a single word "Opera." Sam quietly responded "Carmen." Those were the authentication tokens serving as the password. He opened the suitcase and emptied its contents of weapons and ammunition into the bags.

They did not introduce themselves, did not stop to chat, nor tell him why they needed the weapons. In silence they quickly put the bags over their shoulders, and motioned him to leave. He did not look back.

Sam guessed where these weapons were heading and knew how important they were for his colleagues and co-conspirators. A bit further down Geula Street was the southernmost perimeter position of the Haganah protecting the Jewish civilian population of Tel Aviv from their Arab neighbors to the south in Jaffa. From time to time small bands of Arabs would come up from Jaffa and attack the Jews in the southern portion of Tel Aviv, and this position was meant to repel their next attack whenever it came.

Occasionally, the minaret of Hassan Bek mosque in the Manshiya section of Jaffa would be the perch of an Arab sniper. Any Jew walking down one of the streets leading north was in danger of being shot, and the purpose of the Lee Enfield rifle was to hit that sharpshooter and stop him from killing the pedestrians on their way to buy groceries.

Sam picked up the suitcase and started climbing up Geula Street, taking an alternate return route to his motorcycle. He was no longer in a hurry, yet was still alert to not bump into the same two British Paratroopers he encountered before. He reached Allenby Street, a major north-south thoroughfare in Tel Aviv, and by now he was not alone. The city was waking up and workers were heading toward their daily routines, totally oblivious to the drama that he had experienced but a few moments ago.

He could not relate the incident to anyone, he realized. Not to his bride of eight months, Leah, not to his father who lived with them, and definitely not to anyone else. He knew that Leah suspected that he was a member of the Haganah underground, and he surmised that she was too, but they never told each other what they were up to. A code of silence prevailed, meant to protect the other party more than yourself: Should he get captured and interrogated he could not betray her and neither could she if she were to be captured and under duress. Although the British were not known to torture their prisoners, they still knew how to extract information from "terrorists."

Until circumstances changed drastically in the country, and the occupying British forced to leave, neither of them could share their experiences with the other, and that might take quite a few more years. A strange imposition on their married life no doubt, but he was sure that the same situation existed with many of his friends and colleagues whom he suspected, but did not factually know, were involved in the underground.

He knew very few people within the organization, only those who fairly regularly arrived for training in the sand dunes southeast of the city. The whole underground movement was cell-based to avoid one cell exposing another. From time to time he received messages, dispatches of missions to execute, like the one this morning, or to appear for training, but he would only know the messenger by face, never by name, and in this small city that was incredible in itself.

This time, the messenger had arrived at his ground-floor apartment around midnight, and knocked on the bedroom window. The rap on the window was faint, but loud enough to wake Sam up from his deep sleep. As always, a remnant of his service in the Latvian Air Force, when awakened he was fully alert and cognizant of his surroundings. He quickly yet quietly rose from the bed, so as not to disturb Leah who was sleeping beside him, and swiftly walked to the window. All he saw in the darkness was the silhouette of a man standing in the yard. Sam opened the window, and the man said one word only, "dark," to which Sam replied "skies." The man then produced a small piece of paper out of his pocket, handed it to Sam, turned around and quickly disappeared into the darkness.

By the light of the small candle always burning in the kitchen Sam studied the note, torn from a notebook. Someone had scribbled on it in Hebrew:

"*Two rocks, two whistles, 100 peas, and one stick, Geula 13 06:15—06:18. Left shoe lace. Opera = Carmen.*"

Sam memorized its contents, and then burnt the note in the flame of the candle. He knew what he had to do, and that keeping the note intact would not be wise, and was against orders.

At 5:30 a.m. he was fully dressed and ready to move. He reached under the kitchen sink and quietly lifted the false bottom of the cabinet. He extracted the two grenades, the two pistols, the 100 rounds of ammunition, and the disassembled Lee Enfield, and restored the false bottom of the cabinet to its place. There were a few other weapons in the hiding place, but the orders were specific. He was sure the other weapons were already spoken for—there were not enough of them to go around.

His elderly father sleeping in the next room was snoring comfortably as Sam tiptoed out of the house. He was sure that Leah was awake and praying for his safety—these missions were dangerous, and she never knew if he would be back in the morning, or ever.

He tied the suitcase to the back seat of the Norton and pushed the heavy machine to the corner. He did not want to kick-start it in front of the house, and once he got to the corner he could coast down the hill some before starting the motorcycle by its momentum. The less noise he made, the less attention he attracted, the higher the probability was that he will succeed in his mission and come back alive.

Now, with the mission successfully completed he was back at the Norton. He would have to go get some gas for the machine so in the interim he secured the motorcycle to a fence and walked the one-mile home, suitcase in hand. He did not want to be seen coming home with the suitcase, so he cut through the back yard and entered through the side entrance of his apartment house.

Close call with the British Paratroopers, he acknowledged. Close call with his life.

How did he ever get himself into this? He wondered.

What brought him to risk his life like that?

Chapter 2

Winters in Riga, the capital of Latvia, were always bitterly cold and damp, with snow and ice all around and strong winds coming off the Baltic Sea. Although officially considered a temperate climate it was far from that during the winters, not much different than the climate on the seashores of southern Finland.

Walking back from school 7-years-old Sam was shivering. Even with the multiple layers of clothing his mother had dressed him in, he felt the chill of the wind seeping in under his topcoat and his teeth rattled. It was not more than half a mile distance between his school and his home, but by the time he got home he would feel totally frozen. Thank God for the fireplace in the parlor of his home at 21 Blaumana Street. During the winter months it was almost always lit, stacked with crackling wood, and warming the first floor of the house.

And then there also was the wood-burning stove with its chimney sticking out in the middle of the hallway that spread its warmth to the upstairs bedrooms. The basement also had a stove, and it provided heat throughout the servants' quarters, making the entire house so very pleasant and cozy to come into, especially when there was a storm outside.

Coming home from school Sam was always greeted by his mother, and she doted over him excessively. No wonder, he was her baby. Her next older child, Philip, was already in his late teens, and like most other teens of any generation not too interested in his mother's attention. He was, as were his older siblings Tanya and Isaac, more of a product of their father who was not the warmest and most affectionate individual. A stern disciplinarian who always seemed to barely tolerate them, their father showed no outward signs of caring. Without a doubt Haim did not know how to relate to children, or how to raise them; he wisely then left that to their mother. He insisted that they be educated well, study hard, and be respectful of their parents, other adults, and even the servants, all in the finest of Jewish traditions. But he never spent much idle time with them, never took them to the park or for an outing, or otherwise had much communication with them. He observed them from afar, demanding and foreboding, remote in his world, yet not aloof. The only activity he insisted that the boys join him in—Tanya being a girl was excused—was attending synagogue every Saturday and Holidays and the daily prayers when he was in town. He was a fiercely observant Jew and maintained a strictly kosher home, but his religious learning did not encompass some of the basic philosophy of Jewish life, with its familial closeness and warmth of the heart.

Bella on the other hand was a gentle creature, friendly and warm to everyone, and a wonderfully attentive mother to her children. Her first three came in close succession within the first six years of her marriage to Haim, and she was very happy and content in having them around, and giving them all the attention and affection she could. Along with the love came the caring, and she was extremely attuned to their health, both physical and mental. She was always watching the children's moods, being on the lookout for any issues that might suggest emotional discomfort, especially depression, knowing full well that depression and suicidal tendencies had been not uncommon among her ancestral family. After all, her own niece Dussia, daughter of her late sister Zelda, had committed suicide at 16 years of age, and that was not the only such case within her family.

No wonder then that Sam adored his mother and was deeply attached to her. At the same time, he treated his father with respect and consideration, but with no closeness of the heart. He admired his father, seeing among other things how others treated him with respect. He was recognized as a learned Jew and a successful businessman, a pillar of the Riga Jewish community.

On this cold day in early November 1917, there was a hefty layer of fresh snow on the ground. On the way from school Sam had to cross the open field of the park, then circle past the stadium, and make his way home along the other side of the street, and the snow on the ground made it slow going.

As he approached the stadium Sam noticed something quite peculiar that he had never seen before: Someone had shoveled the snow from the side street to the main entrance to the stadium. He wondered: Why would anyone clear a path, wide enough for a cart or truck to pass, in the midst of winter when the stadium was idle with no games being played there until the spring? "That path is great. It is a gift," he thought. "It is leading toward home, so I can use it instead of walking in the deep snow."

So rather than crossing the field diagonally as he always did, he turned to the right to intercept the path at its beginning near the door of the stadium. As he approached the entrance to the stadium he noticed that one of the doors was ajar.

The curiosity of the 7-year-old boy got the better of him, and he decided to investigate what was going on there. He knew that his mother would not be worried about him arriving a few minutes late from school, so why not check it out?

Gingerly, Sam poked his head through the door. He did not want to be noticed, so he did not open it further lest it might creak or squeak and that would give his presence there away. Once his head was through, he realized that it was open wide enough for his entire body to pass through, school bag and all, so he quietly entered the stadium, staying by the door.

Sam looked around. In the middle of the field he saw a line of people, mostly men but a few women too, all with their hands behind them, standing shoulder to shoulder before posts stuck in the ground. They were all dressed in street clothes, without coats, and probably cold, he figured. He did not understand what was going on, and why this bizarre sight. For the moment he stayed put, trying to figure out what these people were doing in the middle of the field. Then he heard voices, so he knew there must be some other people in the stadium, but he could not see them because the bleachers on his right and left blocked his view.

He started moving forward then stopped. He recognized the second man from the right as his next-door neighbor Mr. Levin, the father of his best friend Moishe. Why was Mr. Levin here? He wondered.

Mr. Levin looked straight at him. There was no question that he recognized Sam, but he did not smile as he normally would do. Instead, with a single movement of his head from left to right he motioned Sam to get away. There was no doubt about it, Mr. Levin was telling him to scoot, scram, and get out of there. But why? Mr. Levin kept looking at him to make sure he obeyed, and he started to turn around and go, but before he could move one step the noise arrived—that terrible sound of a machine gun in rapid fire. He knew that sound so well, the fighting between the Russians and the Germans in and around Riga had been going on for quite a while, but it had stopped a few weeks ago when the Germans took the city back from the Russian invaders. He turned back around and now Mr. Levin's head, as all the others' heads hung low, and their clothes stained red, and Sam knew that all of them were dead.

He ran. He ran for his life, being sure that if the Germans had seen or heard him they would kill him as they had killed the line of people. Why did they shoot these people? Mr. Levin was such a gentle man, so kind and friendly, with a family and children, and now he was dead!

He ran all the way home, his book pack weighing heavily on his back. He ran like the devil was chasing him, terrified and traumatized. The front door was unlocked and he burst inside, closing and bolting the door behind him, and then he heaved this deep cry of torment, coming from the depth of his soul.

His mother ran from the parlor toward him, picked him up and held him to her chest. She did not know what had caused this boy's deep anguish, but she could tell that something very terrible had happened.

It took Sam the longest time, clinging to his mother, before his hysterical crying somewhat subsided, and she could finally ask him if he was all right. Still unable to speak, he nodded confirming he was not injured, something she had surmised already. Throughout the time she was hugging him she passed her hands over his small body and made sure he was not physically hurt.

When his crying changed to sobbing she finally asked him: "What happened, Mulya?"

"Mr. Levin is dead," he sobbed.

"Mr. Levin?"

He nodded.

"Are you sure?" She asked.

Beyond wanting confirmation, she was trying to get him to verbalize. She wanted to hear him speak coherently.

He nodded to the affirmative, still sobbing.

"How did he die?"

"Shot by the Germans," he finally said.

"Where? How do you know?"

"In the stadium. I saw."

"What was he doing there that he got shot?"

"Don't know. He was standing with other people in a row, with his hands behind his back, and they shot them all dead."

"What were you doing in the stadium?" She asked in an inquisitive tone. She was careful not to sound admonishing or critical; the boy had just been through a life-altering trauma, and she did not want to aggravate the situation and exacerbate the damage.

"I was passing by on my way from school, and saw the stadium door open and wanted to see why," he explained, and went on telling her the whole thing in detail. That was precisely what this mother in her wisdom wanted her child to do, to cleanse himself by relating the story, and not keep it bottled up within him.

"He wanted to protect me," said Sam. "The last thing he did before dying was signaling me to get out of there, but I still saw him being shot dead before running home as fast as I could."

"You are a brave boy," Bella said, "and I am glad that you are safe, at home with me. When your brothers come home you should tell them also." She wanted this incident to leave as little a lasting shock as possible, and by retelling the story it would then become more ordinary than otherwise.

She did not suggest he tell his father as he was out of town, and even if he were in town she would not have recommended it. After twenty-four years of marriage to Haim she knew he would not appreciate the significance of the impact on the boy, and would probably dismiss it as the product of a vivid imagination of a 7-year-old, causing more harm to his son than he had already endured.

She waited for a while longer to let her son quiet down before calling Maria, the chief housekeeper to get some food for Sam.

"Mama," Sam finally asked what had been on his mind all this time, "why did the Germans shoot Mr. Levin?"

"I don't know for sure," she said softly, "but I think because he was selling to the Russian soldiers while they were here occupying the city, and the Germans considered him a 'collaborator,' and a traitor to them."

She waited for a few more minutes before putting on her coat and dashing out next door to Yaakov Levin's home to console his wife and children. By now they probably knew what had befallen their husband and father, and if not, then she would have to be the bearer of bad news.

❖ ❖ ❖

Bella wished she could communicate the sad news of Yaakov's Levin's demise to Haim, but he was out of town, and won't return until Friday afternoon. He owned a wood mill in town by the river, and he normally left Monday morning to the forest where his crew was working cutting the trees down and floating the logs down the river to the mill. Each time he was in another part of the forest, having bought the rights to the trees, and as long as the river did not freeze he stayed away at the site for the entire week, every week, supervising the work of his employees.

She planned to tell Haim the sad news upon his return from the mill on Friday, before he went to the synagogue and found Yaakov's seat empty. But then he arrived late, shortly before sunset, and he hurried to wash and change, to go to shul and welcome the Sabbath. She did not want to relate the story around the dinner table as a family discussion lest he dismiss it somehow, so the first opportunity she would have was after the festive meal. The Shabbat dinner was the traditional meal: Kiddush—the blessing on the wine and challah bread—then the soup, and the gefilte fish, and the chicken dish, and finally some dessert and a hot glass of tea.

Throughout that time Bella was anxious, and she was right to be so because while seated at the table with the entire family, just before dessert, Haim mentioned that Yaakov Levin did not show up for prayers at the synagogue that evening, something he had never done before. He was about to ask her if she knew where he was, but she quickly threw him a glance that stopped him cold in midsentence. She clearly did not want to discuss it at the table, and he understood her gesture.

When the meal was over and just the two of them retired to the parlor, she finally told Haim what had happened to Yaakov, and he was stricken with grief. Despite Yaakov being quite a bit younger than he was, they had a special bond between them. They normally sat together in shul, and whenever not in prayer conversed about worldly affairs and their businesses. Yaakov had a small tannery and leather-goods factory, and although not yet as successful as Haim's wood-supply company, he was only in the early years of his business and was hoping for it to grow with time.

Unfortunately, now it will never happen, never.

And who will take care of the family with Yaakov gone?

Chapter 3

Exactly one year later, with the war over and the Germans defeated, in November 1918 Latvia declared its independence with pomp and circumstance. But to Sam, a young boy of 8, it did not matter much. His life did not change in any significant way because of it, neither at home nor at school, with the exception that he no longer saw foreign soldiers, German or Russian or any others occupying the city—they all scared him and he was relieved they were gone. He followed the routine of attending elementary school in the mornings, followed by lunch at home with his mother and occasionally one or both of his brothers, and then dashing over to the cheder for Bible and religious studies for the bulk of the afternoon.

The only significant recent change in his life was that since the event at the stadium his mother would walk with him to school and be there to pick him up after classes, something that he really enjoyed. No kids in his class lived on his street, and walking back and forth was kind of lonely without anyone to talk to, and he thought it was somewhat scary too.

Although he tried very hard, for the longest time he could not shake off the memory of the stadium, and Mr. Levin. The images of Mr. Levin and the others being hit by the bullets, then their bodies going limp and sliding down the posts were not going away. They were as vivid to him a year later as they were the day it happened. Worse still were the nightmares, night after night, dreaming that he is being chased by the Germans who want to kill him, just as they had killed the others.

He frequently woke up, deeply distraught and frightened, and thank God his mother was there, on a chair by his bedside. With a mother's instinct she would calm him down, speak to him softly and reassuringly, caress him, and make him feel safe in her presence.

And so the years passed by, and the two of them grew incredibly attached to each other.

The only other person to whom he had been strongly attached had been his sister Tanya. She was already a teenager of 15 when he was born, and she "adopted" him, playing surrogate mother to him. Tanya would hold him, feed him, dress him, and act as if he were her own child. The housekeepers certainly also took care of him when his mother was busy and Tanya was in school, but it was not the same. Tanya doted over him—he was so cute, with hair that was allowed to grow long—and for some reason, she dressed him in a knee-high dress that she sewed for him herself. No wonder he adored her.

But when he was barely 4 years old Tanya packed her bags and took the train to St. Petersburg to attend the university there. She left, and except for a brief visit during some summers, the only contact with her were occasional letters that his mother would read from to him. Tanya always asked about him and sent him her love, but what he really wanted was to have her hug and kiss him, as she used to do before she went away to school.

The pain and sense of loss lingered with him for some time, and as time passed Sam began to realize that Tanya would probably never return to Riga, and that made him sad. She did come to Riga for his Bar Mitzvah celebration some years later and brought him a nice gift from Berlin where she was finishing her medical studies, but by then he had detached himself from her, or so he thought. And when she left a few days later, he knew that it was the last time he would see her for many years to come, and the sadness returned.

For Sam, his Bar Mitzvah was a substantial life altering event, and he understood its significance. That is the day that a Jewish boy makes the transition into Jewish adulthood and becomes responsible for his own deeds or misdeeds. He becomes a full-fledged member of the adult society, at least as far as his religious duties are concerned, and is a full participant in adult Jewish society, with all the rights and obligations associated with that.

The traditional Bar Mitzvah ceremony in Riga was performed during morning Sabbath services, where the Bar Mitzvah boy participates, for the first time, in leading the congregation in part, or all, of the prayers. In orthodox congregations, including his father's in Riga, Sam was not called to lead the entire service, since only a man can do that, and until the ceremonial induction he was still considered a boy. Only when the time came for the ceremony to begin would he take center stage, sing the blessings, read from the Torah and another section of the Bible, and sing his closing blessing too.

Somewhat shy Sam was very concerned about his first performance before the congregation. He did not want to embarrass his father, or the Rabbi under whom he studied in preparation for his part in the service. He had studied hard for it: For several months before the date he stayed with the Rabbi after classes in the cheder, and prepared for the reading of the specific Torah portion that he would read at his Bar Mitzvah. Clearly, Sam had already learned how to read the unpunctuated, un-sentenced, Hebrew Torah text consisting almost entirely of consonants and with no vowels, as the Torah was originally written; he even knew how to sing that portion in the traditional way; but his Bar Mitzvah would be the first time that he would read the Torah in public, in front of the entire community attending Sabbath morning services. The Rabbi knew that Sam would be nervous and apprehensive, so he trained him, drilling it into him over and over again to avoid any potential mishaps.

Sam's special day finally arrived and the synagogue was packed with all the "regulars," and a lot of others came to participate in the event. His entire family, uncles and aunts, and cousins galore, came to join in the occasion. Almost the entire section of town where the 40,000 Riga Jews lived was empty, with all the inhabitants packed into the synagogue, or so Sam thought. It was his impression that since that time when the world-renowned cantor Gershon Sirota had performed in this shul, never was the place as full and vibrant as on that day.

When it was time for Sam to come onto the bimah, the raised platform at the center of the synagogue, all eyes were on him but he took it in stride. The women had the vantage point of the balcony from where they could observe with an unimpeded view, and also chat a bit in between prayers. When his name was called, "Shmuel ben Haim,"—Samuel son of Haim—he donned a borrowed tallit, the traditional prayer shawl. As was the custom in this congregation he will not get his own tallit until his wedding day.

Sam stepped up to take his place next to the Rabbi facing the Ark, and read his section of the Torah flawlessly to the relief of his Rabbi. Not all students were gifted, and music and singing were not among Sam's known fortes, but reading from the Torah is not true singing, so he performed it well, to the tremendous joy and pride of his well-wishers. Only his father did not show any outward signs of satisfaction or relief that Sam did well, and the boy, now "adult," noticed that. It was so important for him to please his father, he always tried his best to extract some sign of approval from the man, and mostly his wishes were never answered—he never, ever got that word of encouragement from his father whom he so revered.

In his mind, Sam had, by some reasoning, always excused his father's aloofness and coldness, his lack of exhibited warmth toward his wife or children. This time he tried to convince himself that his father's lack of reaction to his achievement was because his father had his own part to perform shortly, and he would show his satisfaction later, but deep inside he knew that commendation would never come.

When he finished his part and stepped back from the podium with the Torah scroll on it, his father stepped up to the same spot and loudly, for the entire congregation to hear, recited the traditional prayer *"Baruch shepetaranu meonsho shel ze"*—— Blessed be He that released us from the punishment of this one—relieving oneself from the sins of the son: The boy just entered Judaic manhood and is responsible for his own deeds, hence the father is no longer responsible to God for them and won't suffer their consequences.

The utterance of this significant prayer signaled the closing of the Bar Mitzvah ceremony, and the ladies on the balcony showered the crowd downstairs with the customary wrapped candy. The whole place burst in singing and blessings, joy and cries of Mazal Tov. Then they hurriedly finished the remainder of the Morning Prayer services and headed out the door.

From there, many of the attendees walked the short distance to Haim and Bella's home where a fabulous lunch was being served. Bella had strenuously worked with the servants to produce a feast for the guests. Not so much the traditional Sabbath lunch—that would be difficult to prepare in a kosher style for such a large crowd—but a well decked buffet laden with cold cuts, and salads, and other goodies, anything that could be served to this large crowd under the strict Sabbath rules.

And, of course, a celebration could not be complete without a lot of schnapps. There were bottles galore of all kinds of alcohol, all strictly kosher of course, and the guests raised a "few" glasses to toast the new adult member of the congregation.

Most of the crowd started dispersing in the afternoon, some going home to catch a snooze before returning to shul for evening prayers, others going home to catch a snooze without returning to shul later. Some even stayed and celebrated until it was time to go back for *Mincha* afternoon services which, it being the middle of March began at 5:35 p.m., and Tanya, who no longer observed the Sabbath, said her good-byes and left for the train station on her way back to Berlin.

By the time the last guests finally left, Bella was overly tired, practically exhausted. It was not like her. Normally, although on the more delicate side, she had tremendous stamina, especially on such a happy occasion as this celebration was. But despite the superb assistance that the servants had provided, by now she could hardly move, and barely had the strength to go upstairs and lie down.

When Haim and Sam returned from the evening services, Bella was nowhere to be found, and that was strange, not like her. She normally waited for them in the parlor, and the three of them would have either a cup of tea if it were early enough, or dinner if it were late as it was today.

Haim sat down and started reading his book as if nothing was out of the ordinary, but Sam was uneasy so he went looking for his mother upstairs.

He never entered his parents' bedroom while his father was home from his trips; he felt that it was inappropriate, and ill mannered. But when his father was away, he would occasionally, gingerly, knock on the bedroom door, even when it was open, to talk to his mother or ask her a question.

The door was open, and he knocked. From the room he heard his mother's voice, faint, sounding tired.

"Who is it?" she asked in Latvian. It could be one of the servants who did not speak Yiddish.

"It's me," answered Sam in Yiddish. Among the family members Yiddish was the language of choice, never Latvian. Because of the unsettled presence of Jews in foreign societies, one year here, next being expelled, they had developed their own universal language, a mix of German and Hebrew with which they could communicate with their brethren, wherever they found themselves.

Still from the doorway, without looking in, he asked, "Are you all right?"

"Come in, Mulya," she responded, ever so weakly.

He walked into the room. She was lying in bed under the covers, and did not raise her head to greet him as she would otherwise do.

He approached the bed, coming into her view. "Are you all right, mama?" he asked again.

"Yes, my sweet, I am just tired, very tired," she answered. "I must have worked on the preparations harder than I thought, and I wanted to rest awhile."

"Thank you so much for the wonderful Bar Mitzvah you prepared. I know it was a lot of work, and I really appreciate what you did for me."

"It is all right," she reached for his arm, brought it to her chest and hugged it. "You deserve it; you are such a great boy." Then she stopped for a moment, as if catching her thoughts, and proceeded, "Now by Jewish law you are no longer a boy, you are a man. Be a good man, my baby child, be a good man."

He nodded.

"I am going to sleep a bit now, please tell Maria to serve dinner for your father and you."

And with that she closed her eyes. Sam put his hand on her forehead, caressed her for a bit, and then walked out of the room.

❖　❖　❖

All day Sunday Bella stayed in bed. Maria brought her breakfast upstairs, and sometime later went back to collect the tray. When she came down Sam noticed his mother had barely touched her food. She was never a "big eater," but after not having had any dinner last night, to have left half of the breakfast on the plate worried Sam. So with his father having gone away for the morning he went upstairs to check up on her.

He knocked on the door, and she must have guessed that it was him because she invited him to come in.

"Good morning, mama, are you better this morning?"

"Much better," she replied, and by the tone of her voice he knew she was not telling him the truth.

"Are you still tired?"

"Yes, and my hips are hurting a bit."

"Do you want me to bring you some aspirin?"

"No, my child. I will be fine in a couple of hours. Tomorrow I will be as good as new."

"God willing, amen," he responded. "Is there anything I can get for you?"

"No, my sweet, I am resting comfortably."

Around noon, Maria brought Bella her lunch, and she nibbled on the food sparingly. Sam knew at that point that his mother was not well, so when his father arrived from shul after the evening prayers, he told him about the fact that his mother had not eaten practically anything all day, and that he was worried about her.

"Moreover," Sam said, "when I put my hand on her forehead last night, I felt that she had a touch of fever."

Haim gave him a stern look, a frown. He was not pleased that his son, now a "grown man," would put his hand on the forehead of a woman, even his mother. That was something that is reserved for himself as her husband.

"We will wait for a few days and see how it goes," his father said. "When I come back from the forest Friday I will decide if she needs to see a doctor. In the meantime, make sure Maria takes care of her while I am gone!"

And with that, Haim rang the servants for dinner. He did not go upstairs to see with his own eyes how his wife was doing; he was hungry and wanted his dinner right then.

On Monday, Haim left early, all businesslike, with barely a grunt toward his son. Bella was still in bed, and since she did not get up, get dressed, and walk him to school as she always did, Sam knew that she must not be well, but she reassured him that she would be fine within a few days.

By Tuesday she felt a bit better, got out of bed and came downstairs, but still did not make the trek with Sam to school and back, as she had done twice every school day before the Bar Mitzvah. Sam knew that the reason she was not accompanying him to school was because she was too weak to make the trips, and not because he was a "grown man" now. So he assured her that he would be fine walking by himself the short distance.

Chapter 4

"Jhyd!" Sam heard the vicious call out in the deserted street.

"Jew!" he heard it again, and before he could react, they were coming from different directions. There were four of them, older and bigger than he was, probably in their late teens, and they were no friends of his.

"жид!! Ebrejs!!" again that derogatory disrespectful term for a person of Jewish persuasion, the battle cry of the anti-Semites, first in Russian then in Latvian.

There was no time for him to run, not with the heavy book bag on his back, and they were closing in on him fast, so he just continued moving forward ready for the beating he was about to receive.

This was not the first time he had been beaten, kicked, and injured. He had been bullied before by other kids in his school for merely being Jewish. He had never harmed anyone, never caused anyone grief, and when they tormented him he never went to the teacher or schoolmaster to complain. For all he knew, they could be anti-Semites as well, and the bullies would not take to it kindly were he to squeal on them.

As a senior in eighth grade in his elementary school, the number of older or bigger kids had diminished, and the ones who could torment him finally relented and let him be, so he had thought he was safe, for a while at least. And next year he would be going to the Hebrew Gymnasia, the local Jewish high school, and he wouldn't have to suffer the humiliation and pain of these encounters anymore, since all the students there were Jews as well, and those would not attack him for no other reason than him being a Jew.

This time it was different, though. He was on his way from school heading home, and these youths were big, and nasty, and outside the framework of a disciplinary institution such as a school where attacking another student was not looked upon favorably, even if the victim was Jewish. This time it was a public street, empty, with no passersby who might intervene and stop them. The sun had already set and within moments it was going to be totally dark.

They started by pushing him from one to another, circling him like a band of vultures, waiting for the kill. Sam did not think they intended to kill him, just beat him up thoroughly, but in their frenzy they might hurt him badly or even inadvertently kill him. Who would know who killed that Jew boy on the street? No one would be held responsible, and they knew it.

Being pulled and pushed back and forth with punches thrown in between, Sam finally lost his balance and fell to the ground. That was the signal to them to start kicking him wherever they could. Thank God for the book bag, and the heavy coat underneath, because those somewhat shielded him from the force of the beatings.

Out of the corner of his eye in the midst of this mayhem, Sam saw a large man fast approaching, a long solid plank of wood in his hand. Who was this man, and what was he going to do with this wood bat? Then Sam saw one of the boys lift a brick over his head to throw it at Sam's head.

The boy had no chance. With one swing of the bat, this burly man now running fast toward them hit the hooligan behind his knees, making him collapse to the pavement, and the brick made a terrible loud crack as it fell on his ribs. Within a split second the man was onto the next closest guy, and the bat connected with his torso in mid back. With a groan, this bully too headed for the ground.

Seeing this, the other two on the far side of Sam lying on the pavement, turned around and ran for their lives, before this man's bat could reach them too. The man stayed focused on the two lying on the ground, and with his bat taught them a lesson that they would not likely forget for the rest of their lives.

It was over as fast as it started, and the man reached out and grabbed Sam's hand and brought him to his feet.

"Are you hurt badly, Mulya?" he asked Sam.

Sam's eyes grew big when he recognized the man. It was Karlis, their chief butler.

"I will be fine," replied the boy. "You showed up in the nick of time. Thank you so much for rescuing me from these thugs."

Then it dawned on him: What was Karlis doing precisely on this street, and precisely at this time?

"Were you following me?" he asked.

Karlis did not respond.

"Did my mother tell you to follow me from school?" Sam insisted.

"Yes, she did," reluctantly replied the butler. "She was worried that since you won't go near the stadium you had to pass through this part of town, and it is not always safe for a Jew to be in this area. She was right."

His mother was always right, Sam thought, and her instincts proved infallible once more.

"Have you been following me every day on my way from school?" Sam asked.

"Every day," answered Karlis, "every day since she stopped."

"You are my savior," Sam told the man. "Will you continue following me every day from school?"

"Without a doubt," responded Karlis, "definitely after this."

"If that is the case, can we walk together? No need for you to follow me, and we can keep each other company on the way."

"That would be very nice," responded Karlis, fully cognizant of his station in life, being the butler of this child's father.

They walked slowly, and in silence, reflecting on the incident. When they approached the house, Sam turned to Karlis.

"Do I have any signs of the beating?" he asked.

"Not that I can see, none visible. Maybe you have some under your coat, but nothing on your face."

"Will you tell my mother about what happened today?"

"Not unless you insist that I do," Karlis replied.

"Good. Actually it would be better that she didn't know anything about it, otherwise she would be worried about me every day, even with you accompanying me from school."

"If that is what you wish, she will not hear a word from me. Just another day like all the previous ones, nothing happened," said the butler turned bodyguard.

"Thank you again, Karlis, you saved my life," the boy was genuinely grateful.

"All in a day's work," replied the man.

Chapter 5

Bella's condition of chronic fatigue did not improve much, and when Haim finally consented to let her go to the doctor all her tests proved negative. According to the doctor there was nothing wrong with her, and he dismissed her symptoms as either stress, or part of her normal aging process.

Bella did not believe the doctor. Until Sam's Bar Mitzvah she never was sick a day in her life, was not under stress once the celebration was over, and yet was not feeling well. Her intuition told her she must have some undiagnosed condition, so she wrote a letter to her daughter Tanya, now a practicing doctor in New York. She described what she was feeling in as accurate terms as possible, and awaited the response.

The reply took some weeks to arrive. Not because Tanya was not responsive, but because the mail was sent by ship, and it took a few weeks for the right ship to collect the letters and deliver them across the Atlantic.

Tanya's reply did not have a diagnosis, or any suggestion of what might be ailing her mother. It carried a very simple and concise directive:

"Go immediately to the Facility of Advanced Medicine in Berlin. See the head professor Dr. Fuchs. Have a thorough exam. Tell Dr. Fuchs that you are my mother. Something is not right and needs to be taken care of without delay."

Did Tanya know what it was? She did not say. Did she suspect something but did not want to scare her parents?

It took another couple of weeks before Haim could break away from his business and accompany Bella on her trip, and they used the time for the preparations. They needed to alert Dr. Fuchs of their arrival and verify that he would be there at the time, and available to see them. Beyond that they expected to be gone for a week or so, and needed to make arrangements for someone to supervise Sam. This would not be something appropriate for the household staff to do, so maybe Sam's half-sister Esther would agree to take care of him while they were gone.

Sam did not mind being left alone in this big house while his parents were away. Firstly, Philip was there, although Philip admitted that he did not like being his brother's babysitter, or "caretaker." At 27 years old Philip was a grown man already, and liked the freedom of coming and going as he pleased, without needing to worry about his teenage brother. He preferred the company of his older brother Isaac—being only four years apart they had more in common with each other than with that "baby" Sam.

So, when his half-sister Esther agreed to come and stay with Sam in the house, and bring her son Misha with her, he was pleased. Sam liked Esther, and more so, he liked her son Misha who was three years younger than him, and whenever they both were free from their schooling they would spend time together.

With all arrangement made, on Sunday morning Haim and Bella boarded the train and went to see the specialist Dr. Fuchs in Berlin.

Sam was anxious, very concerned about his mother, and he missed her terribly. He had never been separated from her for this long, but he could not have traveled with them to Berlin—he had to attend school, and summer recess was still some weeks away. He was hopeful that the doctor would be able to easily cure her of whatever was ailing her, some parasite perhaps, and every morning and evening he prayed for his parents' safe return.

A week passed with no word. On Sunday, a telegram arrived from Berlin saying only: "*Staying another week in Berlin.*" That raised Sam's level of anxiety quite a bit, but he tried to reassure himself that maybe his parents liked Berlin, had decided to take some time off before returning to Riga, and all is really well with his mother's ailment. He knew that it was a bit out of character for his father to simply take a week's vacation away from his work, it not being winter when the river was frozen and his father would normally stay in town. But maybe, just maybe his mother, who had never been to Berlin but wanted to so much, especially after reading about the city in Tanya's old letters, had convinced Haim to enjoy yet one more week with her there to see the sights. After all, there was so much culture in that great city–music, and theatre, museums, and opera, all the things she loved–and since both spoke German fluently they had no problem taking in the sights.

The days seemed to crawl by. Misha's presence in the house helped Sam a lot, and kept his mind from constantly worrying about his parent's trip. The week had passed, and still they had not returned. Sam then realized that because of the Sabbath they could not leave Berlin before Sunday morning, so they wouldn't be back before sometime Monday.

Late Monday afternoon, after a grueling twenty-five-hour train ride from Berlin, Haim and Bella arrived back home. They had covered the 525 miles between the cities with some stops, and fortunately they could afford the first class accommodations in a Pullman sleeper car, so the trip was not too hard or inconvenient.

As soon as they walked into the house, Sam felt that something was very wrong and that things in Berlin did not go as well as he had hoped. Despite his mother's smile and warm embrace, he felt that she was even weaker than when she left, suggesting that the doctor's treatment had not reduced her symptoms, and he did not think the train ride was the cause.

Although Haim said almost nothing when Sam greeted them, his father's face showed an anguish that spoke loudly to Sam, telling him that the news was not so good. Very rarely, if ever, had he seen his father's face ashen as it was that evening.

Within moments the door opened and Philip came in. He had just finished his work at the Laima Chocolate Company owned by his uncles, and came home hoping to see his parents. Still unmarried, both Philip and Isaac were living at home with their parents and young brother. That was the custom in those days in Riga and elsewhere; you did not leave your parents' home until it was time for you to build one of your own, for yourself and your spouse.

Philip's relationship with his parents was practically the opposite of Sam's. He was tremendously attached to his father, much more so than to his mother. Although he loved her deeply, as most sons do, his devotion and first allegiance was to his father whom he adored, respected, and admired. Isaac's feelings towards his parents, on the other hand, were somewhere in between his two brothers—he respected his father but was not too emotionally attached to him, but was not very close to his mother either.

They sat in the parlor, and the servants brought some hot tea to refresh the travelers. They were all there, except for Isaac who was still at work at the tanning factory, so Haim dispatched Karlis to go fetch Isaac.

With Karlis gone, Haim then picked up the suitcases and carried them himself to the bedroom upstairs. Philip offered to help, but the tall, strong man declined. He went upstairs alone and did not come back down until he heard Isaac's voice sometime later.

Isaac was perturbed. Never before was he ever "summoned" like this to his parents' home, and he became very concerned when he saw his mother sitting limp in her favorite armchair in the parlor. She looked pale, and tired, and she did not come forward to greet him as she normally did. Being a very sensitive man he felt something ominous in the air.

He nodded to Sam, querying him with his look, but Sam raised his shoulders and shook his head like saying "I don't know." Isaac then acknowledged Misha who was getting ready to go back home with his mother, gave a brief hug to Philip, and then they heard Haim's footsteps coming down the stairs.

Haim entered the room, and signaled to everybody to sit down, everybody, including Esther who was standing by the doorway on her way out. When everyone was seated, Haim spoke in a measured, matter-of-fact voice.

"Bella is very sick," he said in Yiddish. "After all the tests that the Professor in Berlin performed, he concluded that Bella has cancer."

There was a gasp in the room.

He stopped for a moment, letting the gravity of his words sink in, then continued. "He could not determine how widespread it is, nor estimate how long she will be able to fight the disease, and anyway any statement like that is pure speculation."

Sam did not hear much of the second sentence. The word he heard was "cancer," and with that word alone his world came crashing down around him. His mother has cancer, that awful, terminal, non-curable disease! Oh God in heaven, how could you do this to this gentle soul? How could you do it to me, and my brothers and sister? Why? What has she done to deserve this fate?

He knew enough about the disease to know it was a death sentence, an agonizing painful end to a life, a songbird being silenced. His mother, this wonderful human being who never hurt a fly, who cared for every miserable soul she ever came across, this generous loving beacon of light, would soon be extinguished in the most cruel, agonizingly painful, and inhumane way.

❖   ❖   ❖

Over the next two years Sam saw his beloved mother wither away. Bit by bit the life was being drained out of her, and there was nothing anyone could do for her. If in the early days after the diagnosis she was able to get out of bed, get dressed, and come downstairs almost every day, the frequency of those days diminished over time. More and more she remained in bed, too tired to negotiate the stairs down, and definitely not able to climb back upstairs to the bedroom.

Everybody tried to make her as comfortable as possible, and tend to all her needs. Philip cut his engineering studies in Prague after only one year, and following a short internship at Siemens in Germany during that summer he returned home to Riga to be close to his mother. No one knew how long she was for this world, and Philip wanted to spend as much time with her as he could.

Through the entire winter, when the river was frozen and no new wood was being cut, Haim stayed home. The mill was still operating, cutting and shaping the harvest of the previous summer, but Haim left the work to be run by the foreman. He left the house only occasionally to negotiate the lease of the next part of the forest, or negotiate the sale of the milled wood, but otherwise he remained in the parlor downstairs at all times, available should Bella need him.

He studied incessantly. He read the *Mishna*, the *Gemara*, the *Talmud*, and any biblical text he could lay his hands on. Together with Philip he studied the Rambam, and the other sages, and immersed himself in Judaica, to a large extent to suppress the pain of the inevitability of him losing his wife.

The passing of Bella would be the second time he would endure losing a life-partner, and this time a much more painful loss than before. He had been married to his first wife Zelda for only three years when she passed away, and he was married to Bella for over thirty years by now. Although he rarely exhibited it, he was deeply attached to her in his own way, loving her with that love that creeps up on you after so many years together of sharing life experiences.

He was always grateful to Bella for what she had done for him. When Zelda died in childbirth of his second daughter, Haim was crushed. Not only did he lose the love of his life, but in a split second he found himself a widower with two daughters: Esther who was barely 2, and the brand new baby Dussia. How was he to raise them, and take care of them, especially when he spent over half of each year away from home in the forest?

Bella, Zelda's younger unmarried sister took charge and stood in for her late sister. She moved into Haim's home, something unheard of in Jewish society of the late nineteenth century, and took the girls, her nieces, under her wings. With innate wisdom, kindness, and loving care she tended to every need of the two girls, and no one could tell that they were not her own flesh and blood. She did that because that was her nurturing nature, gentle but firm, caring but disciplined.

A year passed, the period of mourning ended, and Haim proposed to Bella, and she accepted. She loved the girls so much, and could not bear the thought of letting someone else raise them. Thus Esther became both Sam's half-sister and his cousin, in one fell swoop.

Bella was cognizant of the gap between her and Haim—one gentle and warm, intellectual, music lover, literature connoisseur, the other frowning and foreboding, stern, never commending others, although not an evil person inside. Or maybe because they were so different they balanced each other out, and maintained a harmonious home for the children. Soon Isaac, Tanya, and Philip arrived in close succession, and after a thirteen-year gap Sam was born to his father already in his fifties and his mother already in her forties.

❖ ❖ ❖

The notice of Bella's death appeared in Yiddish in the local paper. It read simply:

"After a long and difficult illness, on Tuesday the 14 of December, at 2:30 p.m. my good wife, our great mother, grandmother, sister, aunt and mother-in-law Bella Glickman passed away at the age of 58.

The funeral will leave today, the 15th of December at 2 p.m. from the home of the bereaved, 21 Blaumana Street.

The family."

Bella's funeral procession was immense. A large portion of the Jewish community of Riga followed her to her final resting place. Her ancestral family, the Frenkels, was huge and they all attended the funeral. And then, beyond her husband and children, all those people who knew her during her lifetime came to show her their last respects and escort her on her last voyage.

Following the customs of a Jewish orthodox burial in Riga, there were no eulogies. A simple traditional ceremony was held, with the bereaved walking behind the cart carrying the body, now washed and purified, wrapped in muslin and covered by a tallit, with a cantor chanting the traditional prayer "*El Maleh Rahamim.*" Then at the site the body was lowered into the grave, and the grave closed in a dignified manner, bringing the body to its final destination. The boys recited Kaddish, the cantor chanted a bit more, and the funeral was over.

Harsh. A traditional Jewish burial is harsh, intentionally so. There is no viewing of the body, there is no wake, and no delay. The body is placed in the ground within one day after the person passes away to signify the unimportance of the body itself, now an empty vessel, and thus preventing the possible emotional attachment to it by those left behind. The soul has left the body, an instrument enabling the soul to execute its worldly mission. The person is no more, and the body serves no more purpose on this earth. And when the soul exits the body, the body must return to its origin in the dirt, the place from which God created Adam. From the dirt you came, and to the dirt you shall return.

It does not lessen the pain, but it allows the bereaved to recognize, in the most poignant and cruel way, the finality of the event. Once the grave is closed, there is no question but that the beloved person is gone, forever.

Sam wanted to stay behind for a few more minutes, to say goodbye to his mother in his own way, but his brothers, knowing his pain, urged him on with them. They all circled through the other path to exit the cemetery, and it was all over.

He was barely 16 years old, and his mother was no more.

Chapter 6

For the next two years Sam focused on his schooling. The Hebrew Gymnasia he attended was a very demanding learning institution, providing not only the complete curriculum of a normal high school, but also the full-fledged teaching of a yeshiva, and the workload was heavy.

It was good that his mind was occupied by his studies as it helped keep the pain of the loss of his mother from overtaking him. His father, always demanding excellence, also maintained the pressure on him, and when Sam finally sank into bed each night, he was so exhausted that he had no time to contemplate his fate before falling asleep.

Philip remained in Riga and assumed a leadership position as Secretary General with the Laima Chocolate Company. He resumed his life as a young single man, although he did not participate in any festive occasions during the year of mourning after his mother's death.

The only celebratory events during those next two years were the wedding of Isaac to Gita, a wonderful girl from a respected Jewish family, and a year later, in the summer of 1928, the birth of their firstborn son Marc. The following Saturday Isaac joined his father and brothers to shul, something he had not done for quite some time, and following Halachic tradition announced that the Brit Milah of his son—the circumcision ceremony—will be held in Haim's home in the early afternoon of Tuesday, the eighth day since birth.

And a month later, out of respect for his father, he held the traditional service of *Pidion Haben*—the redemption of his son. And with those obligations out of the way, he was done with Judaism and its rules. Since leaving his father's home, he had shed substantially all of his "Jewishness," became totally secular, and assimilated among the Latvian aristocracy as an industrialist par excellence. He did not keep a kosher home, did not observe the Sabbath, and except for not attending church acted no differently than any of his gentile Latvian friends and colleagues.

❖   ❖   ❖

When Sam graduated the Gymnasia and the Yeshiva, he decided not to pursue ordination as a Rabbi, but follow in Philip's footsteps by going abroad to study engineering. This time however, he chose a somewhat more difficult path to studying: Whereas Philip studied in Prague, at the German University, in German which he spoke fluently as did the rest of the family, Sam decided to pursue his studies at the University of Lille in northwestern France, despite the fact that all his classes would be in French, a language he did not speak a single word of.

What interested Sam in the University of Lille was its curriculum that included a degree in aeronautical engineering. Ever since he saw the military planes of the warring countries flying overhead during WWI, he was drawn to the pioneering field of aviation, and what better way to get close than to become an engineer designing airplanes?

So one morning in August 1928, Sam boarded a train for the 1,500-mile trek to Lille where he expected to spend the next four years. It was hard for him to leave his father behind, but both Philip and Isaac were there, and so was Esther, and they could keep Haim company. And as for Haim, with great trepidations he gave Sam his blessings, and a small stipend, and freed him to pursue his quest. He just insisted that Sam keep kosher and remain faithful to the religion—that was the price he exacted for letting the young man go.

The long trip took Sam through Lithuania, where his fluent Russian was good "currency," and through Poland into Germany where his fluent German presented no obstacles. In Berlin he had a few hours between trains, and he could roam the streets a bit and get the feel of the place, so he strolled about the city.

Then he saw a large sign for the Facility of Advanced Medicine and his heart sank. It reminded him so of his mother, and his home in Riga. Although his mother was no longer there, he became terribly homesick and was questioning the wisdom of having left the comfort of his father's home. He even contemplated heading back to Riga, but then his determination and perseverance intervened, and he went back to the station and boarded the train for France.

The rest of the trip was long, and tedious, but uneventful, until the train crossed the border into France, and his anxiety level rose.

Getting off the train in Lille was a traumatic experience. He had no idea how he was going to manage in France without speaking a word of the language. He did not expect that the French would speak any of the languages he knew, but he was sure that somehow he would manage. He trusted God to take care of him and protect him, and that gave him the strength to step down onto the platform.

Walking out of the train station, Sam did not know whether to turn right or left. Where was the university? He could not even ask anyone. There was no map at the kiosk, and anyway he did not have French currency to buy one, so he stopped, put the suitcase down, and looked around.

Out of nowhere someone walked by, tripped over the suitcase, and almost fell to the ground, his hat flying a few steps further. Instinctively Sam reached out and grabbed the arm of the man and helped him up to his feet, and then he noticed the yarmulke, the skull cap, adorning this man's head. God was watching over him!

Without a second thought, Sam addressed the Jew in Yiddish: "I just arrived in town, and do not speak French. Can you please help me?"

The short man in his 50s looked at him in disbelief, as if he had seen a ghost. Then the look changed into an "ah," as if the man realized something he had not realized before.

"זענט איר א ר טוואקק?" he asked, also in Yiddish. "Are you a Latvian?"

"Yes, from Riga," Sam answered, "how did you know?"

"Never mind. You must come with me, then," the man said, and turned and started walking away.

Sam did not know what to make of the little man, but he followed his instincts and caught up with the guy.

They walked along a boulevard, at one point crossed to the other side of the street and then turned left. The man kept a few paces ahead of Sam, and did not engage him in a conversation.

In front of number 37 the man stopped, turned around and said: "Go ring the bell. Tell them you are from Riga."

"Who is there? Are you coming there with me?" Sam asked.

The man shook his head.

"Go," he said.

Still puzzled Sam dutifully climbed the six steps to the front door. Up on the landing he turned around to thank the man, but no one was there. Sam dropped his suitcase and climbed down the stairs, and looked both right and left. The little man had disappeared into thin air.

Who was this man? Was he real? Where did he vanish to?

❖ ❖ ❖

Sam rang the bell.

The door opened, and a bearded Jewish orthodox man in his fifties stood there, followed by a slightly younger woman in a house dress and apron. They stared at each other for a moment.

The woman gently pushed the man out of the way and took over.

With one look at the strange young man at the door suitcase in hand, she sized him up. She knew right away that he was no threat to them, probably a door-to-door salesman, although too youngish looking for that.

She said something in a strange language. French, Sam assumed.

"I do not understand," Sam responded in that universal language Yiddish.

"Who are you, and what do you want?" she asked, this time in Yiddish.

The pronunciation of this short sentence sounded like something he would hear back home, not something he would expect in this town. Yiddish, while a common language for almost all European Jewry, has a slightly different sound and pronunciation, flavor you might say, depending on the locale. You can instantly and decisively tell the difference between a Polish Jew, a Romanian, Russian, Hungarian, and so on, and unless French Jews spoke that way also, this woman was clearly from either Lithuania or Latvia.

"My name is Shmuel," Sam said, giving his Hebrew name. "I just arrived from Riga, and I do not speak French. I am here to study at the university, and I do not know anyone in town."

"How did you get here?" she meant her home, her address. "Did you knock on our door at random?" she puzzled. Then without waiting for his answer she stepped aside, no longer blocking the door. "Never mind. Come on in, child, and sit down. You must be tired from the trip." She closed the door, and led him toward the parlor.

The parlor was not as big as the one at his father's home, but it was cozy, sparsely but tastefully decorated.

"You must be thirsty from the trip. Let me go bring some hot tea," the woman said, and scurried into the kitchen. If this were a Latvian or Lithuanian home, then there must be the traditional samovar of tea in the kitchen, always ready for the thirsty. The tea is sucked through a sugar cube held between one's front teeth, and thus one enjoys the strong, sweet tea to warm the soul, "*precuscu*" Russian style.

The man motioned to Sam to sit down on the couch, and he occupied one of the two armchairs placed next to each other.

"Did you come by train directly from Riga?" the man asked. He had not introduced himself or mentioned his name, but Sam was not going to ask outright. The man seemed cultured, and it was more a question of it escaping his mind than anything else.

Sam nodded, and then looked around the room. Typical of a Jewish home, one wall of the parlor was lined with a wall-to-wall bookcase, filled to the brim with volume upon volume of books of all sizes and colors. From his seated position Sam could tell that some of the books had Hebrew lettering on their spines, hence were obviously religious manuscripts, but there were also some in Cyrillic lettering indicating Russian literature, and fewer with Latin lettering. These people were well read, no doubt.

"Well, young man, I don't know how you got to our door, but you are home," the woman was carrying a tray with tea cups from the kitchen. She put the tray down and handed Sam a cup, and a couple of sugar cubes.

"We are from Lithuania, from Vilnius, but originally from Riga," she said. "We left a long time ago, before the war. Through some miracle Mendel here was invited to be the local Rabbi of a small congregation, so we came to Lille, and have stayed here since then."

She paused. "We still have relatives there in Riga, but lost contact with them some time ago. Levin is their last name."

"Levin?" Sam asked. "That is a common family name. There are quite a few in Riga. Would you know their first names, or where they lived?"

"Sure. They are Yaakov and Mira. Yaakov and Mira Levin."

"Yaakov and Mira Levin?" Sam asked in astonishment, and his heart skipped a beat.

"Yes. You would not know them by chance, would you? Maybe through shul? We really wanted to know where they are these days."

Yaakov Levin? Could it be? Could this woman be a relative of their neighbor, the late Yaakov Levin?

Probably not, Sam said to himself.

"I don't think so. I knew a Yaakov Levin, but as you know that is a common name among Jews in Riga."

"They lived not too far from the stadium in Riga, maybe two blocks away," she said. "Just before we left, Yaakov had started a new business. I think it was a tannery business."

It could not be! This could not be happening! Sam was dumbfounded. Out of all the people in Lille, he was led to the house of the relatives of his neighbor, the late Yaakov Levin. What were the odds of that?

Who was this little man who led him here and then disappeared into thin air?

Was he an angel sent to guide him to this house?

He was silent for a moment, and the woman was looking intently into his eyes, as if she sensed something.

"Yes, I know the Levins," he finally said slowly. "We live right next door to them. They have two children, Moishe and Rachel, and Moishe is about my age, 18, right?"

"Oh, my God," the man exclaimed, "it is true. How are they?"

"Mira and the children are fine," Sam said quietly. "As a matter of fact, Moishe was my best friend at the yeshiva, and I saw him last just before boarding the train yesterday, or was it the day before?"

"And Yaakov? How is Yaakov?"

"Yaakov died eleven years ago."

"Yaakov is dead? How? He was a young man! How did he die?"

"He was shot by the Germans for having collaborated with the Russians while they occupied Riga. He really had not collaborated with them. They demanded that he provide saddles and reins for their horses, and he had no choice but to supply them. So when the Germans defeated the Russians, they gathered the 'collaborators' into the stadium and shot them. I was there. I saw it with my own eyes."

"Oh my God," the woman exclaimed, taking it all in.

"If Yaakov is dead, how do Mira and the kids survive with no breadwinner in the house?"

"They are being taken care of."

"But how? They had no close relatives in Riga. Like us, the rest of his family went to Vilnius, so they have nobody there."

"When Yaakov died, my father helped my brother Isaac buy the business from Yaakov's widow, and gave her his solemn oath that so long as he lived he shall always share the profits with them. So for the past ten years or so, Isaac is managing the company, and it is doing very well, and so are Mira and the children."

There was a long pause while they were digesting the news. Finally Mendel, who was sitting silently the entire time, turned to Sam.

"How did you find us?" He asked.

"Gabriel," Sam muttered.

"Gabriel?" they both echoed.

"An angel. God sent me an angel to guide me to your door," Sam said, and then he told them the incredible story of the man tripping over his suitcase and bringing him to their door.

❖   ❖   ❖

Sam stayed with Rabbi Mendel and Rebbetzin Rivka until Sunday when it was time to start his classes on Monday. Mornings and evenings the men prayed the daily prayers together, and Friday night and throughout Sabbath, they spent at the little synagogue where Mendel officiated over the services. Mendel even invited Sam to come up on the bimah for an *Aliyah*, a courtesy that he felt honored to receive.

During the few days before the Sabbath Rivka taught him a few phrases in French. She instructed Sam in the basic obligatory sentences so he would be able to buy something, or ask for directions should he need to. Beyond her imperfect accent her French was quite limited and Sam knew that it was not enough. So during one of the early excursions with Rivka he picked up a French language book and a German-French dictionary—there was no Latvian-French dictionary to be had.

On Wednesday, the topic of Sam's accommodations came up. Sam asked Rivka if she would help him find a place to stay, and immediately both of them offered Sam to stay in their home. Since their own daughters were grown, married, and had moved away, they had the place for him, they said, and he was more than welcome to stay. As a matter of fact, they reasoned, it would be very nice for them to have someone to keep them company.

Despite the opportunity to save money for his accommodations, and while feeling comfortable in their company, Sam politely declined. Firstly, they lived in the other side of town from the university, and it would be difficult for him to live far away from campus. Secondly, while he did not tell them that, as an 18-year-old single youngster he wanted to explore his freedom, come and go as he pleased, and living with them would burden him with adhering to their schedule rather than his own.

So, reluctantly they relented, and Rivka went with Sam to look for accommodations. Like most institutions of higher learning in Europe at the time, the university did not have a dormitory, so the student body was dispersed over the neighborhood near the campus.

How lucky could one be? Almost immediately they found a room to rent, with a small bathroom attached, and a separate entrance, permitting Sam to come and go at all hours without disturbing anyone. The room was sparsely but adequately furnished—a single bed, a dresser, and a desk, all reasonably clean, with a window facing the street bringing in daylight, and it was not expensive either, well within Sam's meager budget. The landlady, an old woman in her seventies if a day, explained that the room had been reserved by another student, but just that morning she received word that he would not be coming this year, and the room became available. They grabbed at the opportunity.

Finally, Rivka helped Sam locate a small kosher restaurant, actually a tiny room with a couple of tables, where they served home-cooked meals. It was run by an old French couple, and at least there Sam could communicate in Yiddish, in addition to eating food that reminded him of his home in Riga.

On Sunday Sam thanked Rabbi Mendel and Rebbetzin Rivka from the bottom of his heart, bid them farewell, and they made him promise that he would come and visit them whenever he could spare the time.

He walked through the streets with his suitcase across town, and entered his new home, for the next school year at least.

Once in his room his first official act was to gently remove the large carved wooden crucifix hanging on the wall over the bed and carefully place it against the back wall inside the closet. To his chagrin, the outline of the cross remained on the wall; it probably had been there for many years, definitely since the place was last painted quite some time ago.

The first few weeks at the university were very difficult for Sam. He sat in class totally lost, not understanding one single word of what the professor was saying. The classes were conducted mostly in the form of a lecture, and the professor would ramble on and on, and Sam's mastery of German, Russian, and Latvian, was of no help at all—none of these languages were even remotely related to French. He understood the science classes somewhat, because his schooling in Riga included advanced math and physics, and the first few weeks at the university were a repetition of those classes; they also helped tune his ear to the terms, rhythm of the sentences, and pronunciation of some words. But the other academic classes were a total loss, so he occasionally skipped those and sat at the library studying the language from the books he had previously purchased.

In all other respects, Sam followed the "monkey see, monkey do" principle. He observed what other people did, students at the university or strangers on the street, and followed their examples. Sometimes however, those imitations led to strange and even embarrassing circumstance, but he took those in stride.

After classes, Sam would go to his room and continue studying the language using the local newspaper and a dictionary, until it was time for evening prayers which start about one half hour before sundown. Fortunately, sundown during the early fall months in Lille was still quite late, so his religious practice did not interfere with his classes that normally ended at around 4 p.m.

Following the evening prayer Sam would head to the kosher restaurant for dinner. There he could speak Yiddish with the owners, and that was a relief from the stress of trying to understand the gibberish of a strange language all day. For lunch, Sam mostly ate a salad on a plate and with utensils that he carried with him, and he thoroughly washed those every night. Life of an observant Jew in Lille, without the ability to cook for himself, was a bit complicated.

Back in his room after dinner Sam would prepare for himself a cup of tea with an electric tea pot, a fabulous invention only a few years old that had just come onto the market. He had seen it in a store, and although it was quite expensive it was wonderful to be able to sip a cup of tea in the evening after the meal.

Overall, Sam was managing quite well under the circumstances, but he did not see it that way at all. He did not give himself credit for what he was accomplishing, but that was part of his personality to not acknowledge his successes, not pat himself on his back, and not feel terribly good about himself. Despite his mother's nurturing and encouragement while she was alive, his unquenched thirst for his father's approval, which never really came, caused him a tremendous loss of self-esteem and did not allow him to feel good about that brave young person that he was. Here he was, an 18-year-old, for the first time in his life in a foreign land by himself and without any support, not speaking the language and not knowing anyone except for an old couple on the other edge of town, and yet he could not see or acknowledge the fierce dragon that he was slaying.

To the contrary, the language barrier was to him a serious roadblock. How could it be? Why would he be so traumatized by it? After all, he had mastered five languages before!

Well, he reasoned with himself: Latvian he studied in kindergarten and elementary school; German was taught in school also, since Latvia was under German control for so many years; Russian he picked up in high school, taught as a foreign language because of the Russian influence, and occupation of large parts of Latvia; Yiddish was spoken at home, and Hebrew he studied at the yeshiva, not to forget Aramaic as well. But French? Just listening to it was not enough; he needed to find some other way to immerse himself in the language. Reading the newspaper was a good starting point, but having to check every word in a dictionary was a tedious and time-consuming task. He needed to accelerate his pace, but did not know how.

On his way back home that Thursday evening, the young woman standing at the street corner said "good evening" to him. He had seen her standing at that corner almost every night when he passed by on his way back from dinner at the kosher restaurant, but he never paid much attention to her. He figured she must have noticed him passing by since he walked that same route home from the restaurant.

When she said *"bonsoir"* to him this evening he politely replied *"bonsoir,"* and continued home to his little room. Her eyes continued to follow him; maybe he would get the hint and would stop and come back?

He had absolutely no idea who she was nor what she was doing there night after night at that street corner, so naïve he was.

❖   ❖   ❖

He spent the Sabbath and Sunday with Mendel and Rivka, and it felt somewhat like coming home. The atmosphere in the house, a traditional Jewish home with the same smells of cooking he was used to, the Yiddish, the way that the Rabbi and Rebbetzin thought, all were very comfortably close to what he had seen at his father's home or his friends' homes.

The only drawback was that it reminded him so much of his parents' home and made him miss his late mother that much more, so when he left one Sunday after dinner, he told Mendel and Rivka that he would probably not see them for a while—he had to concentrate on his studies, French in particular.

It was true, he felt he was slipping in school and was starting to worry that unless his language skills improved he would not be able to meet his obligations in school and fail the classes.

He went back to his routine with renewed vigor, "burning the midnight oil," but French is not an easy language to learn, with all seventeen tenses that might apply to a sentence, the accents, similar to but different from Latvian and German, and the gender associated with each object, similar to Hebrew, but confusingly not the same: In Hebrew for example, a table, "*shulchan*," is considered masculine whereas in French it is "*table*," and is feminine. Remembering all these rules is not easy, and it was so easy to make a mistake to possibly disastrous consequences. Not simple.

Another few days had passed, and the lady at the corner and he continued to greet each other each evening. She would say "*bonsoir*" to him, and he would respond in kind

Except that tonight she added another word: "*Bonsoir monsieur*"— "Good evening sir," she said smiling faintly.

Feeling a bit cocky perhaps, Sam responded, "*Bonsoir madame.*"

It must have been his accent, because she smiled at him and said, "*Mais non, monsieur, je suis une mademoiselle, pas madame,*"—"But no, sir, I am a Miss, not a Mrs." She chuckled.

At first, he was embarrassed. On top of being naturally shy, especially around women, he thought his baby steps in French had backfired. But then he realized there was no indignation in her voice. She did not reproach him. She corrected him, and that made all the difference in the world to him.

"Pardon me," he said. Then deciding to really push his luck, he added, "I am sorry."

If she had any doubt about this young man being a foreigner, by now those doubts had evaporated.

"I understand," she said. "You are not a long time in France, eh?"

That was not so difficult, and he acknowledged it to her.

"If you want, I can teach you French," she offered.

Sam was carefully selecting simple words from his limited vocabulary and sentence structures. "You can?"

"Yes," she said.

"I will pay you."

"That is good. I can use some extra money, business is weak."

Sam strained to understand what she said, but he did, a great accomplishment he thought.

Poor Sam still did not know what her line of business was, but it did not matter at this point. She had offered to help him overcome the single most pressing obstacle in his life, and he was not going to reject it.

"You come tomorrow night same time," she was simplifying the sentence so that he would understand, and also was using signs like pointing to her watch to signify time. "We will go to the bistro there," she pointed to the bar at the other corner, "and I will teach you French."

❖　❖　❖

For the next three months, Sam and Brigitte met at the bistro four nights a week, and with the help of his book over a cup of coffee, she taught him the proper pronunciation, grammar, and syntax of French, and he paid her for each and every lesson. (Years later he would look back at that period and chuckle at the thought that he was paying to spend a couple of hours every night with a prostitute, and never for sex!)

After a while they could spend some of the time in conversation. They told each other about their lives and their families, and since there was nothing romantic between them they felt very much at ease to relate some of their innermost thoughts, feelings, and aspirations.

She was nearly five years older than he was, and had a very distinctive perspective on life, quite different than his. She had come to Lille from St-Juste-la-Pendue a small village far to the southeast, to be as far away from her family as she could, especially because of the line of work she was pursuing. She was very curious about Judaism and Jewish life, and he in turn wanted to understand her life, particularly as it related to her profession—how she felt about it, what it was like, in both practical as well as psychological terms—and so they conversed, sometimes quite late until closing time of the bistro.

During Christmas, Brigitte went to visit her family and was gone for almost two weeks. When she returned, she told him that she had decided to change her life.

"Not that you did anything specific to convince me, or tried to influence me, but while talking to you I realized that the life that I was living when I met you was not really what I want for myself. In your kind and gentle manner, you showed me that I am missing something in my life, and I want to try and change course."

"What are you thinking of doing?" Sam asked.

"I think I will be better off in a larger city, so I will be moving to Paris. I have some money saved, enough to give me a fresh start, in a place where no one knows me or my past. I will be going to school first to improve my typing skills, and then get a job in some office, a regular job that pays well enough that I do not have to do what I have been doing here."

"I will miss you, Brigitte," Sam said with sadness in his voice.

"I know, and I will miss you too, my young friend. Promise you will write me, now that your French is on solid ground."

"I will," he promised.

A few days later, in the midst of a cold spell, she boarded the train at the same station into which he arrived not four months earlier, and when the train pulled out of the station Sam felt a void in his heart.

"*Au revoir,*" he called after her, "So long."

"*À bientôt,*" she answered, "See you soon."

Chapter 7

The European teaching method that the university in Lille followed consisted of a fixed curriculum. The course of studies was predetermined for each faculty, with no electives. At the beginning of each semester Sam would receive a schedule in the form of a calendar, with all the courses filling five full days of classes and labs, with Saturdays and Sundays off. All were compulsory subjects, and one had to pass them all. The grading system was complicated and quite strict and demanding: Not only was the student required to obtain a minimum average grade of C+, but he could also not fail a single subject or else have to repeat the entire year, with a dispensation for those courses that the student had received a minimum grade of B+ in.

Beyond his innate intelligence and hard work, two things worked in Sam's favor during his first year of his studies. One was that the university library was stacked with technical text books in both German and Russian, and his absolute mastery of those two languages saved him on numerous occasions. The second was the tremendous help of Brigitte in overcoming the French barrier—by the end of the first semester Sam was able to write an essay in a non-scientific subject and receive a passing grade for it. Between those two assets, Sam was able to squeeze by that semester with the minimal required grade point average, while passing all his courses, and without asking for or receiving special dispensation due to French being a foreign language for him.

To Sam's chagrin though, as the technical studies advanced from pure math and physics into engineering, more and more text books appeared to have been written in English, and there was no translation for those to any other language, French included. In recognition of that fact the university introduced an English language course for the second semester of freshman year, and now Sam had to contend with two new languages. At least with English he was not disadvantaged as compared to the other students—almost none of them spoke the language—so he was at par with them.

At the conclusion of his freshman year Sam returned to Riga for the summer, to be with his father and brothers, but before departing Lille he had a few things he needed to do. Firstly, he confirmed with his landlady that he would have the room for the next year. He liked his room; it was comfortable for him, close to the university, and within walking distance of the kosher restaurant. Secondly, he remembered to retrieve the wooden crucifix in his closet, and hang it back in its unmistakable place over the bed.

He responded to Brigitte's latest letter advising her of his departure and the anticipated return date. On the back of the envelope he wrote his address in Riga should she wish to write him, something he would like very much. Over the year they had been corresponding, and she told him about her new life in Paris. Immediately after finishing her course, she got a position with an insurance company. The position was paying her well, and she was very happy on that front. On the social side, she told him about the gentleman she had met, and how he courted her, and that she really enjoyed the life in the big city.

And finally he went to bid farewell to Mendel and Rivka and promised to bring their wishes to Mira Levin in Riga. Then he boarded the train and slept most of the way home.

Karlis was at the door to greet him, picked up his luggage and took it upstairs to his old room. Sam followed him and looked around a bit, and noticed that nothing had changed during his year of absence; everything had remained the same as when he left home.

Philip was overjoyed to see his baby brother, and Haim was pleased that his youngest child was in good health and spirit, yet he was not terribly pleased to notice—and made it clear to everyone that he did—that Sam was not as observant as when he left for school. He no longer was wearing the tzitzit, that undergarment with the fringes, and from time to time he would skip saying the morning or evening prayers. Yet when his father returned home from the forest for the weekend, out of courtesy to his father more than anything else, both Philip and Sam would join him and attend the Sabbath services at the synagogue.

As soon as he could free himself from the welcoming committee—Isaac, his wife Gita and their toddler Marc showed up some time later to join in the joy of his return—Sam dashed next door to see his friend Moishe, and tell the family about their relatives in Lille, but the house was dark, and no one answered the door. He later learned that Mira and the children went to Warsaw on vacation and would not be back for two more weeks.

When they returned, the reunion between Moishe and Sam was a sight to behold. Moishe could not control himself and after embracing Sam he grabbed him by both shoulders, and they danced around like a pair of Hassids at a wedding. Rachel too was delighted to see him, but being a young girl of sixteen she was a bit shy and reserved, watching him as a young man and not as a childhood friend that he used to be.

Mira came out of the kitchen to see what the commotion in the hallway was, and when she saw Sam she too gave him a wonderfully warm hug.

"How have you been?" she asked, "How did you manage in France? We were worried about you, you know, because you did not know anyone there and did not speak the language."

"Well, I have the most incredible story to tell you. You won't believe it," Sam said.

"What, what?" Moishe eagerly exclaimed. "Tell us!"

And so he did. He told them about his first hour in Lille, and the little man leading him to some seemingly random house and telling him to ring the bell and then disappearing.

"An elderly couple opened the door, and when I told them I was from Riga, they invited me in. They were also from Riga, and then asked if I knew you. Imagine that. Of all the people in the world, they asked about you. They told me that they are your relatives."

Sam stopped to let the tension build for a moment.

"Our relatives?" Mira asked. "Who are they? What are their names?"

"Mendel and Rivka Schneirson."

Mira gasped. "Mendel and Rivka?" she asked, "My God, Yaakov's long-lost cousins!"

Sam pulled out the letter he had been carrying and handed it to Mira. She looked at the envelope, front and back, still somewhat in a daze, and put it on the table.

"How long are you going to be in Riga?" she asked.

"I will be here for the remainder of the summer, until a week after Tish'a B'av. School starts the first week of September, and I need to be in Lille a few days earlier to get my schedule and the like."

"Then I will write them right away."

❖　❖　❖

The summer went by fast, and it was so pleasant for Sam to be home among his closest relatives. He visited his half-sister Esther and his nephew Misha every week, made the rounds seeing all of his relatives on his mother's side, a large clan to be sure, and spent his free time with Moishe, two 19-year-olds about town.

But mostly that summer was a time of transition, with great consequences to Sam's life. He has been on his own for close to a year, independent, away from home, without its support system, and he had managed his year abroad very well. To his siblings he no longer was their baby brother, but their younger brother, an adult in his own rights. Their relationship with him changed, and they treated him with much more respect, as an equal among them. And that change of attitude toward him allowed them to discuss with him issues, and share with him feelings, that in the past they did not.

Throughout the summer Sam had several serious and far-reaching discussions, primarily with Philip, on topics that would influence Sam for the rest of his life. They had long conversations about many topics, heart-to-heart talks, invariably leading to the question of their future.

This summer evening Sam and Philip were strolling through the park by the river, not too far from where Sam had been attacked by the four hooligans some years earlier, and Sam told Philip about that incident.

"Interesting that you had not mentioned it to me until now," Philip commented.

"At the time I was afraid mama would find out about it, through some slip of the tongue, so I did not tell anyone about it. Karlis and I kept it only amongst us, but for me it was a major event."

"Must have been a traumatic experience for you."

"Yes, it was, and it made me think about those guys that attacked me. They did not know me, I have not done anything bad to them for their vicious attack, so why? Why did they want to hurt me, just because I was a Jew?

"But then it was not the only time I was mistreated because of being Jewish, both here and in France," Sam stated.

Both Philip and Sam had been out of Latvia for one year each and had realized that anti-Semites were not limited to Riga, or Latvia, but existed elsewhere as well. Philip recounted events and incidents that happened to him in Prague where he endured being mistreated merely for being a Jew, and Sam had his own tales to relate of being subjected to "special treatments," both in and out of school.

These were not major incidents; neither brother had been physically assaulted like Sam was years earlier. But they still felt on their own skins those sharp barbs directed against Jews, and thus for them, anti-Semitism was not an academic or abstract intellectual topic. It was real, and painfully unpleasant.

The fact that over the centuries Jews had been mistreated by the countries where they lived was not something new to either of them. Both were fully aware of the centuries of discrimination, open and official—laws forbidding Jews from owning land or other property, practicing their religion, or taking positions in government.

And then there were the unofficial acts: Hooliganism, pogroms, rapes, burning of villages, and pillaging, and if not always sanctioned by the authorities, they were nonetheless tolerated by the rulers in the feudal societies of Europe—over the years the hatred for the Jews had spread throughout all of Europe, east and west alike.

"Europe is not a friendly place for Jews, and has not been for centuries, if ever," Philip concluded. "Not that other places were ever very hospitable to us. After being expelled from the Holy Land almost two thousand years ago by the Romans, and dispersed throughout the Roman Empire and beyond, wherever Jews went they were always outcasts, strangers in the land."

"The amazing part of it," Sam answered, "is that invariably the Jews were initially welcomed by the rulers, and helped propel the economy and make the place successful, only to later be placed under harsh conditions or expelled in undeserved humiliation as a 'thank you' gesture."

"It is interesting that the only time that the Jews actually thrived through these nearly 2,000 years of diaspora was during the Islamic Almoravid Empire in Spain and Morocco in the eleventh and twelfth centuries, the time of the illustrious Jewish deep thinkers and Rabbis, Maimonides and Nachmanides," Philip responded.

"True, that was a period that Jews had religious and economic freedom," Sam acknowledged. "The Muslim rulers treated the Jews better than their European counterparts."

"But then came the Catholic Church in the fifteenth century, and the Inquisition, and the forced conversions and the expulsions from Spain in 1492, just when Columbus discovered America."

They reached home, and the conversation ended.

Several days later, after dinner the three brothers retired to the parlor at Haim's home for a glass of cognac from a bottle Sam had brought with him from Lille. Isaac's wife Gita left to put Marc in bed and Haim was tired of the day's events and went upstairs for the night. They all had just spent the afternoon with Misha's great uncle Ben who had immigrated to the United States some ten years earlier, and had now returned for a short visit with his relatives in Latvia.

"Ben seemed to be quite content in his life in America," Isaac commented. "He is doing well financially, and there is a small Jewish community in Pennsylvania where he lives. He says the Jews are quite welcome there, he never felt any antagonism in America because he is a Jew."

"Yes, he said that," Philip responded, "but I wonder how long this welcome of the Jews in America will last."

"What do you mean?" Isaac asked.

"How long before the anti-Semites in America raise their heads," Philip replied.

"From what he said there is no anti-Semitism in America," Isaac was forceful.

"That may be so, Tanya says the same thing," Philip answered. "But the question is for how long?"

They were back to the subject of Jews in the Diaspora.

"What makes you think it will not last?" Isaac asked.

"Because that is what happened over and over again," Philip stated. "As Sam pointed out to me the other day, Jews were initially welcomed to the society by the rulers, and were allowed to contribute to the success of the place, but once they did, they were made outcasts, or even expelled. Poland in the sixteenth and seventeenth century is an excellent example, but it happened in other societies as well."

"But America is different," Isaac contested. "America is made of many different peoples, the country of emigrants, not a homogeneous society, so they would not pick on the Jews."

"Again, the question is for how long?" Philip insisted. "Once that society becomes integrated, why would they not be like the European societies that mistreated the Jews over the centuries?"

"That reminds me, Philip," Sam said. "The other day you mentioned the Catholic Church and the expulsion of the Jews from Spain in 1492, and that made me think."

"And?" Philip asked.

"I spent some time this week at the Yeshiva library reading about the history of the Jews in the Diaspora, and found that there were significantly more places from which the Jews were expelled than I had previously known about," Sam said.

"More places?" Philip asked.

Sam reached into his pocket and pulled a folded piece of paper. "I made a list. Since the year 1000, in this millennium alone, France expelled the Jews in 1182, England expelled all the Jews in 1290 to 1657, Belgium in 1370, France again in 1394, and Austria in 1421," Sam read from his notes.

"And that's not all," Sam continued after a brief pause. "As you mentioned the other day Spain was in 1492, then Portugal in 1496, and Poland in 1648, and I am sure I had missed one or two."

He looked up from his paper. "All these in addition to the many cases where a local Baron threw the Jews off his land during Feudal Europe."

"True, there is even a Yiddish idiom about that: When the Baron evicted the Jews, and sent his dogs after them, or issued another edict against them, they always said to not worry, things will improve: 'either the Baron will die, or his dogs will perish.'" Isaac chuckled.

Philip was stunned, shaken by the facts. "I knew that in addition to Spain there were other expulsions, from other societies, but I had no idea there were so many."

The three brothers sat for a while in silence, nursing their cognac.

"Seems the Jews are a subject of hate and scorn, and have always been," Sam stated.

"But why are the Jews so picked on, so disliked, so mistreated?" Philip asked the inevitable question. "There must be serious reasons why this hatred. After all, we don't cause trouble to the population, and try to be good citizens wherever we go."

They sat quietly pondering the dilemma.

"That is a very difficult question to answer," Sam finally said. "I had asked myself this question many times, and did not come up with any definite answer. There may be many reasons why the Jews were and are so hated by their host societies, not the least of which is the Christian belief that it was the Jews who crucified Jesus. For centuries, the Catholic Church taught this falsehood to their believers, instigating them against the Jews when in reality it was the pagan Romans who crucified him because in their view he was an insurrectionist against the empire, and he had to go.

"But I think the main reason for this hatred may be this: We are a small minority, and different, mostly well educated, and despite the limitations imposed on us, and regulations against us, we are quite successful wherever we go and hence are resented by the local population."

"That does not make sense," Philip objected. "If we are successful, would not the goyim look at us with favor, and appreciate and like us more?"

"You certainly would think that, but the opposite seems true, and I can understand why," Sam was forming a conviction. "Psychologically, it is easy for people to look *down* on others, but very difficult for them to look *up* to others. It's as if they themselves are diminished, an unpleasant feeling of inadequacy," he concluded.

"Interesting theory, maybe even plausible. But if so, what is the solution? We are not going to stop educating the children, diminish ourselves, and be less successful to please the goyim," Philip contended.

"Right. There is only one solution. The Jews have to not be dependent on the goyim, The Jews must have a place of their own, their own country where they are not the minority, and not dependent on another ruler."

"You are right," Philip replied. "Our own place, our own country, our own homeland."

"But where?" Sam asked. "Where can we go? Where can we create our homeland?"

"There is only one place where we can create a homeland. The only place is the place from which we have been evicted some 1,900 years ago, the Promised Land, the Holy Land, Eretz Israel—the Land of Israel. That is the only place where we won't be subjected to this rampant anti-Semitism."

"Isn't that what Theodore Herzl's described in his book Altnouland?"

"I read it," Philip replied.

"I read it in its original German in Lille. What a fascinating uplifting story about a future state of Israel in the Land of Israel, which is now under the British Mandate of Palestine," Sam said.

He paused for a minute and then continued. "But how could we accomplish that? How could we fulfill the dream when the British High Commissioner to Palestine is not cooperating, to say the least, and the British government is so hostile to the notion of Jews immigrating to Palestine?"

They were silent for a moment.

"With great difficulty, I presume," Philip responded. "With great difficulty and sacrifice" He paused deep in thought, then proceeded. "But we shall prevail. We *will* create a homeland for the Jews in Palestine. It is our home, our land, promised to us by the Balfour Declaration, by the San Remo Conference, by the League of Nations. And before all that, and above all, promised to us by God."

And so, the Zionist aspirations which had been seeded nearly two millennia earlier, since Jews were evicted from their home in the Holy Land, now took roots and sprouted in these two young men.

Their eldest brother Isaac dismissed their discussions and conclusions with disdain. He felt quite comfortable where he was, and the position he had attained in society.

"I don't share your views at all. I don't feel anything like what you described. I am being treated with respect, have many friends, and am quite comfortable living here in Riga and running my business. I don't consider myself a traditional Jew, and am perfectly assimilated in the society.

"If I were to leave Latvia, leaving all my friends behind, and my business and my comfort, then it would have to be for something better, not worse," Isaac said. "I would then follow Misha's uncle, or better still Tanya, to the United States, to America. At least there, with the money I have, I could establish a comfortable life like I have here, and not a primitive existence in some desert piece of land which has nothing," he told his brothers.

Tanya and Adolf had arrived in the United States in 1923 after having graduated from the University of Berlin, each in his own field—Tanya as a medical doctor, Adolf as an attorney. They were ready to start their new life but soon realized they were required to pass the qualifying exams in order to practice their professions: Tanya would have to pass the medical board exam, and Adolf would have to pass the bar, both of which required fluency in English. Adolf's hurdle was more difficult than that of Tanya, since the laws and judicial system in Germany which he had studied were substantially different than those in the United States, whereas medicine is medicine regardless of where it is practiced.

So Tanya and Adolf set out to expeditiously pass the exams. They struck a deal between them: whoever passed the exam first would start practicing their profession, while the other would take on the responsibilities of a homemaker. Tanya passed the medical boards first, and was certified as an obstetrician and gynecologist, and Adolf became the homemaker. Over the next few years he continued studying for the exam, and finally passed the bar, and could practice as an attorney in New York. But in the meantime their two daughters arrived in close succession, and he raised the girls and never practiced law in his life.

Poor Adolf, a man walking around New York streets in the mid-1920s pushing a baby stroller, and doing the shopping at the local grocery store, or buying clothes for the girls. In those days men did not do these things; those were relegated to women only. The roles were distinct: Men were the breadwinners, worked outside the home, and women were housewives taking care of the needs of the family and raising the children; and here was a couple that reversed the roles. But while Tanya's practicing medicine as a female doctor was rare but not unheard of, Adolf had no equivalent among people of his gender and he endured abusive glares and stares of passersby snickering behind his back.

To be fair, in 1929 when the girls started attending school, Adolf finally entered the workforce and joined a financial firm, not as an attorney but as an investment advisor managing a few portfolios of friends and acquaintances. But he still was the girls' primary care giver, although by now there was no need for him to be humiliated by pushing them in a baby stroller.

And then came the crash of 1929, and being an investment advisor managing a portfolio was not the best profession to be in.

Chapter 8

When the summer of 1929 was over, Sam returned to Lille for another year of engineering studies. He came back to his old room, put the crucifix back in its spot in the closet and settled in the normal routine of a sophomore at the university.

He spent his first weekend with Mendel and Rivka, and they were overjoyed to see him. During the past year they had gotten to know him quite well, and liked him as if he were their own son who, regrettably, they never had.

"I have the warmest greetings for you from Mira and her children," he told them. "Mira is doing fine, although she has not remarried, probably still grieving for Yaakov even after so many years. She says: 'What do I need some other old guy to take care of? My life is fine as it is.'"

"Yes, she wrote us some of that," Mendel replied, "but it is not good for a person to be alone, without companionship."

"The children tried to convince her she should find someone to share her life with, especially since they will soon be leaving the home and establishing their own families, and then she will really be alone, but she would not hear of it. She likes her freedom to come and go as she pleases. She is an emancipated woman." Sam said. "She draws beautifully, portraits and nature scenes, and is very happy doing that. With the profits of the company that my brother Isaac is sharing with her she is also able to put quite a bit of money aside, and even go on vacation during the summer, free of obligations. This summer she went with Moishe and Rachel to Warsaw for a couple of weeks, and enjoyed the culture of the city and especially the museums."

"In that case, good for her, my blessing to her," Mendel said.

Since it was still early in the day, Rivka hurried to prepare Sam's favorite dish for the Sabbath, a very special concoction of beef with potatoes and plums cooked for hours over a small flame. It so reminded him of his mother's cooking!

After evening services at the end of the Sunday, Sam returned to his room ready to go back to school the next morning.

In early March Sam received a letter from Brigitte telling him that she wanted to see him. Would he be in Lille toward the end of the month?

He immediately responded to her that yes, he would be there, and was very excited about seeing her. He offered her that she could have his room during her stay, and he could stay with the Schneirsons while she was in town.

He met her at the train station, and she looked wonderful. She had radiance about her, the aura of someone who is positive and happy. They embraced for the longest time, and then they went to their old neighborhood. Sam carried her suitcase upstairs as she followed him.

Brigitte had never been to his room, so she looked around at the simple accommodations and sparse furnishing: A single bed, a small dresser, and a desk with a table lamp for his studies, and books, lots of books. She noticed the electric tea pot and two cups on the dresser, and chuckled at seeing the empty place where a large cross must have hung over the bed. He showed her the hiding place of the crucifix out of view and she smiled understandingly.

They went to their favorite bistro for a cup of coffee and a chat. Sam could tell that she was eager to tell him something important, but she needed to get to it on her own terms, so he did not ask. They spoke of everything that had happened to them since they saw each other last, describing every event in minute detail, exposing their innermost feelings without concern or care.

Long after it became dark outside they walked to the kosher restaurant. Drinking a cup of coffee in a non-kosher bistro was as far as Sam was willing to go violating his religious obligations, but dinner was a different matter, and Brigitte did not care one way or another, so long as the food was decent, which it was.

The woman feeding them sized Brigitte up and down, to make sure she was worthy of that nice boy Sam, but she made no comment or asked any question, and Sam decided to not satisfy her curiosity. Instead, he focused on his friend, waiting for her to share with him what she was so excited about.

"I have some good news," she finally said, "but it is not all good news."

"What is it, Brigitte? Tell me."

"Remember the man I wrote you about?"

"Of course I remember. Is he all right? Is he treating you well?"

"Oh, he is wonderful. He reminds me so much of you. He is kind, and gentle, and considerate. We spend every free moment with each other. He even comes every day at midday and we have lunch together. Sometimes when it's warm, he brings sandwiches and some wine and we sit on the bench in the park. It is so pleasant."

"Sounds wonderful," Sam was genuinely happy for her and his voice showed it.

"And best of all, for the first time in my life I believe that I am in love."

"You are? How wonderful! That is great!"

"I did not think that I would ever feel that way. You know, with all the men I had, I sort of closed myself to men. They were clients, not a subject for love.

"But then you came into my life, and I got to know you in a different way. You were not a client, and after a while I got attached to you anyway, and that made the difference. You restored my ability to connect with men in a different way, as people, and not as potential clients who wanted me to satisfy their sexual urges.

"Do you remember the first time I said hello to you? I had seen you walk by every night for a week or two, and you never paid much attention to me. I knew you saw me there every evening, but you did not approach me, and that made it a challenge. Like a spider I wanted to draw you in into my web. You were mysterious to me, an anathema, why would you pass by me night after night and not try to use me?

"And then I found out you were a person, not a potential client. You were a man, naïve and uninitiated perhaps, not the kind of man I was used to in my profession, but a man nonetheless. And that told me that maybe there were more men like you, men for whom a quick sex act with a stranger for money was not as important as getting to know the woman before engaging in sex with her.

"My boyfriend Armand is like that, like you. We dated for the longest time before he even kissed me in earnest, not the peck on both cheeks as we French do. He wanted to know me, about me, and

I wanted to know all I could about him, and it was such a wonderful feeling to be free from that darkness I was in for so long."

She stopped for a while, looking for a way to tell him the rest.

"Well, a month ago Armand proposed. We were walking along the Seine near Place Vendome and he pulled a red rose from the inside of his topcoat, and asked me to marry him."

"Congratulations, Brigitte," Sam exclaimed, "I am so happy for you!"

She was quiet, saying nothing.

"And you accepted, of course?" Sam inquired enthusiastically.

She took her time.

"You accepted, right?" Sam repeated, a bit hesitatingly.

"I told him I needed some time to think about it."

"You did *what?*"

"I needed some time. I had never told him about my life here in Lille, so I would be starting a life with him based on a lie, and that would not be good. Regardless of whether he eventually finds out or not, it is wrong to hide it from him."

Sam looked at her in silence, thinking about what she had just said. She paused, waiting for his words.

"I think you are right," he finally said. "If you want to have a life with him, if you truly love him, you must tell him. He should know. And if he loves you, as you think he does, he will make his own decision if he accepts it or not."

"I thought that is what you would say. I came all the way here to make sure of it. That was the other reason I needed more time, I needed time to hear you say that."

They walked back to his room, arm in arm. He walked her up the stairs, and was about to go across town. She would not hear of it.

"Stay here," She said. "Don't go. You can sleep on the bed. I will sleep on the floor."

He hesitated.

"I will stay, but *I* will sleep on the floor."

They took the comforter off the bed, and folded it in three, and he lay on it next to the bed.

She turned the light off and lay on her back on the bed. Then she let her arm dangle off the side, until she found his hand. She held on to his hand for a moment, then tugged on it and pulled him onto the bed.

❖ ❖ ❖

When Sam woke up the next morning Brigitte was gone. On the dresser he found a note scribbled with her distinctive handwriting:

"My dearest friend,
I am going back to Paris to speak with Armand.
If you do not hear from me again, it means that he understood and accepted.
Thank you for everything. You are my guardian angel; I love you dearly.
God bless you,
Brigitte."
He never heard from her again.

Chapter 9

During the rest of that year Sam's studies took front and center place in his life. His visits with the Schneirsons from time to time broke the routine somewhat, and his discussions with Rabbi Mendel about Jewish law and custom added color to the otherwise bland and dry engineering studies. Despite being quite a large city, Lille was not known for cultural excellence and except for occasional lectures by visiting dignitaries at the university, not much else was happening on the intellectual plain. If one sought to watch an opera or attend a concert or theatre, one would have to travel to Paris—which for Sam, an observant Jew on a limited budget, was not only too expensive but complicated as well. So through the entire time Sam remained in Lille, regrettably he did not visit Paris even once.

When summer arrived, Sam returned to Riga to spend time in his native city, with his father, and more so with his brothers, and his dear friend Moishe. Sam's father was mostly out of town tending to his business, and Sam joined him for one of those outings. It was not an exciting event for him, he preferred to remain in town, but his father surprisingly offered him to join him on his trip, and Sam accepted. It gave him the opportunity to observe his father at work, away from his home environment, something he was always curious about. Primarily he wanted to find out how his father interacted with his employees, and if he were as stern with them as he was with his own sons. To his great surprise and relief, the answer to that question was a resounding "no." While not terribly warm toward them, Haim treated his employees with respect and consideration, and he even uttered praise for some, drastically different from his behavior at home.

Sam also joined Philip at his work at Laima chocolate factory on a couple of occasions, and Philip gave him a tour of the plant. For

Sam, an aspiring engineer, it was extremely interesting to see the manufacturing process, and especially the complex machines producing, wrapping, and packaging the sweets to be sold in stores.

Philip became engaged that summer to Miriam, a wonderful girl from a well-known and respectable family in town. Miriam, who went by her nickname Manya, was liked by all who knew her, and Sam was so happy that his brother had found a soul mate. They adored each other and were planning to get married during the coming year, and Sam hoped to be able to come back to Riga for the wedding.

So it was a great summer all around, but alas it too ended, and by middle of August Sam had to return to his studies. This year Sam had a special reason for arriving to school early: He was not returning to Lille for his junior year. He had decided to transfer to the Engineering School at the University of Nantes, a town in the southwest region of France, near the Atlantic coast. Although a smaller city, with a smaller university, Nantes had become an industrial center and therefore a hotbed for engineering studies.

Moreover, the University of Nantes had the reputation of having the best aeronautical engineering department, and if Sam were to spend two years of his life studying the subject, then why would he not attend the best school he could?

He boarded the train heading for Paris, and from there he took another train to Nantes. He wished he had a few hours in between trains so he could explore the city some, but the train schedule did not allow for that, and he was not interested in having to spend the night in a hotel in Paris.

He arrived in Nantes in the morning, and as he stepped out of the train station he recalled his first arrival in Lille, and bemused over the difference. By now Sam spoke French perfectly like a native, with a slight accent attributed to his northern Lille pronunciation. For all intents and purposes he appeared as a local, the classical beret always on his head, and the mannerism of a native. Like a chameleon, Sam could pass as a regular Frenchman, and he melded into the crowd.

Before leaving Lille he did some research at the library about Nantes, and also asked some of his French classmates who knew the city for recommendations concerning housing and the like, and was well prepared.

He spent the first two nights in a hotel, while scouting the neighborhood near the university for the "essentials:" a place to stay, and a kosher place to eat. To his pleasant surprise he found both without much effort. Moreover, he also found a small synagogue within walking distance of his new quarters, so he was all set for the new academic year.

❖ ❖ ❖

Except for Sam's aeronautical engineering professor Claude Brunet, none of the other teachers and instructors at the university cared much for him or paid any attention to him. Firstly, through his records, they discovered that he was not native French, and that was a big minus for them. Secondly and more importantly, he was a Jew, and they had no use for those. Their blind dislike of the Jews was much more pronounced than the anti-Semitism he had experienced in Lille, and he wondered why it was, but never came up with an answer.

For some reason that Sam also never uncovered, Professor Brunet took a liking to this blond and blue-eyed foreign student. He appreciated Sam's efforts to master the subjects he taught, and in his eyes Sam was, without a doubt, at the top of the class.

There were only fifteen students in the faculty. Aeronautics in 1930 had not yet taken off as a prime destination for engineering students, so it was not difficult to be noticed by the professor. But in this case, Claude Brunet went beyond the normal professor-student relationship and invited Sam to visit his office at will.

Maybe it was the professor's curiosity more than anything else that led him to extend the offer. Ever since he started teaching engineering at the university a few years earlier, he had never had a Jewish student, and in his life overall he had had very limited interaction with orthodox Jews. He wanted to understand that strange sect, with their bizarre customs and restrictions. What made them tick? How come this clan, this tribe, had survived all these centuries in exile without being totally absorbed and crushed by the massive forces of the enveloping societies?

Sam was delighted to have the opportunity to spend time one-on-one with this distinguished professor—this was the man whose reputation brought Sam to Nantes in the first place, and being able to meet with him at his office was a godsend. An offer like that gave him a golden opportunity to maximize his time at the university and come out of it not only as an aeronautical engineer, but the best aeronautical engineer ever. Nevertheless, he was reluctant to take advantage of the professor's offer. He was never a pushy type or one who felt a sense of entitlement, and being extremely polite and well-mannered he did not want to intrude. So gingerly at first, more boldly as time progressed, Sam would visit Professor Brunet at his office whenever time and courage permitted.

During the first few times when Sam visited the professor's office he brought up some issues on which he wanted clarification. Some of the discussions during class did not convince him and he asked Professor Brunet if he would expand on some of the notions described in class. On other occasions he would ask the professor to review some of the formulas that acted as the basis for some calculation or other: lift-to-drag ratios, wingspan computations, and the like.

While always being responsive to Sam's needs, the professor would eventually guide the conversation to more personal terms. He first asked Sam about his overall impression of the class, and solicited his comments and suggestions to maybe alter the order of the material, or anything that would improve the comprehension of the other students. Then on one occasion he explained his reasoning to Sam:

"I consider you the brightest among the students in my class," he stated. "If you do not understand something, or need clarification, in most probability the other students did not understand it either. Knowing that fact helps me rearrange the lecture and dwell on the issue in question, making the class so much more valuable to all of us."

"I understand your point of view, professor."

Claude Brunet looked at Sam, mulling something in his head.

"Glickman, eh? You are not French, are you?" he asked.

"No sir." Obviously Professor Brunet had not checked his dossier carefully.

"Where did you come from?"

"Latvia. I was born in Riga."

"And you came to France for your studies, or before?"

"I came to France and directly to the university in Lille just before my freshman year."

"Did you speak French when you arrived?"

"No, Professor Brunet, not a word."

"Remarkable. I have seen your grades from Lille, and saw that you had some difficulties in the first semester, but finished both the first and second years as an 'A' student."

"That is true, professor."

"I believe that you are Jewish. Is that so?"

"Here goes," Sam thought. "One more time I am going to find out that my religion will be held against me in some way." But the truth was unavoidable, so he nodded in the affirmative.

"I have not met many Jews in my life, and none of my former or current students, except you, are Jews. I heard a lot from people who resent the Jews for being so smart and successful and I always wanted to understand more about your people."

He took a deep breath as if he were about to say something difficult to say.

"I would very much like to hear about your people, but my office is not the right place for it. Would you mind meeting me outside the university, after school hours?"

Sam thought it was an interesting proposition, one that he could hardly refuse. The professor seemed sincere, and even if he were not, he could see no harm in acquiescing.

"I will be honored," he responded.

"Would Friday evening be convenient for you? Say around eight o'clock?"

"I am afraid not, professor," Sam said, sheepishly. "Fridays are the only evenings that I am not free, but any other evening will be wonderful. Would Saturday evening at the same hour be good?"

"Saturday will be fine," the professor said enthusiastically. "I will tell Madame Brunet to prepare dinner for us."

"If it is all right with you professor, I am on a strict special diet. Would it be all right if I came after dinner?" Sam asked.

"Oh, that will be fine. Let us make it for nine o'clock then."

He scribbled something on a piece of paper and handed it to Sam.

"This is my address, and I look forward to seeing you on Saturday evening."

"Thank you, I do too."

❖ ❖ ❖

At nine o'clock sharp on Saturday, a bouquet of flowers in his hand, Sam rang the bell at Claude Brunet's house. With a smile Claude Brunet greeted him at the door and invited him to come in.

They sat down in the parlor. It was a nice room, decorated in Louis the XIV style furniture, but delicate, not overdone, and in good taste.

"You found the place without much difficulty, I hope."

"No problem at all, professor. I have a map of the city as a guide."

Soon Madame Brunet came in. Sam rose to his feet and waited. Europeans maintain the tradition that the man never extends his hand to shake a woman's hand; she is the one who initiates the handshake, and she did.

"*Bonsoir monsieur,*" she greeted him, "I am Yvonne, Claude's wife."

"*Enchanté madame,*" Sam replied, "I am Sam. I am a student of Professor Brunet," he responded.

"Yes, I know. He told me a bit about you."

"Please call me Claude," the professor had also risen to his feet when his wife entered. "Outside the university I am Claude to all my friends and acquaintances, so please do call me Claude, and I will call you Sam if you permit."

"That would be very nice, I like that," Sam said.

Yvonne sat down on one of the armchairs facing the center coffee table.

"Please sit down," she said to Sam.

"Thank you."

"Would you like some cognac?" Claude asked.

"With pleasure," Sam replied. Although not a drinker, a good snifter of cognac was a treat he had learned to enjoy from time to time since his arrival in France.

Claude walked over to the cabinet, pulled out three cognac glasses and a bottle of Courvoisier VSOP. Yvonne signaled him that she did not want any, so he returned one glass to the cabinet.

"Would you prefer Courvoisier, or Remy Martin?" he asked.

"Either would be delightful," Sam replied.

Claude poured them both a generous snifter, then sat down.

"Please tell us about yourself some. What made you come to study in France? Is there no university in Latvia—that is where you said you came from, right?"

"Yes, I was born and raised in Riga, the capital. I wanted to study engineering, aeronautical engineering in particular, so after high school in 1928 I came to Lille."

"Tell us a bit about Riga. We have never been there."

And so they conversed for a few hours. Primarily they asked the questions, and Sam answered, but from time to time he would seek an equivalent response from them. They were delightful people and he really enjoyed their company.

Time passed so quickly and before he knew it he heard the grandfather clock chime twice, it was two o'clock in the morning.

"I must go now," he said during a break in the conversation, "I have kept you up too long."

"Not at all, it was such a pleasure," said Yvonne, "we must do it again. You are a fascinating young man. You must come back and visit, and soon."

"Thank you. I would like that very much. And thank you for your hospitality."

"I will see you in class on Monday. *Bonne nuit*," said Claude as Sam stepped out into the night.

❖   ❖   ❖

Over the next two years while Sam was in Nantes, he was invited numerous times to the Brunets' house, and he looked forward to the opportunity every time. They discussed everything: University life, politics and current affairs, both domestic and international, history and geography, and even religion. Like most of Nantes' population they were Catholic, and although they attended church every Sunday they were open minded and interested in other forms of worship, Judaism especially.

Over many nights Sam shared with them some of what he had studied about Jewish law and custom, and more so about Jewish philosophy, a subject that intrigued them most. He explained the uniqueness of Jewish history as he understood it, and what in his view allowed Jews to survive the hostile environments they had endured for nearly 2,000 years.

Both Claude and Yvonne, who taught humanities at the university, were extremely interested in understanding Sam's narrative at a deeper level, and in between their meetings, all three read any book they could find that covered the topic being explored. Together they learned about the treatment of Jews in the various societies, from Babylon to Spain, from Siberia to Morocco, and through the different periods of the Greek Empire, the Roman Empire, the Crusades, the Dark Ages, all the way to Ottoman Empire and the modern era.

Then at one of their discussions, when they were thoroughly versed in what had befallen the Jews over centuries of hardship and abuse, Yvonne raised the question of the future of the Jewish people: Were they going to be shuffled from place to place, being initially welcomed to revive the local society, breathe new life into it, and then when the economy flourished and the situation stabilized be expelled with their shirts on their backs as it had happened in Poland and Hungary and Russia and England?

Sam was quiet for the longest time, deep within himself, searching for the right words. They patiently awaited his reply.

"The solution is for the Jews to have a place of their own, to not depend on others, to be masters of their own destinies, and free of the hatred and abuse they have suffered for so long.

"The Jews must be able to return to their roots, to the land with which they have historical ties, the land that had been taken away from them by force almost 1,900 years ago, the ancient Land of Israel, the Holy Land, the land that God promised them in the Old Testament."

"How can they return to the Holy Land, to Palestine?" Claude asked.

"That is a difficult question to answer," Sam said. "That land which had been under the Ottoman Empire for the past four hundred years is now in the hands of the British Empire. The British have a mandate from the League of Nations to govern over the area from the Mediterranean to beyond the Euphrates River to the border of Persia.

"In 1917, the British Foreign Secretary Lord Balfour made a declaration that the British Government 'views with favor the establishment in Palestine of a national home for the Jewish people and will use their best endeavors to facilitate the achievement of this object...'.

"Then there was the 1920 San Remo Conference that further strengthened the rights of the Jewish people to settle in Palestine.

"The Balfour declaration was later incorporated into the mandate given Britain to govern over the area, but the British, under the influence of their Arab friends are refusing to obey the mandate as written. First they cut off an area of their mandate and created Iraq; then in 1924 they further cut off a very large area, seventy-seven percent of the remaining area to be exact, and gave it to an Arab tribe to create Trans Jordan, leaving only the area west of the Jordan River for Jewish Palestine; and now they are compounding the problem by preventing Jews from returning to even that small remaining area of their declared homeland. Until they relent, it is not likely that the Jews will be allowed to create their homeland there as promised over and over again. They are also preventing the existing Jewish population in Palestine from arming themselves to defend themselves and their homes from hostile Arab mobs.

"Just three years ago, there was a two-day massacre of sixty-seven Jews in Hebron by the Arab population of the city, and the British did nothing to stop it.

"So, the answer to 'how can Jews return to Palestine' is: 'with great difficulty'," Sam concluded.

They sat in silence for the longest time digesting what Sam had just said. It was obvious the Brunets understood the situation.

"That said," Sam continued quietly, "by hook or by crook, my brother and I are going there as soon as we can."

"You will go to Palestine?" asked Yvonne.

"Even if I have to smuggle across the border," Sam said with determination, "I will be there. Nothing will stop me, I will be there."

Chapter 10

It was not before two months later that the subject of Palestine came into the conversation once again. This time it was Claude who raised the subject.

"Are you serious about going to Palestine?" he asked Sam one evening, out of the blue.

"Yes," Sam answered.

"I have been thinking about it a lot," Claude said. "I wonder what you'll be doing there."

"I don't know. Quite frankly I never gave it a serious thought. I will do whatever I can, whatever they need me to do."

"You understand of course that there is no aviation in Palestine, no need for aeronautical engineers."

"True."

"So what can you do? How can you contribute and also feed yourself?" He was obviously leading somewhere with these questions.

"I will do whatever I am asked to do."

"Do you know anything about agriculture?"

"No, Claude."

"I know that you can speak many languages, but is there a need for it in Palestine?"

"I don't know for sure, but quite frankly I don't think so."

"What do they need? What profession would be useful there?"

"I am not sure," Sam said. "I know that it is a desert, with limited agriculture. There is no major industry, mostly a trading society."

"I can't imagine you taking on a trading job. You don't look to me like a good salesperson."

"I am terrible at that," Sam agreed.

"If you are serious about going there, you must find an occupation that may be in demand. Doesn't that make sense? Think about it and so will I."

A week later Professor Brunet asked Sam to his office.

"I was thinking about our conversation of the other day. Did I understand you correctly when you said that Palestine is mostly desert?"

"That is my understanding."

"How hot is it there?"

"I think it can get very hot. I don't know for sure, but it makes sense that it would be hot."

"I think that I have the answer to your dilemma, Sam," Claude said.

"You do?"

"I think so. If the country is desert, and hot, then the thing that they will need is refrigeration. Does that make sense to you?"

"Yes it does," Sam agreed.

"If so, I want you to come with me, I will introduce you to Professor Hisleur. He is a good man, the top expert in refrigeration this side of the Atlantic. Let's go talk to him and see what he suggests."

They walked down the hall a few doors down from Claude's office. Claude knocked on a door.

"Enter," they heard a deep voice. They did.

Behind the desk sat a man in his sixties sporting a long silver beard, and wearing rimmed glasses. He took his glasses off, raised his eyes and looked at Claude.

"Oh, hello Professor Brunet. Please come in and sit down." He turned and looked at Sam, sizing him up. "And who might this young man be?"

"This is Samuel Glickman. He is one of my students. Actually he is the top student in my class."

"Glickman, eh? German? Please sit down."

"No, professor, actually Latvian," Sam replied sheepishly.

"So what can I do for you, Professor Brunet?"

"Samuel here is planning to immigrate to a place that is mostly desert, hot, and quite primitive." Sam noticed Claude did not divulge the destination as Palestine, just defined it by its attributes.

Claude continued, "He will not be able to practice his profession as aeronautical engineer for many years to come, if ever, so I thought that maybe a change in major to refrigeration engineering is a wise move for him. What do you think? Would you agree to add him to your class?"

Until this moment Sam had not realized that what Claude had in mind was to hand him off to this professor and thus have him change major. But what about his dream, his desire to be part of the emerging aviation profession? Isn't that why he had come to Nantes in the first place?

Professor Hisleur stroked his beard, looking at Sam.

"You are in your junior year, is that correct? Because if you are in senior year then there won't be enough time for you to study and pass the exams."

"Yes, I am in my junior year."

Professor Hisleur continued stroking his beard for a moment in silence.

"Then I have a better proposal for you, young man. Entering the class in the middle of the year would be difficult, especially this late in the year. Instead I would suggest you continue studying under Professor Brunet and finish the semester. During the summer I will work with you and provide you all the material and guidance that you need in order to pass the exams. You will have to do some additional work during next year, but probably not more than you can handle."

He paused again for a second or two.

"This way you will graduate with a double major, with two diplomas as aeronautical engineer as well as refrigeration engineer. What do you think?"

Claude looked at Sam to see his reaction.

"How wonderful," Sam thought. He would be able to continue studying aeronautical engineering which he loved, and at the same time gain another degree in a practical topic!

Ouch. There goes his summer vacation. If he accepts, then he would have to stay in Nantes and study with Professor Hisleur during the summer.

But it was the best and most logical solution, and his summer vacation will simply have to be the price to pay.

"That sounds wonderful Professor Hisleur. That is absolutely great!"

"So it is done. I am staying in the university this summer anyway, which is slow time for us professors, and it would be interesting to have you study with me. By the end of the summer we will know if you can make it, putting the extra effort during the year. And if not, we will find another solution. Maybe an extra year at the university?"

"Thank you so much, Professor," Sam said.

"Come and see me the first day after school is out," Professor Hisleur instructed him. "Arrive not too early, around ten o'clock. *N'est pas?*"

"*D'accord*," Sam replied, "I agree."

"Thank you, Professor Hisleur," Claude called over his shoulder as they left his office.

❖   ❖   ❖

Sam had one minor problem with the new arrangement—his allowance. The stipend he received from his father did not include him staying nearly three months extra in France over the summer, and he somehow needed to cover that shortfall.

He weighed his options. Firstly, he could explain to his father that he wanted to take another major in school and needed to stay in France over the summer. That was the truth, and under normal circumstances that would be the most reasonable route to take. But he did not think his father would really be receptive. He would probably scoff at the idea, especially since he had just paid for a lavish wedding for Philip and Manya, a wedding that Sam regrettably was unable to attend.

He could ask either Isaac or Philip for help, but again he felt uncomfortable about that. Isaac never went to a university, and resented the fact that both Philip and Sam did: If he could go to work at eighteen, right out of high school, why were they different? He also never forgave Sam for being their mother's favorite, as if it had been Sam's fault. And Philip was just married a few months ago, and was setting up his new home, and on top of that Manya had just told him the good news that they would be expecting a baby early next year.

The alternative was for him to get a summer job, and work and study throughout the summer. He did not expect that the refrigeration engineering course would require his full time, because he was already taking all the regular engineering basic courses such as math, physics, fluid dynamics, and materials sciences, so that was an option, the best option.

When the summer arrived, Sam had no difficulty finding a job. Nantes was an industrial city with a lot of manufacturing plants around it, and almost immediately, with the help of Professor Hisleur the soon-to-be engineer was offered a mechanic's position at the French railroad maintenance yard.

It was a terrific part-time job. Beyond the flexible hours it paid well, well enough for him to mostly plug the hole in the budget. It also gave him an excellent opportunity to see how engineered products were designed, from a mechanic's point of view. He quickly saw that the products that he worked on could have been designed with minor adjustments, and those minor changes would have made the world of difference for him, the maintenance man. He understood that those observations would make him a much better engineer.

And above all, he learned how to use hand tools, identify which problem each tool was aimed to solve, and what the dangers of misusing them were. That is a most valuable lesson in life, and a major asset to add to his other capabilities.

For the next three months Sam worked on every component of the interior of a railroad car. He became adept at fixing plumbing, replacing wood trims, seats, and tables that needed repair or adjustment, the intricacies of the electrical system and the heating system. He liked the work, not realizing in his wildest dreams how instrumental this summer's job would be for the rest of his life.

And he also studied, studied hard, always burning the midnight oil.

The summer flew by, and the new school year started, his last year in the university. Sam was determined to make the best of it and he studied diligently. His goal of dual diplomas, aeronautical and refrigeration engineering, was now within his grasp, and he was not going to let either degree fade away.

Professor Hisleur took a tremendous liking to this hard-working young man, and mentored him both in and out of class with dedication and enthusiasm, to the chagrin of his colleagues. It would not be positive if it became known that someone could graduate from the University of Nantes with a full double major within four years; it might suggest that the school is not demanding enough, and the institute wanted to portray an image of a tough school in order to retain the accolades of a top tier world-class university.

Despite his added income from his job during the summer, Sam realized he would still end up short of funds. Although he earned a nice salary for a summer intern, after deducting his taxes and dues, and accounting for his living expenses, he was not left with much, and his expenses were rising while his allowance was not.

Sam pasted hand-written notices on campus offering his services as a translator to other students and faculty in the university, but the net he cast remained empty for some time. So he composed a new notice to offer private language tutoring in Russian and German, and as an afterthought, he added Latvian and Hebrew as well. He did not expect anyone would be interested in either, but he figured that if adding those did not help, it probably could not hurt either.

To his amazement, two days later he received a note requesting his assistance with Hebrew. The signature was that of a Father Joseph Masson, a priest with a local Catholic congregation. Sam did not hesitate a moment, and at the first break in his classes, he dashed to the church off campus in search of Father Masson.

When he saw Sam entering the church and looking around, Father Masson emerged from behind a partition, and started walking toward the confessional booths. Sam did not follow him there, so the priest realized that Sam must be seeking something other than a confession, and approached him.

"What can I do for you, my son?"

By Sam's estimation the priest was in his mid-forties, medium height and build, and with a calm and pleasant disposition.

"You responded to my posting concerning language tutorial in Hebrew, Father," replied Sam.

The priest noticed that Sam had not removed his cap as he entered the church, and immediately put two and two together.

"You are Jewish I presume?"

"Yes, I am," Sam answered in a matter-of-fact voice.

"Ah, perfect, and your Hebrew is correct, and you are familiar with biblical text?"

"Yes, truly so."

"Then please come to the study, and we will talk there."

Sam perfectly understood the priest's concern about "Hebrew being correct." Many Jews, the Ultraorthodox and especially the *Hassids*, consider Hebrew a sacred language that should be used only for biblical studies, and not for normal conversation and communication. Over the generations, they had developed an intentional mispronunciation of the language to serve as a basis for communication amongst themselves, and even with God during their prayers. That mispronunciation even received a name, "Ivris," as compared to "Ivrit" which is the proper Hebrew name of the language. Obviously Father Masson was interested in the unadulterated form of the language, which Sam had also studied at the yeshiva.

They sat down at the opposite sides of his desk, and discussed the needs of the priest and how Sam could best serve those. They covered the usual subjects—Sam's qualifications, the schedule, and also Sam's minimal fee for the lessons.

For the next few weeks Sam and Father Masson met in the church almost every day for one hour. Sam started with the basics, the twenty-two letters of the Hebrew alphabet, which was not an issue for the priest who mastered those quickly.

But then, when it came to reading whole words, Father Masson ran against a brick wall. For some reason, he could not get himself to read from right to left, the way Hebrew is written. No matter how hard he tried, dyslexic he was not.

It was a major obstacle requiring a special solution.

Sam tried placing the book in front of a mirror and having Father Masson read the words that way, from left to right, and it worked to some extent, but Father Masson was not pleased at always having to carry a mirror in order to read the text. Moreover, since they were sitting side by side to study, Sam would have to read the words backwards, all the letters were reversed, and it clearly was not a good solution all around.

For a few days they struggled with this handicap. Sam was patient, trying to help the priest, but it was not going anywhere.

The solution appeared to Sam in his dream, and he was eager to get to the church and try it out. He sat across the table from Father Masson, placed the book right side up for himself to read, and asked the Father to read from left to right, from the bottom row up.

It worked! Hesitatingly at first, and more solidly within a few minutes, Father Masson was reading Hebrew with the letters upside down, from left to right and from the bottom line up.

Hebrew is a relatively "small" language, with barely 4,000 roots, and therefore should be an easy language to learn. However, since the normal written text, especially biblical texts which were the priest's focus, have no vowels within them, the sound of the pronunciation is determined by the context of the word within the sentence, and it is difficult to discern how a word should be pronounced. For example, if one saw a word as "brd," is it "board," "beard," "bared," "broad," "bread," etc.? In Hebrew the only clue is its context within the sentence, and it takes substantial practice to be able to read such a text.

So once the basic mechanics of reading the language were out of the way, that was what Sam and Father Masson concentrated on, and by the end of the school year, when Sam was leaving Nantes, Father Masson was reading Hebrew, pronouncing the words mostly correctly, and understanding most of what he was reading. The mission was accomplished.

❖　❖　❖

Almost up to graduation day Professor Brunet repeatedly tried to convince Sam to remain in Nantes. He even secured for Sam a position of engineer in the engineering department of the railroad where Sam had previously worked as a mechanic.

Sam graciously declined, thanked the professor for all his efforts and help. He intended to return to Latvia for his military service, and then on to Palestine, he said. For him, he explained, achieving his goal of going to the Land of Israel was more important than the convenience of a steady well-paying job in France or elsewhere. It was his life's dream, and he would not be dissuaded from pursuing it, no matter what.

The day after graduation Sam bid his two favorite professors, Madame Brunet, and Father Masson farewell, and with two engineering diplomas, a Bachelor of Science degree in mathematics and a Bachelor of Science degree in physics under his arm, he boarded the train to Paris, and then home to Riga.

Not a bad haul for a young man who did not even speak the language when he arrived less than four years earlier.

Chapter 11

Sam's reason for joining the military in Latvia was simple: He wanted to make sure that no one could ever say he owed the Latvians anything, and since Latvia had been his home for eighteen years he felt obligated to complete his military service in the country. He probably could have saved himself from enduring this hardship by not returning to Riga, but that was not his style. It was something he had to do, a question of honor.

Being an aeronautical engineer gained him entry to the fledgling Latvian Air Force.

Being a Jew gained him entry to the Latrine Squad at the base with the rank of private.

All other college-educated entrants to the military were automatically granted an officer's rank of second lieutenant, with the normal privileges associated with it. Beyond upscale housing, officers' dining hall, authority, transportation, and the like, there was the opportunity of practicing one's profession, which in Sam's case would be in aeronautics. But Sam was a Jew, and a Jew was not even a second class citizen; a Jew in the Latvian military was a person to torment, mistreat, and abuse.

So for six months past his basic training Sam cleaned toilets, a job normally assigned to new recruits. Every day at morning parade he would be singled out, without any provocation on his part, and sent to his station of the day, the same one of the previous day—the latrines.

No furloughs, limited weekend passes, no privileges of any kind. But Sam, this young man who spoke seven languages and held two engineering degrees, nevertheless made the best of it.

"You want me to clean your toilets?" Sam said to a fictitious Latvian. "Fine, then I will clean them like no one else has done so before."

And he did. Within days, the latrines were shining, sparkling, spotlessly clean, and ready for the "White Glove Inspection" that never really came.

Even then, for six months Sam scrubbed the place over and over again, in a silent frenzy to show the Latvians that the Jew could teach them a lesson or two in excellence.

But the torment was not limited to his days. Being a private, never getting a promotion while others of his recruit class were already corporals or even sergeants, he was also part of the Night Watch Squad. Others rotated in and out of the squad, but Private Samuel Glickman was a permanent fixture there, being assigned guard duty almost every other night.

And the abuse was ongoing in the Mess Hall as well. Forget *kashrut*, the religious decree to eat only kosher food which Sam maintained even during his time away from home in France. In the Latvian Air Force, to the officers supervising lunch or dinner in the mess hall kosher meant that they must plop a piece of pork onto Sam's plate, contaminating the meager other portions of the meal that he could otherwise eat.

Sam had no choice. For self-preservation he was forced to eat the pork, and he never complained, never showed his anguish, and never gave the tormentors and harassers the pleasure and satisfaction of seeing him in discomfort.

After a long while they relented somewhat. Abusing someone in new and different ways requires effort, and by not showing them that they were getting to him Sam obliterated their gratification from seeing him hurt, so they lost interest and after some time stopped their harassment. The hatred and disdain did not abate, but the other manifestations did.

It was not long afterward that a delegation of French officers was arriving, and the staff desperately searched for a French speaking officer to assist in the translation. They found none, but they found out that Private Samuel Glickman spoke the language fluently, so out of the latrines they dragged him, and into the Office of Public Relations of the airfield.

And that became Sam's role for the next year and a half, to escort visiting dignitaries and translate for them. Whether they were Russian or Ukrainian, German or Austrian, French or Belgian, English or American, wherever the foreign delegation arrived from, or whatever letters and communications were required, they could rely on Sam to translate for them. His incredible knack for languages was so strong that he was even able to translate a document that arrived from the Italian Air Force although Italian was not a language within his repertoire.

No, this position did not garner him either a promotion or a relief from his guard duties, but the demand for his services as translator did raise his standing among the officers in the unit, and no longer did he have to make the latrines spotlessly clean.

But he still had to do guard duty. Most nights Sam's guard assignments were the most difficult: He usually landed the middle shift, positioned at the remote ammunition bunker far from the main section of the camp. Aside from it being dark and frightening, with cold winds blasting, and with strange noises and weird animals running across his post and putting him on alert every few minutes, it required someone to drop him off at this remote site and come and pick him up at the conclusion of his shift. Those drives back and forth from the main camp would rob him of at least one hour of well-deserved sleep every watch night, and there was no other time when he could catch up during the day.

On rare occasion Sam was assigned to man a guard position in the hangars where the planes were kept during the night. The hangars were dimly lit, but at least he was not in complete darkness, and somewhat protected from the elements. From time to time some mechanic or another passed by to work on a given plane, and very infrequently a pilot would show up early in the morning for a pre-flight check.

On one particular night his shift was the usual middle shift, which is the worst. One doesn't sleep enough before it, then has to be wide awake for the 4 hours of guard duty shift, then get another shuteye for a couple of hours before the new day begins. Sam was drowsy but wide awake. Getting caught snoozing on guard duty could lead to a firing squad, guaranteed for a Jew.

Around 1:30 a.m., Sam heard noises of footsteps, and he jumped into readiness. Two mechanics that he recognized came into view, one carrying a small container. Following the rules Sam challenged them for the password, and they recited it to him and he returned to his position.

They went out of his line of sight, and he heard them doing something. There was a plane blocking his view, so out of sheer curiosity he walked around the plane to see what these two were doing.

They had removed the gas cap, had made a cone out of a sheet of paper, and they were pouring something from that container and into the gas tank. It was a bit strange that they would be doing something to this plane in the middle of the night, but Sam did not make much of it until one of them placed his index finger in front of his own mouth signaling Sam to be quiet.

With the gas cap back in its place, they removed the step ladder they had used, and left the hangar, again signaling Sam to stay quiet.

That triggered his alarm. Why would they motion to him to stay silent? What was it that they were doing there? With them gone he went to the plane to take a look. He saw nothing unusual, but was still uneasy so he grabbed the ladder and stepped on it to see from above.

He immediately spotted it. Around the gas cap he saw a small patch of white powder, more like grains of salt, or even thicker. He wet his index finger in his mouth, and touched the powder, bringing some grains closer to his eyes.

He thought that it looked like sugar, so he tasted it carefully. It was.

He now knew what the two mechanics were doing, and why they wanted him to keep quiet about it. Sugar dissolves in gasoline, creating a thick paste which, when sucked into an engine, clogs the carburetor and causes the engine to stop. And while these WWI planes were light, they were not immune to crashing when the engine stopped in mid-flight. Moreover, in a crash with a tank full of gasoline the plane most likely would burn to a crisp, destroying the evidence of the sabotage, and also killing the pilot.

Observing the flight schedule hanging on the wall Sam now knew that Captain Manelis was their target. They must have had some dispute with him, and sabotaged his plane for him to die in, as their act of revenge. And no one would ever know.

What was he to do? Sam thought furiously. If he kept quiet about this incident Captain Manelis would most probably die in the morning. And although he did not know him too well, the captain was a human being who was about to die, and he might have a family, wife and children perhaps.

If on the other hand Sam informed the watch commander about these two, he no doubt would be sacrificing his own life. If they found out, they would kill him. And who knows, the watch commander might be a friend of theirs, or in cahoots with them.

He struggled with the dilemma, mulling over the two options in his head. He still had some time before the end of his shift to decide, and the plane was not scheduled to take off until after dawn.

What was he to do? Keep quiet or expose the attempted murder?

He walked back and forth in the hangar like a caged animal. There must be a solution that was neither of the two obvious ones. He must think creatively and come up with a unique solution.

As an engineer he systematically analyzed the situation, and the conclusion was obvious: He must not let the plane take off. He must do something to disable the plane and prevent it from taking off in the morning.

But what?

How could he disable the plane without being executed? If the plane was somehow disabled there could be only two possibilities: Either he himself sabotaged the plane, or he was asleep during his watch and someone else came in and damaged the plane. After all, he had inspected the hangar before starting his watch, and the next shift would be coming soon and his replacement would also inspect that all is well.

He went back to the plane and looked it over. He had to do something that not only disabled the plane, but would also appear to have been caused naturally without his intervention. And finally the damage had to be such that if repaired it must prevent the sugar from causing the engine to freeze.

Then the solution came to him.

He ran his finger along the bottom of the gas tank. There was a seam running along its length, a weld seam connecting the two halves of the tank together. If he could cause the gas tank to leak, the plane will be disabled and not be ready to take off in the morning. This would not be a suspicious leak since these gas tanks often leaked without anyone's "help," and to repair the tank they would have to flush its contents thoroughly before doing any welding to not have it explode on them, thus ridding it of the sugar.

He grabbed a screwdriver from the toolbox that was on the floor next to another plane being repaired, and gently pried the seam open. Gas started dripping slowly from the tank and onto the hangar floor. Not a major leak, just enough to render the plane inoperable.

He returned to his station. When his replacement arrived they walked together and saw the leak, not an unusual event, and Sam returned to his bunk for the rest of the night.

Chapter 12

During the latter part of his first year in the Latvian Air Force, the family grew again: Philip and Manya had a healthy boy, Daniel, and there was great happiness in Haim's home. He joined Marc, Isaac's first son who was born while Sam was in his sophomore year in Nantes.

"Boys galore," Philip commented when Daniel was born, "the three of us brothers, and now two baby boys. Thank God Tanya had two daughters."

Shortly afterward, the British authorities in Palestine granted permission for the family who had just recently sold the Laima Chocolate factory in Riga, to open a similar factory in Palestine.

To build a chocolate factory in Palestine the company needed machinery, supplies, and records, and also the know-how and leadership. That's how Sam's brother Philip, and his nephew Misha, being part of the senior leadership of the company, received the necessary immigration papers from the British authorities in Palestine.

Sam was on duty that day in early 1933 when Philip, Manya, and Daniel boarded the ship to sail for Palestine, thus becoming the first pioneers of the family to immigrate to the Land of Israel; Misha had already left via France where he spent some months studying agriculture, dreaming of becoming a farmer in the Promised Land.

In their last get together before the departure, during Sam's most recent furlough, they discussed how to get the rest of the family to Palestine and Philip promised to do his utmost best, and spare no effort with the British authorities, to get them certificates to join him there. Their goal was that by the time Sam concluded his two years of service and he was released from the air force the papers would be ready and they could board the first ship out to Palestine.

Upon arrival in Palestine Philip went to work on two fronts: Firstly, he was busy getting a factory built and operational as fast as possible. Secondly, he constantly pestered the British authorities to issue the immigration papers for his brother Sam and his father Haim.

After the end of WWI, the large area conquered from the Turkish Ottoman Empire was parceled by the League of Nations between France and Britain, with Britain gaining a mandate over most of the Middle East. Included in that mandate was the area called Palestine, an area that had been repeatedly declared to be the site for a homeland of the Jewish people. In the early days of the British rule they grudgingly allowed some Jewish immigration to the declared Jewish Homeland. But after a few years the British Government, not being particularly friendly to Jews, and under pressure by their friends in the Arab population, tightened the immigration rules to this God-forsaken desert, and only through special provisions or some extraordinary circumstances could Sam and his father be allowed to join Philip in Palestine.

Getting his father and brother into Palestine was therefore a real ordeal and took an enormous effort on Philip's part. He spent endless days at the High Commissioner's offices of the British Government in Jerusalem, and at the port in Jaffa, doing everything short of bribing the British clerks to obtain the entry visas for his immediate family members. His excuse was that Sam was an engineer, a specialist in chocolate manufacturing machinery, and that his services were desperately needed in the Elite chocolate factory—formerly the renowned Laima factory in Riga—where Philip now held the prestigious position of Secretary General.

It took over a year for the papers to be issued. Sam had already finished his military service when a letter from the British Consul General in Riga notified him that he and his aging father had been granted the long sought-after immigration visas to Palestine.

Sam was overjoyed. Not only would he be going to the Holy Land, something he had dreamt of for so long, but he was leaving Latvia, a country he did not particularly like. Latvia represented to him unpleasant memories of war, brutal occupation, killings, rampant anti-Semitism, and most of all the death of his mother. He was anxious to leave everything behind, ready to board any bathtub-size boat, cross any stormy ocean, fight whatever dragons crossed his path, only to arrive at, and live in, his dream world of Zion.

Sam was a true Zionist. Not the flaming boisterous kind, but the quiet type devoted to the mission without the fanfare—the fanfare that other Zionists had created with their conventions and organizations and congresses and booklets and leaflets. His desire to move to the Promised Land was a fire burning inside, kindled by his attachment to his Jewish roots and the feeling that no matter how assimilated his friends and neighbors were, the Latvians did not accept them as equals, regardless of their level of education, wealth, or contribution to the society.

The only misgiving and sadness he had about leaving Riga, was the fact that his half-sister Esther, and his brother Isaac, Isaac's wife Gita, and their son Marc, remained behind. Esther was married, and it would mean leaving her husband's family behind. As for Isaac, it was his choice to stay in Riga—Philip could probably have arranged a visa for him and his family too, but Isaac was an "important industrialist," or so he thought of himself, very well off, rich you might say, one of those Jews who assimilated into the High Society of Riga, with a mansion in town and a summer home on the seashore some distance away, and servants galore.

Sam and his father implored Isaac to join them, to sell the business and come with them, but no level of appeal and argument could persuade him to leave all those good things behind and go to the deserts of Palestine.

"What will I do there?" was his retort. "My life is here, my business and friends are here, I have an obligation toward Mira and her kids, and you want me to leave all this behind and go to Palestine? In Palestine I will have nothing. I will have to start from scratch, so why do I want to do that?"

But when he saw them off at the port, the reality of their departure finally hit him and Isaac hugged Sam for the longest time, holding on to him with the desperate understanding that it would be a long time before they saw each other again. Then he took one step back, looked at Sam with teary eyes, and whispered to him in Yiddish: "God willing, once you settle there, I will come to visit you," but Sam sadly felt it was idle talk, and for all he knew he might never see his oldest brother again, at least not in this lifetime.

❖ ❖ ❖

It was a miserably hot day when the ship docked in Jaffa. By the time the British frigate shadowing this rickety boat swung around to deeper waters, the vessel was almost at the mouth of the port. The heat inside the ship was unbearable, not a lot better on the deck, and the humidity was suffocating. A typical summer mid-day in the Holy Land, not especially hot, but for the Northern European passengers who were used to much cooler climates, it felt quite intolerable.

The ocean voyage was uncomfortable but otherwise uneventful. This ship was crowded, with mediocre facilities, but it served the purpose and got them to their destination safe and sound. The winds of turmoil were already in the European air, and the passengers were happy to be out of harm's way. Little did they know that their future in the Holy Land was fraught with danger and difficulties—although nothing equal to what their brethren who stayed behind in Latvia would endure once the decade ran out.

After being guided into the port by small tugboats for what seemed like an eternity, the passengers finally heard the clank of the gangplank being lowered to the dock, and from the deck of the ship Sam and his father watched as the British Immigration Officers paraded up the plank below them, and into the belly of the ship.

Sam's older brother Philip was standing on the pier, sweating profusely, scanning the deck for a familiar face, and when he spotted them he waved to them with enthusiasm. He had not seen either of them for over a year, and for him being reunited with his closest relatives, and especially with his father, was a tremendous joy and the happy culmination of months of intense efforts and anxiety.

So, on this steamy hot day in early September 1934, only days from the High Holidays, Philip was elated that all the hard work and persistence in obtaining the immigration certificate had finally paid off, and he would now be reunited with his aging father whom he admired, and the little brother whom he adored.

Within the hour the passengers were beginning to disembark with their minimal belongings. Due to lack of space on this small vessel they were not allowed to carry much on this boat, at most two pieces of luggage each, and quite a few did not have much anyway. Those who did have more than two suitcases' worth had to leave those possessions behind. And to make matters worse they were searched at the departure port, and any valuables were confiscated by the Latvian authorities. No gold, no jewelry, not even family heirlooms.

And now in a few minutes they would disembark the ship and start their new life in this ancient land, a dream come true. Sam, his father, and Sam's "wife" Tzipora stood patiently in line for the final steps of the process, the immigration and customs inspections. If

Haim was apprehensive it was well hidden behind his tall bearded façade, and Tzipora, that happy-go-lucky free spirit, was flirting lightly with the ship's crew members standing by, so Sam felt the burden of leading this pack through the inspection. He was nervous worrying that the British Immigration officers would challenge his marital status or something like that, and send them back to that hated Latvia.

Tzipora was his wife only on paper, a fictitious marriage hastily arranged to help bring yet another Jew into the Holy Land, despite the strict immigration rules established by the British. When the visas arrived in Riga they were only for himself and his 75-year-old father, but it was an unspoken rule among the Jews that no young single man or woman would immigrate to Palestine alone. The British allowed the certificates to cover a wife or husband as well, so a fictitious marriage would be immediately performed by the local rabbinate, with the understanding that once the couple arrived in the Holy Land the marriage would be dissolved in a similarly fictitious divorce. All pre-arranged, agreed to, and honored by all. Thus Sam's cousin Tzipora was chosen by the extended family to become his "wife" in a partial religious marriage ceremony, without the traditional breaking of the glass but with the official signed documents showing them as man and wife. Would the British accept the Latvian documents?

The Immigration official carefully scanned the papers and passports, glanced at them both with Tzipora dutifully hanging on Sam's arm like a newlywed, and without batting an eye handed Sam the papers and motioned to them to proceed through the door, and into the sunshine.

At long last they were out of the boat, and onto the pier. Still a bit shaky from the voyage, hot and sweaty, they were gratified to feel their feet on solid ground. No more rolling and shaking with the waves and the constant humming and clanking of the engines.

Philip came toward them, tall and lanky, and faced his father. For the longest time they stood still, silently gazing at each other and recording the effect of the past year. Both were tall, straight, and slim, and the resemblance remarkable, sunken eyes, longish nose, solid head of hair, one more graying than the other. Philip was an exact image of his father, in all respects except that his face was clean shaven while his father sported a beard, and he also was not wearing a skull cap covering his head as his father did.

Philip spoke first, addressing his father in perfect Yiddish.

"I am so happy to see you, papa," he said. "How are you feeling?"

"I am fine, thank you," was the old man's terse response. "I am happy to see you too."

And with that, the encounter was over. It was not cold, but there was not much manifestation of affection or warmth between them. It was obvious that Philip respected his father, and cared deeply for him, but the casual observer could have been misled to thinking that they had no emotional connection between them.

Philip turned to his brother, scooped him in his arms and hugged him, lifting him off his feet in the embrace. Then he let Sam down, held him at arm's length, and looked at him.

All the while Tzipora was observing the dance carefully, and she was amused by what she saw. After all, her "marriage" to Sam was a fake, and she intended to return to the position of being an unmarried cousin from his mother's side, so the relationship between the old man and his sons meant very little to her. She hastily said farewell to them, and trotted off to find her own relatives waiting behind the barricade.

Now that they were just the three of them Philip turned to Sam once again, grabbed him by the shoulders, and with the utmost earnestness asked him the question that was on his mind ever since he learned that Sam was actually on his way to Palestine.

"Mulya," he said, referring to his brother by his nickname. "You need to know that this is not France, or Latvia, and conditions here are very different from what you are accustomed to. Now that you are here, you need to decide very quickly how to establish yourself. In simple terms, you need to decide if you want to live, or do you want to die."

Stunned, Sam remained silent for the longest time looking at his brother with astonishment. He was trying to understand what his brother had just asked him. Was he serious? What was this all about?

After a pause Philip repeated. "You need to decide, and fast, if you want to live, or if you want to starve to death. I know that you are very learned, an engineer with multiple degrees and all, but if you want to live you have to forget your engineering degrees, and your fancy diplomas, and your other credentials, and become a mechanic, a technician, a laborer. There is no work for engineers in the country, and you will starve to death, but there is a need for people who work with their hands, who build roads, who clean the streets, who take on menial work despite the fact that they are all 'Herr Doctor,' and 'Herr Professor.'

"So make a decision what you want to do, and live by it.

"Now let's go."

And with that he picked up his father's suitcase, turned around, and started walking toward the exit where they could catch the bus to his home in Ramat Gan.

Chapter 13

Philip and Manya's apartment, on the fourth floor of a residential building in Ramat Gan, a suburb due east of Tel Aviv, was spacious and airy, with an abundance of light. It had three bedrooms, one occupied by Philip and Manya, one reserved for Haim, and one shared between their son Daniel and Sam.

The building was situated perfectly: It was on a small hill providing it an exceptional view south and west, and a cool breeze coming from the Mediterranean. It was within walking distance of the newly built Elite chocolate factory, a replica of the Laima factory of Riga, and only a few doors up the street from a synagogue where Haim could attend services. Finally, despite its suburban location it was only a couple of miles from the center of Tel Aviv, and less than two miles from its commercial area, the train station, and the bus depot. There were bus routes from the Elite intersection to most destinations, and that served the neighbors quite well since almost none of them had cars.

With his experience as a technician, his knowledge of refrigeration and his impeccable command of Hebrew, Sam landed a job as a refrigeration technician with the Levinson Westinghouse Dealership within a short time after his arrival.

Abraham Levinson had the exclusive dealership to import and service Westinghouse refrigerators in the area covering Palestine, Trans Jordan, Lebanon, and Syria, and since the quantity of refrigerators imported and sold was very small, practically a trickle, he also provided service to commercial refrigerators for butcher shops, grocery stores, restaurants, and institutional kitchens. In the hot climate of the eastern Mediterranean, keeping food cool was a must, and the ice factory in northern Jaffa could not supply the growing populations of Jews and Arabs in the area who were using ice boxes to keep the food from spoiling.

Slowly at first, and then at a growing rate, all commercial establishments dealing with food were forced to move away from ice boxes and into electricity-driven refrigerators. Notwithstanding frequent electrical outages, almost a daily occurrence in the country, the departure from ice boxes was especially acute in places further away from the population centers where ice delivery was available, so the Levinson Commercial Refrigeration Department with its three technicians was in high demand.

How grateful was Sam now to his two professors in Nantes who had guided him to add refrigeration engineering as a profession! And after settling down some he sent them both a letter telling them about having arrived in Palestine, and thanking them profusely for their wisdom and help.

One of the main issues he faced though was that of transportation. He had to travel by bus to clients while carrying a heavy toolbox, to install or repair refrigerators wherever they were located, sometimes some distance away. Worse still, if he did not happen to carry with him the specific part that was required to repair a particular refrigerator, he had to waste valuable time and go back to the shop to get the part. Moreover, in many places he could not leave his toolbox behind, so he would have to carry this heavy weight with him, and travel by bus with an unpredictable and infrequent schedule there and back. Not an ideal situation.

"Listen Abraham," after a few weeks Sam approached his employer, "it is very difficult, and not efficient, to get to all the clients we serve using public buses. I don't have money to buy a vehicle. I may be able to borrow some from my brother, but it would not be enough. Can you help?"

"I understand, but there is very little I can do," Abraham was very sympathetic. "The business does not have any extra money at the moment, and nor do I. What I can do though, if you find some good vehicle, is to help you negotiate a better price—a lot of people know me and owe me one favor or another, and I may be able to squeeze them on the price some."

Sam started looking for another mode of transportation, but he was not too optimistic about it. He could not afford anything beyond a bicycle, and a bicycle wouldn't do with the big toolbox.

A few months had passed and he was still going by bus.

As described in the book of Genesis in the Old Testament, the creation of the world took six days. At the conclusion of each day, except Tuesday, God reflected on His accomplishments of that day, and remarked that "it was good." On Tuesday God remarked that "it was good" not once, but twice, so Tuesday is considered in Judaism the day of good things and good fortune. It is then the most favored day for weddings because God blessed it twice.

This particular Tuesday Sam had a service call at a dairy store and lunch counter in Tel Aviv. It was his first visit to the store, and he did not know what to expect, how easy or difficult the repair might be, or equally how nice or difficult the owner would be. Some owners were not nice when he walked through the door—understandably so, their livelihood was at stake and they were anxious and upset that this thing, the refrigerator, had broken down, and naturally it had to be his fault.

To his delight, he owners of this particular store seemed very nice. They introduced themselves in hesitating Hebrew.

"I am Herman," the man said, "and this is Rosa."

The accent was unmistakably German. It was not unusual to hear German on the streets of Tel Aviv those days as quite a few Jews had already run away from Germany or Austria to Palestine in the early 1930s, fearing the rise of Hitler.

Sam introduced himself.

"We are so happy that you came so quickly," Rosa said.

"Do you speak German?" Sam asked politely, "It would be easier for me."

He did not want to suggest to them that their terrible Hebrew was terrible, but he wanted to make it easier for them, and as an added advantage also practice his own German a bit.

"What is wrong with the refrigerator?" he asked in German.

They described it in terms that they certainly could not have done so in Hebrew.

He was curious about them. Almost every immigrant to Palestine had a story to tell, and he wanted to hear theirs, so while checking the refrigerator he struck a conversation with them.

Rosa was very gregarious, the hyperactive type, and Herman was more sedate and calm, but both were very nice and friendly, especially that they could now communicate with him in their native tongue. They told him they had had a business in Koln in Germany, a successful business, and then when Hitler came to power and things started deteriorating for the Jews, they left everything behind and decided to flee. They had some money stashed away and in early 1932 they still were able to extract the money, came to Palestine and opened this dairy luncheonette and store.

Rosa also told him that when they arrived in Palestine Herman was stricken with Typhoid Fever. Within a few days he was taken to Hadassah Hospital in Tel Aviv.

"He had very high fever, and they figured that he was not long for this world. After a couple of days, they decided that he was in a coma and was dying, so they moved him out of the room and into the hallway to make room for another patient. A doctor passed by and took a look at him and declared him dead, and asked the nurse to wheel him to the morgue.

"When Herman heard that he was dead and heading to the morgue, he got up from the gurney. The nurse fainted, and Herman wrapped himself in a bedsheet and ran out of the hospital. He was not going to stay there—they had just declared him dead!" she laughed.

"A truly funny story," Sam joined her. He imagined this burly man, Herman, running through the streets of Tel Aviv in the middle of the day, wrapped in a bedsheet. What a sight that must have been!

After a while Sam discovered what had caused the problem with the refrigerator but he did not have the replacement part with him.

"I have to go get a part for your refrigerator," Sam said, as he started packing his toolbox. "I don't have it with me, so I have to go to our shop. I will be back in about an hour or an hour and a half."

"One and a half hours? That's how long it will take you to get there and back?"

"I am sorry," Sam said sheepishly, "it is not too far, by the train station, but I have to go by bus, and they do not run so often."

"You mean you do not have a car, or motorcycle?"

"No, I don't. It is all right; I am used to taking the bus."

"That is unbelievable. Then I will take you to the shop," Herman said. "I have a motorcycle outside."

Then he noticed Sam carrying the big toolbox in his hand. "You can leave the toolbox with Rosa here. It will be safe."

"Thank you so much." He put the box out of the way near the wall, and they left.

They were back in fifteen minutes. The whole trip was two miles each way.

Rosa had prepared lunch for them: Salad, white cheese, a couple of slices of herring and a cup of coffee.

"Please sit down and eat," she said.

Rosa was all up in arms. "Is this how you work, young man?" she asked. She was a few years older than Sam, but not by much, maybe seven or eight years, so calling him "young man" was not an insult to him.

"What do you mean?"

"Going to work with this big box by bus, and if you need a part you have to go back to the shop by bus?"

"Yes, unfortunately they can't give me a car or motorcycle."

"Can't you buy one?" Rosa was direct.

"I have not worked long enough to save money to buy a motorcycle," Sam said apologetically.

"That is preposterous!" she said. "That you have to go by bus. I will give you the money and you go buy a motorcycle. You will pay us back when you can!" She was forceful.

Sam thought. "They had just met me this morning, they know nothing about me, and they are offering to lend me money to buy a motorcycle without any guarantees? This is unbelievable! It couldn't be, and I can't accept it from them."

He opened his mouth to decline, but Rosa raised her hand to silence him. "I will not take 'no' for an answer."

Herman got up, went around the counter to the tiny office in the back, and came back with a thick envelope.

"I hope this is enough. Go find a vehicle. If there is anything left, you will give it back to us."

And that's how the Norton became Sam's trusted mode of transportation, so long of course as Sam put some gas in the tank.

It was an excellent and reliable machine. This British-made motorcycle had been brought to Palestine by a British officer who later rotated back to England and sold it, probably at a significant loss. The motorcycle then passed through two or three hands before Abraham Levinson was able to wrench it from its current owner at a very good price.

That little investment in the Norton paid off in spades to both Abraham and to Sam. For Abraham, it enhanced Sam's efficiency in getting to the customers quickly, not being dependent on public transportation, and extended his range to places he could not have reached before. Being fair minded, he offered Sam to pay for gas and repairs for the bike, and even gave Sam cash to pay Herman and Rosa some of the money back, and even that, with no strings attached.

It also gave Sam the mobility that every young man in his mid-twenties desires. Although his weekends were dedicated to joining his father at the synagogue, and out of respect for his father he would not ride the bike on the Shabbat, once the Sabbath was over he would hop on the two wheeler and head for the center of Tel Aviv, or the promenade by the beach, wherever other young men and women congregated in one of the local coffee shops.

Before too long Sam became a member of the local young scene. Alcohol was not an attraction, but almost everyone smoked. They never found out what the cigarettes were made of, clearly not tobacco, but they smoked those awful smelling things anyway while sipping the traditional cup of Turkish coffee so typical of the Middle East.

Sam was well mannered and educated, a worldly type, and also kind and gentle, not pushy and aggressive as others were, so people took to him and embraced him into their midst.

During one of those summer evenings, Sam met Leah. He was sitting with a few friends at Café Piltz in the promenade and Leah and another girl approached. His friends asked the girls to join them for a cup of coffee, and introduced them to each other.

Sam was instantly taken by this pretty brunette with dark eyes and complexion in her early twenties. He noticed that she was modestly dressed, and that her manners were fine, indicating a good upbringing. His friends treated her with the utmost respect suggesting that she was from a good family, and when she spoke, he noticed how impeccable her Hebrew was; she must be a native-born he concluded. But when he heard her conversing with her friend in Russian, his trained ear detected the richness of a true Russian sound, tugging at his heart with childhood memories. Where did she learn such perfect Russian? He wondered.

Leah on the other hand took one look at the scrawny blond blue-eyed young man with light complexion and concluded that he must be a newcomer, and that he was still a boy, maximum of 18 years old if a day, and she decided she had no further interest in him.

On the way home, Leah and her friend Mira chatted about the evening.

"I really liked Sam," Mira said. "He is one handsome guy. We spoke for a while, and he is quite interesting."

"Yeah, he seemed very nice and cultured."

Something in the tone of voice told Mira that Leah was not impressed.

"You mean you are not interested in him?" Mira asked.

"Not in a million years," Leah sneered. "He seems nice, but he is still a baby. He could not be one day older than 18. For me I need someone 25 years or older, not a '*Pisher*' like him." She used the Yiddish derogatory word suggesting he was still in diapers.

"Why do you call him a '*Pisher*?' He looks young, but he's probably 23 or even older."

"No way. He looks 18, maybe 19."

"He could not be younger than 23. He is an engineer, so he must be older than 22. Figure it out yourself."

"I don't think he is an engineer. There is some mistake here, he is 20 at most, and I am not a babysitter. I am not interested in him, but if you think he is so interesting why don't you date him yourself?" Leah was never one to beat about the bush.

"No, thank you. I have my boyfriend, and I have no intention of dumping him. But you should date him. I know he is interested, I could tell."

"Not me."

Mira knew that when Leah decided something, it was difficult to convince her otherwise, so she dropped the subject. Anyway, they had so much else to talk about. A few blocks later they bid each other good night and parted, Leah turning right to Bograshov Street, and Mira continuing straight ahead, each heading to her home.

❖ ❖ ❖

One Saturday night, returning to Ramat Gan on his motorcycle, having just spent an enjoyable evening with his friends, another motorcyclist passed him on the road. A few hundred yards later Sam saw the same motorcycle rider on the side of the road tinkering with his engine in the dark. Sam stopped to offer his help to the motorist, and his life was changed forever.

"Do you need help?"

The man stood up and shined his flashlight at him. He pointed it at Sam's face for a minute, and then dropped the beam to the ground.

"Yes, that would be very nice, thank you. My magneto seems dead, and I have another one at home. Would you mind giving me a ride? It is not too far from here."

"Sure, hop on and tell me where to go."

"Great, thanks."

The man hopped onto the back seat of the Norton and had Sam make a turn into a dirt road leading into an orange grove. They came to a stop by a shed.

"I will be right back," the man said, and hurried toward the far side of the shed.

Sam turned the engine off but stayed on the bike, waiting for him to return.

He heard some noise behind him, but could not see anything in the pitch dark. Probably some small animal, he thought. Then he heard a voice close behind him, a man's voice.

"Don't look back," the man said in perfect Hebrew.

Before he could react, a blindfold covered his eyes. He realized he was being kidnapped, but there was nothing he could do. Someone else was in front of him, holding the handlebars of the Norton.

"Please put the kick stand down and get off the bike," the voice from behind him said.

Sam complied. He was not terribly worried. It was obvious that the men did not mean him harm, otherwise they would have killed him by now. And if they knew anything about him at all, they knew he did not have money or anything else worthwhile. But what did they want of him?

He felt a hand on his left arm, moving him away from the motorcycle, and then another hand on his head pushing his head down. He bent his head and could tell that he was now in the back seat of a car.

They drove for a short while making a couple of turns, probably to disorient him. All he could tell judging by the smells coming in through the open windows was they were in a rural area, and by the sound of the car that it was old, really old.

He was brought into a shed of some sort, placed on a chair and the blindfold removed. He was facing a table with a desk lamp on it pointing at him. There were people on the other side of the lamp but he could not tell even how many, let alone who they were.

Then a voice from behind the lamp started asking him questions, about himself, his friends, his colleagues at work, his family, and his habits. Why did he come to Palestine? What did he study in France? Why? What did he do in the Latvian Army?

Although it must have taken no more than fifteen minutes for the questions, for Sam it felt much longer than that, and by the time they stopped, and got to the point, he was sweating profusely.

"We are from the Haganah," the questioner finally said, "and we want you to join us."

Sam could not say that he was surprised. By now he was somewhat prepared for that. After all the questioning, he was sure that whoever they were on the other side of the table had done their homework and knew quite a bit about him, so it had to be something like the Haganah, or maybe the Irgun, the two most active Jewish underground movements in Palestine. Who else would go to all the trouble to do the investigation, and kidnapping, a well planned and executed operation. Not the British, that's for sure, and definitely not the Arabs.

Ever since Sam had disembarked from that boat in Jaffa in September 1934, he was anxious to do something for the sake of his brethren, the Jewish population of Palestine. Something extra, something meaningful and useful, helping safeguard the community; something way beyond his normal daily activities, but he had not known how or where to start.

He had heard about the underground movements working to "convince" the British to terminate the mandate, return home to their own country and free the Jewish population from their oppressive controls. He knew some about the Haganah, the military arm of the Jewish Agency—the pseudo government dealing with Jewish matters within the territory. He had also heard about the more extreme two underground movements, the Irgun and Lehi, groups that also worked to protect the Jewish population but were more focused on aggressively trying to evict the British from Palestine.

Sam was dedicated to the Zionist idea that the Promised Land belonged to the Jews, and that the British had no business in running it, and an independent Jewish state should be established in its stead, but he found closer affinity for the Haganah's methods than those of the Irgun and Lehi. Those two resorted to more violent encounters against the British garrison, and Sam did not agree with their aggressiveness and brutality. He was more intent on the welfare of the Jewish population than the elimination of that foreign force imposing its will, laws, and regulations, on the civilians.

"I will do whatever it takes to help protect the Jews in Eretz Israel," Sam said.

"Including giving your life for the cause?"

"Yes, if that is what it takes."

There was a moment of silence.

"Since you have served in an army and have gone through basic training there, you will be assigned as an infantry squadron leader. Unfortunately, we do not have an air force yet," he chuckled, "but someday we will.

"You will get specific instructions in due time.

"You will not discuss anything that has transpired here tonight, nor will you communicate to anyone that you have joined the Haganah or anything about your activities. You understand the utmost need for secrecy?"

"I do."

"Not even your closest relatives may know, and whenever possible you will try to camouflage your activities under some excuse or another."

"I understand."

"Please step forward, put your hand on the gun on the table, and swear your allegiance to the Haganah and the Jewish People of the Land of Israel."

"I swear."

The blindfold went back on, and the return trip to the motorcycle seemed to track the same route.

"Keep the lights off until you hit the paved road," he was told.

He hopped on the Norton and very carefully headed back to the paved road. There he turned on his lights and backtracked to an area from where he knew the way home.

He was gratified, and relieved. Once he had understood the nature of the three underground movements he had wanted to join the Haganah, but could not find the door, the entry point, to this clandestine group. No one would admit to belonging to it or offer to introduce him to the organization.

And now, finally, thank God, they had come knocking on his door.

Chapter 14

At the dawn of 1936 things were weary in Palestine. The strife between the Jewish and the Arab populations was increasingly unfriendly to say the least, and the British were no help in defusing the situation. Whenever an incident occurred they mostly sided with their Arab "friends," and life for the Jewish population was often imperiled by their unfair actions.

It came to a head in April of that year. Provoked by the chief Islamic religious authority, the Mufti of Jerusalem Haj Amin al-Husseini, the Arab Higher Committee led a campaign of incitement against the local Jewish population. Animosity toward Jews flourished. The Mufti and lower ranked Muslim religious leaders spewed their venom from every pulpit of every mosque during services five times a day, and that incitement turned violent on many occasions. Not satisfied with that, the local Arab population declared a national strike, despite the fact that such a strike would cripple the economy and hurt the meager subsistence of the entire population, Jews and Arabs alike.

The effect of this turmoil on Sam was substantial from its first day. It became too dangerous for him to travel far to service customers outside the immediate Jewish areas of Tel Aviv. He was unarmed, riding a motorcycle, and that made him an easy target for marauding gangs of Arabs who blocked the roads and shot at any non-local vehicle. Worse still were the wires between trees on two sides of the road, aimed at motorcycle riders: as the motorcycle approached, the Arabs would pull the wire taut, exactly at the level to behead the rider.

Beyond that, Sam's calls to duty by the Haganah became more urgent and frequent; no longer was it a sporadic endeavor. He would be ordered to take on various assignments on a regular basis: Passing messages, transporting people and materiel, standing guard duty, or participating in an ambush when intelligence indicated an imminent attack on a Jewish neighborhood.

And then there was the weekly training of unnamed men, every Saturday. He would get up at dawn, quietly dress and sneak out of the house before anyone woke up. Out of respect for his father he would not start the Norton right away, but push it up the street some distance before turning it on. Then he would head south toward the sand dunes of the Manshiya section of town where his squadrons gathered for training.

Sam never knew the names of these people, only their faces, so he could not identify them should he be interrogated. They were equipped with sticks made of branches of the bitter orange tree, known for their special attributes that made them perfect weapons for hand-to-hand combat. These branches were strong but not heavy, and when used as a club would issue a punishing blow to the opponent. And when the bitter orange branch connected with its target it would not send shockwaves up the arm holding it, as would other types of wood do.

It was more than a bit awkward and artificial to practice "shooting" using wooden sticks and no ammunition, or throwing fake hand grenades which were really small rocks, but it did provide some basic training and discipline to this ragtag group of otherwise non-military men. They came from all walks of life, from office workers to road construction workers, all sewn together with the thread of a desire to protect themselves and their families from harm.

It did not matter what the weather was, rain or shine they all gathered on the same sand dunes every Saturday, and stormed the imaginary enemy up the hills with determination and fervor. All the while the sentry would be watching from one of the nearby hilltops for any British soldiers, because these training exercises were strictly forbidden by the High Commissioner and his henchmen—God forbid if the Jews could defend themselves, what will happen to the British Empire?

To be fair, some remote Jewish outposts were provided some arms by the British army, but only sparingly and only for self-defense. These old weapons, ancient bolt action rifles, were not much of a defense against a well-organized military force with tanks and mortars, but against some disorganized militia they could act as a deterrent.

So throughout that year Sam trained several hundreds of young men in khaki shorts and knee high khaki socks running up and down the hills of Manshiya, and those were supposed to be the future defenders of the Jewish population in Palestine.

It was mid-July, while the general strike was raging on, when out of the blue Abraham Levinson called his employees to a meeting. Despite it being the midst of the summer busy season there was not much work so everyone was at the shop. They gathered in the small showroom of the dealership.

"You guys know," he opened, "that business has not been going very well. Mostly because of the general strike by the Arabs, and the violence, our business has suffered. The dealership is not selling any new refrigerators, and anyway because of the work stoppage at the Jaffa port ships are not being unloaded. Even if we had orders for new refrigerators, which we don't, we could not get them out of the ships. And it is not just refrigerators; business is stopped all around, and I don't see it changing very soon. This strike is crippling any business activity, including ours."

They listened attentively as he continued.

"Over the last few months I did everything I could to keep the business going. Personally I stopped taking any money from the business months ago. To be honest the business was not doing so well even before the strike, and now it is really bad."

He paused for a minute.

"I am very sorry, but I can no longer afford you guys. Good business sense tells me that I should let you all go, and close the shop, but I know this will place terrible hardships on you, so I have a proposition for you.

"I will walk away from this business without taking anything. It is all yours to do with as you please. You can sell the equipment, the inventory, the tools, whatever, and you owe me nothing. This would be your severance pay. You were good employees and good to me, and this will give you a head start until you find somewhere else you can go. There are not many other places to go, there is not much competition, so it will be tough, but that is the best that I can do."

All three stood in stunned silence for the longest time. "What a decent man to make this offer to us," Sam thought. "He built this place, it was his baby, and now he is walking away from it with the shirt on his back, leaving it all to us."

"I can pay you your normal salary until the end of August," Abraham continued. "After that you will be on your own."

And with that he turned and walked into his tiny office and shut the door behind him. Was it a tear in his eye?

They went back to work, and agreed to meet after hours and have a cup of coffee at a coffee shop nearby.

Sam looked around the room. He had become fond of this place, and the workshop, and it would be a shame to leave it all behind and walk away. He was not concerned about finding a job with one of the competitors, they knew him by then, had seen the quality of his work, and would grab him in a minute. But the others?

"What do you think guys?" Sam asked when they met that evening. Typical Sam—listen first, speak later.

Between the two of them, Yehuda was first to react. With a half-smile on his face he was looking forward to dismantling the place, and making a quick buck. Although he did not say that, he knew he wasn't much of a technician anyway, and could not carry his weight, so this was an easy way out for him. Maybe he could take the money and run, and go join the Dan Bus Company as a member of the co-operative, and in the meantime his wife was working and would bring a paycheck home.

Meir was more deliberate and thoughtful about it. He was more concerned about having a steady income than having a short-term gain and then facing the consequences, but he could not suggest an alternative at that moment.

Sam looked at these two men. Meir had just married a few months before, and his wife did not work. As a technician he was mediocre, nothing special, but he was solid, always on time, pedantic and consistent—some Germanic qualities Sam respected.

Yehuda was a bit of a problem. As a technician he was totally useless, barely knew which end of a screwdriver to hold. He knew refrigeration principles, although not at an engineering level. It was obvious that Abraham Levinson knew this all along and had placed Yehuda on the business side—selling, and keeping the books, although he always double checked Yehuda's figures to make sure nothing was remiss. But Abraham kept him as an employee, so he must have found some value in him.

They were silent for some time, sipping the coffee.

"I think there is another alternative," Sam broke the silence. "There is another alternative to breaking the business apart."

"Like what?" Meir asked.

"We could try and keep the business and run it without Abraham."

"You think you can keep the business when Abraham could not?" was Yehuda's immediate question.

Did Sam detect a sneer in Yehuda's response?

"It may be possible. You should know best, you worked on the books," Sam retorted.

"We will all have to take a serious pay cut and cut expenses to the bone to maybe make it work," Yehuda stated.

"What is your flexibility, guys?" Sam asked. "Can you take a pay cut?"

"It won't be easy," Meir said.

"I can probably take a small cut, but why would you do that? I would rather sell my share and go looking for something else."

Practical and pragmatic Sam summarized his thoughts. "It is not the time to go looking for another job right now, what with the general strike and its aftermath. Nobody is hiring, and nobody has money to buy the inventory and tools.

"This strike is not going to last forever. When it is over, there will be pent-up demand by all those who could not get refrigerators during the strike, so we may be able to pull it off.

"What do you say we sleep over it, and try and figure out how much we can shave off our salaries to make a go at it? In the meantime, Yehuda, please check to see what would be a reasonable level of income for the next few months, and accordingly what level of expense we could tolerate."

They parted that evening, each with his own thoughts.

Sam knew he was taking a big gamble proposing that they keep the business going. His gut told him it was a risky move on his part, maybe even a mistake, but he was inclined to shove his misgivings aside for the benefit of these two coworkers.

Personally, he had a particular issue to resolve. As Abraham's employee he was making a salary of six British pounds per month. While not a high salary, it was fair by the existing market prices for technicians, a salary on which one could feed a family of four. His problem was that he was handing a large portion of that to Philip and Manya for the upkeep of his father and himself.

That left him with a small discretionary sum for all his personal expenses, and there was not much he could do to reduce his costs to fit within a smaller budget. Not much wiggle room there, unless he could convince his brother that he, Philip, needed to contribute a bit more toward the upkeep of their father. Until now Sam had been saddled with most of the costs, and he would not be able to carry it going forward, and anyway it was not fair. After all, Haim was his father too! True, Philip gave Haim a room which he otherwise could maybe rent out, but how much was that worth? In addition, Philip was earning a very nice salary from Elite, and he could afford to not charge the old man with part of the rent, a rent that he had committed to long before his father and brother arrived in Palestine.

Sam had a heart-to-heart talk with Philip that evening, and he was able to negotiate a one-pound reduction in his monthly contribution to Philip's household. That would allow him to take a one pound pay cut to keep the business going. He knew it was going to be rough for a while, or longer, and that the three-legged stool had two weak legs, but against his instincts and better judgment he was willing to give it a try.

They got together the next day, after business hours and at the same spot.

"I checked the books, and if we can reduce our expenses by fifteen percent, and increase another ten percent on the revenue side, we might be able to make it over the next few months, but as Abraham said, we must take action quickly."

"I am able to give back one pound from my income, which is sixteen percent," said Sam. "That is the maximum I can do."

"I checked with my wife, and we can also reduce our income by one pound per month and still survive, but no more than that, and only for some time," Meir said.

"I am reluctant to do this, but I will go along with you guys," Yehuda's verdict was in. Sam and Meir should have dumped him right then and there, but foolishly they did not.

"Are you guys willing to give it a go?" Sam asked.

"As three partners, right? Equal shares, one third each?" asked Yehuda.

"That's what I thought," was Sam's response.

"How are we going to divide the work amongst us? You know I can't very well go out on the road outside Tel Aviv because I don't have a vehicle."

"That's okay, Yehuda. I will take the long routes when necessary, you will cover locally, and do the books, and Meir will manage the workshop and all the servicing done here. Is that all right with you?"

They nodded.

"Who is going to manage the outfit?" asked Yehuda, hoping to be named.

"Sam will," Meir said. "He has more experience, and the university degrees. He will be the president, you will be the secretary and treasurer, and I will stay out of your way." Meir had a dry sense of humor after all.

And so Coldomat was born. Officially formed a few weeks later, the three became equal partners in the business—share and share alike.

It did not take long for Yehuda to slow down on customer visits. After Sam realized the high rate of repeat visits to customers previously serviced by Yehuda, he concluded that it would be better if Yehuda did not go out on service calls in the first place, and he took on Yehuda's workload added to his own.

For the longest time there was no rush on the workshop either, not many new commercial refrigerators ordered, and so Yehuda and Meir were having tea at their favorite watering hole several times a day while Sam was riding his Norton and doing most of the client service for the company.

Times were rough, and they barely met payroll for the longest time, but Sam never complained, nor did he ever confront the two for their meager contribution to the revenues of the company. Complaining, he felt, was counterproductive and unfair, since it was his idea to resuscitate the business rather than letting it die, and he had walked into it with eyes wide open. Confrontation was just not in Sam's nature, not part of his makeup, so these two were getting an almost free ride month after month, living off his sweat while he worked long hours until the work was done.

❖ ❖ ❖

Since the early 1930s and over a period of a few years, the Haganah had been gathering Jewish musicians from Europe who had been put out of work by the anti-Jewish sentiments and laws enacted by the different countries there. By 1936 some seventy-five such musicians, all experienced instrumentalists of all kinds, had been recruited by the Jewish leadership and brought to Palestine to form the core of a Jewish Symphony orchestra.

On his own and without external persuasion, the world famous maestro Arturo Toscanini decided to come to Palestine to conduct this fledgling orchestra for a series of concerts, the first concert to take place at the new Tel Aviv port on December 26, 1936.

The appearance of such a world renowned figure and the gathering of hundreds of people in the audience presented a substantial security risk of an Arab terrorist attack, and required special security provisions. The British High Commissioner concluded it was up to the local population to protect itself and its esteemed guest, and refused to provide any personnel to secure the event. Supposedly his forces were busy elsewhere.

Even if the British were to have offered a security detail, the Haganah was not prepared to blindly hand over that role to the unreliable British, and it was determined to provide a security ring of its own operatives to protect the venue and the distinguished guests.

Sam was ordered to lead the Haganah unit protecting the event and its occupants. He designed the plan as follows: The unit would be placed at specific spots around the venue, mostly out of sight and armed with pistols, ready to take on any potential terrorist threat. A few snipers were also to be deployed, hidden from view on some of the rooftops of adjacent buildings.

For a few days after receiving his marching orders and before the event, Sam and his team scoured the neighborhood to identify avenues of potential terrorist attack, and also received intelligence briefings about what to expect, and whom to watch out for. While no specific threat was identified, Sam's unit was ready for whatever it might encounter.

It was a tremendously important event for the country, its Jewish community, and its morale. It meant a lot to have such a famous and respected musician show his compassion and worldliness to come to this insignificant strip of desert and provide his moral support, that in addition to the terrific music that this orchestra would produce under his baton.

The key to the success of the security detail was its ability to be invisible to the naked eye. The perimeter protectors were to stay as much out of sight as possible and prevent any unidentified person from attending the open-air concert from the rooftops—only "cleared" personnel were permitted to be on the roofs, and they provided cover for the Haganah security operatives stationed there. Any neighbor having a balcony or windows facing the venue were screened as well, ensuring that they were "safe," and other "uninvited guests" were kept away as much as was reasonable.

The venue security detail was supposed to meld in with the crowd and, as much as possible, not be identified as to their role and responsibility. They were to be in civilian clothes, not khaki of any kind, but appear to be normal attendees of the concert. They were either assigned specific seats dispersed among the guests in audience, or were "pretend" venue ushers or other workers, while keeping an eye on any potential trouble spot.

It was a very tense evening for all who belonged to Sam's detail. In advance of the event they had arranged a form of signal communication between them, each one of those signals representing a specific condition, and there were those among them whose primary role was to watch out for any signal by any of the others that suggested potential risk.

Despite it being the end of December, the weather in Tel Aviv was very cooperative, chilly but not rainy—just chilly enough to require an outer layer able to camouflage the fact that among the audience was a group of men armed with pistols.

Sam was so intent on his mission that he did not even hear the concert. He heard the music, but did not listen to it, and since music was not his forte, even if he were interrogated he would not be able to tell what pieces the orchestra played, or even how long they were.

To Sam's enormous relief the event passed without incident, and once the guests and players left the site, his unit could stand down. He signaled the rooftop detail that they were free to go, and they dispersed among the crowds leaving the area.

From then on, other units would cover the security of the orchestra and its director in its follow-on series of concerts in Jerusalem and Haifa.

Part II

LEAH

Chapter 15

It was a stormy night, Leah remembered, when her mother picked her up from her crib and carried her to the master bedroom of the big house. Sleepy Leah could not understand why her mother woke her up in the middle of the night and whisked her to the other room. She had never done that before, why tonight?

Pessia walked into the well-lit master bedroom with the child in her arms. Leah noticed that her sister Ida was standing by the bed next to Nahum, her older brother. Her father was lying in the bed, propped by two pillows, frail and gaunt looking, worse than she had ever seen him before.

"Pessia, gather the children around me," she heard her father speak in a faint voice. "I want to say good-bye to them."

"Good-bye?" Leah thought. "Where are you going, papa?" she asked timidly.

"My darling Leah," the man said gently, looking at her with his dark loving eyes. "I am going away in the morning, and I will be gone for a long, long time."

She could hear her mother whimper next to her. Pessia stepped closer to the bed and lowered the child next to her father. Ida and Nahum climbed on the bed from the other side and reached and hugged their father. They, being 4 and 7 years old understood the significance of the moment: They knew this was the last time they would ever see him, but Leah still could not fathom the event; after all she was barely 2 years old and the concept of life and its end were not within her grasp.

Clinging to his children the man turned to his wife who was weeping in the corner.

"Don't cry, Pessia, please don't cry. We had eight wonderful years together, and now it is time for me to go. I love you all, but God is calling me, and I will not last the night."

He took a deep breath. "I always dreamed of taking you and the kids to Eretz Israel, our ancestral homeland. We talked about it many times, and you agreed, for the sake of the children. We, they, belong there. All Jews belong there."

He paused. "Now it is clear that I will not make it there. Unlike Moses I will not even see it in the distance."

Pessia was sobbing and barely keeping herself from wailing.

"What I want you to promise me, swear to it, is that when I am gone you will take the children and go to Eretz Israel. Leave this place. Sell what you can, and buy a passage. Bribe whomever you have to, follow my parents and go to Palestine. Palestine is our home. That is where all Jews should go. That is the land God gave us many centuries ago, and that is where we had two states in the past. Go there, and you and the children will help create the third Jewish State in the Holy Land."

His voice faltered as he spoke, he was tired.

"Promise me that you will go, Pessia. Promise me, on the life of the children, it is my dying wish."

And with that, at 33 years old, this tower of a man, Chaim Bernstein of Kharkov, Ukraine, succumbed to the cancer and he was gone.

Pessia could hold no more. The painful scream she kept bottled inside finally came out, and she ran to his bed, grabbed his hand and put it to her face with the tears streaming down her cheeks. She stayed by him whimpering and crying in agony.

Nahum gently gathered his sisters around him and in silence herded them back to their beds, leaving their mother to suffer her pain and grief in peace.

❖　❖　❖

It was barely nine years earlier, in early 1907, when Pessia met Chaim at her parents' home. He had come to discuss a business deal with her father, the renowned Shimon Appel. At the time her father was constructing a section of the Trans-Siberian Railroad and Chaim came to offer him his top-of-the-line railroad ties. Merely 24 years old, Chaim was already quite a successful businessman, owner of a wood mill specializing in construction materials. Weather conditions in the area of the planned route of the railroad were extremely harsh and Shimon Appel was looking for the best quality railroad ties he could buy, and Chaim had precisely the product he was looking for.

Chaim was a tall handsome man, sporting a mustache that added a distinguished look to his otherwise impressive figure, and Pessia fell in love with him at first sight. The business arrangements with her father took some time to negotiate, and during that time Chaim came to visit quite often. She suspected, but could not be sure, that he was also interested in her, and was dragging the negotiations far longer than necessary so as to have the opportunity to see her and get to know her a bit better before proceeding to ask her father for her hand. He also timed the meetings to late afternoon, and thus was frequently asked by her mother, who liked him, to stay for dinner.

Alas, Chaim was not deemed orthodox enough by her father, and when Chaim approached him asking for Pessia's hand her father adamantly refused to allow the young couple to get engaged and be married. He would not hear of it! He was even ready to cancel the deal they were negotiating if the young man persisted. He was not going to relent; he was not going to allow any daughter of his be married to this infidel, he said.

"How could I approve of this man?" Shimon said to his wife, "He looks like a goy, not a truly religious Jew. He shaves, does not wear a yarmulke except when he prays, and although he is quite learned in Jewish matters, he does not follow the 613 commandments as every Jew should. For all I know he may not even say all his prayers. I can't agree to have my daughter marry a goy!"

But by then Pessia and Chaim were deeply in love, and Pessia was not going to let such a small thing as her father's disapproval stand in the way.

One evening after dinner in 1908 they flawlessly executed their plan and eloped. During the few weeks leading to this night, Chaim had secretly negotiated to sell his business and found a similar mill in Gomel in Belarus some 450 miles away, far enough from the reach of her all-imposing rich and powerful father. He had also arranged for an orthodox Rabbi to marry them as soon as they arrived according to the strictest Halachic rules.

They settled in their new home and soon started a family. Nahum came first, almost a year to the day after their wedding, and he was a delight—a wonderful baby, good natured and calm, never fussy even when teething. Oh, how cute he was!

Mark was next, but unfortunately only lived a few months. When Nahum was three, Ida arrived, and two years later, on the last day of

June 1914, just a few months before the war started in Europe, Leah was born.

Pessia and Chaim were ecstatic, deeply in love, and having a solid middle-class Jewish life. Chaim was a doting father, taking care of the children whenever the servants were not hovering over them. His construction wood business was doing well, and the war, consuming Western Europe, did not affect them at all. Life was good, with lots of light in the house, warmth, and caring. For this couple, these were seven wonderfully blissful years.

Leah was barely a year old when their idyllic lifestyle came crashing down: Chaim had been diagnosed with a very aggressive form of cancer. During that year, Chaim was rapidly getting weaker, was absent from his company more often than not, and the business faltered. No new major land leases, no new timber to cut, most of the employees laid off, an economic decline of serious proportions.

And now, after Chaim's death, Pessia realized their savings were mostly gone, the business was in shambles, and with no other means of support she would have to sell it to put food on the table.

Within days after sitting shiva this little feisty woman disposed of the business, dismissed the servants, and put the big house up for sale. Alas, the war raging in Europe and the uncertainty had caused a serious economic decline, and the proceeds were not enough to keep them going but for a short time—definitely not to purchase a passage to Palestine, or as her late husband properly called it Eretz Israel, the Land of Israel, the Promised Land.

But she had sworn to it on the life of her children!

Chapter 16

Pessia sat motionless in the straight back wooden chair, and once again tears were streaming down her cheeks. She had been sitting there for many hours, since shortly after sunset, staring into the darkness outside. The wind had picked up during the night, was howling furiously, and the little wooden shack creaked every time the wind shifted direction.

The inside of the shack was bare—barely any furniture, just the crude wooden country style table and the three other chairs around it. Her two little girls were sleeping peacefully huddled together on the thin mattress on the floor. In the two other corners were two other mattresses on the floor, the bigger one was hers, and the other for Nahum.

She had extinguished the lantern as soon as the girls fell asleep, pulled the chair to the window and sat there weeping, agonizing, and dreading the worst.

Nahum had not returned.

As he did nearly every morning since they had moved to this God-forsaken little village outside the town of Gomel, Nahum had left this morning with a sack of freshly baked bread to deliver to the grocery store in town. There he would trade the sack for a sack of flower, and a few miserable coins which on Fridays he would trade for groceries for the Shabbat.

He always made sure to return before dark because the roads were not safe for a defenseless little boy walking alone back from town with the heavy load on his back. The Bolsheviks were roaming the countryside in groups, looking to cause trouble, especially to the Jews. If they so much as even remotely suspected he was a Jew he would be as good as dead, so he removed his yarmulke as soon as he left home, and did not put it back on until he returned.

Tonight his mother was in total agony wondering if she would ever see her son alive again. He was not the type to have dawdled around in town, and if he had not returned as usual it was only because he was unable to do so, and that meant that he was either very sick, or worse, dead.

She was emotionally drained and physically exhausted. What could have happened to him? Was he kidnapped to serve in the Czar's army? Did the Bolsheviks capture him? Although a strong boy he was still too young for that—they were looking for boys in their teens, and Nahum was barely 9 and did not look older than that.

She was desperate. She could not go looking for him, and leave the two little girls behind. She could not take them with her because if she had any encounter with a robber, or the Bolsheviks, she could never protect all three of them out on the road.

How could God put her through this agony? What had she done to deserve this? First she lost her husband, becoming a widow with three little children, then piece by piece losing all their worldly possessions and livelihood, ending in this little village in abject poverty, and now Nahum is missing.

With all her strength she prayed.

"Please God, do not take Nahum from me. I already lost one son, and I could not bear the thought of losing another one, especially not Nahum, without whom I would be totally destitute and helpless.

"I do not know anyone in this village to ask for help, we have been here only a very short time, and most of the people are hostile to Jews, anti-Semites. You know I did not want to come here, a village without a Jewish community or a synagogue, but without Chaim I had no choice. It was the only place I could go to with my limited means.

"Please guide me, God. I try so hard to follow your ways and obey your commandments and *mitzvoth*. I try to be kind to others, and be a good mother to my children, and I feel like Job who suffered but did not forsake you. Please do not punish me anymore. I have suffered so much already, be kind to me and save and protect me.

"Please bring my son back to me, and I will be an even more devoted servant to you and to your light."

And with that she recited the prayer exalting God, the Kaddish: *"Yitgadal veitkadash shmei raba. Bealma divra kirutey…"*

Just as dawn started to break, out of total exhaustion Pessia fell asleep.

❖ ❖ ❖

She heard the door creak open and in an instant she was wide awake and on her feet.

Nahum stood at the door. He looked disheveled but he was alive, and in one piece. He put the sack of flour he was carrying on the floor.

She ran to where he was standing and scooped him in her arms. She hugged and kissed him all over his face, and he did not resist. He stood there in her frantic embrace for the longest time—he probably needed her warmth and closeness as much as she did. Finally, she took one step back and looked him all over. He did not have any bruises or injuries, so he was not beaten by those damned Bolsheviks or robbers along the road. He just looked exhausted.

"Come sit," she told him in Yiddish. "Do you want some hot tea?"

The samovar, one of the few possessions she clung to in the turmoil of the last two years was almost full, and she picked up two glasses, filled them, and brought them to the table.

Nahum sat down and sipped the hot tea, and his mother waited patiently to hear what travails he had endured since the previous morning.

"On the way to town yesterday morning I was attacked on the road by two guys on horseback. They did not beat me, but they stole the bread."

"Thank God. Thank God they did not hurt you."

"They were more interested in money than hurting me," he said "and I did not have any money so they took the bread, and the sack. I am sorry, mama."

"Sorry? Why are you sorry? For the stupid sack?"

"Not only that. I know you needed it for me to carry the bread to town, but I am sorry that you worried about me."

"I was very worried. I thought I had lost you forever," she admitted quietly. "So what did you do?"

"I went to town and told the grocer that I did not have his bread, and he was very nice and was sorry for me. He asked me if I needed more flour and I said yes, but I can't pay for it because I did not sell the bread to him.

"He was very kind, and said that if I needed the flour he would let me work at his store and he would pay me enough to buy the flour. So I did help him in the store all day, and by the time I had enough money to buy the flour it was already dark, and I didn't want to take the chance of walking back the five kilometers here in the dark.

"So he let me stay in the store and sleep in the corner until he came back in the morning and let me go. All day I watched every customer to see if I recognized them from the village, but no one I knew came. I was going to ask them to tell you that I was working in the store so you wouldn't worry."

"You are a good boy, and very considerate to me. You did very well."

She thought in silence for a moment, and then her divine guidance came through and she sounded determined. There was no way she would put her son through this anymore, and she herself couldn't ever again endure this fear and worry.

"I didn't have flour to make another load of bread last night," she said. "Tonight I will make a new batch, and tomorrow we will all go together to town, and with the money we will buy tickets for the train to Kharkov to your *Zaidi's* home."

❖   ❖   ❖

At first light the next morning, in unwavering determination, this little barely five-feet-tall woman carried out her mission with military precision.

She left her meager possessions behind—the chairs and the table and the pots and pans, but not that samovar—and with only a small suitcase with few clothes and the girls' dolls, and with Nahum carrying the last batch of bread on his back they all headed to the store in town.

Many hours later she stood with her three children in front of the mansion in Kharkov, looking at the front door up the flight of stairs. She stopped at the landing and looked around. As far as she could tell not much had changed in this upscale neighborhood, and her childhood memories flooded her and gave her the confidence she needed. She still hesitated for a moment, finally assembled the courage to knock on the door.

Chapter 17

The door opened, and the maid looked over the woman with the worn suitcase and the three children standing on the landing. She did not recognize the woman, and by her looks she must be a beggar.

"Go to the servants' entrance," the maid said, and started closing the door when a woman's voice from inside queried.

"Who is it, Monica?" the woman asked in Russian.

"It is me, mama," Pessia replied with all the strength that she could muster.

"Pessia?" bewildered, but a mother's instinct is rarely fallible.

"Yes, it is me, mama," Pessia replied, this time in Yiddish.

A portly woman came to the door, pushing the maid aside. She took one look at the foursome outside the door, then reached and grabbed Pessia by the arm, dragging her forward and embracing her with all her being.

She finally let her daughter go. "Come in," she said in Yiddish, "and you too, children."

Pessia picked up the suitcase and entered the hallway. She handed the suitcase to the maid and stood looking at the place where she had grown up. Nothing that she could notice had changed, same wonderfully warm home that she left some ten years earlier, left to never visit until this evening.

"Where did you come from?" mama asked.

"Gomel."

"Gomel? Have you eaten anything?" Yiddishe mama.

"Not since we left. We only had some bread I baked before leaving. Nothing on the train is kosher."

She led them to the dining room.

"Then you and the children must be famished." She instructed the maid to get the kitchen staff to put out food for these four hungry souls. "Sit down, kids, you must be tired."

She looked at her daughter whom she had not seen or heard from since the girl had run away with Chaim in 1907.

"Where is Chaim?" she asked.

"He died almost two years ago."

"He died? How?"

"He had cancer, and within a year he was gone. At least he did not suffer too much pain."

"*Baruch dayan emet*," mama said, the saying after the dead. "I am so sorry; he was such a fine man. I liked him. It was your father who objected to your marrying him because he did not think Chaim was religious enough for his taste.

"After you eloped I had serious conversations with your father and he was very sorry that you had to run away and get married without his blessing. For months I used to hear him crying in his study, he was so attached to you.

"After you eat something I will go and call him and then you must tell us everything that had happened during these ten years. I would have written to you but I didn't know where you were! Chaim's parents were already in Palestine even before you two ran away, and they didn't write from there so I could not ask them where you were either."

The servants came with plates full of food of different kinds and the children, hungry as they were, waited politely for their turn. Pessia served them and they dove into their plates in silence, only throwing glances around from time to time to get acquainted with these strange surroundings.

❖ ❖ ❖

Pessia and her children remained at their grandfather Shimon Appel's house for several years. Years later when Leah recalled the time, she couldn't identify those years as happy. Although they were being taken care of by their mother and the servants, that period in the Ukraine was not peaceful, with the revolution happening next door, and the upheaval of the First World War, all combining to create a somewhat unsettled and tumultuous era.

After the revolution of 1917 when the Bolsheviks took over in Russia, her grandfather's work travelling to the railhead and attending to his business became quite dangerous. Quite a few times his payroll wagon was robbed on the way to pay his employees, and being a caring and conscientious employer he ensured that his workers were being taken care of in all respects, even at his own expense and peril.

When laying out a railroad track the railhead constantly moves forward, and in the tough winter conditions the workers needed shelter, so every so often he would erect a new railroad camp for his people with sturdy structures as shelters, and not flimsy tents as would be expected. He brought his workers' families to the camp, and ensured those encampments were supplied well and that there was always medical care for the sick and wounded, schools for the children, and a good paycheck at the end of the week.

But still, safety was a dominant major concern, especially for a Jew, and a practicing orthodox Jew no less. The Bolsheviks did not appreciate the rich aristocracy, to which Shimon belonged, and anti-Semitism among the marauding bands was rampant. For him to be exposed, as he was, meant a real risk to life and limb.

Shimon appreciated all this and took safety precautions but he could not avoid being harassed and threatened. At one point the Bolsheviks actually came to his encampment searching for him to kill him, and his employees formed a cordon around him rescuing him by placing themselves between the attacking Bolsheviks and himself.

On that day Shimon finally realized it was not long before one of those gangs would actually get to him, and it was time to retreat from the risks that he was taking. After consultation with his wife, he sold some of his business holdings, including some coal mines and other assets, and converted them to diamonds and gold. On one of his last trips out he hid the diamonds and gold in one of his remaining coal mines, and then flooded the mine, thinking that once the situation settled down and the Communists were gone, he would come and recover the treasure.

He never did.

At home, the growing tension was being felt by the children. They could feel the nervousness and angst of their grandfather who was concerned about his properties, his businesses, and even the personal safety of himself and his family. Trying to keep a very low profile he released some of the servants who were not to be trusted, and without an outside activity he imposed more of his authority over his grandchildren.

He was an avid music lover, so he forced Ida to practice the piano in the attic, an unheated room, for hours each day. Being a very religious orthodox Jew he forced the little girls, Ida and Leah, to recite the prayers over everything, prayers they did not understand as they did not speak Hebrew well enough yet. He was a strict disciplinarian with both of them as well as with his wife: If he did not like something at dinner he would grunt at her, not speak to her, yet he spoke well with the servants. One time when he was not pleased with the way the dinner table was set for the second course, he grabbed the edge of the tablecloth and pulled the whole thing off the table, dishes, utensils, everything, scaring the children half to death. He then motioned to the staff to set a new table, all the while not uttering one word. It was not a calm and peaceful environment for the children to grow up in.

The girls' protector and benefactor was Nahum, who would defend them and watch over them. But before too long Nahum, now a teenager became potential fodder for the Ukrainian army. Under threat of a twenty-year compulsory military service, he had to be whisked out of the house in the middle of the night, secretly sent to Odessa, and from there he boarded a boat to his paternal grandparents the Bernsteins in Eretz Israel, with whom contact was just recently reestablished. Thus, part of Pessia's promise to Chaim was fulfilled, but it left the girls exposed to their grandfather's whims and wrath.

Their salvation, if one could call it that, was the time they spent in school. Beyond a solid education it provided them a structure and discipline outside the house, and the opportunity to socialize with other children their ages. At that Jewish religious school, the girls studied Hebrew, finally making the prayers less alien to them, but they still did not like being forced to recite them morning noon and night.

With the passage of time things settled down into a routine, but Pessia never gave up on her promise to Chaim to take the girls to Eretz Israel. In 1922 she was introduced to Yitzhak Ostrovsky. Yitzhak, a widower with one son of Leah's age, a banker by profession and a learned man in both religious and secular affairs, was deeply orthodox, definitely to Shimon's liking. He was a warm and loving man who took to the girls from day one, and promised Pessia that if she married him he would care for them and love them as if they were his own daughters—in later years he admitted that he liked them more than he liked his own son who turned out to be a decent but totally unimpressive person.

One evening he asked Shimon for Pessia's hand in marriage.

"Reb Shimon," he said, "I would like to marry your daughter, and would like your blessing. I can promise you that I will treat your daughter and grandchildren as best I can, with love and kindness following Jewish tradition. We will keep a kosher home, following God's will and commandments."

"You are a fine man, Reb Yitzhak. I know you will treat my daughter and the children well. You have my blessing," Shimon replied without reservation.

They raised a glass of schnapps.

Shimon was well aware of the fact that Pessia had promised her late husband Chaim on his deathbed that she would take the children and immigrate to Palestine as soon as she could. Until now he would not let her travel there by herself, but being married to Yitzhak that would no longer be an issue, and Yitzhak professed to being a Zionist with strong aspirations to immigrate to Palestine; he was being held back by his inability to obtain an immigration certificate from the British, he had said. Yet that did not stop Shimon from blessing the marriage knowing full well that once again his daughter will be far away.

But maybe, God willing, with the situation in Ukraine being what it is, with the turmoil and dangers, maybe he and his wife will follow their daughter to the Promised Land.

For the girls, and especially for Leah, the presence and affection of Yitzhak Ostrovsky meant a lot, because her mother, while devoted to her own children saw less value in her girls than in her sole remaining son Nahum, and at every opportunity dismissed them as silly unimportant human beings.

"Boys grow up to be men, the heads of the household like your late father and grandfather, the breadwinners of the house," she told Leah and Ida on a number of occasions. "Girls need to know how to be good wives to their husbands, keep the house in order, cook and sew, and bear their children. That is all a woman has to do in life. Men are important, girls not so much."

Only later in life did she realize that her daughters were as important, if not more so, to her own existence and survival in the Holy Land.

❖   ❖   ❖

It was late in the year of 1924 when they were finally able to book passage on a ship headed for Palestine. The British allowed them to immigrate since their grandparents, Chaim's parents, had arrived there during the Turkish Empire rule before the British Mandate took effect–the Turks were not concerned about allowing Jews to enter their empire. Once the British took over with their immigration restrictions Chaim's parents, under the premise of family unification, requested immigration certificates for their daughter-in-law and grandchildren.

Leah was on the deck of the ship and was the first to spot Jaffa port. She ran up and down the deck screaming, "*Yaffo, Yaffo,*"—the Hebrew name for Jaffa—at the top of her lungs, as any 10-year-old excited child might do. At the sound of her voice, others came and joined her on the deck.

It was some time later, as they neared the shore, that she saw these weird looking animals walking up and down the pier with boxes on their backs.

"What are those?" she asked her stepfather who was standing next to her.

"Those are camels," he answered. He had seen pictures of camels and knew what they were, but not much more than that. "They are like the horses of the desert."

They stood there watching the activities on land until it was time to disembark. She had been told that her late father's parents would be there waiting for them, but as she had never seen them before she could not point them out of the small crowd on the pier. When they came off the boat an elderly couple approached them and she assumed it was her other grandparents, clearly not the ones who had remained in Kharkov. Then she saw Nahum behind them. She had not seen him for some years, since he had left for Palestine.

"Nahum!" she squealed as both she and Ida ran toward him.

"Easy girls," he said in Russian as he hugged them both. "You look great, are you okay?"

"We are. You grew so much!" Ida took the lead.

"I am almost 15, I had my Bar Mitzvah almost two years ago," he said with pride. "Let me go talk to mama."

"Nahumchik!" It was his mother's turn to call out to him. She hugged him so hard he thought his bones would be crushed.

She pushed him away from her to arm's length. "How are you, my big boy?" she asked in Yiddish.

"I am fine, mama," he answered also in her favorite language.

Her in-laws came over and they all exchanged embraces. "Wow," Pessia thought about her father-in-law, "how much he reminds me of my Chaim! Same build, only older," and tears flooded her eyes.

Her father-in-law stood there, tall, slender, with a head of gray hair, and a respectable beard to match. His wife, still a handsome woman with all gray hair was standing by his side. They all remained motionless for what seemed like a long moment, and then Pessia turned and grabbed Yitzhak's arm.

"This is my new husband, Yitzhak, and his son," she introduced them. "These are my late Chaim's parents that I told you about."

The crowd of other passengers disembarking grew around them, and they started moving ahead out of the port.

"Where is Motya? And how about Dora?" Pessia asked her in-laws about Chaim's siblings. Chaim had three brothers—Mordecai referred to as 'Motya,' Uri, and Morris—and a sister Dora.

"Motya is in the United States. He went to visit his brothers Uri and Morris in New York a few months ago, and he will be staying there for a while. Dora is in Ramat Gan, she could not come," Nahum volunteered. Dora and Pessia had met only twice in Kharkov when Chaim brought her to introduce her to his parents, before his parents' departure for Palestine, and the two women did not like each other during those two encounters.

They all boarded a bus and headed to the Bernstein's home on Ben Yehuda Street in Tel Aviv, where Nahum had been staying since arriving in Palestine.

❖   ❖   ❖

The small house on Bograshov Street that Yitzhak had arranged to buy was perfect for them—three bedrooms, a nice living room and dining room, an enclosed balcony overlooking the back yard, and a good kitchen, all on street level. It was centrally located, and literally across the street from one of the main synagogues of Tel Aviv, which was important to both Pessia and Yitzhak.

This was the house where Leah and Ida would spend their teenage years. They shared a room, Yitzhak's son had the smaller bedroom, and Pessia and Yitzhak had the bigger bedroom; Nahum preferred to remain living with his grandparents on Ben Yehuda Street.

Based on his experience as a banker in Kharkov, Yitzhak took the reins of Mizrahi Bank as its president. He hired the staff, trained them, and established all the procedures for proper banking. Soon he earned the reputation and the respect of presiding over an honest and friendly banking institution.

Pessia wasted no time in setting up the house. She furnished it with solid practical furnishing, mostly new from local stores. From the Ukraine all they could transport were kitchen silver, an old mantle clock, and a few other small somewhat valuable heirloom items. With a foot-pedal mechanical Singer sewing machine that she bought in the flea market in Jaffa, Pessia set out to make drapes, bedsheets and pillow cases, and of course tablecloths for a Shabbat table. It seemed that in no time at all, this tiny woman had established a new traditional Jewish home in the Land of Israel.

And of course, there was the samovar in the living room, always warm with a typical hot cup of tea for an occasional visitor.

❖   ❖   ❖

Life for a young girl in Tel Aviv in those days was uneventful, so long as she did not stray too far into the less-than-friendly neighborhoods of Jaffa. The streets were safe; a girl could walk anytime day or night in the Jewish neighborhoods of the city and most of the countryside without fear of being molested, or worse. Cases of burglary were few and far between, there were no robberies, and most people knew each other. Better still, they knew about each other, and cases of people going astray were not common. So, except for the occasional terror activity by the Arab population attacking a kibbutz or a moshav, individual security was not an issue.

Alcoholism and drug use within the Jewish population were practically unknown, so cases of violence resulting from either were unheard of. In the hot climate of the Middle East, who had in mind to drink themselves to death?

In this carefree environment Leah enjoyed the freedom of roaming around Tel Aviv, going to school on foot and unescorted, going to the beach and frolicking with her friends in the town. Since most people could not afford the high cost of commercial entertainment, there was very little of that; social life centered on personal contacts, visiting friends in a very informal easy-going manner, and at a very low cost too.

Soon after Pessia finished arranging their home on Bograshov Street and making it livable, she set her eyes on a grocery store, and with the help of Yitzhak she purchased and managed it. Since managing a grocery store all by herself was a very tough assignment, what better than the help of two daughters, who, in her mind, did not need an education to succeed in life? Girls needed to know how to cook, clean the house, wash the clothes, sew, and make a good home for their husbands, and did not need any of the formal education taught in school beyond basic math, reading, and writing. So Pessia conscripted Ida and Leah to help her in managing the store, dealing with the customers, stocking the shelves, washing the floors, and all the other tasks normally associated with running a grocery store.

Life for Leah in her early teen years consisted of going to school, helping her mother at the store, and enjoying the outdoor informal life that Tel Aviv had to offer. On weekends, which spanned Friday afternoon and Saturday only, time when all stores were closed, Leah would walk the short distance to the beach to meet her friends and enjoy a nice swim in the warm waters of the Mediterranean.

Ida, being her senior by two years, had her own crowd of friends and so the two girls socialized in different circles. Neither had any interest in religion, but would honor Yitzhak and their mother by attending Shabbat evening Kiddush, and Shabbat midday meal which were always strictly traditional.

Leah liked Yitzhak very much and respected him greatly. Not having her father to guide her, and with Pessia's views being quite narrow-minded as far as being a role model for her girls, Yitzhak took it upon himself to guide the girls, especially Leah, in a different approach in life, more attuned with the conditions of Palestine in those days—where girls in the kibbutzim acted as equals to their male counterparts and were responsible for even back-breaking manual labor, plowing fields, sowing and harvesting, as well as guarding the kibbutz at night. Yitzhak realized that was the modern way of a pioneering society, and adapted to it, and taught his girls those principles in a special way without demeaning or openly contradicting his wife.

Yitzhak insisted that the girls remain in school as long as they could, and hopefully obtain their high school diplomas. He would spend many hours teaching Leah things not taught in school, open her mind, engage her curiosity, and form her personality to be much more universal and sophisticated than that of a small-town girl of the Levant under the dismissive attitude of her mother.

During the summers Yitzhak insisted that Leah attend "Children's Village," a summer school in an agricultural setting where the children performed all farm tasks: Tend to the animals, milk the cows, feed the bull and clean its pen, plow the field, pick the fruit, whatever the chores of the season required, all in an effort to expand their horizon, stiffen their backbones, and prepare city youth for life in a kibbutz or another agricultural type community.

Under his guidance Leah grew to be quite independent and free spirited. And while she heard her mother demean those girls who actually took on professions rather than the role of subservient wives, she did not allow that thinking to shade her own actions and personality. She rose way above her mother's prescribed role, exceeding even her own expectations, and definitely garnered the respect of her friends, peers, and contemporaries.

So, when the Haganah sought an exceptional operative, loyal, independent, reliable, a true Zionist who came to love the country and believed in its future, what better asset could they find? She knew every nook and cranny, could move about the city with total ease, fearlessly and silently, day or night.

Leah was just 15 when the Haganah came knocking on her door, or was it on her window?

❖   ❖   ❖

Leah suspected that her stepfather knew about her "extracurricular" activities—requiring strange comings and goings, mostly sneaking out of the window of her bedroom in the middle of the night, returning before dawn—but he never ever uttered a word about it to her. At the same time, he did tell her on a number of occasions that he expected her to remain a respectable young lady, and that she should maintain the decorum befitting their social standing in the community—he being the president of a major community bank, an honest and compassionate banker, hence part of the elite of the Jewish population of Tel Aviv.

Ida in the meantime, being 18 and a grown up, decided that dancing was her calling in life, and becoming a professional dancer was what she strove for. She ignored her mother's strong objections that dancing girls were nothing but glorified hookers, and that no respectable girl of hers was going to demean the family's reputation by becoming one. Instead, she packed her bags and left the home and, with the tacit acquiescence and support of Yitzhak, joined the famed Russian dancer Mia Arbatova and became one of her students. She was good, very good, and soon began appearing with the group performing in Palestine, and not long afterward traveled to Europe and North Africa appearing in various venues as a full-fledged member of the troop.

Leah was happy for Ida actually fulfilling her dream, although deep down she resented her sister for abandoning her to the greater scrutiny and criticism of her mother. Pessia's critical focus, previously divided between her two "useless" daughters, now concentrated on the younger one. Moreover, Ida's departure meant that Leah lost her best friend and closest ally, the only person she could trust to share her innermost feelings with, and she never found a friend who could completely replace the closeness of spirit these two had.

Over the next two years Leah continued attending the local prestigious high school Gymnasia Herzliya, where her uncle Motya, upon returning from the United States, was hired as headmaster, although because of circumstances she never received her diploma. Not that she was not a good student but just before her final exams a series of assignments for the Haganah late into the nights robbed her of the opportunity to study and pass the exams.

She spoke Hebrew like a Sabra, Russian like a native Ukrainian, Yiddish fluently, and because of the British presence all around, she picked up some English as well, although not to the level she would consider satisfactory. She was like a sponge, soaking up knowledge at every opportunity, both academic and practical.

Her competence and efficiency were extraordinary. Without fanfare and wasted motions, throughout high school she had helped her mother in the grocery store in the afternoons, helped with the household chores, and also did her homework. The light in her room would stay on late every night while she devoured books at an incredible rate. Since during the summers she had spent time in the Children's Village, animal husbandry and farming were not alien to this city girl. Her favorite advice to anyone who ever tried to pick a fight with her was to tell them about the bull who decided to go after her when she entered its corral one day to clean it.

"He came charging at me with all its might. I stood fast, did not move, and let him gain full speed. When he was only a foot away I ducked sideways, and he hit the post behind me with his head. The poor bull, he learned his lesson and stayed away from me after that, and so should you!"

As with most of the girls in those days, upon graduation from high school Leah could marry, join an agricultural settlement, or go to work. There was no university she could attend in Tel Aviv, and no money to go to Jerusalem to The Hebrew University that had opened just a few years earlier, and definitely no money for her to go abroad.

So among these choices, fiercely independent Leah chose to go to work. Almost immediately she was hired as a salesperson in a textile store in town, not too far from her home. It was not that large of a store, but it had a fabulous collection of textiles imported from all over the world. The owner had formerly owned a shop in Germany and knew the ins and outs of textiles like the back of his hand, and thus his merchandise was the most cherished in the whole of the Middle East.

Seeing how competent Leah was, within six months after she came to work in his store the owner promoted her to run his establishment, and good for him that he did—it did not take her long to guide him into bringing in the kind of merchandise the clientele wanted. Surely he knew the business of textile inside out, but this was not Germany, it was a backward Middle East swath of land with customers coming from all over the Levant, with their special needs, desires, and tastes. He followed her advice, and the store grew in prominence and reputation to become the busiest store of its kind in the entire Middle East.

It was located on Nahalat Binyamin Street, a main north-south thoroughfare not too far from Jaffa, and the cream of Arab women would come from Jaffa to buy the exquisite cloth materials that the store carried. Silks from India and China, cotton from Turkey and Syria, wool from Persia, the store had everything the clientele wanted.

As soon as they would walk into the store draped in their black attires from head to toe, and faces covered with just a slit for their eyes, Leah would motion her boss to scoot—he would scurry into the office in the back of the store, out of sight. The women liked that because now they could unveil their faces and feel comfortable in the presence of this young woman who tended to them. They would never dare remove the veil with a man around—that would be against their custom and no respectable Muslim Arab woman would do that. And Leah always marveled at their facial skin, smooth as a baby's bottom, without a blemish, thanks to it always being covered up outdoors out of the damaging sunlight.

They loved to come in and browse, always in a group of two or three, conversing freely in Arabic, and it was not long before Leah picked up some of the language and could understand what they were looking for, and help them find it.

Sales grew, and the reputation of the store spread in the entire Middle East, and soon women from Amman, Damascus, and Beirut came in to shop. Despite the local politics and strife between the Arabs and Jews in Palestine, the flow of tourists coming to the seashore, especially from Amman, was a constant source of new customers. So Leah was very busy keeping the store open even during the customary mid-day break normally from one to four in the afternoon; she used to grab a hurried lunch at the dairy luncheonette next door, and became friendly with the owners, a nice German couple, Rosa and Herman.

Leah's boss was an honest man, and he rewarded Leah handsomely. She was earning sixteen British pounds a month, an enormous sum of money. Alas, between financially helping her mother's grocery store and a few of her not-so-fortunate friends, not to mention charity, Leah kept only enough of the money to modestly get by. There were many people less fortunate than she was, she would say, and they could really use some help.

At one point a local real estate broker approached her with a proposition.

"I have a tract of land for sale," he said. "It spans from the Yarkon River south to near your home on Bograshov, and from Dizengoff Street all the way to the beach. Right now it is all sand dunes, but it could be made into a really good piece of property. I can sell it to you for 300 British pounds, and you can pay for it in installments, at five pounds a month."

She turned the offer down because she was committed to helping her friends, and there would not be enough for that investment.

Today, this is the prime tract of land of Tel Aviv worth many, many billions.

Chapter 18

Sam met Leah again in the summer of 1937, at the home of one of his friends. He had looked for her on many occasions and was hoping she would show up at Café Piltz, the place where they first met, but she had vanished as if into thin air. Even his friends could not tell him much about her. Was she dating anyone? They were mum; they said they did not know. It was strange that during all this time he never bumped into her on the street, or at some event. After all Tel Aviv was not such a big place that one could be hiding for so long.

Nor was she hiding, not from him and not from anyone else. Actually since he was not of interest to her she had forgotten all about him. She was going about her business, doing what a normal young hard-working girl would do in Tel Aviv: During the week she was at the store, or at her mother's grocery, and she spent her free time most Saturdays at a specific spot at the beach with her group of friends, and then there were the missions for the Haganah at all hours of the night, and some Saturdays too.

They just were in two different circles of friends and happened not to run into each other at some random place. Sam's light complexion prevented him from going to the beach often, or for long durations, and anyway he was mostly spending his Saturdays on the sand dunes of Manshiya.

So one night when she walked into his friend's house, he was determined that he would not let her vanish again. He was interested, intrigued, and that was enough for him to overcome his natural shyness related to girls, although it wasn't easy.

She recognized him, he noticed, and nodded her head in a way of greeting. He still looked young, but he had a darker complexion, tanned, probably due to being more in the sun than when she saw him last.

With a faint smile at him she sat down at the other end of the couch.

Sam gathered all the courage he could muster and slid down the couch closer to her.

"I have been looking for you all over," he stated simply.

"You have?" she asked, a bit puzzled.

"Yes. You caught my attention the first and only time I saw you almost two years ago at Cafe Piltz, and I wanted to get to know you a bit better."

"I was here all the time," she answered innocently. "I saw you a couple of times riding a motorcycle in town, but you didn't see me."

"I asked all my friends, and no one knew where you lived."

"I am surprised. You must have asked the only people in town who do not know me," she said whimsically.

One of the young men came over and asked her to join him on the balcony for a cigarette. She excused herself, and headed after him.

Sam did not follow. He felt it would be rude, and he expected she would return to her seat as soon as she took the last drag of that cigarette.

She did not. She remained on the balcony for some time mingling with some other people. At one point he could hear her laughing although he could not hear what was being said that made her laugh.

He watched her most of the time, trying to get a feel of who she was. All his life he had been blessed with an innate ability to assess people fairly quickly, and with tremendous accuracy, and he liked what he saw in Leah. She seemed down to earth, unassuming and unpretentious, well-mannered and cultured, and the people around her seemed to like her. Certainly a positive personality.

At one point he caught her glancing at him, and it meant a lot to him. Was she suggesting that she wanted to get back to her seat on the couch next to him? Did she want him to come join the two men talking to her?

He finally got off the couch, and started walking toward them when she broke off from the two and beckoned him to join her on the balcony for another smoke.

"When did you arrive in the country?" she asked after he lit her cigarette for her.

"Almost three years ago, in September 1934. And how about you, you were born here, right?"

"Oh no," she chuckled, "I was not born here. Many people make that mistake. I came here ten years ahead of you, in 1924."

"Where did you come from?"

"From the Ukraine."

"That explains your fluent Russian."

"And you, you speak Russian?"

"*Немножко*," he said modestly, "a little bit."

"Where did you come from?"

"Latvia. Riga."

"Then you must be fluent in Russian, not just 'a little bit'," she chided him. "Did you not study Russian in school there?"

"Yes, I was understating it. I am fluent in Russian."

"How old were you when you arrived?"

"Twenty-four."

"You don't look twenty-four even now. Are you sure?"

"Yes, I am sure. I was born in 1910. After high school I studied engineering in France for four years, then did my military service in Latvia, and then came here. You can do the calculation; in 1934 I was 24."

"When I met you last I was told that you were an engineer, but I didn't believe them; you look so young!"

"My mother's family, they all looked younger than their age, and I take after them."

It was getting late, and he had a full schedule the next day, and maybe even a callout during the night. It was time for him to go.

"I have to get up early tomorrow, so I'd better go. Would you be staying?"

"No, I have to be up early too."

"Can I offer you a ride home?"

"I have never been on a motorcycle."

"You don't have to do anything, just sit there, hold on, and tell me where to go."

They thanked their host, and left. He released the kickstand, and boarded the bike.

"You can sit sideways over here," he said pointing to the rear seat.

"I live at 70 Bograshov Street," she said, anticipating his question. "Do you know where it is?"

"I know the street. We have a client there, a grocery store by the circle."

He started the bike, and off they went. He could not see the surprised look on her face. She knew who he was! He was the young man her mother had talked about so many times for the past two years.

They rode the short distance in silence. It is a bit difficult talking over the engine noise of a Norton, especially when he was facing forward and she was facing sideways.

In front of her house he helped her off the bike, lowered the kickstand and walked her to the front gate.

"Good manners too," Leah thought.

"Could I see you again?" Sam asked, his heart thumping.

"That would be nice. Would you be able to join us for dinner next Saturday night after the Shabbat?"

"Us?"

"Yes, my mother, my stepfather, and me."

"I would love nothing better."

"Great. Good night."

"Good night." He watched her walk by the side of the house, up the three steps and without looking back she was gone through the door.

When Leah entered the house her mother was still awake, sitting in an armchair on the rear veranda reading the Yiddish paper. Leah glanced at her watch, and was glad that it was only 10 p.m. Her stepfather did not approve of her running around town till all hours of the night, and she really liked him and did not want to aggravate him, so she normally tried to arrive home within a reasonable hour. She also had to get up early the next morning for work, be at the store at 7:30 a.m. to open it at 8:00 a.m. sharp. The walk from her parents' home to the store took about fifteen minutes, so her wake up hour was 6:30 a.m., come rain or shine.

She was tired by now so she wasn't going to dawdle about but she had to tell her mother about Sam.

"You remember that young man you have been telling me about, the service guy that comes to the store from time to time?" she asked her mother in Yiddish.

"Sure, I told you many times he is a fine boy from a fine family, and you should marry him, a match made in heaven."

"I finally met him tonight at some friend's house. You are right, he really is nice."

"*Nu,*" the mother asked, "so?"

"He'll be coming for dinner next Saturday night after Shabbat."

"Mazal tov," her mother said sarcastically.

Leah kissed her mother on her forehead, wished her good night, and headed directly to bed. She hoped there would not be a mission awaiting her during the night, delivering messages to other Haganah operatives or any other assignment.

❖   ❖   ❖

The knock on her bedroom window was loud enough to wake Leah up, yet carefully muffled to not disturb anyone else in the house. Her stepbrother was sleeping in the next room, and he was a light sleeper and she was almost sure that he did not belong to any of the underground movements trying to depose the British from their occupation, legal as it was. From conversations they had had over a Shabbat dinner table she could tell that his political views were not at all advanced; he had no interest in what was going on around him, and no Zionist tendencies whatsoever. He definitely was not a member of the Irgun she could tell—those boys had an aggressive attitude toward the British and would resort to violence trying to eject the British from the country. Nor did he belong to Lehi, another right-wing underground group. Equally she sensed, although did not know for sure, he was not a member of the Haganah either.

If anything, she wondered how she herself ended up with the Haganah when her views were much more radical than those of the Haganah, which was trying to have the British leave the area without resorting to violence against them, instead focusing on the welfare of the population and its security from the antagonistic Arabs.

She rose from the bed and opened the window.

"I need two piasters." The woman standing outside said.

"All I have is a shilling," Leah replied.

Password verified, the woman handed Leah a note and disappeared into the darkness. Leah was so familiar with this routine–she had been the messenger like that so many times before, and probably would be so many times more. She knew that the note would give her the details of her assignment, and she needed to validate that it was not urgent or she might have to get dressed and go out to carry on the mission sometime during that night.

She turned on the night lamp and read the note. In coded language it ordered her to be at the high school at 8 a.m. on Saturday and be ready to teach a class. While the note did not say what she was to teach, or whom, or provide any details, Leah knew the drill—she would be teaching a few new Haganah female recruits how to handle a revolver, or a 1908 Parabellum pistol, or a more modern Luger pistol that clandestinely had made its way to Palestine, as contraband. Or, on occasion, it would be a Lee Enfield rifle popular with the British, or a Karabiner 98, another weapon issued to German infantry during WWI. She was familiar with all of them, had been trained to assemble and disassemble these weapons blindfolded.

"Well," she thought, "there goes the beach Saturday morning, but this is more important. And anyway, an order is an order even if the British thought that those were illegal." She would be there.

She would not know where the weapon itself would be arriving from—that would be the responsibility of another operative, who would not know the purpose of his or her delivering the weapon to the high school on Saturday and retrieving it back two or three hours later. Everything was on a "need to know only" basis.

She destroyed the note, and went back to bed.

❖   ❖   ❖

On Thursday Sam asked Philip to buy him a box of sweets at the Elite factory store, so that when he came to visit Leah's family on Saturday night he would not walk in empty handed. He could not get accustomed to the local ways in Palestine, where people who immigrated there intentionally shed a lot of their former European manners, and adopted a simpler, less formal and more down-to-earth style of life, crude in his eyes.

Saturday night he waited until his father finished the Havdalah service separating the end of the Holy Sabbath from the rest of the week, then he quickly hopped onto the Norton for the short ride to Leah's home.

He knocked on the door, and she welcomed him in. Somehow he was able to suppress his anxiety and nervousness to offer the "shalom" greeting followed by the traditional "good week" wish reserved for the end of Sabbath.

"Good week," she responded, "come on in."

She led him down the hallway and into the living room. Her stepfather was sitting in an armchair reading a book, and her mother was in the kitchen making final preparations for the meal.

"Come on in, young man, and sit down," Reb Yitzhak called from his perch on the far side of the room. No formal introductions, easy going atmosphere, Sam was elated to note to himself, just like the environment his late mother always fostered in her home.

He heard footsteps behind him, and he turned around and stopped in his tracks, stunned.

"Finally, young man, you finally found your way to my home," she said in Yiddish.

All of five-foot-tall if an inch, still dressed in Sabbath clothes stood Pessia, his favorite client, the woman who ran the grocery store down the block near the circle.

"Oh my God," was all he could exclaim, and then it dawned on him how close he had been so many times to bumping into Leah during the past two years.

He had spent countless hours at her store. He liked her so much; she filled that void in him of a motherly figure, something he so deeply missed and longed for since his mother passed away. Whenever he had a free moment he would drop by the store, supposedly to check up on the converted icebox-now-refrigerator he had built for her, but truthfully to soak up a bit of that home environment that she represented to him.

She had invited him to come for supper on many occasions, but somehow he never could make it, primarily because of his father, but also because of his unpredictable schedule: He would be free in the morning, enough to spend an hour or more at her store, with no clients to visit and no service calls to address, but then at noon he would be called to assist one of the out-of-town clients, and not return till very late at night. When a butcher's refrigerator goes bad, it is urgent that it get fixed lest all the merchandise and the livelihood of the butcher would be lost.

"Come, sit, food will be ready shortly," she said in her motherly tone. It was obvious that she liked him very much; he reminded her of her brother who died when he was only 15 years old—the same soft and kind disposition, the same gentleness, the same old soul.

Leah could not miss the exchange between her mother and Sam. It was no surprise to her that her mother recognized him. What did impress her was the way she reacted to him, and the warmth and kindness she projected toward him, something that until then had been reserved for only one person, Leah's brother Nahum—the sunshine of her mother's life.

Pessia showered her affection on Nahum, and admired him, but was not very kind to her two daughters, never appreciating them or their accomplishments. They were girls after all, and in her mind girls were meant to be good wives and mothers, and nothing more. Keeping a good kosher home and raising the children well, that was their mission in life, she stated many times. An old-fashioned mentality, remnant of the nineteenth-century thinking in the small villages of Eastern Europe.

Yet she did not apply that way of thinking to herself. Fact, she owned and managed a grocery store, working outside the home many hours of each day, and in many other respects she was ahead of her time. But that did not change her attitude about her girls: they did not need a profession or anything beyond a basic education.

They sat around the dinner table, said the prayers over the food, and had supper—a typical evening meal composed of a salad of fresh vegetables, scrambled eggs, and white cheese on a slice of home baked rye bread. And as a special treat, a piece of Matjes herring that melted in one's mouth, all washed down with a hot glass of tea, Russian style, accompanied by a delicious piece of homemade Strudel.

The conversation flowed easily at the table, with Reb Yitzhak asking Sam about his childhood, his home life, his parents, and the synagogue in Riga. When Sam mentioned that the famous cantor Gershon Sirota had come to their shul Reb Yitzhak admitted to being jealous.

"I have heard him perform on the gramophone, but never in person."

After a while Pessia and Yitzhak excused themselves, Pessia had to get up very early and open the store, so Leah and Sam retired to the veranda on the other side of the house.

"You told me that your family arrived in Palestine in 1924, but you did not tell me from where, and why, and how? I am curious."

"It is a long story," she said, "but I will give you the short version." She told him about her family history and her grandfather's disapproval of her father.

"When my grandfather forbade them from seeing each other, my mother and her love eloped. Yes, eloped, can you imagine that? They ran away to Gomel, got married there, and soon started raising a family. My father had been in the forestry business, so he built a wood mill and would lease land, cut the trees, and make wood for construction and furniture."

"Amazing, my father did the exact same thing in Latvia," Sam said softly.

"Nahum was born, then a boy who died very young, then Ida, and finally me."

She was quiet for a moment.

"I don't remember my father, he died of cancer when I was only 2 years old," she was fighting the tears.

Leah then told him about their life in the little village, and the poverty, and the ordeal that finally made Pessia swallow her pride and come knocking on her parents' door. She described the life in Kharkov, Nahum's departure, and the fear from the Bolsheviks.

"Some time later my mother met Reb Yitzhak. He was a widower, taking care of his young son. He liked my mother and she liked him, and he promised her he would take care of us to the best of his ability, as if we were his own children. They got married. I don't know how much love there was there in the beginning, and how much it was a marriage of convenience on both sides, but I, for one, would never complain. He loves me and treats me like I am his own daughter, his own flesh and blood, and he is also kind to Ida, and takes care of her whenever he can."

"But how did you end up in Palestine?" Sam asked.

"On his dying bed my father had my mother swear to him that she would bring us all to Eretz Israel. He was a true Zionist and believed that the Jews belong here and nowhere else."

She was getting tired, Sam could tell. He wanted so much to hear the rest of the travails of this family, but it was getting really late.

"When can I hear the rest?" he asked gently.

"Whenever you would like, Sam, I am here. I rarely leave the house in the evenings, except for Saturday nights, so you are welcome to drop in whenever you can."

He wanted to kiss her, he felt so close to her, but it would not be right, so they parted with a smile.

❖ ❖ ❖

Over the next few months Sam spent as much time as he could with Leah, and she told him the rest of the story. She described how they traveled by train to Odessa, where they stayed for several months until their papers arrived, and a ship was ready to take them to Palestine. While in Odessa they heard about the death of her grandfather from a heart attack, and not a week later her grandmother also passed away, probably from sorrow and sadness.

So aside from some cousins on her mother's side, the entire family was scattered all over creation, and no one she could recall remained in the Ukraine, and good that they all left—the atmosphere in the Ukraine for Jews was becoming not very hospitable.

On her father's side, uncles Morris and Uri immigrated to the United States, and had settled in a section of Brooklyn called Sea Gate, in the city of New York. Her grandparents who had preceded them to Palestine were living not too far from her mother's home, and although she was not very close to them, she still wanted Sam to meet them someday soon. And finally her uncle Motya and his sister Dora had purchased a citrus grove in Ramat Gan, and were living on the property. It was around the corner from the Elite factory.

Sam and Leah became inseparable, and spent every available moment together. Sam would pass by in the morning on his way to the workshop, pick her up and drive her to the store, and he would pick her up on the way back and bring her home. By now she recognized the unique engine noise of the Norton as there were not many of them around, so upon hearing it she would dash out and they would take off without delay.

They worked out an arrangement, however. If he were not there by a certain hour to pick her up in either direction, she was not to wait for him, especially not in the evening. He explained that sometimes he had to go out of town, or be on a service call, so he might not be able to give her a ride. Neither one had a telephone in the house nor at work—there were not many telephones in the entire country—so he could not notify her if he were detained.

What he could not tell her was that sometimes he was called to special duty by the Haganah, and that would not permit him to pick her up as planned.

Chapter 19

During the remainder of 1938 and beginning of 1939 the British were becoming more and more dependent on Arab oil, and as a result in Palestine they were leaning further and further away from a balanced approach to resolving conflicts, and were clearly aiding and abetting the Arabs in their violence against the Jews. No longer were Jews allowed to carry weapons of any kind, under penalty of death. The British threatened the Jews to not retaliate against Arab violence, and actually executed by hanging two members of the Irgun underground who did retaliate, while at the same time none of the original Arab perpetrators of the violence were ever brought to justice.

In Europe serious anti-Jewish sentiment grew, manifesting itself in a string of legislations issued by various countries, especially Germany and Austria. These laws were aimed at stripping Jews of any and all semblance of humanity, confiscating their property, throwing them out of their jobs, and limiting their movements. One by one their freedoms were being curtailed or completely taken away.

Those who saw what was happening and had the means to do so, fled to wherever they could, but not many places accepted them. Not even the United States, the land of "Give me your tired, your poor, your huddled masses yearning to breathe free," would allow these persecuted refugees entry beyond a small trickle, the lucky ones. The Jews were not welcome almost anywhere.

To appease their oil rich Arab friends, the British blocked almost all immigration into Palestine, and not even Christian pilgrims, once their pilgrimage was over, were permitted to remain. Marjory, a Christian and British subject, a single woman who had immigrated to Palestine in the early 1930s, and lived on Motya and Dora's property, was affected by this closure of the borders: When she had to travel back to England to tend to a sick aunt, the British government would not permit her to return to Palestine, under the guise that it was "too dangerous." She ended up having to smuggle across the border from Beirut, in the dead of night, and go underground once she arrived in Palestine.

Those were the conditions of the time, a world entering a period of turmoil.

Sam was very aware that these deteriorating conditions were not limited to Western Europe. He knew that also Russia, Poland, the Ukraine, Belarus, and even Romania, were following in the footsteps of Germany and taking their aim at Jews. Philip, Sam, and Misha, tried to convince their huge extended family spread over Latvia and Lithuania to pack up and go, but they did not meet with much success at all. Only few of their relatives heeded their warnings and actually fled. But where could they go?

Leah on the other hand did not have those worries about relatives left in the old country; most who were still alive had run away from the Bolsheviks in the 1920s and only some remote cousins remained under Russian rule in Moscow.

Despite all of that upheaval and uncertainty, both at home and abroad, Leah and Sam became convinced they were meant for each other, and decided to tie the knot toward the end of March 1939, Tuesday the 28th to be precise.

Two weeks before the date, Leah went before the Rabbinical Council, the organization presiding over weddings, to obtain the required marriage license. Sam was out of town for the day, so she went by herself to face the council. It was supposed to be a routine appointment, where she would provide the names of the bride and groom, their dates of birth, etc., and they would issue her the license.

Instead they started asking questions about her, about Sam, how well does she know him, and for how long, and finally they asked if she knew Tzipora.

"Sure I know Tzipora. She is his cousin from his mother's side," Leah replied.

"What do you know about her?" one of the Rabbis inquired.

"What do you mean?"

"Do you know about her background?"

"Well, she comes from Riga, the same place Sam comes from."

"Yes, we know all about that. Do you know anything else?"

"She is an artist, a painter. She lives not too far from here."

"Yes, yes, yes. Not that. Do you know that she is married?"

"No, but what does that have to do with me?" she asked.

"She is married to your intended husband," the Chief Rabbi said.

"Oh my God," Leah exclaimed. Now she remembered. Sam had mentioned it to her once when he told her about his arrival in Palestine. But then in the excitement both totally forgot about it.

"She must ask him for a divorce, a *get*."

"But this was a sham wedding. They were not really married; it was for her to come under his immigration certificate!" She was absolutely distraught.

"We know, we know. So it will be a sham divorce, but nonetheless it has to be."

The head Rabbi saw that she was frantic, and tried to calm her down a bit.

"I want you to understand," he said in a reassuring voice, "we are not being harsh on you. I am sure your stepfather Reb Yitzhak will confirm that what I am telling you is true. A normal Jewish wedding is always made up of two parts: *Kiddushim*, the sanctification of the union, and *Nissuim*, the actual marriage ceremony. In the old days there was a period of time between the two parts. After the *Kiddushim* the bride and groom went back to their own parents' home. A year or so later they would get back together and celebrate the *Nissuim* part and then they would be able to consummate the marriage. Nowadays you young people are in a hurry, so we do it together in the same event, separating the two parts with the reading of the *Ketubah*, the marriage contract."

He looked down on the papers in front of him.

"It says here that Sam's and Tzipora's ceremony consisted only of the *Kiddushim* part. Even so, according to Jewish law it still requires a *get* in order to dissolve the marriage.

"But don't fret, girl. We understand the circumstances and will make it easy on them."

He looked at the other two Rabbis sitting next to him and they nodded their concurrence.

"Have the two of them come here in the next few days and everything will be all right," he said reassuringly.

"גייט מיידלה, גייט," he told her in Yiddish. "Go girl, go."

Leah went looking for Tzipora. She knew where she lived and went to her apartment but she was not home. She asked her neighbors but they did not know where she was, she had not been seen for a few days.

"She may be on vacation. Sometimes she goes away for a few days near Zichron Yaakov to paint there. She likes to paint trees and bushes."

By now Leah was getting nervous. All the guests had been invited, and the preparations were underway, and her future brother-in-law Isaac, his wife Gita, and their son Marc would be arriving soon from Riga, and no wedding?

She took a bus to Ramat Gan, to the Elite factory. Between Philip and Misha they might know where Tzipora was, and there was no time to waste, the divorce proceedings needed to be completed before the wedding night, less than two weeks away!

Misha told her not to worry. "I know where she is," he reassured her. "She is near Zichron as the neighbors suggested, which is not too far from my home in Binyamina. This evening I will drive to Zichron to tell her to get back to Tel Aviv immediately."

"Thank you, Misha, you are an angel," she was grateful.

Tzipora was in no hurry to return. Although she herself was engaged and was planning to get married, her wedding was not scheduled until late summer, so there was no urgency on her part. She showed up in Tel Aviv on mid-day Friday, when everything closes for the Sabbath.

Tuesday morning was the earliest that Sam, Leah, and Tzipora could all meet at the Rabbinate. When the Rabbis saw their sham marriage certificate they annulled the marriage, without forcing them to go through the unpleasant divorce ceremony, and they both became single again, able to marry.

With a big sigh of relief, the marriage license in hand, Sam and Leah knew their wedding would go ahead as planned in one week!

❖   ❖   ❖

A few days before the anticipated celebration Isaac and his family arrived from Riga. They used the new Flying Boat service, and landed in the Sea of Galilee near Tiberias, then came by bus the rest of the way.

Isaac met Leah for the first time, and from the first moment he laid eyes on her, or maybe even before, he made it very clear that he did not like his little brother's choice of a mate. He and his father were the only two people in the whole world who did not approve of the match.

Haim did not want Leah in their lives—he said she was not orthodox enough for Sam, and wouldn't keep a kosher home, but in her heart Leah knew that that was not his only reason. She understood the old man was concerned she was taking his baby son away from him, and he could not suppress his selfishness and accept their upcoming union.

As for Isaac, his reason had to be something else; it could not be that she was not religious enough, since he himself was totally secular, assimilated, and agnostic. He made no bones about the fact that he simply did not care for her, her personality rubbed him the wrong way. He told Sam he did not approve of her and that Sam should call off the wedding and find another girl to marry at a later date—surely there were more deserving girls in Tel Aviv for his brother, more suitable than this high-school dropout!

Many times during the last few days before the wedding Isaac tried to convince his younger brother to abandon his marriage plans. Almost incessantly he exerted tremendous pressure on the groom to call the whole thing off. There was no fight, no voices raised in anger, just a discussion kept in respectful tones, despite the hurt felt all around. But neither side was going to budge.

His efforts failed; Sam would not hear of it. He loved Leah, she was his soul mate, his "*bashert*," and the wedding would take place as planned. He would not even tell Leah about these conversations to keep her from being hurt.

Hearing that, and seeing his brother's determination, and although no harsh words were exchanged, Isaac was angry. This powerful businessman and industrialist, a pillar of the community, was not used to being disobeyed, especially by his baby brother and on a matter of such importance. He was determined to not remain for the wedding.

When Isaac announced his imminent departure back to Riga, it was a tremendous blow for Sam. Beyond his sadness about his eldest brother's decision to forego his moment of happiness, the separation from Isaac was very difficult for him—Isaac's rejection of Leah notwithstanding, Sam still was very attached to his brother.

His concern was much deeper than just his desire for his brother to remain close to them. The winds of war were already blowing in Europe, especially after the capitulation of the British, French, and Italian governments to Nazi Germany, allowing Hitler the annexation of Sudetenland, part of Czechoslovakia in September of 1938. Then there was the awful *Kristallnacht*, the "Night of Broken Glass" in November of that year, the ongoing expulsion of many Jews from Germany to Poland, and the many other atrocities committed by the Nazis, all of which caused Sam, Philip, and their father terrible unease about Isaac returning to Latvia. They tried so hard to convince him to stay.

"You are already here, with Gita and Marc. Things are not good over there. Who knows what will happen next. Why would you not stay here?" they all pleaded with him. "At least for a while until things settle down there."

"I have my responsibilities to my workers, to the future of my family, to all the people who depend on me, not to forget Mira," he argued.

"All that is nonsense. If that madman Hitler decides to go after Lithuania and Latvia next, what will you do then?"

"What makes you think he is interested in that place?"

"Latvia was under German control for hundreds of years. Why did he go after the Sudetenland and would not go after Latvia?" Sam argued.

"Sudetenland was something else. There were Germans living there, and he wanted to unite them under one country."

"No difference. He might come after Latvia too," Philip added his voice.

No matter how hard they tried to persuade him, Isaac was going to return to Latvia and resume his life there. It was not even Gita's family he was concerned about—her parents had already passed away, and she was an only child. He was determined; they were leaving, and not coming back except to visit from time to time. Was it his status in the society, or the financial security, or the aura of being a pillar of the community, all the glittering material things that were blinding him to the situation in Europe and tearing him away from his family?

Two days before the wedding Isaac, Gita and Marc left by bus to Tiberias where they boarded the Flying Boat air service on their way back to Latvia.

Leah's brother Nahum and his wife Rivka hosted the wedding celebration in their apartment in central Tel Aviv. All their friends and family gathered around the canopy under the clear skies on the roof of the building, and witnessed a traditional orthodox Jewish wedding. Nahum, Philip, Misha, and Leah's uncle Motya held the four posts over which the chuppah was draped, and Reb Yitzhak gave away the bride, his stepdaughter whom he dearly loved. Pessia's cousin Rabbi

Fischmann, head of the Rabbinical Court in Jerusalem, had travelled to Tel Aviv to officiate at the wedding, and even Sam's father, glum faced of course, blessed the couple and wished them a long and happy life together.

Leah was dressed in a long white satin gown, Pessia's superb handiwork. Weeks before the wedding Leah went on a scavenger hunt at the store where she worked, and found the material, a remnant not an inch too long. Pessia sat by her Singer sewing machine, measured Leah with her eyes, without the help of a tape measure, and sewed for her a perfectly fitting dress. As for Sam, Pessia also tailored a hand-me-down suit donated by Philip from his closet, and it also fit him like it had come from a tailor's shop.

Even without music—Rivka's father had passed away a short time before and she was still in mourning—it was a very joyous occasion for all the friends and family who came to wish the couple Mazal Tov.

Their honeymoon was a weekend in Tiberias; that was all that this couple could afford. Like many in Palestine in those days, they too were quite poor: Leah's wedding ring was so thin, like a gold wire wrapped around her finger it was almost invisible, and Sam did not even receive one, and come to think of it, never wore one his entire life.

Sam had a single pair of shoes, two pairs of pants and a few shirts. A few days before the wedding he brought his entire wardrobe to Pessia, and she did her magic to repair his underwear, and mend his socks—the groom had very little.

But despite it all they were very happy. Newlyweds.

Part III

LEAH AND SAM

Chapter 20

Leah and Sam settled down in their small apartment in Tel Aviv, not too far from Pessia's and Yitzhak's home. They were very much in love, and very happy, except for the fact that Sam's father Haim came to live with them.

Once they wed, Leah resigned from her lucrative position at the textile store. She would have liked to continue working but Sam forcefully insisted that as a married man he now had the responsibility of being the breadwinner of the family, and his wife should be the homemaker. He insisted, notwithstanding the fact that Leah was earning sixteen pounds a month, and his income was only six.

Or was his lower income also a reason for his insistence? Was it that her higher salary made him feel inadequate? To be fair, it was the common family structure in those days, he claimed, and that was the arrangement he preferred.

It meant that they had to reduce their expenses, and live much more modestly than they otherwise could, but that was his demand and Leah acquiesced. The immediate effect was that they no longer could afford the high cost of financially supporting Haim living with Philip, and instead he moved in with them.

The first year of marriage is often difficult for couples who have not lived together before. The adjustment is not trivial. In many ways, one forsakes his or her independence for the pleasure of having a loving companion. Having a third person in the house at that adjustment time is not a good idea, but neither of them anticipated just how much more difficult Haim's presence would be for them.

From Haim's perspective things were not going well either. He no longer had his favorite seat at the synagogue, and the companionship and respect of people whom he had been accustomed to and liked there—having graduated from the yeshiva himself, he was considered a learned Jew, an authority in all Jewish matters second only to the Rabbi in this synagogue. He occupied a seat in the "elders" section against the eastern wall of the shul, and would be consulted on matters whenever the Rabbi was not available.

But in the new synagogue he was attending now, he became "rank and file" again, sitting in a non-prestigious section, and treated like all the others attending the services.

He was bored, restless, and depressed by the circumstances, living with his son, and a daughter-in-law whom he did not particularly care for, so he set out to pick on Leah at every opportunity.

He would wait for Sam to return home, and even before the couple could greet each other properly he would start complaining to Sam about something or other that Leah did, or said, or did not say, or did not do, that was not to his liking. The worst parts of his hard character manifested themselves, and placed Sam between the proverbial rock and a hard place.

And Leah tried so hard to accommodate him, to tend to him. She kept her home strictly *glatt* kosher, much more so than she would otherwise have done, and it was an encumbrance on her. She had to do twice the laundry, by hand, make sure he had clean towels and ironed bedsheets and the food was to his liking, and on top of that entertain him somewhat and keep him company when she really did not care to.

She was very considerate to Sam and never complained to him about his father's attitude toward her. When Sam was present Haim was a bit more civil toward her, so Sam, although mildly aware the old man's presence was bothering her some, did not perceive just how much. The old man was just seeking attention, he thought.

Sam was so absorbed in trying to make a living, working long hours. And then there were the other activities for the Haganah that kept him tense, life-threatening events like being chased by the British near Geula Street. Obviously that did not add to Sam's peace of mind, and despite his love for Leah his attention to his father's behavior toward her did not attain center stage as it should have, and would have in normal times.

And anyway, what could they do? Sending him back to live with Philip would put a serious dent in their finances. If Haim were to go back to live with Philip it would only be fair that they contribute some of their miserable livelihood for the upkeep of Sam's father, and forget the fact that Philip was earning several times more than what Sam was bringing home.

Then in December 1939, Leah became pregnant with their first child, and that further complicated matters. She suffered morning sickness almost every day, and was irritable, and the consistent bad behavior of her father-in-law got the better of her. She bore the discomfort as best she could, but the irritation of the old man's behavior was becoming intolerable.

When Sam came home one evening in early February, expecting his father to complain once again about his wife having done something wrong, it was Leah who was waiting for him at the door.

She did not mince words. "I love you like nothing else, and I don't want to hurt you ever. But either your father goes, or I go." She lay down the law of the land. There was no mistaking how serious she was.

"What?" was Sam's astounded response. He was in total shock. Did he hear her correctly?

"Either your father goes, or I go. I cannot take it anymore. Pregnant or not, I go."

She did not need to explain to him why she made that statement; he was mildly aware of his father's cruelty toward her, but not to the level that he now realized it had reached. On a couple of occasions, he had gently asked the old man to change, but he now realized he had failed. Obviously Sam had been too careful about not hurting his father's feelings, and did not balance it against the damage being done to his wife and himself.

That was the first time that Leah saw Sam in tears.

"I am so sorry for your pain," he said as he reached out and hugged her and held onto her for the longest time. "I did not realize how hurtful he had been to you. I can't let you go, and I won't. I will do whatever I need to do to make sure that you and I stay together. Whatever it takes."

"What can you do?" she asked.

"I will find a solution."

He thought for a moment.

"Can you stay with your mother and Yitzhak for a few days until we resolve this? Obviously my father has to stay someplace, but not here with us. I will talk to Philip and see if he can go back to Ramat Gan to live with them—I think it would be best all around. There he has his friends, and the synagogue where he can spend his mornings, and here he has nothing to do. So it would be better, and I think Philip will understand that."

"But if we have to share our income with them to cover his expenses, how will we survive?"

"We will find a solution."

The next morning Sam drove Leah to her mother's store. By the afternoon he had sold his trusted Norton at a very good price. Since September the British were at war, they needed all the Nortons they could lay hands on, and here they were presented with a very clean and well maintained motorcycle, so they pounced on it offering Sam a price way above market value.

But he needed a vehicle, or else he would lose his livelihood. By the next afternoon he was the proud owner of a German 1937 BMW R16 twin carburetor motorcycle with a sidecar that he picked up for an unbelievable low price. What a bargain it was! This was probably the only motorcycle of its kind in Palestine. It was the motorcycle that the German army used, and there were no spare parts for it to be had. If you bought it as a form of transportation, you were on your own. If anything broke, you might be without a bike for a long, long time.

Sam was aware of all that, but he had advantages others did not have. First of all, he trusted the BMW brand—the Germans built them like tanks to never break down. Second, he had a fully equipped mechanical workshop at his disposal, and good contacts among machinists who could fabricate almost anything out of nothing. So he felt confident about his decision.

And anyway, he now needed a sidecar. Being pregnant, Leah would not be able to ride behind him on the motorcycle but she could sit comfortably in the sidecar. And when the baby was born, it would definitely be a good thing to have her sit with the baby without having to hold onto him or her.

And to top it off, he also had a few pennies left in his pocket.

He picked Leah up that evening in his new motorcycle, and she was amazed at his wheeling and dealing. Although three years old it looked brand new, and when she heard at what price he made the exchange, she was even more impressed. Sam was never known to be a salesperson, and financial dealings were not his strongest suit, so Leah marveled at his ability to have risen to the occasion.

The next thing was finding a place to stay, a lower-cost dwelling.

"Your Aunt Dora used to have the ground floor apartment in Ramat Gan in that building in the citrus grove. Do you know what the story with it is?"

"No, I don't. Dora now lives with her parents on Ben Yehuda Street, but I don't know what happened to her apartment."

"Maybe she is willing to lend it to us?"

"I can check with her tomorrow morning. It is a great idea."

The next evening Sam picked Leah up from her mother's home, and with a smile on her face she dangled a set of keys in front of him. They went home, had supper with Haim, and then they headed to see the place.

It was not really an apartment. At one time it had been a chicken coop, and later had been converted to an apartment, dark and dingy. It was attached to a two-story town house where Leah's Uncle Motya made his living quarters. But it had two bedrooms, an old kitchen, a bathroom, and a nice size living room which opened to a large veranda. There was an area of overgrown vegetation that could be converted to a yard, and obviously there were citrus trees all around. With proper care and some handy work, it could be made into livable space once again.

It was perfect. Now they had the perfect excuse as to why Haim had to leave them and go back to Philip's place—in their new place they did not have a bedroom for Haim, and the nearest synagogue was up the hill, quite some distance away, too far for him to walk to.

Within days Leah and Sam moved to their new quarters, and both went to work improving the place and making it habitable.

Leah's dream was to clear a patch and grow some vegetables, and she soon went to work at it with a vengeance. Alas, the gophers were there too, and they demanded their share of the crop, and for a few years Leah did battle with those critters, fighting them for every radish, potato, kohlrabi or carrot.

❖ ❖ ❖

Times were getting tough all around. In Europe the war was raging, Hitler had already occupied Poland, France, Holland, and Belgium, and stories started leaking about the horrible treatment of Jews. Refugees who succeeded in escaping to Lithuania, which had declared neutrality along with Latvia and Estonia, were sharing horror stories about mass round-ups and executions, deportations in cattle cars, and people disappearing to never be heard from again. In the beginning this trickle of stories consisted mostly of rumors, or at best third-person accounts, but soon that trickle grew into a more sustained flow of troubling and substantiated events happening all around the continent.

In September 1939 Misha traveled to Riga to marry his girlfriend Rachel but the British dragged their feet in issuing her an immigration certificate, so he had to return to Palestine alone. Only nine month later, in June of 1940, did she receive the permit, but by then the war was raging and she had to circumvent all of Europe and travel via Helsinki to arrive in Palestine.

Isaac and his family were still well. He would not budge from his position that since Latvia had declared neutrality, Riga and its Jewish population were safe, and assured his family there was nothing to worry about.

But wasn't Denmark also neutral, they argued, and still the Germans occupied it in April 1940?

Isaac's written response was long and well thought out:

"Denmark was in the way for Hitler to occupy Norway, and to recover the large German population of South Jutland which Germany lost during the Treaty of Versailles after the end of WWI. No such minority exists in Latvia.

"And anyway, since April the Russians are occupying Latvia and protecting it. Furthermore, between Germany's forces and Latvia lie East Prussia and Lithuania, so we will have enough notice if the Germans decided to move north and will escape if needed, either east to Russia, or west by sea.

"And finally, there is the Molotov-Ribbentrop non-aggression pact between Russia and Germany that ensures that Germany won't attack the Soviet Union or its satellite countries such as Latvia."

The family tried, but no amount of cajoling and pleading would change his mind. In a later letter he wrote:

"I love you all, but my home is here, and everything I have built all these years, and I have not much interest in that desert that you call Eretz Israel. To me it does not mean the same thing."

In Palestine, the impacts of the war and turmoil were felt in almost all aspects of life. Firstly, there was a complete stoppage of any economic activity. Not having anything to offer, namely no natural resources or manufacturing of war materiel, Palestine became just a nuisance for the British who had to concentrate all their efforts on stopping Hitler's advance—they did not want Trafalgar Square to become Bismarck Square. They kept only a small garrison that was substantially ineffective in keeping the peace between the Jews and the Arabs, and did not invest a single shilling to make the place any better. But under pressure from their "friends," and their oil, they made sure the borders to Palestine were practically sealed shut, in compliance with the May 1939 White Paper of Neville Chamberlain's government which, among other provisions, limited Jewish immigration to Palestine to 75,000 over five years. They interdicted and sent back any ship, boat, or rickety ferry that carried refugees from the war zone, refugees running for their lives to Palestine.

At the same time, the local Arabs were cheering the Germans on, with the Mufti of Jerusalem befriending Hitler and openly supporting him in the quest for extermination of all Jews anywhere in the world. He would deliver fire-breathing sermons, instigating the crowd and inciting them to violence, with total disregard for his position as a religious leader. Is that what his religion professed, or was it a vicious misinterpretation of what Allah really would have wanted?

The British were of absolutely no help in protecting the Jewish population from Arab terrorist activities of murder, rape, and pillage. The protection of the "*Yishuv*," the Jewish population in the country, was left primarily in the hands of the Haganah and its smaller rivals the Irgun and Lehi underground movements

If that were not enough for the Jewish population of Palestine to deal with, World War II came knocking on their doorstep. Of all people, the glorious Italian Air Force decided to bomb the port of Haifa and between June 1940 and July 1941 they showed up in the skies over the city and caused damage to the oil refineries in that city.

Against this backdrop Sam and Leah carried on with their lives, both the ones open and known, and those hidden and camouflaged. By now they both understood that the other partner was also a member of the Haganah, but they never spoke about their activities to each other.

Coldomat's clientele was expanding, but ever so slowly, and while the three partners were mostly able to pay themselves the meager salaries they had agreed upon, it was still tough, touch and go. There were many a week when not enough money was in the cash register to spread the wealth, so to speak.

There was not enough money to hire any help, and Sam was constantly on the road, carrying the load of single-handedly servicing all the installations at their clients' sites. They were in no position to forego any client, regardless of how far Sam had to go, and what dangers were involved in these excursions.

He went on service calls to Ramallah, and Jenin, and even as far as Amman in Trans Jordan, Beirut in Lebanon, and Damascus in Syria, as well as many other places that were not terribly hospitable to Jews. Not all the clients were in friendly territory, and whenever Sam had to go to a client in one of those hostile neighborhoods, or villages, he would represent himself as "Mr. Engineer from America." That gave him some measure of cover, because the local Arabs had no quarrel with America at that time. They never challenged him about his origin, or the fact that he was riding a motorcycle with Palestinian license plates, but when in doubt he would take those plates down before entering those communities.

His worries were highest not while he was at the client site—as customary in the Arab culture they always treated him well and set a table loaded with fruit and nuts, and cakes and cookies, and before too long the aroma of Turkish coffee would permeate the place. But it was when he left that he was mostly concerned. Arab custom, reigning down from the Bedouin culture is that when a person, even a sworn enemy, is "guest in their home," the hosts have the obligation to defend and protect that person to the death, but the moment the person leaves the person becomes fair game to be pursued and killed, even if by the former hosts.

The long road trips were emotionally hard on Leah who wondered if Sam would come home safely, or become another statistic never to be heard of again. Now pregnant her worries were growing as the baby she was carrying was starting to kick inside her. And her worries for him were double: Not only was he traveling on unfriendly roads, in areas sprinkled with hostile Arab villages, but he sometimes was carrying with him some very valuable cargo, way beyond his refrigeration tool box. His frequent road trips and his profession gave him perfect cover for the urgent need to ferry small weapons or ammunition to remote kibbutzim or other settlements. So working alone in the shop one night, he fitted the sidecar with a double bottom, into which small weapons could be placed.

In his "spare" time Sam had dug a "septic tank" in the back of the property camouflaged under layers of leaves from the surrounding trees, and from time to time he brought small arms and grenades home and stashed them in the hiding place—a *slik*—all under the orders of the Haganah. From time to time he also received orders to deliver some specific quantities to a specific place. Sometimes he had to go out during the night but mostly the Haganah tried to work his "courier service" such that he could weave it into his trips to clients. But about those missions Leah felt that if something were to happen to him, at least there was a broader purpose and justification; more worthwhile than some stinky refrigerator at some client of his in a hostile village..

So if the hostile Arab villagers didn't get him, the British were also a serious threat. Carrying any kind of weapons and ammunition was a death sentence for Jews, and he was very often stopped at the British checkpoints and they inspected his toolbox to ensure he was not carrying weapons, but it never occurred to them however to lift the heavy toolbox and check underneath.

In the meantime, Leah's pregnancy was progressing well, but that however did not stop her from continuing her battle with the gophers who were after the vegetables that she planted in the little patch behind their home. So she also was digging in the backyard.

❖ ❖ ❖

This tense life was hard on the young couple, and the secrecy they had to maintain, both at home and outside the home, added additional stress. Sam had to keep his undercover work hidden from his business partners whom he did not trust; he definitely could not divulge to them the detours in the routes he had to take for the "courier service" he was running behind their backs. Not that they would rat him out to the British, but they could slip up at some point, and say something that would endanger him and his missions.

Leah, now in her seventh month of pregnancy, with tremendous anguish and regret notified her handler at the Haganah that she no longer could undertake any missions, and was honorably and with quiet commendations discharged from the movement.

Things were weary, and to make matters worse, on September 9, 1940 the glorious Italian Air Force attacked the open city of Tel Aviv. They were actually on their way to the port of Haifa once again, but this time they were intercepted by British aircraft stationed at Ramat David Airfield, and in their retreat targeted the port of Tel Aviv instead. Unfortunately, their aim was not good and the bombs fell some two miles away, hitting the central bus station, very close to Coldomat's shop, and killing 137 civilians.

This tremendous loss of life shook the Jewish population of Palestine to their very core, and made them realize that World War II was not so far away from them after all. Yet aside from a small British garrison, and a single British air squadron, there was nothing to protect them from these aerial bombardments.

Not eight days later, in the early morning of September 17, 1940, Sam and Leah welcomed their newborn daughter Bella, named after her grandmother, at Assuta Hospital in Tel Aviv.

Like most other couples they were elated that their baby seemed healthy, with all her limbs, and for a few weeks they allowed their concerns and fears to be pushed aside by the wonderful feeling of bringing a new life to this world. But this reprieve from the worries did not last long, and "normal" life had to be resumed with the stresses and pressures of trying to stay afloat financially, as well as physically, in this dangerous world.

And then came Rex.

Just shortly after their daughter was born, Rex appeared out of nowhere and adopted them as his family: A very large totally black from head to paw German Shepherd, he showed up one day, and settled down as if he owned the place. No one knew where he came from, or why he chose this particular family to adopt, but that he did. He scouted the area the first day, checking the boundaries of the large property that ran all the way to Wadi Musrara, staking out his new domain. He must have liked it, because he stayed.

Rex was a godsend for Leah who was spending many hours alone in this isolated and remote place. If anyone was interested in causing mischief, then that place certainly offered privacy for an intruder. True, Uncle Motya did live upstairs, but as the president of the Publishers Association, and a publisher himself, he was rarely home during the day, and during the evenings this ladies' man was always gallivanting around, chasing women and not always returning for the night. And with Sam out on the road so much, sometimes returning very late at night, or, on occasion, when gone to Beirut or Damascus and being away overnight, it was very comforting to have this large, ferocious looking animal around.

Rex became the bodyguard, the watchdog, and protector. Leah would put her daughter Bella in her carriage under a tree, hang some noisy colorful toy on one of the branches, and Rex would lie by the carriage and not move for hours on end. God forbid if anyone, Motya included, tried to approach the baby, Rex would be fierce in his objection.

Now Leah could tend to her garden without worry and, a few months later, even dash into Tel Aviv for an errand or two without concern for the well-being of Bella. In addition to having Rex, a new family moved to another shack on the property, with a baby just a few months older than Bella and the mother was homebound and able to help in case of emergency. And as the last resort, should it ever get to that, there was that British woman Marjorie who had settled in another converted chicken coop, and although she knew nothing about babies, was at least an adult who could take reasonable action in case of need.

When Sam had an errand to run to courier something he was not supposed to be ferrying around, he would sometimes "invite" Leah to join him on the trip, using her and Bella to camouflage his true activity. No British soldier would be as rude as to ask a lady sitting in the sidecar of a motorcycle with a baby in her arms to get up to allow the sidecar to be thoroughly inspected. They would not think any man in his right mind would endanger his wife and baby to this extent, because if the stash under their feet was found, they would all be shot dead on the spot. That was the logic Sam counted on, and obviously he was right—although they were stopped and searched on numerous occasions, not once was Leah asked to get out of the sidecar for a more thorough inspection.

Leah of course knew what they were doing. It was not something Sam would mislead her into, and although they never discussed it openly, she gladly agreed to do her part. This undercover escort duty then became her continued contribution to the cause.

And so their lives continued to be very serious and intense. There was no time or the mindset to frolic around and just relax. There was always something more urgent, a higher calling for their time. The only entertainment they could indulge in from time to time, was to visit with Pessia or Nahum in Tel Aviv, or Haim, Philip and Manya in Ramat Gan. And on a rare occasion they even would ride the motorcycle to take Bella to the beach on a late sunny Saturday afternoon.

In the meantime, the war in Europe in 1941 was not going well at all. The Nazis were advancing on all fronts and solidifying their grasp over the continent, with horrifying stories about mass deportation of the Jews and rumors that concentration camps were really death camps, slaughter houses. The Jewish Agency was trying to rescue as many Jews as it could, by whatever means it could, but theirs was a list of small successes within a massive genocide. Whenever Jews did escape the grip of the Nazis they had nowhere to go, no one to take them in.

The only ray of sunshine in the bleak news all around was a letter they received in mid-June from Isaac; at least he was in good shape. In it he gave them mostly good news about his business, the family, and the relatives. He also mentioned that their former neighbors—Mira, Moishe and Rachel—were well; both Moishe and Rachel were married to people from the community, and Rachel was expecting. He briefly wrote of stories he had heard about concentration camps in Poland and Germany, but he was not sure what was going on inside the camps. They were touted by the German propaganda as Work Camps, but he didn't know much more than that. Isaac also reported the Germans were making no advances toward Latvia, and he said he was not terribly concerned about the future. As soon as the war was over, he wrote, he planned to come visit them again in Palestine.

That was the last communication they had with Isaac or anyone else from the large family in Latvia.

In mid-July, the Germans entered Riga.

Chapter 21

On December 7, 1941 the United States was attacked by the Japanese at Pearl Harbor, and entered the war. With the United States' might and production capacity of tanks, trucks, aircrafts, and ships, from soup to nuts, it was only a question of time before Germany would be defeated, but time was precisely what the Jews in Europe and the Middle East did not have. The round-ups, and the transports and mass executions continued unimpeded for three-and-a-half more years.

Given the events happening in Europe and especially North Africa, the Jewish population in Palestine was growing nervous and anxious about the Germans overrunning Egypt, and then nothing would be between them and the extermination of the remnants of the Jewish People in the Promised Land.

In North Africa, the Germans were advancing eastward, and by July 27, 1942 Field Marshal Rommel had taken El Alamein in Egypt, only sixty-six miles from the deep port of Alexandria, a prized possession for an army needing to be supplied on a large scale. The Jewish population in Eretz Israel was preparing for the worst—it became obvious the British were stretched too thin, and unable to stop Rommel from reaching Cairo, and beyond Cairo there were no Allied defenses at all. Beyond Cairo was only a stretch of 170 miles of road through the Sinai to Tel Aviv.

The Haganah was accelerating its recruitment and training, and the smuggling and distribution of weapons to the settlements throughout the country. But what good would this ragtag civilian militia be against the well-trained, well-armed, organized and disciplined Wehrmacht with their tanks and airplanes, a well-oiled military machine?

One evening that October Sam and Leah, now seven months pregnant with their second child, sat on the veranda and had a short but earnest and very serious conversation.

"I was at Herman and Rosa's shop for lunch today, and they sent you regards," Sam said. "They are fine, but like the rest of us, very nervous about the German advance.

"They have a radio and we were listening to the BBC broadcast from Egypt, and it doesn't look good at all. Of course the BBC wanted to sound encouraging, but we were not convinced."

"What did the British radio say?" Leah asked.

"They spoke about Churchill being friends with the American President Roosevelt, and they have been getting some help from the United States in weapons, equipment, and supplies, and it is going to help them in the war effort. But I don't think it will be enough to stop the Germans, at least not in the short term." Sam said.

"Do you think the Germans will invade England?"

"Who knows? They have all of Europe and Russia to deal with, on both the eastern and western fronts, and the British will fight them very hard, and now with this help from the United States it is less likely, but it still could happen."

"But that won't stop the Germans advances elsewhere. Will it? Like in Egypt?"

"I don't think it will. The German army is well equipped, and by now well trained and seasoned in combat. They are a formidable force, with all their tanks, and air superiority."

"But you just said that the British are getting supplies from America," Leah challenged him.

"Even so, that is a drop in the bucket. There isn't enough to go around. The British will use the equipment and supplies they get from the United States to first defend their own country, especially after what happened in Dunkirk. You read Churchill's speech in the papers then. He said they will fight the Germans everywhere, on the beaches, in the streets, but he did not say Cairo, or Alexandria. He meant in London, or Manchester, or Birmingham. That is where this equipment and supplies are going to, to defend Britain, not to bolster Egypt."

"What will we do if the Germans pierce through the British forces and break out from El Alamein? Is there anything to stop them from taking Cairo and Alexandria?

"I don't think there is much to stop them there. Alexandria port is very important, and if the Germans can take that, they can pour equipment and supplies to the Afrika Korps of Field Marshal Rommel, and he will be unstoppable. He will go through the Sinai and be here in no time."

"Why do you think he will want the Sinai?" Leah asked. "It is all desert with nothing in it but empty space."

"First, he is the Desert Fox, that's his nickname, and he loves fighting in the desert with his tanks. He can move very fast through the open desert—you saw him advance in Libya. Once he takes the Sinai then he has excellent access to the oil fields of Saudi Arabia. The Germans don't have oil and they need it to continue conquering the world.

"And he can also come north, to Palestine. That will allow him to create a land bridge through Syria to Turkey and to Europe. Encircle the entire Mediterranean."

"Then you think Hitler's army will come here?"

"Makes sense to me," was Sam's reply.

Leah was silent for a while.

"I don't want to be captured by the Nazis. No. I don't want to be captured by the Nazis."

"Neither do I. I am not going to let it happen," Sam said. He was deadly serious.

"What can we do? We have nothing that can stop Rommel, or Hitler."

"No, we don't," Sam said, and then paused before continuing, "but I am not going to be captured by the Nazis."

Leah was quiet, trying to decipher Sam's two opposing statements—they can't stop Rommel from coming to Palestine, and if he does he will capture them, unless they fled somewhere else. But flee where? There was nowhere to run to with hostile Arab nations encircling the small Jewish minority in Palestine.

"What do you mean?" She finally asked.

Sam was quiet for a long time, as if looking for the right way to express his thoughts.

"Masada," he finally said.

"Masada?" Leah asked.

"Yes, Masada—like the 900 Hebrews on the top of Masada who killed themselves to not be captured by the Romans 2,000 years ago, I will kill myself before being captured by the Nazis."

"Kill yourself?"

"I know, suicide is not allowed in Judaism, but regardless, I will kill myself and not get captured by those monsters." Sam was determined.

"Oh no you won't! You can't do that. You won't kill yourself and leave us to the Germans!" she said emphatically. "You will kill me first, then Bella, then you can kill yourself."

Sam looked at her. They were of a single mind. He was silent for a long moment.

"That is what I will do, then," Sam said, "in that order. You, then Bella, then myself."

In their concentration on the discussion they did not notice that Bella had come into the backyard and was listening to their conversation. At two years old she absorbed these shocking words, and for the next seventy years she kept that memory deep inside of her. But she never forgot.

❖ ❖ ❖

Then one month later, on the 11ᵗʰ of November 1942 news came of the end of the second battle over El Alamein—some good news for a change—and a slight reprieve for the Jewish population in Palestine: The Germans were being pushed back in North Africa, at least for now. Between lack of supplies and sickness of his troops— jaundice, diphtheria, dysentery and skin sores, Rommel's Afrika Korps was seeing defeat on the battlefield, forcing it to retreat westward in the Libyan desert, further away from Palestine. Oh, what a relief!

That relief however did not translate to improved conditions, increased economic activity, more work, higher pay, or anything that would make Leah's and Sam's life easier. They struggled like most of the population, Jew, Arab, and others. The only person Leah and Sam knew to be somewhat well off was Motya who was double-dipping, getting paid by both his Dvir publishing house where he worked as the president, and the Publishers' Association where he was chairman. But charity and goodwill toward others were never part of his makeup, so he was also collecting hefty rents from Marjorie, and the other tenants of the orchard. That was Motya the Miser.

And then two days before Christmas Leah delivered their son Ofer at the same hour and the same hospital where his sister Bella was born twenty-seven months earlier.

When their second child arrived things got really tough for Leah and Sam. Now there were two babies in the house, and the good Dr. Cohen was summoned to take care of one or the other frequently. Fortunately, both Bella and Ofer were mostly healthy, since there was no medical insurance to cover the costs of any significant illness.

Leah valiantly fought the gophers, and Pessia, now living off Yitzhak's pension rather than his salary, would slip her a coin or two from time to time, or bring a chicken or some cheese and bread, but things remained tough. On rare occasions Sam could bring a piece of chicken or a piece of meat, mostly cuts the butcher would be willing to part with, but that was not a constant source of food for the house.

In times like these families normally circle the wagons and help each other, but due to Sam's and Leah's foolish pride no one except Pessia was aware of their situation. Motya had to know but pretended not to notice, which was hard to believe—after all they lived in the same two-family house and saw each other almost daily. And Nahum, who by then was doing quite well was oblivious to what was going on, and was intentionally kept in the dark lest Rivka might say something demeaning to Leah as she had done to Ida once before.

"Sam, we are struggling," Leah spoke to him one evening in the spring of 1943. "You work so hard, long hours, and the income is not enough for a family of four, plus a big dog."

"I know," Sam said with deep sadness in his voice. He had been depressed for the longest time. His inability to provide for his family was very painful to him. It signaled his biggest failure in life: Isn't that the primary responsibility of the man, head of the household, the breadwinner? Regardless of the external circumstances—a stalled economy, suffocated, where almost nobody had money—these facts did not relieve him of his duty as husband and father of two to provide food and shelter and all the family's other needs.

Worse, he did not see a way out of the situation. As hard as he had tried, a solution escaped him. There was nothing he could see to do that would bring more income to the family. He felt caged, stuck, losing ground, and sinking in a sand trap with no relief in sight.

His pride had taken a tremendous beating, and that was not good. This man who had so many things to be proud of in his life, so many accomplishments, was being beaten by his own doing, his ego crushed.

Would they have been better off had he not formed Coldomat with his two partners, and gone and worked for someone else instead? The competition was not doing terrifically either, but he would have had a salary, a decent salary, definitely better than what he was bringing home now.

Perhaps he should have a heart-to-heart talk with his partners Yehuda and Meir? It was difficult to support three families with the revenues of the company, but maybe the revenues would be sufficient to support two families? If so, who would leave, and how could they work it out?

The least productive partner was Yehuda, a glorified bookkeeper, whose contribution to the success of the company was limited and easily replaceable by an inexpensive part-time clerk, definitely less burdensome to the bottom line than Yehuda's salary. But if Yehuda were to leave then they would have to sell his share of the inventory and tools, and compensate him for the goodwill they had with the clients. The company did not have any reserves to buy his share out, and who else would buy it now? And if someone were to buy his share, wouldn't that person expect a salary?

He had talked with Abraham Levinson in confidence about the situation, and Abraham saw the dilemma but had no recommendations.

"What if you left the company and went to work for the competition?" Abraham asked.

"I checked around, and everybody is in somewhat of the same boat we are in. Nobody is hiring. I bring in most of the revenues and Meir brings in some through the workshop repairs. Yehuda does the books, as he did for you, and is in the office as the dispatcher. If I leave, Yehuda and Meir will be up the creek without a paddle."

"Is that your problem? That is their issue, not yours."

"That's not how I am built," Sam replied. "I just can't do that, not in this situation. It is like the captain abandoning the ship."

"Yeah, I know, that is you, and that's why I like you. You are a decent human being," Abraham said.

"Thank you."

"But if you stay, I am afraid I have no suggestion for you, and the ship might still sink."

He stayed, praying for better times. Leah watched him become more and more depressed and she was more and more concerned for his health.

She thought of going to work for a few hours a day, leaving the children with the neighbors, the new arrivals at the orchard. They were a fine couple, trustworthy, and could use a little boost to their own income. The old store owner where she had worked would love nothing better than having her back, and would pay her handsomely, he said. But she was sensitive to her husband's feelings and did not want to suggest it because that would be an even bigger blow to Sam's ego–it would affirm his feeling of defeat, worthlessness, and failure.

But something had to be done, and she finally approached him one evening.

"I feel bad for Rex," she said. "It is not fair to the animal. We share our meager rations with him but he is still losing weight, always scavenging and foraging for some food. Yesterday he even tried to eat a dead gopher."

"I am trying my best. I have become a scavenger myself. Whenever I can I ask the butchers for any meat they don't use to bring for the dog, but they are using everything they can these days, every gram of it. Things are tough for everyone. They strip the meat off the bones, so bringing him those won't help either."

"I understand, but all our efforts are not enough. I give him three-quarters of our daily loaf of bread soaked in water, but it is not enough. He can't live on bread alone." She paused. "As much as it hurts me—you know how I love dogs, and how I love this particular dog—but I am afraid we will have to let him go," she fought the tears.

"Let him go? We can't just throw him out!" Sam exclaimed.

"No, no, I am not talking about throwing him out; you know I wouldn't do that. We need to find him another home, somewhere where he can be fed regularly. Can we find someone who can take him? At least for a while until conditions improve?"

"I don't know of anyone who can take him."

"How about one of your clients, a butcher, grocer, or some institution, or a kibbutz, someone who can feed him properly?" she asked.

"I can ask around, but I don't have much hope. I will ask."

A few days later Sam told Leah he had a conversation with Abraham Levinson, and he said he could take the dog. He had a small orange grove some ten miles south of town and he could put the dog there to watch the property. There are people there during the day who would take care of him, and there is a shed for the dog to stay in, out of the rain. Abraham promised to feed the dog well.

With a broken heart, over the weekend Sam put the dog in the sidecar, and drove him out to meet with Abraham Levinson on his property. Abraham tied the dog with a long chain to a post, made sure Rex had water to drink, and made arrangements for one of his workers to feed the dog every day.

It took only two days for the dog to free himself and make his way back to Ramat Gan with half a chain dangling behind him. How he found his way back no one knew, but he did. And he did it again two weeks later.

"I can't bear it anymore," Leah cried in tears. "He clearly wants to stay with us but we can't keep him. As it is I give him every scrap of our rations, but he can't survive on three-quarters of a small loaf of bread a day."

Sam was tormented as well. While he was not as attached to the animal as Leah and especially Bella were, he too loved the dog, and it tore him apart to have to send him away again.

"I am going to take him back tomorrow, for the final time," he said. "If he comes back then I won't take him away again. I can't, I simply can't."

Rex did not come back.

From time to time Abraham told Sam the dog was fine, but they never saw that beautiful animal again.

Having to give the dog away was a big blow to them all. They missed this gentle beast, and for the longest time they would wake up in the middle of the night thinking they heard his whimper outside the door. It was hard, as if a member of the family was missing. But of all of them Bella took Rex's departure the hardest. She had known him since she was born. For her he was a person, her big brother, her constant companion and protector, her guardian angel. Whenever she went someplace on the property, all Leah had to say was "Rex, where is Bella, where is Bella?" and he would trot away and only when he found her, and she was fine, would he return, tail wagging.

Way beyond that, the trauma of the dog being sent away was very significant to the little girl. Bella decided Rex must have done something bad and that's why he was sent away. She concluded that if someone did something her parents didn't like or approve of, they send that person away.

"I must be good, must never do anything bad, never make them mad, or they will send me away too," was her conclusion and decision. That's how the mind of this child worked. That's how the mind of most children works.

It never occurred to Leah and Sam to sit down with the little girl and explain to her why they had to send the dog away, and that it hurt them terribly, not just her, and they would never, not ever, never, never, never, do anything like that to her. In their state of mind at the time, with their worries and stress, the effects of that event on their child did not come to the forefront.

But for Bella, the scar lingered for many years.

❖ ❖ ❖

Two years later the family had to move out of that converted chicken coop. Bella was having difficulty breathing, and after examining her Dr. Cohen concluded that due to the constant dampness of that concrete box they called home, she was developing asthma. By then the finances of Coldomat were a bit better, the war in Europe was turning around, so a few days after D-Day they packed their few belongings and rented an apartment in Tel Aviv.

They moved to a fourth-floor walkup on the main drag of northern Tel Aviv, three blocks from the sea. It was a fairly modern building, as most of the northern part of Tel Aviv was at that time, a concrete and cinder block structure with a flat roof. On the ground floor were some stores, and in the next building over were a butcher shop, a fish monger, and a grocer, while fresh vegetables could be had in the vegetable store one building over to the other side.

Location-wise this apartment was perfect—not too far for Sam to get to his workshop, in an upscale neighborhood, and a school for the children almost directly behind the building. The area was safe for the children to come and go as they pleased. Not many cars were passing, no one would harm the children, and to top it off, if a child got hurt and needed medical attention then the pharmacist directly across the street could, and did, render whatever first aid was needed. And finally, the most important other advantage of this place was the affordable rent, so critical an issue for Leah and Sam.

The irony of this rented apartment was that it was smack in the center of that affordable tract of land that had been offered to Leah some ten years earlier for 300 British pounds and which she had turned down; now she was paying rent for only one of the apartments in one of the buildings on that street.

Just before they moved out of Dora's apartment Uncle Motya had a conversation with them.

"I want to remind you," he said, "you owe Dora the rent on the apartment for all the time while you lived here."

"Rent? What rent?" Leah asked flabbergasted. "She owns the place, and was not living here, it was vacant. So what rent?"

"You weren't expecting to live here for free, were you?" he asked sarcastically.

"Exactly. She let us stay here because we needed a place to stay, and she did not need the place, and she is our aunt, and there was no discussion of rent."

"I don't know, I was not involved in your discussions with her," Motya insisted, feigning ignorance. "I am managing her financial affairs and I would not have agreed to give you the place rent free."

"But that was not part of the agreement with her," Leah was getting angry. "And since you were not involved, you cannot come now and demand back rent retroactively. That's not how it works."

Miser Motya would not relent.

"She told me otherwise. But don't worry, you don't have to pay it now, pay it when you can. I will just keep it on the books until then."

"Not on your life! I am going to talk to her and see about it."

The next day Dora put the matter to bed: Motya had never discussed it with her; he was not telling the truth. No rent was due, and that was that! "Family members help one another and I was glad I could do it," Dora told Leah. Anyway, she did not want to live there anymore, for now she preferred to stay with her parents in Tel Aviv.

"What was your uncle Motya trying to do here?" Sam asked Leah that evening when she told him what Dora had said.

"I think he was trying to pocket the money and never tell her a word about it. It goes along with something else I had heard about him that I didn't believe until now. Now I have no doubt that it is true."

"What was that?"

"Do you remember I told you that after we arrived here in Palestine Nahum was sent to study electrical engineering in Grenoble, in France?"

"Sure I remember," Sam said. "You told me he graduated and then came back to Palestine in 1930 or so, right?"

"Right. How do you think he financed his studies?"

"Your grandfather, I suppose."

"No. Neither of my grandfathers could support him. Pessia's father was already dead, and my father's father did not have enough to send from Palestine. Instead, our uncles Uri and Morris in the United States paid for his education. They were both engineers with the City of New York, and were earning decent salaries, so they could help their nephew with his education.

"When Nahum came back from Grenoble, Motya approached him and said he was managing Morris' and Uri's finances in Palestine, and had him sign a promissory note that he will pay them back. All of a sudden that help that they extended became a 'loan.'

"Over the years Nahum paid Motya every penny back, except I suspect Motya never gave them the money. Instead he bought properties in his and Dora's name in Palestine.

"Do you remember that just before the war Nahum went to America for that Philco deal?" Leah asked.

"Sure. What a coup that was, getting that dealership in Palestine was a great success."

"During that trip he went to Sea Gate in Brooklyn to visit his uncles Uri and Morris and the rest of the family, and to thank them for all the help they extended to him while he was in France. He did not even have the chance to tell them Motya made him sign a promissory note, and that he had already paid Motya all the money they had sent him, because as soon as he started thanking them they hushed him up and dismissed his thanks.

"'Don't even mention it,' they told him, 'it was our duty as your uncles to do that. That's how things go with families. We helped you, you will help someone else in the family when and if you can,' they told him.

"That sounded strange to Nahum, considering that Motya had collected the money from him in their name, so he told them he thought that they had asked for the money back through Motya. They told him to not insult them, it was a grant, not a loan. It came out Motya never discussed collecting the money back for them, never mentioned his intention to them, and probably was not planning to give them the money at all. Now his goose was cooked and when Nahum asked him about it he had to 'share the information that he recovered the money for them' with them. They were very angry with him, how dared he do that in their names?"

"He would do that to his own family?" Sam was shocked.

"Didn't he try to do that to us just now?" was Leah's response. "He is a miser and a scoundrel. Never gives anything back.

"I never pictured him as a con man though, and from his own kin too!" Sam was really perplexed. "I guess that is what he is."

Chapter 22

The war in Europe ended in May of 1945, and although it was still raging on in the Pacific, as far as the Jews in Palestine were concerned the war was over, and Hitler was dead.

The story of the Holocaust was unfolding to its deepest of horrors, and the utter devastation of the Jewish population of Europe became clearer with every day passing. Like an image emerging from fog the atrocities committed by the Nazis were coming to light, although the complete horrific picture would not be exposed for years to come, if ever.

Sam's primary preoccupation was the home front. His most pressing focus was trying to make ends meet. With time Coldomat was gaining some grounds, albeit slightly, and although income was still sporadic they were able to hire two technicians to work at the shop. They repaired refrigerators that could not be repaired on site, and converted old ice boxes into electric refrigerators by fitting them with a compressor and a freezer box instead of the old ice block holder.

Sam broke the Yiddish idiom "אלע שוסטער גיין באַרוועס"—"all shoemakers walk barefoot," meaning they themselves have no shoes, and on their anniversary surprised Leah with one of those converted ice boxes. Was she ever thrilled to not have to go downstairs every day and wait for the donkey-drawn ice wagon, and then carry this heavy half block of dripping ice up four flights of stairs to the apartment!

All in all, except for the more frequent curfews enforced by the British, on the surface life was improving. Bella was starting grammar school in a four floor walkup apartment building in the back street, now serving as a school. And Ofer was in kindergarten in a ground floor apartment with a tiny yard, in the building next door, so educationally the kids were in good hands.

Socially they were doing well as well. Because of the proximity to the school the neighborhood had many kids their age and they were free to come and go as they pleased. Safety was not an issue, and the door was never locked. And since none of the kids had store-purchased toys, the kids built their own, and let both their imagination and ingenuity run wild.

Leah and Sam had made a few friends in the neighborhood, and although Sam was still on the road a few days of the week and came back mostly late, it was important for Leah to have a circle of friends she could go to the market and share other experiences with.

To top it off, with the end of the war Sam pulled off another fast trade: he sold the BMW for a very good price—with the defeat of the Germans there were spare parts galore for it now—and in its place Sam bought a car, a small 1940 Opel that needed some attention but nothing Sam's shop could not provide. Now Sam drove in more comfort to his clients, carried more tools and supplies, and did not have to come back to the shop for replenishment in between service calls. He also was less concerned things could be stolen from the sidecar as they were now less visible, locked in the trunk of the car. And finally, now he could pack the family into the car, and go for a short trip during the Sabbath.

Like so many other members of the Jewish population in Palestine, Sam, Philip, and Misha, made every effort to find any news about the fate of members of their families that were caught in the grip of the Nazis. Information was scarce, communication was sporadic at best, and for the longest time any effort by these three to locate any member of the extended family, and through them maybe get some knowledge about the others, were futile and did not yield anything.

Sam's activities in the underground changed as well. He was no longer transporting weapons to remote sites as he had done during the 1930s and early 1940s. Instead, his squadron was called on to execute night missions, sometimes armed but frequently not. Those missions were more dangerous than before: They were mostly resistance actions against the British, and this time, shots were being fired by British soldiers, veterans of a war, a well-armed and well-trained force, rather than some garrison, or poorly trained and undisciplined gang of Arabs as before.

In Europe, hundreds of thousands of refugees emerged from the Holocaust starving, without clothes, sick and dying, and with nowhere to go. The Allied forces, primarily the British and Americans, knew they could not leave them in the former German concentration camps, so they established another type of camp called Displaced Persons Camps and moved the refugees there. Albeit, the conditions in those camps were not to be compared to the horrendous conditions of Hitler's extermination camps—food and medical treatment were available, housing and clothing were provided—but to the refugees it still was a camp, with a fence and a gate and guards with guns keeping them from leaving. And except for the Soviets who demanded the return of their former citizens, either resettlement or repatriation was not forthcoming for the rest of the survivors.

Only Brazil offered to resettle these refugees in the Amazon jungle. No other country volunteered to open its borders to them. Those who could return to their former countries, now under Soviet rule reluctantly did so, to be under the totalitarian regime of Stalin—Romania, Yugoslavia, Czechoslovakia, Poland, Russia, and Ukraine among others, but anti-Semitism had not been wiped out in those places by any stretch of the imagination, not to mention that life under Communism was now different than what they were accustomed to before the war, and many of the returnees found themselves in the gulags, or worse were executed by Stalin.

Not even that shining star of democracy, the United States, was willing to open its gates to these poor down-trodden people. During the war President Roosevelt proved to be no friend of the suffering Jews in Europe, unwilling to divert even a single bomber to fly over Auschwitz and destroy the crematoria. Bombers were targeting less strategic installations only sixty miles away but he would not allow them to take a swipe at the death factory spewing the smoke of incinerated human beings day and night, and there is no denying that he and his administration knew what was going on in that camp. He even had refused entry to the 900 Jewish refugees on board of the St. Louis arriving in Miami back in 1939, and shamefully sent them back to be slaughtered by the Nazis.

And his successor, President Truman, was equally unfriendly in his policies, allowing only a select few remaining scientists to be admitted to the U.S., ironically together with the Nazi scientists the U.S. whisked out of Germany before they fell into Soviet hands. There may have been a practical reason for the U.S. actions, but no morality in them.

By and large these Holocaust survivors were held, for years, sub-stantially against their will, in refugee camps supported by the United Nations Relief and Rehabilitation Administration, under lock and key and armed troops of the Allied command.

The Haganah had dispatched emissaries to provide a framework and order for these displaced people, with the goal of getting as many of those poor souls as possible to the relative safety in the Land of Israel, a place where they would no longer be persecuted for simply being Jewish. They provided structure, schooling for the children, Hebrew lessons for the adults, and other social services not otherwise provided by the camp administrations.

But most of all they wanted to bring these refugees to Palestine. Immigration ships were heading toward the shores of Palestine, but under heavy pressure from the Arab leadership, the British did not let them come ashore. Ships would evade the British, and try and bring their human cargo to the beaches of Eretz Israel, and the Brit-ish would try and intercept those ships, either on the high seas or on the beaches. And since the war had ended the British had many more resources at their disposal to deal with the "Jewish Issue" in their own way.

In a cat and mouse chase, the Haganah would start some diver-sion operation to keep the British from rounding up those who came ashore and sending them back to wherever they came from, or to other camps where they could be held indefinitely. And although it was not illegal for the British to turn these people away from the shores of Palestine—as part of their mandate over the area their rule was absolute—holding these people in detention *was* illegal, but since no one opened their gates to them where else could they go?

Sam and his squadron mostly knew when a ship was due to ar-rive. They were told to meet at some specific point in the evening and draft a plan of action to block and delay the British forces from arriving at the seashore. In the interim another group waded into the water where a ship had run aground, and helped unload the passen-gers and quickly disperse them among the population, making it very difficult for the British to round them up and deport them.

Before dawn, on the incoming tide the ships that made it ashore would try and escape into international waters where the British could not arrest the crew and confiscate the ship.

Whenever Sam left in the evening Leah's heart would sink. She did not know what his mission was, each time at a different place, but after the fact she knew what he had been doing those nights—she heard about another ship that had either made it through or was captured by the British and turned back.

He used to kiss her and the children good-bye and leave, and that was her sign that something was about to happen. She would take the children' mattresses off their beds, lay them out on the floor and make sure Bella and Ofer were on their mattresses, away from the windows. She would then sit on the floor next to them until Sam returned in the morning. Sometimes she could hear the gunshots of the British Sten guns, or even heavier machine guns mounted on top of the armored personnel carriers, and her heart would beat hard in her chest. On one occasion one of those bullets actually came flying through the bedroom window and sprinkled shards of glass on Bella's now-empty bed; other times she heard the bullets hit the building on a lower floor, making a thudding noise when connecting with the concrete. And while the children slept through it all, Leah was awake watching over her young all night so no harm would come to them.

Thank God she had the wisdom to put them on the floor, in a safer place.

Tel Aviv had turned into a war zone.

Inevitably the next morning the British would declare a curfew, and the orders were "shoot on sight." Anything that moved was fair game for the "Red Berets"—the British paratroopers who watched the streets. Somehow Sam could still sneak through back alleys and secret passages and come home tired, disheveled, but uninjured.

To be fair, not all the British hated the Jewish population, definitely not rank and file. Some were even sympathetic, but orders were orders. One such Red Beret, a tall handsome lad, was frequently stationed at the door of the pharmacy across the street from Leah's and Sam's apartment. He seemed nice enough and definitely helpful to her, but despite her curiosity Leah never had an opportunity to speak to him or really get to know him—he was there only during curfew when she could not be on the street.

On a number of occasions Leah needed to buy something at the grocery store in the building next door during curfew. She would poke her head out through the side entrance of the building to peek outside. When he noticed her, he would scan right and left to make sure no one else could see her, and then he would move his head sideways to signal her "all clear" for her to dart from the side of the building through the hole in the fence to the side of the next building, and enter the store through its back door that was always open. Returning with the goods was a similar process, and with his acquiescence and help Leah could dart back into her apartment building with mission accomplished.

But beyond the curfews and the shootings at night, the children went to school, people went to work, and life continued as well as could be expected under the circumstances.

❖　❖　❖

Philip arrived one day, with Misha in tow with some news from Riga. They had a grave look about them.

"We received a letter from my sister Laura in Riga," Misha said. "As you know she was in Moscow when the Nazis entered Riga, and only now was permitted to go back there."

"And?" Sam anxiously asked, "What did she find in Riga? How is the family?"

"Terrible news," Misha said. "First, she found out our poor mother Esther was deported to a concentration camp, and has not returned. Witnesses who did come back said she was murdered by the Nazis. No doubt about that."

"I am so sorry for your mother, Misha. It is a great loss to the family." Having lost his own mother years earlier Sam was truly sad and empathized with Misha. He also liked his half-sister Esther very much.

"Thank you, I sort of expected it. When I did not hear that she had succeeded escaping when the Germans entered Riga I did not think she will survive," Misha replied, "so I had time to get accustomed to the idea that my mother is gone."

"But it still is painful."

"True, but there is finality to it."

"How about Isaac?" Sam asked.

"She did not mention him in her letter," Philip said, shaking his head from side to side.

"How about the rest of the family? We had 128 cousins in Riga before the war."

"She says two succeeded in escaping before the war and are in the United States, one she thinks is in Canada, and the other two were already here in Palestine that we know of, including Tzipora."

"Only three escaped?" Sam was horrified. "So from 128 only five remained alive after Hitler?"

"That's what she wrote in her letter," Misha said. "Here, read for yourself."

The letter from Misha's sister did not mention Isaac. Had she found out what had happened to him, she surely would have written about it. Nor did she mention anyone of the family by name. They were all gone, she wrote, no one left to tell her anything.

"We had to share this with you," Philip said. "At least Laura is alive and presumably well."

"Ask her if she can find out about Isaac," Sam asked Misha.

"I will write her tonight, but it will take at least a month to get a reply. The mail is still very slow."

Not a week had passed, when they were back, excited and breathless, having run up the four flights of stairs like the devil was chasing them.

They banged on the door, and when Leah opened it they ran past her all the way down the long corridor screaming "Isaac is alive, Isaac is alive!"

Sam jumped off the couch where he was taking a short nap before going back to work.

"How do you know?" he screamed.

Philip was waving a letter in his hand. "Here, read for yourself."

The letter was postmarked two weeks earlier in Italy addressed to Philip's home. Sam quickly pulled the single sheet of paper out of the enveloped.

Torn from a notebook, it captured a scribble in almost indecipherable handwriting. Was it Yiddish in Latin script? For a moment Sam was confused. He finally realized it was Latvian.

"*Philip,*" it said, "*I am in a D.P. camp near Rome. Gita and Marc are dead. I have no money. Please send some money. Isaac.*"

It was like reading a telegram, so brief and concise, it sounded harsh and brutal. But at least he was alive!

"Thank God Isaac is alive. How is father?" Sam asked Philip.

"Incredible. He is relieved I am sure, but it will take some time for him to comprehend. All along he was sure Isaac was dead, so he said."

"That is interesting. Leah and I had wanted to name our son Yitzhak, in honor of her stepfather Yitzhak Ostrovsky who died in 1941, but Yitzhak is the Hebrew version of Isaac and we were concerned father would think we knew for sure that Isaac was dead, and were naming the boy after our brother, his son."

He glanced at the note again. "Isaac says Gita and Marc are dead, so sad. He must be devastated."

"Without a doubt," Philip replied. "Can you imagine losing a child? God help us, that is the worst fate, and he was so much in love with Gita, it must be horrible. I wonder how they died, but I am not going to ask him."

They had a cup of coffee in the kitchen and discussed how to proceed, and how to get the money to Isaac, and how much they could afford to send him. They agreed that British pounds would be the best currency. Before too long it was Sam's time to go back to the shop, so they all left, thrilled to know that their eldest brother Isaac was alive.

Over the next few days they collected the money and sent it to the address on the envelope, the address of the Displaced Persons camp near Rome.

From that point on, every few weeks they received a short note from Isaac, each a bit more descriptive about his life at the camp, and invariably asking for money, more money. They could not understand why he needed so much money when most of his needs were being taken care of at the camp, including food, shelter, medical services, and clothing. Nevertheless, they scraped together whatever they could of their meager resources and sent it to him as he requested.

He never wrote about what happened to Gita and Marc or how he survived the Nazi occupation. The only mention of that period was to tell them that Baruch, one of the 128 cousins of theirs, died in his presence, but he did not elaborate on when or how. He was living in the present, and seemed to blot the past out of his memory. Philip, Sam, and Misha decided not to pressure him for any details, figuring the memories must be painful, and he was not ready yet to relive those times.

❖   ❖   ❖

In the middle of January 1948 Sam's father Haim came down with a seemingly innocuous intestinal infection. For a few days Manya and Philip thought he must have eaten something that did not quite agree with him. They were baffled because they all, their sons included, had eaten the same food and none of them was sick.

Maybe it was his age, they speculated. Otherwise strong as a bull, at age 89 the stomach may be more sensitive to food that was not the freshest. It was possible that he suffered from food poisoning, they speculated. He was not complaining much, and was not running a fever, so they figured he would overcome it on his own.

Over the weekend Leah, Sam, and their children came to visit, and Haim was strong enough to get out of bed and reach for the box of candy he had above the tall bookcase, offering the children one piece each. Outwardly he did not seem terribly sick, but the pains and discomfort persisted.

"I think he has a bacterial infection in the intestines," The trusted Dr. Cohen pronounced his diagnosis on his second house call.

"Is there anything we can do for it?" Manya asked.

"Keep his food simple, nothing too oily or fat, and let's see if it goes away by itself."

Manya tried to sooth his inflamed intestines by giving him lean food, some toast or crackers, some tea, and that miracle Jewish medication—chicken soup. Even that did not help.

When Haim's conditions did not improve Dr. Cohen became concerned.

"What we need is some penicillin. It is a new class of drugs that kills bacteria. By the articles I read about it I am sure Haim's condition will go away with it, and he will be fine once again. His constitution is strong for his age, but this thing is eating him from the inside," was Dr. Cohen's conclusion.

"Where can we get some?" Philip asked.

"I don't know," was Dr. Cohen's answer. "I don't know who has any in Palestine. It is being mass produced already in the United States, and the price has been coming down there. But the British are not bringing it in for some reason."

"Is it available in the United States?"

"Yes. I don't know how easy it is to get there, but in the article they said it is available for one dollar a dose."

"I'll send a telegram to Tanya tomorrow morning," said Philip. "My sister Tanya is a doctor in the United States, so she should be able to send us some. How many doses do we need?"

"I don't know precisely, but I would think ten doses will be enough. Better ask for fifteen or twenty. If she can get that many, that will be good, and whatever we don't use we can always give to Hadassah Hospital."

"I will do that," Philip promised. And he did.

The next morning he sent a telegram to Tanya.

Two days later he received a response back from her. It read:

"20 DOSES PENICILLIN EN ROUTE STOP EXPEDITED POST STOP TANYA"

Haim's condition continued to deteriorate. By the end of that week Dr. Cohen arranged to have him moved by ambulance to Hadassah hospital in Tel Aviv.

He died on the last Saturday in February with two of his three sons by his side.

The penicillin arrived three days too late.

The funeral, held on Sunday, was not large: Philip and Sam and their wives, Misha and Rachel came from Binyamina, some of Philip's coworkers as well as Sam's partners, a few other relatives and friends, and some men from the synagogue came to pay their last respects to Haim, the last patriarch of his generation in the family.

Haim had asked to be buried in the Jewish Cemetery on Mount Olives in Jerusalem. According to tradition, that is where the resurrection will begin when the Messiah comes, so that is where Haim had purchased a burial plot. But when the time came, they could not inter him there: Since the outbreak of hostilities by the Arabs, which were kindled by the 1947 Partition Resolution of Palestine by the United Nations, the road to Jerusalem was impassable except by armored convoys, and even those were not always safe. So the family hurriedly arranged for him to be buried in a temporary grave in another cemetery in Holon instead.

They sat shiva, the customary seven-day mourning period, in Philip's house.

Nineteen years later, after Israel reclaimed Mount Olives from Jordan during the Six Day war, his remains were transferred to his final resting place.

Part IV

OTHERS CAME

Chapter 23

April in New York City is special, and although you can probably say that about each and every month in this phenomenal city, including September when it is hot and muggy and quite possibly unpleasant, this second Sunday in April of 1948 was a very pleasant day for Maurice. He had just enjoyed a wonderful lunch with his mother at a restaurant near her home on Madison Avenue, and now he was strolling down the avenue, breathing the clear air and enjoying every minute of it.

He was very close to his mother, an easy-going young-looking woman in her mid-50s, a socially active woman, intellectual, bright and friendly, always involved in some charity or another. She was not rich but comfortable, living off the estate her late husband left when he died prematurely at a relatively young age.

Like any mother she was concerned about her son, but unlike other Jewish mothers she never pestered him, gave him grief or sent him on a guilt trip. After all, he was 30 years old, handsome, bright, educated and well-spoken with a terrific sense of humor, and how come he had not been snatched already by some nice Jewish girl? The truth was he simply enjoyed his life as a bachelor living in New York City, with a well-paying job and not many worries in the world. "Why would I shackle myself?" he would tell his friends. "Why settle for one dish when there is a smorgasbord around?"

Maurice was an adventurer, always open to new and exciting things to explore, and not ready for the mundane nature of married life with children, and a dog, and a mortgage, and a mediocre suburban existence. He had a circle of friends who appreciated him as he was, and they enjoyed his company, whenever he could free himself from yet another pretty face hanging onto his arm.

As he did most Sundays, this afternoon he was going to meet a friend for a drink down at their normal hangout on 42nd Street by

Lexington Avenue. The air was crisp, but it was not cold by any means, and the short walk was rejuvenating.

He turned the corner from Madison Avenue onto 42nd street heading toward Grand Central Station.

There was someone walking behind him. Maurice suddenly had that strange sensation of his hair rising on the back of his neck. The person was too close for comfort. He started turning around to see who it was behind him when he felt a hand on his left shoulder.

"Keep looking ahead," a man's commanding voice said behind him. The man was a bit taller than Maurice's own 5'9" frame.

"Get into the car," the voice said. At the curb was a black Pack-ard limousine. A man was standing by the rear door with his back to Maurice, and as Maurice approached he opened the door and gently pushed him in. Maurice could not see his face; the man made sure that his back was turned to him at all times.

Maurice was not about to resist. He had seen this scenario many times before, had abducted a few people in his time himself, and knew these were professionals. He had not the slightest chance of making a run for it; the best course of action was to go along with it, in the off-chance they would make a mistake and he could escape. In the meantime, compliance and acquiescence were the orders of the day.

Anyway, it was an adventure. Getting snatched in the middle of New York City in broad daylight was not a common occurrence. If you said East Berlin, or even West Berlin, that would be something else, it happened there often by American, British, or Soviet spies. But in New York? His curiosity got the better of him. What did these men want with him? What did he have to offer?

As soon as he got in, or better still nudged into the back seat of the car, the door closed, and the car moved into traffic. The window between him and the chauffer was darkly tinted, and he could not make out even the most basic features of the man behind the wheel.

They crossed the bridge heading for Brooklyn. On the other side of the bridge the driver made a few turns, and they were in an indus-trial area not too far from the river. Maurice did not know this area, and would probably find it hard to retrace the steps to this place, but by the smells he could tell they were not too far from the ocean.

The car stopped in front of an industrial warehouse, and the car door opened. He stepped out onto the sidewalk, and the man who opened the door grabbed his arm and led him through the door in the building and into a dark hallway. The man had a gray overcoat with the collar turned up under his fedora hat, and very little of his face was showing. There was no way Maurice could identify him in a lineup or otherwise.

He was led through a door and into a room. There was a table in the middle of the room, facing a mirror. A one-way mirror Maurice presumed.

"Please sit down." A voice with a distinct British accent boomed through a loudspeaker.

"Thank you," Maurice said. He understood what was coming. He would now be interrogated, and possibly tortured, but for what he had no idea.

Toward the end of WWII as a major in the U.S. Army Air Corps he had been assigned to the Office of Strategic Services, the famous OSS, and was operating with his men behind German lines in an attempt to capture German scientists along with their technologies. The United States was anticipating a potential adversarial relationship with the Soviet Union and was seeking to advance their scientific and military posture by leveraging Nazi research. Should the OSS locate any solid scientists the likes of the rocket scientist Wernher Von Braun they were to kidnap and interrogate them for as much information as they could, or even abduct them and bring them back with them to American lines. So Maurice and his OSS unit were taught the tricks of interrogation, and, since they were operating behind enemy lines it was possible they themselves could be captured, and so they were trained in the art of being interrogated as well, torture notwithstanding.

Now Maurice knew he may need to apply the principles taught to him regarding being a captive: Cooperate with your captors, do not antagonize them unnecessarily, be alert for an opportunity to escape, be smart at what you say or do, and above all stay tight-lipped. Stay focused, answer the questions in the narrowest possible way, and no more; don't volunteer any information you were not asked, but try and find out what they are really after.

The initial questions were straightforward. The booming voice asked for his name, his occupation, and his address and he replied truthfully. He had nothing to hide, and he suspected they knew all those answers already anyway—they did not grab some stranger off the streets of New York in broad daylight just "for kicks;" they had a goal in mind, and kidnapped him, Maurice, for a reason. One thing he was sure of: These were no amateurs, they were professionals.

And as if to prove him right, the voice asked: "How is your mother?"

"My mother?" Maurice was surprised. He stalled for time to assess the situation further.

"Yes, your mother, Elizabeth. How was lunch?"

They knew. They knew a bit more about him than he had expected.

"She is fine," he answered.

"How is your father doing these days?"

Trick question. They must know his father had passed away some time ago.

"He passed away."

"Do you have a university degree?"

"Yes, I do."

"What was your major in school?"

"Aeronautical engineering."

"Which school?"

"NYU."

They wanted him to know they knew quite a bit about his life. But why?

The voice had an accent, probably British with a minor twinge of something else. He was definitely not American born, but it was not a Russian accent, nor one from the Slavic countries, nor Germany. Middle Eastern, perhaps? Being interrogated by a Russian would make sense—the Soviets were actively spying in New York, and they could be interested in something he had uncovered while at the OSS.

"Now tell me about your military service during the war."

"I was in Army Air Corps."

"Yes, major. We know. Tell me about the OSS."

"Son of a bitch," Maurice thought. They knew that all along, and were just testing him to see if he would tell them the truth.

"OSS?" He played dumb anyway.

"I ask the questions here, you give me the answers, not the other way around. And don't be a 'smart Aleck' with me. What was your role in the Office of Strategic Services?" the voice asked.

"I can't discuss it," he tried. Let's see if that is the core of the interrogation. If it is, then they will insist.

"Do not play games with me, and answer the questions. I am sure as a professional you know we have means of extracting whatever information we want out of you, and we won't hesitate to use them."

"Fair enough." Maurice was convinced they had the means. They were no hoodlums holding him for ransom. These were guys who knew the tricks, and probably had the tools too. But they did not seem inclined to use them or go rough on him, at least not yet. He wondered why.

"What was your role in the OSS?"

"I told you I am not able to discuss it." He was taking a calculated risk. Now either they would burst in and harm him, or accept his refusal and approach it differently. If the reason they kidnapped him was because they were after some information concerning the OSS, then they would come down hard on him. He did not cherish being beaten or tortured, but he had been sworn to secrecy, and only the President of the United States or the Secretary of War could release him from that oath by declassifying the information.

"All I want to know is if your missions for the OSS were due to your aeronautical engineering expertise. I am sure you can answer that without violating the secrecy of the missions."

Maurice sat there for a brief moment digesting what the man was asking. He tried to think if answering the question would put him in jeopardy as a spy, giving secrets to a possible enemy, but he could not see any harm in answering that particular question. If however they persisted with more questions, he would still be able to stop giving information.

"Yes."

The loudspeaker remained silent for the longest time, and he stayed in his chair waiting.

"Okay. Thank you. I am now going to give you some instructions, and you will follow them to the letter, major. Please pay attention; I will say them only once." His tone was somewhat less harsh, but still authoritative and pointed.

"You will be driven back to where we picked you up. You will go directly to your apartment and speak to no one. You will pack the duffel bag that is in your front closet. You will take only those things you would take if you were going on a long term OSS assignment. Bring your binoculars and your .45, you may need them, and the ammunition you have in your night table. Do not load the weapon; keep the ammo in your bag.

"Write your mother a note saying you are going to Europe for the Army Air Corps assignment, and you will contact her when you return. Do not date it, and do not seal the envelope.

"You will be picked up at 19:00 hours sharp at your apartment. Do not be late, and do not try to escape, we will be watching you. Do not talk to anyone. I repeat anyone. And have your passport with you. You may need it. Also, have dinner before pick up time."

There was silence for a moment.

"You got all that?"

"Yes, sir. But what is this all about?"

"I told you I ask the questions here. Do as you are told and everything will be all right. All you need to know is it is nothing against the United States or its interests, and this will not jeopardize your standing as a U.S. citizen.

"One more thing," the voice said. "Do not concern yourself with your job, your boss will not be expecting you at work tomorrow, and while you are gone your rent and bills will be taken care of. Also, your friend is no longer waiting for you for a drink. Good-bye."

Son of a bitch, they knew everything!

The door behind Maurice opened, and he walked outside. It was dark already. The car door opened, and he stepped in.

Now that he was no longer in the eye of the hurricane he could calmly analyze the unexpected events of the last hour, and his curiosity and sense of adventure got the better of him. He was not too concerned about the clandestine nature of the events. He understood by now his services were needed for some special operation, doing something he was probably best suited for by his training and experiences, and they had assured him it was nothing against the United States interests and wouldn't jeopardize his standing as a citizen—for all he knew maybe it is even a mission for the U.S. intelligence service overseas. Why else would they want him to pack his gun, his binoculars, and his passport?

Whatever it was, he would go along with them, probably on a mission not too dissimilar to those missions during WWII behind German lines. Maybe Berlin? Maybe a mission for the newly established Central Intelligence Agency founded only a few months earlier?

And they said not to worry about his job, and his mother, and even his drinking friend, so if it will be a couple of weeks before he returns, no harm in it, and he will have another exciting experience under his belt. Little did he know that it would be much longer than a couple of weeks.

So at 19:00 hours sharp Maurice stepped out of his apartment building, duffel bag slung over his shoulder, ready for a strange and mysterious adventure.

A car came to a stop at the curb. A man approached on foot. He reached for the duffel bag, opened the trunk, and dropped the bag in it.

"The note to your mother, please," he had his hand extended.

Maurice handed him the note, and the man put it in his pocket.

"Now your keys"

Maurice handed him the keys. The man did not ask him for his .45, and Maurice found that strange. They must trust him that the gun was not loaded, as they had instructed.

The man opened the car door, motioned to Maurice to step into the back seat, shut the door from the outside and walked away.

There was another man sitting in the back seat. In the dark Maurice could not see his face, but the man was tall he could tell.

"Hello Maurice," the man said without extending his hand for a handshake, "I am Al Schwimmer. We are going out on a mission."

"What kind of mission?" Maurice asked.

"To help create a homeland," was the answer.

❖   ❖   ❖

The car headed into the Holland Tunnel in downtown New York City and exited on the New Jersey side. The driver then headed south on Route 1, and they drove in silence for over two hours. Al had fallen asleep at the tunnel and did not wake up until they arrived at their destination of Millville Airfield in southern New Jersey. Maurice suspected the poor guy must not have slept for ages for him to sleep through the ride.

The driver entered the field, made a couple of turns and stopped the car at the entrance to a large hangar. Al woke up immediately when the car stopped. He opened the car door on his side and stepped out into the night. Maurice did the same, emerging through the other door. He reached for the trunk lid, and retrieved his duffel bag.

There were about a half dozen other men, all in their mid to late twenties and early thirties, milling about and waiting for them on the tarmac. Maurice looked around trying to find a familiar face, but it was dark and he did not recognize anyone.

The hangar was large and dimly lit. In its center stood a massive plane, and by the moonlight coming through the open doors Maurice had no difficulty recognizing it as a Curtiss Wright C-46 cargo plane. "Curtiss Commando" being its official name, it had a number of nicknames in the service, mostly derogatory like "Flying Coffin," or "Curtiss Calamity." It was the largest and heaviest twin-engine cargo plane in WWII able to carry large loads of troops and equipment. But it had an abysmal maintenance record with hundreds of design changes, so much so ground crews nicknamed it "Plumbers' Nightmare"—hydraulic and fuel systems consistently failed. It also had a questionable flying record, with quite a few of these planes inexplicably crashing or worse, exploding in midair.

And now they were being led to this C-46 cargo plane. Maurice could not see the markings on the plane, and it seemed somewhat different from the C-46 planes he was accustomed to in the Army Air Corps, but in the haste of boarding the plane in the darkness he hardly had the opportunity to inspect it more carefully.

Al Schwimmer disappeared into the cockpit, and Maurice remained in the cargo area with the other men. No one spoke or introduced himself, at least not during the initial phases of the flight; they scattered along the jump seats on both sides of the plane and strapped themselves in.

Maurice had no idea where they were heading. Cargo planes do not normally have porthole windows, so he was not able to see in which direction they were taxiing. He was familiar with this Millville Airfield, having spent several weeks here before shipping overseas during the war, and by the motion of the taxiing he knew they would probably be taking off on runway 10, heading almost due east. Beyond that, it was anyone's guess.

The cargo area was mostly empty, except for a couple of large crates secured well in the front. There were some cots strung overhead, and the entire cabin was only dimly lit. Maurice was bored, so he pulled out his pipe and sucked on it, without lighting it up—he knew better than to light a fire in the fuselage of a military plane, especially one having a reputation of leaking flammable liquids galore.

They rode in silence, and only the droning noise of the engines was permeating the poorly insulated cabin. Maurice was listening to them and concluded they were extremely well tuned. He could tell because having been a technical officer with the Army Air Corps, he had to deal with the C-46 on a regular basis, and only his best maintenance crews could reach this level of competency with these engines.

An hour passed and they stopped climbing. They had reached cruising altitude and leveled off, and Maurice was expecting the engines to be throttled back, but the change was only slight. By the sound of the engines it seemed the pilot was keeping the plane going at higher rate of speed than normal. What was his hurry? Maurice was curious.

A few minutes later Al walked out from the cockpit. He beckoned the men seated spread throughout the plane to come and join him in the middle of the fuselage. They stood in a semicircle around him, and over the noise of the engines he finally explained to them what the mission was.

"We are heading to Žatec Airfield in Czechoslovakia," he said, "where we will be disassembling Avia S-199 fighter planes the Haganah Jewish underground in Palestine had purchased from the Czechs. The Avia is the Czech version of the Messerschmitt ME-109 German fighter plane you may be familiar with. It is being produced by the Skoda factory for the Czech Air Force. They are somewhat inferior to the ME-109, but that is what the Haganah could buy, and that is what we are going to transport to Palestine."

"We are headed to Czechoslovakia with this thing?" one of the men asked. "It doesn't have the range to get there from here."

"Right, but for other reasons also, we are not going there directly," Al answered. "We are going in an indirect route."

"What do you mean?" another man asked.

"We have to get this aircraft and several others out of the United States air space before April 15, that's four days from now," Al said. "The U.S. Government banned any shipment of any military grade materiel, including this type aircraft, to Palestine. Any weapons or military supplies must be cleared by the State Department, the same State Department that had been hostile to Jews living in Palestine and elsewhere for years. Anyone shipping this stuff without permission goes to jail.

"We are supposedly a civilian air cargo company, LAPSA, headquartered in Panama. We are heading to Tocumen Airport in Panama, and from there we will be traveling to Czechoslovakia.

"We believe the State Department and the FBI are suspicious of us, and we may have to alter plans on the spur of the moment. Before we land you will receive instructions about contacts in Panama, should we have to split as a group."

Now Maurice understood why they were in such a rush, flying at top speed.

"Any questions?" Al asked.

There was one raised hand. "How long before we return stateside?"

Al Schwimmer paused for a moment before answering. He raised his right hand up above his head with his index finger pointed upward, looked up and said without fanfare: "Only He knows for sure. All I can tell you is that it will be in a long, long, time from now."

Then he turned around and walked back into the cockpit.

Chapter 24

As she did every morning for the past two years or so, Ruth made her way to her job at the hospital in Brooklyn. This was a typical April day in New York City, a sunny day, the air crisp, and the temperature hovering around forty degrees. With the slight breeze blowing gently from the river it felt a bit colder, but Ruth was dressed in a warm coat over her nurse's uniform and she was quite comfortable.

She reached her destination a few minutes early, and went upstairs to the Intensive Care Unit, checked in with the nurse manning the desk, and checked her schedule for today.

The calendar for Tuesday April 13, 1948 showed her attending to Jacob Goldfarb in room 716, and after depositing her coat and purse in her locker she headed to start her work day.

Mr. Goldfarb was recovering from a moderate heart attack he had suffered a few days earlier, and he was being kept in the Intensive Care Unit under observation for a few more days, just as a precaution. Barring any unforeseen circumstances, he would probably be discharged by this weekend or, worse come to worst, sometimes next week.

Mr. Goldfarb greeted her in his usual jovial mood with a smile.

"Good morning, Nurse Ruth. How are you today?"

"Good morning Mr. Goldfarb. I am fine, thank you. Now let's see how *you* are," she said.

"I am fine, getting better every day, thanks to the excellent care I am getting here."

"Are you trying to bribe me with your platitudes again?" she joked with him.

"Not at all. I love all the attention I am getting here, resting without a worry in the world, happy as a clam. So long as I am home for Passover next weekend I will be fine."

"Why? Don't you want to sample the fine Passover Kosher cuisine in this delightful place?"

He laughed. That would be the day when they serve good-tasting Passover Kosher food in an institution.

"I would rather have a Seder with my wife and the family. There will probably be thirty people for the Seder, and I am the Patriarch, so I must lead the services."

"Good for you. Knowing this hospital, I will probably be on duty that evening."

"That's not nice, they should let the Jewish staff off for the holiday, and let you compensate during Christmas."

"True, but it is too complicated to schedule it that way."

During this entire discussion she was leafing through his medical chart, noticing the regimen prescribed by the attending physician.

All looked clear, Mr. Goldfarb was recovering nicely, as nicely as can be expected after a serious heart attack. She proceeded to take his blood pressure, temperature, and pulse. Then she waved to him and went to see her other patients in the ward.

When she came back a couple of hours later, his wife was sitting by his bed, her face ashen. She had been spending most of her days keeping her husband company by his bedside. They seemed to have a solid marriage, and liked each other's company.

"He works so hard," she had told Ruth on one of her visits, "we do not have enough time together during the week. He leaves pretty early and returns very late, and I miss him. Sad circumstances with this heart attack, but this is the opportunity for me to be with him and catch up on all that is happening in the world, and even have a laugh or two."

Today though, they both were very quiet when Ruth entered the room, both distraught about something.

"Is everything all right?" Ruth was worried.

"With Jacob? He is fine, but did you hear what happened in Jerusalem?"

"No, what happened?"

"Oh, it is horrible." she started saying when the door opened and Doctor Edelstein walked in.

"What is horrible?" he had overheard.

"What happened in Jerusalem."

"What happened in Jerusalem?" he asked.

"There was a massacre there. A convoy of Jewish doctors and nurses were ambushed on the way to the Hadassah Hospital on Mount Scopus, and there are many, many casualties."

"Many casualties?" Ruth asked.

"I heard it on the radio, they still don't know how many casualties, but the convoy had around 100 people in it. They think most are dead, burnt to death in the vehicles or shot by the Arabs."

"Oh my God," Ruth exclaimed. "Tell me again, what did you hear on the radio?"

"The information was still sketchy, not detailed, but what they were saying was a convoy of doctors and nurses and a small security detail was traveling to the hospital on Mount Scopus and they were ambushed by hundreds of Arabs. There was a battle and the Arabs burnt the buses and most of the people in them died. There were about 100 people in the convoy, and the British came and didn't do anything to stop the carnage."

They all fell silent for a moment absorbing the terrible news. Why would anyone attack a convoy of doctors and nurses going to the hospital? And why would the British not stop it?

It took a while for Ruth to get over her shock. "This is horrible. Can you imagine being burnt to death, knowing you will die?"

"What is going on there is so sad," Dr. Edelstein said. "Jews are being attacked almost every day, mostly civilians."

"So sad, I wish I could help," Ruth said.

The doctor looked at her for a moment, then he reached for the chart and they all returned to the present, attending to Mr. Goldfarb in the hospital room in Brooklyn.

❖ ❖ ❖

Two days later on Thursday Ruth bumped into Dr. Edelstein in the staff lounge. He was sitting in the corner, sipping a cup of coffee from the "always warm" coffee urn. When he saw her he motioned to her to come and join him.

When she sat down he looked around to make sure they were out of earshot of others in the room. He leaned forward toward her and spoke in almost a whisper.

"Were you serious the other day?" he asked.

"About what?"

"About helping." Direct, no hemming or hawing.

Ruth was taken by surprise, and was slow to react. She was trying to recall the context of the conversation, and it took a second or two.

"Yes," she said quietly, "I was serious."

"Then after work go to the Bristol Hotel in Manhattan and ask the desk clerk for Zvi."

That was it, he did not elaborate. Ruth was about to ask him some questions, but he rose to his feet and without uttering another word made a hasty exit out of the lounge. She stayed seated for a moment longer, absorbing what had just transpired, then headed back to her station.

What did he mean? What kind of help? Doing what, and where?

She had no idea, but was definitely going to find out. When her shift ended she headed home, and was delighted to see that Maggie, her best friend and roommate was already there.

She told Maggie about the entire incident, from her utterance in Mr. Goldfarb's room to her extra short conversation with Dr. Edelstein.

"What are you going to do about it?" Maggie asked.

"I'm going to find out what it is all about. First I have to go to Manhattan and look up that Zvi character at the Bristol Hotel."

"Wait, I'll go with you."

They rode the subway to Manhattan without exchanging more than a few words. The car was noisy, as New York subway trains always are, and they preferred to be quiet.

The concierge at the front desk of the Bristol was a small man with a thin moustache. He was occupied with some paperwork and did not pay attention to the two young women approaching.

"We are looking for Zvi," Ruth said when he finally looked up.

He gave them a curious look, trying to size them up. He hesitated a moment before uttering "Suite 822," and then went back to his papers on the counter. As soon as they were out of sight he reached for the phone, dialed a number, and spoke with the party on the other end in Hebrew.

"Two women, late twenties on their way up."

Almost immediately when Ruth and Maggie knocked on the door of room 822 a tall tanned young man opened the door, and without a word motioned for them to come in.

Zvi, if that were his real name, watched the two young ladies as they entered a typical living room of a moderately upscale hotel suite, and motioned for them to sit down on the couch. He then closed the door and proceeded to take the armchair across from them. He did not offer them something to drink, but went directly to the purpose of their visit.

"What can I do for you?" he asked in perfect English with a New York accent.

Ruth and Maggie exchanged glances. "We don't exactly know," Ruth finally replied. "Dr. Edelstein told us to come to the hotel and ask for you."

"I wonder why he would do that. How do you know him, and why would he send you here?" It was obvious he was still unsure about them.

Ruth relayed to him the events of Tuesday, and her short conversation with the doctor in the staff lounge at the hospital that morning.

"What is your function at the hospital?"

"We are both Registered Nurses. I work in the Intensive Care Unit; Maggie here is an Emergency Room nurse."

"I see."

Zvi asked a few more questions about their experience as nurses. By his questions it was obvious to both of them he was not well versed in the medical field, so they replied with as few details as were necessary.

"If I asked you to go somewhere for a few months, could you go?" he finally asked.

"Go where?"

"Please answer my question, then I will explain."

They consulted each other.

"I guess we could," Maggie said.

"How long would it be before you could go?"

"About a week, maybe less. We will need to let the hospital know, and sublet our apartment."

"Are your passports current?"

"Mine is," Maggie said.

"So is mine," was Ruth's reply.

He handed each a piece of paper and a pencil.

"Please write your name as it appears on your passports, and your address."

They were curious, but they complied.

"Listen carefully. Please do not sublet the apartment; I will sublease it from you. Let the hospital know you have decided to go to

France for a while to help Holocaust survivors in a Displaced Persons camp there. Tell the same thing to all your friends who ask.

"Can you be back here next Wednesday evening at 9 p.m., packed and ready to leave Thursday morning?"

They consulted each other. "I guess we could."

"Good. You will be departing directly from here. Bring me a copy of the apartment and mailbox keys, and keep the originals with you for when you return."

"You did not tell us where you want us to go."

"Right. What I am going to tell you must be kept in absolute secrecy. No one should know, not family or friends. You will be going to Palestine where there is a shortage of medical staff, to work in a hospital.

"Isn't that what you offered to do?"

"Yes," Ruth said.

"Then I will see you back here Wednesday next week."

❖   ❖   ❖

Exactly at 9 p.m. a week later Ruth and Maggie walked into the Bristol Hotel, suitcases in hand. This time the same concierge noticed them coming in, and without anyone uttering a word motioned to them with his head toward the elevator.

Zvi answered the door of the suite and directed them to the bedroom to drop their luggage.

"Have you had dinner already?" he asked.

"Yes, we grabbed something on the way," Maggie answered.

"Good. I suggest you try and rest tonight, you are going to be on the road tomorrow morning and it will be a long trip, so get to sleep early. I'll be out here in the living room if you need anything. Otherwise I'll see you very early in the morning."

He went back to the living room, closing the door behind him. They could hear him speaking to someone on the phone, but they could not make out what he was saying.

It was still dark outside when he knocked on the door and woke them up. They alternated in the bathroom taking a shower and getting dressed, and when they emerged there was a pot of coffee and some pastry on the table in the dining area.

"Help yourselves, you don't want to be hungry on the way," he said.

"Where are we going?" Ruth asked.

Zvi walked over to the desk in the corner and picked up two envelopes and handed one to each.

"You are going to Idlewild Airport and boarding a Sabena flight to Paris. There you will get further instructions. In the envelopes you have your tickets and some French money for cab fare and the like. The flight is not direct, makes a couple of stops, and you will be changing planes in Brussels. That is why it was good that you rested last night—this trip will be long."

He glanced at his watch. "You still have some time before the car will take you to the airport, so have some breakfast."

They sat down and sipped the hot coffee in silence. Zvi was all business, working on some paperwork at the desk, and they did not want to disturb him with his activities. After a while the phone rang, and he picked up the receiver and listened.

"Okay. Thank you," he said. He got up and came to their table.

"The car is waiting for you downstairs. In the envelope you will each find a piece of paper with a telephone number. That is the number of your contact in Paris. Memorize it and discard the paper. As soon as you land in Paris call that number and you will be directed further where to go."

Ruth handed Zvi the duplicate keys to the apartment. "We checked them, they work fine," she said.

The two young ladies picked up their suitcases and headed for the door. He opened the door, looked outside and motioned for them to proceed.

They passed him on the way out into the hallway.

"Have a safe trip, and thank you. You don't know how grateful we are for your help."

He said "we," not "I," but they understood what he meant.

❖   ❖   ❖

They boarded the Sabena Constellation and began the trip into the unknown. The flight was mostly uneventful, stopping for refueling twice, first in Newfoundland, then in Shannon, Ireland. They remained on the plane until they had to change flights in Brussels for the last leg of the trip to Paris.

They were both excited and somewhat apprehensive not knowing what to expect at their destination. Although the flights had been smooth, with no turbulence en route, they were tired of the long hours on the plane and were relieved when they finally landed in Le Bourget Airport in Paris.

They collected their luggage, passed through immigration and customs, then headed toward the bank of telephones in the arrivals hall.

Ruth dialed the number they had memorized. The phone rang and rang but no one answered the call.

She frowned, hung up and redialed. No answer again. She tried a third time with the same result.

Maggie went to another phone and had no better luck. Maybe the party they were trying to reach had left for a while and would come back, so they waited for nearly a half hour before trying again. No luck this time either.

They were somewhat concerned, but not worried. They were bright and capable women who could manage well even in a foreign land, especially since Maggie spoke a little bit of French. No matter what, they knew they would be all right.

But it was disconcerting nonetheless. The tickets Zvi gave them were only one way, and the cost of tickets back to the states might be more than the money they had between them, but they knew that if worse came to worst, they could always get some assistance from the United States Embassy in Paris.

They waited a while longer and tried that phone number again, but again there was no answer. While Ruth was trying to call, Maggie used another phone and got through to someone because she was exercising her broken French. She scribbled something on the back of the envelope Zvi had given her, then hung up.

"Come, Ruth, I have the address of that phone number. I got it from the telephone operator. It is in Paris proper. Let's go there, maybe the people will be back by the time we arrive. No sense waiting here any longer."

They took a cab to a Paris neighborhood and finally arrived at their destination, a typical apartment building in the city.

"The operator told me apartment 201," Maggie said, so they climbed the stairs to the second floor.

They knocked on the door, and waited. Knocked again and waited some more. They rang the bell but still no one came to the door.

Resourceful Maggie walked over to Apartment 202 and rang the bell. A little old lady opened the door and Maggie spoke to her pointing to where Ruth was standing outside apartment 201.

The lady explained something to Maggie, then went inside and came back with a piece of paper, handed it to Maggie, and then Ruth could hear Maggie thanking the lady.

"*Merci beaucoup madame*," Ruth understood that phrase.

"Come, Ruth, I have another address."

On the way down the stairs, Maggie explained. "The neighbor told me a young woman had rented that apartment. The building manager was getting concerned about all the men who were coming in and out of the apartment, maybe she was a prostitute, so the girl had to move. She moved to another building a block away with a less nosy manager."

They walked the block and entered another apartment building. On the third floor they knocked on the door.

A young woman greeted them and let them in. They had finally made contact and were no longer abandoned.

The apartment was full of young men milling about, and it seemed like Ruth and Maggie were from another world: Here were two young ladies, dressed in fashionable clothes, Maggie with her red hat, totally out of place in this room full of what looked like members of a Kibbutz.

Their hostess asked them to follow her.

"I was expecting you. I am glad you found me, I was sure you would. I had to leave the other apartment, you understand. You must be exhausted from the trip, and hungry. There are some sandwiches in the kitchen, and some wine too. This is France after all." She smiled.

"You will stay the night here. This is your room. In the morning you will continue on your way to Marseilles, and from there to Eretz Israel." She used the Hebrew term "The Land of Israel," not "Palestine."

They dropped their bags and followed her to the kitchen to eat something.

The next morning, they met Reuven, their guide and companion and the threesome headed to the train station where they boarded the train to Marseilles, another uneventful ride. Reuven led them through the streets of this town to yet another nondescript building, where they were introduced to another agent of the Jewish Agency, a slim woman in her late thirties.

The woman was primarily interested in their experiences as nurses. "I understand from Zvi neither of you has experience in surgery, is that right?"

"That is correct," Maggie volunteered. By now she was a full-fledged partner to the adventure, not merely Ruth's companion.

"In that case we need to get you trained as operating room nurses. We desperately need OR nurses who are able to assist a doctor during surgery. We will therefore delay your departure to Eretz Israel for a few more weeks, and you will spend time in a Displaced Persons camp near here and be trained there by a surgeon. Better to be trained here where there are other nurses and doctors who can guide you than learning on the job under stress, and maybe under fire too, with no one to help."

Reuven nodded, he understood what needed to be done. It was getting late, too late to set out to the camp, and instead he guided them to a room where they could spend the night.

"Tomorrow morning I will take you to the camp," he said. "By the way, I hope neither of you is orthodox, because tonight starts Passover, and unfortunately, under the circumstances, we cannot celebrate it this year."

After washing up they each sank onto a cot laid out with clean linen, and were soon asleep.

They spent the next few weeks—they lost the sense of time—working seven days a week fifteen hours a day or more. There was so much need for their services. Although WWII had ended three years earlier, these Holocaust survivors being kept in D.P. camps were still in bad health, and needed much medical attention.

Chapter 25

Maurice and crew stayed in a hotel in Panama for a few days. Nothing fancy, a very basic hotel, not much better than some sleazy hotels they had all stayed at in Europe during the war.

Other teams and other planes arrived. Maurice got to know some of the other members of this group; they were from various units of the U.S. Air Force, or the Army Air Force. Some were mechanics, some flight crew, all having worked either in the cockpit or on the guts of a variety of aircrafts.

By their last names he guessed not all were Jewish, but they were all recruited by clandestine means. Not kidnapped as he was, some had volunteered and through various contacts were introduced to what everyone assumed were Haganah operatives.

Finally, on May 8, they were transported to the airfield at Tocumen. Once again Al Schwimmer addressed the group, this time including the air crews.

"Let me brief you further about our plans. We have here five C-46s which we have to fly to Czechoslovakia," he said. "We are taking off in formation heading together toward Paramaribo in Dutch Guiana and from there to Natal, Brazil. There the planes will be readied for the Transatlantic crossing of nearly 1,700 miles to Dakar in French West Africa."

Just like a wartime military briefing these men had frequently attended, he pointed to a map nailed to the side of the building.

"If you look at the map, Natal to Dakar is the shortest route for crossing the Atlantic, well within the range of these planes. From there we plan to proceed to Catanya in Sicily where we will refuel again, and from there to Žatec in Czechoslovakia.

"For those of you who are not familiar with this plane, the C-46 is a slow aircraft. Its normal cruising speed is only 150 knots, so the trip from Panama to Czechoslovakia will take two full days in the air, plus time on the ground at each stop, a very long and tiring trip.

"You will have to maintain these aircraft in top notch condition. At each stop you will do whatever maintenance is required. There is a tool box in each plane for that purpose, and if you need supplies or parts we will somehow arrange for those. Each crew includes one former C-46 mechanic who had worked on these aircraft during the war, so they will become the crew chief for the journey.

"Go to work, make sure no one has to ditch in the ocean." Al concluded the briefing. There were no questions.

Maurice marveled at the logistics: All the arrangements, from procuring these planes to establishing the company in Panama, getting all the permits, ensuring fuel arrangements, food for the crews, all that required a very sophisticated operation

A few hours later, after all the planes checked out, they took off.

❖   ❖   ❖

Maurice was lucky to arrive at the Žatec Airfield in the lead plane, with no delays for any reason. Other planes from that flight of five had mechanical problems on the way and were delayed, thus extending the ordeal of the crews getting to their destination, but thankfully none had to ditch in the ocean. The only salvation during the trip were those cots hanging in the cargo area where they could nap during the long hours of flight and when on the ground in between the legs of the trips.

Maurice's plane landed in pitch dark. When the engines stopped, and the large cargo door opened, Maurice grabbed his duffel bag and he and his fellow passengers walked out into the chilly night. It felt to him as if he could not have stayed on the plane one moment longer.

It was not much of an airfield—a runway, an apron, and a small shack across from where the plane had stopped. The flight crew started walking toward the shack, and Maurice and the other four men on his plane followed.

There was a very sleepy man in uniform in the shack, presumably the immigration and custom officer, and he stamped their passports without uttering a word. He probably was well briefed or bribed beforehand, and he probably spoke no English and no one in the group spoke Czech. There was a small bus waiting for them at the other end. They drove out of the air strip for a few minutes, stopped by a hotel where they did not have to check in. Finally, at long last, they could take a shower, change their clothes, and sleep in a real bed.

At first light they were summoned and headed back to the field. On the tarmac were the ten shiny brand new Avia S-199 airplanes the Haganah had procured, ready to be disassembled and transported to Palestine. Each Avia was to be broken into four: the fuselage, the two wings, and the propeller. The fuselage and propeller would fit into one C-46, and the two wings into another.

Working diligently, this motley crew of mechanics and aviators meticulously proceeded to disassemble the planes, and ready them for the trip to Tel Aviv, or wherever the Jewish leadership, acting as pseudo government, instructed them to deliver the planes.

One by one the other C-46s arrived and after some rest their crews lent a hand to the effort. A C-54 Skymaster plane also arrived, leased from an American company, and it was able to carry a complete disassembled Avia in its fuselage.

There of course was a risk of an intelligence leak. Not all Czechs were friendly to the Jews, and they may disclose the activities at the airfield, so to reduce the risk, the ground and air crews were confined to the base, and since there were no suitable barracks for them, they slept in the planes on the cots hanging from the ceilings.

One more time Al assembled the entire group in front of one of the C-46s. They sat on the ground for the final briefing.

"The airlift is about to commence," he said.

"You may have lost track of time. Today is May 17. You have not heard, but three days ago, the British mandate over Palestine ended. The Jewish population in Palestine declared independence, and the creation of the State of Israel. So there is a change in plans: we are not going to Palestine anymore, we are going to the State of Israel."

He paused to let the news sink in.

"Sadly," he continued, "the Arab countries declared war on Israel, and attacked the new country. Therefore we are now heading into a war zone."

He motioned to two men to come forward and hold the map for the others to see.

"Since the war broke out," he continued, "the United Nations imposed an embargo on all military equipment to the Middle East. If we fly the normal route with stops in Italy or Greece we will be stopped by the authorities—we are basically carrying contraband, war materiel; we will be arrested, the planes confiscated and all the good work and money invested will go down the drain, not to mention that this vital equipment will not arrive to help Israel.

"So, the flights to Israel have to follow a specific route, and the whole operation has to be conducted in urgency and secrecy. There is no room for error, or failure.

"The C-54 Skymaster will go first. It has the range to go directly to Ekron Airfield in Israel, with no stopovers. The loaded C-46s don't have the range of the Skymaster, and will therefore have to refuel on the way. Because of the embargo the only refueling stop we could negotiate is Ajaccio in Sicily.

"After refueling you will make the ten-hour trek to Israel. You have to arrive at night to avoid Egyptian Spitfires flown by experienced British RAF pilots. They do not operate at night, so that is some relief.

"In Israel you will have to land in Ekron. There is no alternate airfield designated at this time.

"Welcome to Operation Balak."

On May 20, after an eleven-hour flight squeezed into the C-54 carrying the first Avia, along with some Czechoslovakian mechanics and some Jewish, now Israeli pilots, Maurice landed at Ekron Israeli Air Force base.

Not ideal conditions, but you do what you have to do to help create a homeland.

Chapter 26

Meticulously planned, hastily executed, the British ended their mandate over Palestine just before midnight Friday, May 14, 1948, but not before handing over all their strategic strongholds, the Taggart Police fortresses, to Arab militias, in total violation of the spirit and the letter of the Balfour Declaration of 1917, the San Remo Conference of 1920, and any and all other international decrees, including the U.N. Partition Resolution of Palestine from November 1947.

A few hours earlier that same evening, the Tel Aviv population erupted into a giant celebration immediately after David Ben Gurion declared the establishment of the State of Israel, a Jewish state in its promised homeland, effective at midnight that same day, in accordance with the boundaries established in that U.N. Partition Resolution.

Leah and Sam joined the enormous throng of people dancing in the streets and along with their friends they celebrated all night in song and dance and an elevated mood of ecstasy. Their dream had finally come true! The Jewish homeland had been reestablished in the Holy Land, the Promised Land, from which the Jews had been evicted by force nearly 2,000 years earlier.

Actually, the Jews had never completely left. Throughout the two thousand years of exile, ruled by the Babylonians, Assyrians, Persians, Greeks, Romans, Crusaders, and Ottomans, there had always been a Jewish presence in that land—a caretaker group of families always lived in places like Tiberias, Safed, Hebron, and Jerusalem. And now they were being joined by all the other immigrants returning to this country to rebuild it and make it a shining source of national Jewish pride, a homeland for the Jewish people anywhere.

Alas, the well-deserved celebration did not last long. Upon hearing of the declaration of the Jewish statehood, seven Arab armies aided by armed Arab militias declared war and descended on the fledgling country with their armor, air forces, well equipped troops, and even the battleground leadership of some British officers. In front of them stood a ragtag collection of individuals with poor training and no structure or military order, trying to stop this onslaught with sticks and stones and a few weapons illegally smuggled into Palestine under the noses of the British.

On Sunday May 16 Sam went to work with a special objective in mind. Now that the country was at war he had to meet with his partners at Coldomat and discuss and coordinate the future with them. He had to find out what their plans were, tell them what he was about to do, and come to an agreement with them on the near future of the company.

They met in their tiny office next to the workshop.

"We need to discuss what we are going to do in the near future. I don't know what your plans are guys," Sam said.

"Plans? Like what? What do you mean?" Meir asked, either innocently or stupidly. Sam had determined he was both.

"I am sure you heard we are at war," Sam said. "As of yesterday a war is raging. We were attacked by the Arabs on all fronts. Are you planning to join the fight?"

"And do what?" Yehuda asked.

"What do you mean 'do what?'?"

"I won't speak for Meir, but I have had no military training, so I don't know what I could do in the war," Yehuda said. "I never joined the Haganah, or the Irgun, and never fired a weapon. I am not much of a soldier."

"Neither are most of the people in the front, in the kibbutzim being attacked. Are you going to let them be butchered without trying to lend a hand?"

"I will just be in the way," Meir said.

Sam looked at his partners with total disbelief.

"What is it with the two of you? Are you telling me you are not going to try and defend ourselves? We just came out of a Holocaust where millions of us went to the gas chambers. Do you want a repetition?"

"Of course not," Yehuda said, "but the situation is not serious yet, I will wait and see how it develops."

"And you Meir, how about you?"

"I am with Yehuda. Let's wait for some time and see how things go."

"Nonsense. I am not waiting to be slaughtered by the Arabs! They will throw us into the sea after slitting our throats. I am not going to sit here drinking tea while they overrun our country."

"What are you going to do?"

"I am going to help protect the country, and my wife and my children—and yours too!" He was furious. "I am joining the Israeli Air Force. That is where I can help most."

He took a deep breath and continued. "I have already spent my weekends and every spare moment I had with Sherut Avir, the air wing of the Haganah at Sde Dov Airfield. It is now becoming the Israeli Air Force, and I am going to stay with that, but now full-time. We are at war, for God's sake! No more weekend duty, this is the real thing.

"And you guys, you could become mechanics in the army, help fix things, but you won't...." He wanted to tell them how he despised them for being the cowards, useless leaches that they were.

"You mean you are going to leave us to run the business?" Meir asked.

"Precisely. Our country is in danger, our children's lives are in danger, and you are worried about the business? What good is the business if we are all dead?" Sam stood up and angrily pushed his chair into the table.

"How will we be able to make money and cover our expenses if you are gone?" Yehuda was visibly frazzled.

"You will have to work harder, I guess, Yehuda! I am putting my life on the line here, you might as well at least put out a little sweat while I am gone."

The three were silent for a long while. Finally, Meir said:

"We will do what we have to do. Do not worry about us."

"But I *do* worry, very much so," Sam said. "My wife and kids need to eat while I am gone. They depend on you almost as much as your daughters, Meir, and your sons, Yehuda, depend on me. I want your assurance that our agreement of 'share and share alike' holds. While I am gone I want you to take care of Leah, and make sure you give her my salary and portion of the profits without fail."

"You have nothing to worry about," Yehuda said. "Of course we will take care of her. Whatever money comes in will be divided as if you were here working with us."

"You won't fail me. I hope you will be true to your word. And if anything happens to me and I don't come back, Leah's share is one third of the business. My share goes to her."

"Nothing will happen to you, you will come back healthy," Meir said.

"Yeah, sure, I have your guarantee of that, right?" By now his voice was filled with disdain. "I hope you are right, but I want your word you will take care of Leah and the kids. Do I have your word on all this?"

"You do."

"Absolutely."

❖　❖　❖

The next morning, with Leah's full support and encouragement, Sam donned on a pair of khaki slacks and a khaki shirt, and headed for Sde Dov, a small airstrip outside Tel Aviv where the seedlings of the Israeli Air Force planted by the Haganah in November 1947, were beginning to sprout. Sherut Avir—Air Service—consisted of a few civilian planes: Piper cubs, Austers, a Bonanza, three Fairchilds, and a Dragon Rapide, smuggled into the country primarily from South Africa. This assortment of airplanes, some in miserable conditions, had to be converted to military use and be made safe and airworthy. Sam was determined to lend his hand to this effort.

Based on his credentials—being an aeronautical engineer, and his two years of service in the Latvian Air Force, plus his technical abilities and his leadership role in the Haganah—Sam was commissioned as an officer with the rank of captain, and within days assigned his duties as the chief technical officer of Ramat David, an airbase in the outskirts of Haifa being vacated by the British. He was charged with helping create the Israeli Air Force from the ground up. But, as an Israeli Air Force officer he was required to change his name to a Hebrew name, and so Samuel Glickman officially became Shmuel (Samuel) Gielan.

The British did not abandon Ramat David until May 26, so for the few days until then Sam stayed at Sde Dov and led the conversion of the few airplanes there to military use. On May 27, he kissed Leah good-bye, hugged the kids, started the Opel and headed to the Ramat David Airfield near Haifa.

Before evacuating the airfield, the British had swept it clean of anything usable that was not nailed to the walls. Nothing was left there beyond the Quonset huts, huts that now would serve all purposes, from quarters for the mechanics and air crews to operation center, mess hall, parts supply, and everything else.

It was time to get to work, work until you collapsed, sleep a few hours, and then back to work. There was no time to waste, the war was going badly, and the Egyptians were wreaking havoc with their air supremacy. They bombed and strafed with surprising competence, with their American made Douglas DC-3s as bombers, and Spitfires providing fighter cover. Only later did the Jews, now flying the Israeli flag, find out that in the cockpits of the Egyptian planes sat British pilots, former RAF WWII veterans.

And what did the newly born Israeli Air Force consist of? Beyond the disassembled Avia S-199s trickling into Ekron, the rest were a slowly growing miserable assortment of planes in Sde Dov, some of which were being shipped to Ramat David. And personnel? Hundreds of volunteers from abroad, Jews and non-Jews alike, the Machal, a collection of young airmen from more than sixteen countries, mostly former airmen during WWII.

Sam's main task was to militarize the civilian aircraft and make them usable as fighters, bombers, supply or reconnaissance planes, and make sure as many of them as possible were airworthy at any given moment.

The delay in the British vacating the base cost those British dearly, and left somewhat of a gift for the Israelis. One morning after the war began but before Ramat David was vacated by the British, four Egyptian Air Force Spitfires showed up over the base. Not knowing the British still occupied the base and thinking they spotted Israeli planes on the ground, they dove and strafed the Spitfires parked on the tarmac, and a transport plane that was just landing, making them into piles of rubble in no time whatsoever. The "Egyptian" pilots then pulled up and disappeared into the bright blue skies, triumphantly heading back to their base at El Arish in the Sinai. Little did they know they had just torn apart a squadron of *British* Spitfires. They even returned twice more to complete their mission, but this time they were intercepted and shot down by British fighters. British flyers were fighting other British flyers.

When the British Royal Air Force finally evacuated the airfield a few days later they left the damaged planes on the ground. They never thought these carcasses of airplanes had any value to anyone.

But those six piles of destroyed Spitfires and cargo plane turned into a treasure trove for Sam and his mechanics. Like a swarm of locust they cannibalized these carcasses. They salvaged every usable part off those planes and with some of those parts their colleagues at Sde Dov were able to repair an Egyptian Spitfire that had crashed on the first day of the war after strafing Tel Aviv. It had been shot down by an Israeli machine gun, crash landed on the beach, and the pilot captured as the first prisoner of war. Thus, a fully functional Spitfire, courtesy of the Egyptian Air Force, now painted with the Star of David entered the war on the Israeli side, and a gift it was, later scoring victories against the Egyptians themselves.

The planes kept arriving from all corners of the world, and included a prize possession: With the help of Charles Winters—an American friend of Israel, who later paid a heavy price for it by being thrown in jail by the "friendly" U.S. Government—three B-17 bombers arrived. Also in short succession other planes started flowing in, or flying in, primarily through that small airfield in Czechoslovakia, circumventing the American and UN embargo.

Sam's crew was working around the clock. There was no specific work time: You worked until you could no longer think straight, rested for a few hours and went back to the line. There was more work to be done than the meager crew of sleepless men could handle.

By and large Sam operated independently, without any interference from his command structure. He was getting all the production out of his crews with no bureaucracy, and the camp commander saw no value in interjecting himself into the apparent success.

One early afternoon in the beginning of June, coming off a full night work shift directing the assembly of bomb racks on a DC-3 cargo plane, Sam was surprised to be summoned to the office. He was tired, not having slept for God-only-knows-how-long, and he was irritable. What did his commander want from him?

He entered the office and faced the base commander. What he really wanted was a bed, but an order was an order.

"You called, Ezra?" Sam asked.

"Yes. I wanted you to meet your new leader," he said.

"Great," Sam thought, "all I need now is some schmuck telling me what to do." But he said nothing.

In his fatigue Sam had not noticed the man dressed in strange colored khakis sitting in the chair under the map hanging on the wall.

Until now the exchange had been in Hebrew, but now Ezra turned to English.

"Sam, meet Maurice, a major in the United States Army Air Corps. He has been assigned to take over as chief technical officer of the base. You will be his deputy."

Maurice rose to his feet, and extended his hand to Sam. He was taller than Sam by an inch or two, slim, and had a pleasant disposition about him.

They shook hands. "Nice meeting you," Sam greeted him in English, a safe bet. "Do you speak Hebrew?"

"I am afraid not," Maurice said. "I used to read Hebrew, but since my Bar Mitzvah had no opportunity to practice it."

"It is never too late to learn," Sam said jokingly. "What brings you here?"

Maurice chuckled. "A car, A C-46, a C-54, and a car," he said. Obviously it was a joke although Sam, in his state of fatigue, did not quite get it.

"I was kidnapped," Maurice summarized it.

"Oh, you are a Machalnik?" a term used for volunteers from abroad who came to help Israel in its fight for survival.

"I guess so. I heard the term before, and although I did not quite 'volunteer' I am here, from abroad," Maurice said with a broad smile on his face.

"Well, whatever the reason, you are here now. Welcome aboard, major."

"Thank you, Sam."

"Come, let me show you to your quarters. Nothing fancy, we will be sharing a room in one of the Quonset huts."

"Sounds good to me," Maurice said jovially.

They walked across the airfield to another Quonset hut.

"I am bushed. You must be too. How was the ride from the U.S.?"

"Long and roundabout. We were in many places on the way, and arrived some time ago in Ekron. I stayed there for four weeks or so assembling the Avia S-199s we brought from Czechoslovakia. This morning they reassigned me here and drove me here by car."

"So you must be exhausted. I, too, need some shuteye before getting back to the line. We are retrofitting a couple of civilian planes with bomb racks that we are fabricating by hand with practically no metal shop machines, and I need to get back and help the mechanics."

"Sounds like fun. I may be able to help."

"That will be fabulous. When we get up I will show you around and have you meet some of the folks here. Most of them speak English fluently, a collection from the United States, Canada, South Africa, and even New Zealand are here. A couple of Georgians too, Soviet Union Georgia that is. They are good mechanics but hot tempered. I would not want to bump into them on a dark night."

"I desperately need a shower and a change of clothes. I have been in this uniform forever, for so long it almost sticks to my skin," Maurice said. "It is left over from my US Army Air Corps days."

"That explains the strange khaki color. We are used to the British uniforms. As a matter of fact, that is what we will eventually use ourselves, when the country can afford it of course."

They entered the hut, walked through a barrack type area with cots on both sides. To Maurice it looked quite familiar, similar to barracks he had seen in England during the war. To Sam it was a delightful sight, exhibiting the incredible competence of the fledgling Israeli Air Force—only a few weeks old, it is quickly getting organized. Just a week ago the people were still sleeping on the floor, without blankets unless they brought their own. They were still missing so many things to be a real air force, but the leadership was working hard on getting them what they needed, from food to socks.

They entered the small room at the end of the barrack. Maurice dropped his duffle bag next to the vacant cot—the other one had some of Sam's belongings on it—and dove into his bag for some clean clothes.

Sam handed him a clean towel, one of the two Leah had helped him pack, and a bar of soap. He led Maurice through the other exit from the barracks, pointed the showers hut out to him, went back and collapsed on his cot. He never heard Maurice come back; he was asleep long before his head hit the pillow.

Chapter 27

Over the next few days Sam introduced Maurice to the environment, the people, the working conditions, and guided him in a very helpful and effective way. Sam's motives were not completely altruistic—he needed Maurice to be productive as soon as possible because there was more work to be done, more decisions to be made, more engineering to be designed, and more original inventive thinking than he could accomplish by himself. He did not mind that technically Maurice outranked him and was officially his commanding officer. To the contrary, he welcomed the opportunity to defer the strategic decision-making to someone else so that he could concentrate on the tactical aspects of the mission.

It was part of Sam's personality: He was not a born leader. Yes, people did follow him through thick and thin; they all liked and respected him for his abilities, kindness, and consideration toward them. But Sam always felt more comfortable in the role of a deputy to someone else, the co-pilot so to speak, rather than being thrust in the role of the captain of the ship. Thus Maurice and Sam worked very well as a team with Maurice taking charge and relying on Sam's engineering ability and willingness to deal with the technical crews, and anything else requiring experience with the local culture.

They spent many hours together working on various engineering problems, making decisions about how to retrofit or patch or maintain the aircrafts under their command. From time to time they would have a smoke together: Sam would light up a cigarette, and Maurice would puff on his pipe. As everyone else who smoked, and most did, they were careful to light up away from the planes, the fuel, or the ammunition. Even a minor fire could cause a major issue in the mostly dry weeds growing anywhere the ground was not paved.

Planes kept arriving—an assortment of junk and relics from all over the world, in all sorts of conditions, requiring maintenance, arming, patching of holes. And when a plane was deemed beyond repair, the maintenance crew was instructed to cannibalize it to provide spare parts for other more deserving aircraft. Every bolt, washer, nut, piece of metal, pipe or tubing that could be used elsewhere was one less item that needed to be brought, bought, or machined.

The ground crews were doing their best to get as many aircraft operational as they could, but despite the trickle of new hands arriving sporadically the teams were terribly understaffed and lacking the right fabrication tools. There was even a shortage of hand tools, so great a shortage in fact that Sam had already sacrificed his own personal refrigeration toolbox he had been using at Coldomat, and now donated to the war effort. It was a godsend: Among the normal collection of pliers, screwdrivers, adjustable wrenches, hammer, and mallet, in that box were also the refrigeration technician's tools: tube cutter, flaring tool, pipe-bending spring, and two pressure gauges, all very rare gems, critical to the repair of the hydraulics of a plane. The hydraulic systems in airplanes were susceptible to fatigue cracks, needing to be repaired or replaced quite often, and without those tools it would have been very difficult to keep these planes aloft.

The work was relentless. Neither Maurice nor Sam nor any of their crew could drop everything and take a weekend off to rest. The work was intense, grueling and demanding, and the only relief this bunch of men ever had was an occasional rough game of Rugby they played to blow off steam. Surely it was a good bonding environment, and quite a few friendships grew from working under these conditions and relying on each other for survival, but at the same time this tense and intense atmosphere sometimes caused friction between the exhausted crews, and those required Sam's intervention.

Sam missed Leah and the children, and thank God for Herman and Rosa—Sam's former Coldomat clients who became Sam's and Leah's friends—they now became his lifeline to the civilian world. Several years earlier they had sold their luncheonette in Tel Aviv and moved to the village of Nahalal, an agricultural community bordering with Ramat David. Nahalal was a cooperative, a *moshav*, but not a kibbutz—each family had its own tract of land they independently cultivated, their own farm where they raised animals, primarily chicken and cows, and produced eggs and milk, or grew vegetables. Yet the products were handled through a cooperative: The cooperative sold the products of the individual farms as a unit and then disbursed the proceeds to the members according to their crop. But unlike a kibbutz where the land and buildings and the equipment belonged to the collective, here each family owned its farm and equipment, lived by itself, and was responsible for its own success or failure.

Herman, having been a former businessman in Germany before escaping the Nazis, volunteered to be the cooperative's representative to the outside world, dealing with the union of *moshavs* in Tel Aviv and also interacting with the airbase next door. Several times a week he drove the short distance from the cooperative to the base in an old British-made WWII "Bulldog" truck with large milk cans, some produce, eggs and chickens, whatever was available, and that meager supply helped feed the airbase crews.

He also traveled to Tel Aviv on a regular basis to purchase equipment and supplies and also sell the surplus produce, and during those trips he made sure he visited Leah and her children. That is how he found out Sam was at Ramat David, right next door to Nahalal, and he of course offered to ferry letters back and forth between Leah and Sam, as well as provide his own observations on how things were going at either end.

On his second or third visit to Leah Herman realized that although she was not complaining, she was not coping well with the situation. Not that she was incapable of handling the stress and pressure of being left alone, with limited resources with two small children in the house, but the food shortage in the country was making her life, as well as most other people's lives, quite difficult.

Until the war began on May 15, most of the food brought into Palestine came from the surrounding Arab countries. The area of Palestine west of the Jordan River, had very limited agriculture, enough to feed only the agricultural settlements of the kibbutzim or other rural communities themselves, but not enough to feed the growing urban centers of metropolitan Tel Aviv, Haifa, Jerusalem, Ashkelon, and the others.

The normal supply of foodstuffs came from Syria, Lebanon, Trans-Jordan, or Egypt. Once the war started however, literally overnight all shipments stopped. Not a single egg could pass through the embargo imposed by the Arab countries. From the Arab perspective it was logical—you don't feed your enemy with whom you are at war, and whom you have vowed to annihilate and push into the sea.

An immediate shortage ensued, and it affected national policies as much as it affected normal families trying to survive. For the leadership it meant the enormous task of prioritizing the use of the few transportation resources available: Bring food to feed the population, or weapons and ammunition to protect it? Tough choice: Without food the population could not survive, but neither could it exist if it could not defend itself. Every resource was put into double duty and in tremendous efficiency. From the leadership on down, both fronts had to be coordinated as best as could be, and they were.

Complicating matters was the almost absolute embargo on any war materiel imposed by the United Nations, the same U.N. that supposedly blessed over the creation of the State of Israel. "With one hand giveth, with the other taketh away," as the biblical saying goes. Bringing anything to defend the population required extraordinary efforts and extraordinary means, using fake front companies, indirect routes, hiding one's tracks, and undercover and covert operations on a massive scale. The few ships and airplanes arriving had to be loaded with care, and sometimes in the shadows.

Now it was Leah's turn to scavenge for food. Her friendly grocer was very cooperative, and tried his best to safeguard for her some of the meager rations of supplies he was getting.

The other problem was that Sam's partners were not quite forthcoming with his salary. All too often one of them would pass by on Friday on his way home from work, hand Leah a couple of Israeli pounds, far short of Sam's former salary.

"This is all we have this week," Yehuda or Meir would lie.

"Is that *all* there is?" Leah would ask incredulously.

"I assure you this is one-third of the money that came in this week. We would not cheat Sam and you, you know that."

"Well, if that is all there is, then that is all there is." She would reluctantly accept, but in her heart of hearts she did not believe it. If she was having a tough time managing with the amount, which was in addition to the small military salary of two and a half Israeli pounds a month she was receiving from the government, how could they survive when they did not have that supplemental income from the government? Yehuda did have his wife's meager salary as a secretary, but Meir had no other source of income. It did not add up, but there was very little she could do about it, at least for the time being.

Leah kept a record of how much money they gave her each week, but never told them that she did so. She figured that when Sam came back from the war he would check the books and compare it with her notes. And she did not write to Sam about it either, he had enough on his plate, so why cause him anguish when he could do nothing about it? There would always be time for him to deal with it later when hopefully, God willing, he came back safely. She made Herman swear on his mother's grave he wouldn't tell Sam about it.

What Herman did instead was bring some vegetables, or eggs, or a live chicken from time to time, and then it was Leah's turn to share it with her mother, who no longer had the grocery store and was dependent on her late husband Yitzhak's meager pension for survival.

Whenever Herman brought a live chicken Leah took it to a kosher butcher, who lived in a small house up the side street, to slaughter the chicken following strictly kosher rules. Leah would then have to pluck the chicken, and burn off the short stubs of new feathers over an open flame. That always left a specific smell in the house, and when Bella and Ofer arrived from school it told the children there would be a piece of chicken for dinner that day.

No piece of the chicken was ever thrown out, every gram of it was savored and used. Whatever was not humanly edible, which was just the head, was a delicacy for the stray cats roaming the back yard for a scrap of food. They, too, were hungry.

Next door to this primitive slaughterhouse lived a milkman who owned one cow and one donkey. Every day around midday he came out with the donkey pulling a cart on which he had one large ten-gallon milk jug, and he would sell his wares on a first-come-first-served basis. At the sight of this man and donkey people would run out of their homes with a pot of one shape or another, and buy a quart of milk, if they could afford it of course. No matter how hard one pleaded he would not sell anyone more than one quart so that more people and more children could benefit of the fruits of his cow.

Leah wondered how one single cow could produce enough milk to fill the large container, but after a few days she realized the milk that came from his cow was augmented by a substantial amount of water. It was seriously diluted, and only marginally did it resemble what actually came from the cow.

Still, it was better than nothing. Bella or Ofer would run downstairs, get the quart in a pot, and Leah would boil to pasteurize it before anyone could drink any of it. On rare occasions there would be some crust on the top of the pot, and one of the children would enjoy a special treat. And of course, the unmistakable aroma of a pot of milk boiling, over the kerosene flame, was always inviting and comforting, and signifying to the children there would be a warm glass of milk before bedtime that evening.

Leveraging her agricultural experiences and know-how, Leah planted a couple of eggplant bushes in the back yard. Although the bushes got very little sunshine or nourishment they nevertheless produced some fruit, and when those were not stolen by some hungry soul they augmented the lunch or supper menu of the family. She also resurrected her neglected garden at Aunt Dora's backyard and that saved the day on many occasions, producing lettuce, or cabbage, or horseradish roots, anything the gophers did not steal.

And of course she had eggplants, and more eggplants—they do not require much attention, and grow as fast as weeds. Her recipe book was growing by leaps and bounds, and within a short period of time she had the never-to-be-published "Encyclopedia of all the ways you can cook an eggplant you never dreamed possible." Thanks to Leah's resourcefulness and competence, the children never went to sleep hungry, although on occasion she herself might have.

She made sure Bella and Ofer were taken care of in whatever manner possible. Their clothes and shoes were all "hand me downs." Among her friends Bella and Ofer were the youngest children, so whenever any of the other children outgrew their clothes, her children were the beneficiaries of those "donations." And when their shoes were too small for their growing feet, and there were no other donated shoes, then the upper part of the current shoes at the toes were cut off to give the toes some wiggle room.

Things were weary. Money was in short supply, and even if you had money, and very few did, you still could not buy what you needed, everything had to be imported and there were items more critical to the survival of the nation than shoes for kids.

❖ ❖ ❖

Knowing the stress the population was under, the crews in the Israeli Air Force did their best to maximize the air worthiness of the aircrafts entrusted in their care. Day and night these men worked till they dropped, slept some, and then went back to work. Furlough was not in anyone's vocabulary; a weekend pass was not ever heard of. Even the most orthodox religious men worked on the Sabbath, with the permission and blessing of the Rabbis—survival trumps the Sabbath.

Eight weeks had passed since Sam had left for Ramat David, eight weeks since he had seen his family, and only because he needed a special part to be fabricated for a plane was he able to drive down to Tel Aviv, a mere seventy miles away. What a treat it would be for him to spend two days with Leah and the children while the part was being fabricated! Alas, he could barely keep his eyes open, and after arriving home and giving each a big hug and kisses, he collapsed in bed and within a split second he was fast asleep; he slept through the two days.

❖ ❖ ❖

Sam was barely awake long enough to say good-bye to Leah and the children when it was time to go, grab the part from the machinist, and head back to the base. He had not realized how tired and robbed of sleep he had been when he arrived, but he acknowledged now to himself he must slow down some, and try and get at least a few hours of sleep on a regular basis.

Heading back to the air base Sam stopped for a few minutes at the Elite chocolate factory which was on the way, to see Philip, and see if he had heard from Isaac. To his disappointment he was not there, and since Binyamina was on his way to the base as well, he decided to take a few minutes and stop there and see his nephew Misha.

Misha greeted him at the door. After the warm reunion Sam asked Misha if he knew anything about Isaac and his whereabouts.

"He is no longer in Italy," Misha said. "Philip received a letter from him yesterday saying that he is in a camp in Cyprus. He did not explain how he got there, but he said representatives of the Israeli government were trying to get a ship or airplane to transport him and the rest of the survivors to Israel, and hopefully he will see us soon."

For Sam it was great news. A step closer and a bit of relief: No longer could the British Government hold these miserable souls in illegal captivity. Now that there was no more excuse to limit immigration to Israel, the British could not stop them from heading to their new homeland.

Or so he thought.

But then the British would not relent, and the saga of the refugees continued.

Chapter 28

As he drove on to Ramat David Sam thought about his family. They looked good, and the children seemed happy, but then he was not awake long enough to find out how they were really doing. On the surface everything was all right.

The only thing he was worried about was physical danger to the family, that of the Egyptian Air Force bombing the cities. Just as the Italians had done years earlier, the Egyptians tried to bomb Haifa's port and oil refinery, albeit not successfully. Leah's sister Ida who lived in the Bat Galim section of Haifa, not far from the busy port, had to leave her apartment and move in with Leah and the children for safety. But now Tel Aviv itself was getting attacked from the air.

Sam worried about that, and it gave him an extra impetus to get as many aircraft airworthy as possible, thus providing air protection to not only Tel Aviv but to the rest of the country as well. He had to strike the delicate balance between working himself to exhaustion again, possibly making mistakes due to fatigue, and the need to arm, maintain, and repair as many airplanes as his crew possibly could.

Over the next two weeks he tried to moderate his and his crew's schedule, and with some better organization, courtesy of Maurice, they were able to get more consistent sleep while at the same time maintaining the activities at the highest possible level.

In mid-August, Herman showed up in Tel Aviv and visited Leah.

They sat in the kitchen, and Leah made him a cup of Turkish coffee.

"Sam is fine, I saw him just two days ago," Herman said. "He is better able to moderate the workload and get a reasonable night's sleep every so often."

Despite the fact that he had been in the country for sixteen years already, Hebrew was still a bit difficult for Herman, and Leah spoke Yiddish but not German, so it was a mixed-tongue conversation.

"I miss him badly, and I think the children miss him even more. Until he went to Ramat David he never was away from home for more than a night at a time. Before the war started, when he had to go see a client in Beirut or Damascus, even then he would come back the next day. And now he has been away for more than two months, almost three."

"I have an idea," Herman said. "Why don't you and the children come with me to Nahalal for a few days? Since we are right next door to the base, I think he will be able to come by, and you and the children can see him."

"Oh, that would be wonderful. Do you think he can get away for a few hours while we are there?"

"I don't know for sure, but the children are out of school anyway, and I can drive you there and back. Rosa will be so happy for you to be with us, she likes you so much."

"How about the children, won't they be in her way?"

"Don't worry about it, they won't. We have a couple of acres and they can run free there. And on top of that you won't be here with the air raids—the Arabs don't dare come near Ramat David."

"Great idea. Let me talk to Ida and pack some clothes for Bella and Ofer, and then we can go."

"Sounds good. I have to go downtown, I will be back in two hours, and then we will go. I want to be in Nahalal before dark. Sam will be so thrilled, I am sure."

Although it was already one o'clock in the afternoon, Ida was still sleeping on the couch in the living room. Ida was one of those people who could sleep hours on end, and even through a hurricane.

Bella and Ofer soon arrived for lunch, and jumped up and down with joy when they heard the news. They helped Leah pack some clothes for them, and then they woke Ida up and told her they would be back in a week or so. She was happy for them, and said she might take the bus to Haifa and check up on her apartment while they were gone.

Herman arrived as promised around three o'clock, and they set off to Nahalal. Leah joined him in the cabin, and the children climbed up on the back of the truck, suitcases and all. The back of the truck was covered with a tarpaulin, and loaded with large ten-gallon milk cans, so the children sat on those uncomfortable things for the entire trip. After a while, Bella suggested they use some of their clothes as cushions so as not to sit on the bare metal and have a sore behind when they arrived. A great idea, the rest of the trip was so much more comfortable.

They arrived after 7 p.m., about a four-hour drive, and Bella and Ofer were ever so glad the bumpy ride was over. They collected their "seat cushions" and jumped from the back of the truck. Rosa came out to welcome them, so pleasantly surprised at the guests, and Herman turned the truck around and headed to the airfield. He came back shortly afterward followed by the Opel with Sam inside.

What a happy reunion. Despite his hard work Sam looked good, and he hugged first Leah and then his children. They sat down for the supper Rosa had prepared in the meantime.

Bella and Ofer, so tired from the trip soon went to sleep, and the four adults sat on the porch and spoke for a while. Sam told them about the conditions he was working under, and about Maurice and the rest of the gang gathered from all corners of the world.

Not much later, the two children showed up in their pajamas.

"We could not sleep," they said. "It is so quiet here, and we are not used to it." There were no cars passing by and honking their horns, no truck engine noises, no British loudspeakers announcing curfew like just a few months before, and no air raid sirens, only a few crickets and a dog barking from time to time. So strange! Where are all the people? Of course they were also excited by seeing their father and were curious to hear what the adults were talking about.

Soon afterward Sam kissed them all and headed back to the base, to sleep a bit before getting up early in the morning for a new tough day. He did not come by the next evening—they were retrofitting an aerial camera onto a Norseman airplane, and it was not going well, and before he noticed it, it was way too late to disturb Leah and her hosts.

Despite the pressures Sam was able to spend three more short evenings with Leah and the children before they returned to Tel Aviv to prepare for the new school year starting soon. Onto the back of the truck the children went, but this time there was plenty of space to sit on the floor. They used the suitcase as a seat, and suffered the four hours ride back to Tel Aviv without complaints. It was well worth the trouble and pain to see their father, this time clad in the uniform of the Israeli Air Force, with his rank and insignia decorating his shirt and beret.

❖ ❖ ❖

Like most civilian cities around the world, Tel Aviv was not prepared for an aerial bombardment. No buildings had an air raid shelter, or a basement, and there were no public shelters either. Nor did Tel Aviv have an underground railway system, as London had during the German Blitz, so there were no places to hide from the bombs dropped by the Royal Egyptian Air Force or by the Jordanian equivalent.

They would come in a foursome in broad daylight, two DC-3 bombers escorted by two Spitfire fighter planes. In its original design, the DC-3 was not a bomber at all. It was a troop-carrying or cargo plane, and as such did not have the traditional bomb bay with doors that opened under its belly, and bombs that could be released at the right moment, guided by a bombardier looking through his sophisticated bomb sights. Instead, the bombs were carried inside the fuselage, and manually dropped through an open door in its side. It was not a very accurate set up.

Consequently, it was never easy to predict where the bombs would actually fall when the next attack came. Surely the Egyptians had some targets in mind, such as the bus depot, the Reading power plant, or the Tel Aviv port, but their accuracy was so deficient, any building in the vicinity could be hit instead.

To limit the casualties of these bombings on homes and apartment buildings, non-military civilian targets, the Israeli Civil Defense Department decreed each building create a pseudo bomb shelter within an apartment or store on the ground floor. The "shelter" consisted of lining the outside walls of a room with sandbags, floor to ceiling. In addition, the entrance to the lobby of the building had to be protected with two overlapping walls of sandbags as well, leaving a small zigzag passage between them for people to enter the building. That was the extent of the protection afforded the civilian population of the city. Primitive, and barely effective.

The only protective fire power Tel Aviv had was a single Bofors 40 millimeter anti-aircraft gun on the roof of the reinforced-concrete Engineers' Society building diagonally across the street from Leah's and Sam's home. Unfortunately, between that gun, the large bus company depot some 300 yards away, and the port a bit further, that area of Tel Aviv became a prime target for the Egyptians.

The air raid system was very primitive and ineffective as well—it consisted of a few people standing watch on some rooftops throughout the city, each with a pair of binoculars, or sometimes even without. When they saw or heard the enemy planes approaching they would shoot a flare to alert the central command post, and the wailing sirens would be turned on. After the enemy planes dropped their bombs, and headed back to Egypt, the "all clear" sirens would be heard throughout the city to the relief of the frightened citizenry.

More often than not the bombs would start dropping long before the sirens went off, but by then it was too late, the damage had already been done, and people suffered injuries.

Whenever the air raid siren went off, Leah would grab the children, and they would run down the three flights of stairs to the ground floor. There they huddled together with the other neighbors in the makeshift shelter created in a room belonging to the tenants living there.

It was nearly impossible to get Ida to wake up and run with them. She slept on the couch in the living room, and no matter how they pleaded with her she did not budge. One time a bomb fell and exploded not 200 yards from the building, and then the sirens went off, obviously after the fact. Bella and Ofer ran to wake her up, and tried to get her off the couch by yanking at her legs, with no success.

"Ida, Ida, the bombs are falling!!!" They cried, with part excitement and a lot of fear.

"They already fell," she said, sleepily. She never made it to the shelter that day.

On another occasion, Leah and Ida were in the children' bedroom sewing a patch onto some clothes. The window was open, and it was a bright sunny day. Bella was somewhere in the neighborhood playing with her friends, and Ofer was on his bed, running a fever.

"Spitfire," Ofer called out.

The women paid no attention to him; they were involved in their activity.

"Spitfire, Spitfire," Ofer frantically called out again.

"It is the refrigerator making the noise in the kitchen," Leah dismissed his alarm.

"No, it is a Spitfire," Ofer insisted and pointed to the window.

Ida walked to the window to listen for the sound and saw the construction crew working across the street running for their lives into an adjacent building. Then she knew.

"Spitfire," she said, and the two women started running to the door leaving the child behind.

Ofer was terrified. He somehow jumped out of the high bed and started running after them. There was a long dark hallway leading to the front door of the apartment, and half way down Ofer caught up with Leah, and like a monkey jumped on her back and they both crashed to the ground. Leah got up, grabbed him in her arms and ran downstairs. Only there could she assess their injuries which, while not life-threatening by any means, were not trivial either: She had two scraped knees, a bruised hand, and Ofer had hit his head on the floor and was whimpering.

When the siren sounded the "all clear" Bella came home trembling.

"We were playing in the back street and saw him diving toward us," she said. Normally a calm and serene girl she was clearly traumatized.

"We ran into the nearest building, and heard the guns of the plane going off."

"I wonder what he was shooting at," Leah said.

Ida was looking out the window again. "He got one of the construction workers across the street. The ambulance is there, and they are carrying him on a stretcher."

"Poor guy, and for us it was a close call. Good that Ofer gave us a warning, he was better than the air raid sirens."

And so it went, day in and day out, until the Israeli Air Force sent an Avia one morning to intercept the typical foursome—two fighters escorting two bombers.

Although the Spitfire is a superior plane to the Messerschmitt 109, of which the Avia is a poor copy, seeing the Israeli Avia the Egyptian fighter planes hightailed it and ran away, leaving the two bombers to fend for themselves. And without fighter cover those two DC3s stood no chance and were shot down by the Israeli pilot to the tremendous cheers of the people on the ground who witnessed the encounter.

That was the last time the Egyptian Air Force bombed Tel Aviv.

Chapter 29

Ruth and Maggie could not believe how time flew by. It was already mid-August, Israel was already three months old, and all this time they were still tending to the poor souls in the DP camp outside Marseilles. So when the announcement came that they were to pack up and leave together with some of the residents of the camp and sail to Israel it brought them tremendous excitement—they finally would make it to their desired destination, and original goal.

They boarded the Malla, a rickety small 2,700-ton ship to cross the Mediterranean on their way to Haifa. They thought it was not really a passenger ship, nor a cargo vessel, and it looked awfully familiar to them.

"I know," Maggie finally said. "This is the old Mayflower, Theodore Roosevelt's yacht. I saw its picture in a book a friend of mine had about navy vessels."

"This is Roosevelt's yacht?" Ruth asked incredulously.

"Yes, Theodore Roosevelt, not FDR."

It surely did not look like what they would expect from a presidential yacht. But it had changed hands, was twice decommissioned, and then sold by the US Navy.

"Let's go see the infirmary," Ruth said, all businesslike. "We probably will have some patients suffering from sea sickness during the voyage, and better be ready for them."

They went below deck and found the cabin where they would spend the next few days of the voyage.

Fortunately, the weather cooperated, and the sea was mostly smooth and calm. The Malla labored at fifteen knots across the sea, carrying her passengers and crew over the 1,700 mile distance between the ports of Marseilles and Haifa in Israel.

It took nearly five days before the boat docked, and the passengers disembarked. Ruth and Maggie were met at the customs house by representatives of the government and given directions and bus passes to Tel Aviv. They initially were assigned to the Tel Litvinsky military hospital outside the city, but once they arrived at the headquarters in Tel Aviv they were told they had been reassigned to a military base, an Israeli Air Force base called Ramat David about thirteen miles outside Haifa.

So back to near Haifa they had to travel. This time however, they were offered a ride to the base via a military jeep, arriving toward the evening of September 3, 1948. It had taken them over four months from that fateful day in April and Ruth's utterance in Mr. Goldfarb's hospital room to finally reach their destination.

They were escorted to the base commander's office. Walking from the Jeep to the open front door of the office they thought they heard English spoken, and that was a tremendous relief, because neither spoke Hebrew. Not only English, but American English no less, unmistakably delivered with a New York accent!

Their driver entered the office while they stayed outside. On his entry, the conversation stopped, and he said something in Hebrew to whoever was in the room. Someone responded in Hebrew, and through the door the driver beckoned Ruth and Maggie to come in.

They walked into the office. A medium size man in khaki clothes was standing behind a table that was supposed to be a desk. There was a strong smell of pipe tobacco in the air.

"Hello, I am Ruth, and this is Maggie. We are both nurses."

"Yes, I know, I was expecting you ladies," the officer behind the desk said. "We surely could use your expertise in this place. I am Ezra, the camp commander, and this is Maurice. He is our chief technical officer. He is also from the United States."

The other man sitting on a chair rose to his feet, removed the pipe from his mouth and extended his hand to Ruth.

"Nice meeting you," he said, then did the same with Maggie. "Where are you from in The States?"

"New York," Maggie volunteered, "both of us."

"Great, so am I," Maurice replied, but his gaze was still on Ruth. Clearly, she grabbed his attention more than her friend.

Ezra called out to the driver, and he rushed back in.

"Please take the two ladies to their quarters. They must be tired from the trip."

Then he turned to Ruth and Maggie.

"We are quite informal here, but we prefer everyone to be in khakis. After you rest for a while please find the quarter master and see if you can select some military work-clothes. Those are not uniforms but are better than civilian clothes."

"I will be glad to guide you ladies to the quarter master's hut," Maurice volunteered.

"Thank you. That will be nice."

"Dinner will be in the main dining hall at 18:00, that's 6:00 p.m., and I will keep seats for you at the table tonight," Ezra said. "Other times seating is open, no distinction by rank or position, everyone mingles."

"Thank you," Ruth said.

"Delighted," Ezra mimicked the British.

Chapter 30

The Piper Cub coming in for landing was clearly in trouble. With half its stabilizer gone and the tail section full of holes, it was having difficulties aligning itself with the runway, and the cross wind was not helping any.

It had been on a mission attacking Egyptian ground troops south of Ashdod and must have taken some serious ground fire to be in this condition. The Piper Cub was not a fast plane, not anything like the Avia, but was a pretty resilient aircraft that could take punishment and still stay in the air. However, this much damage was way beyond the anticipated life expectancy of the plane, and how it stayed aloft was a miracle. Or was it that its pilot was just that good?

It had to go around and try landing again, and the emergency crews were already lining up at the side of the runway by the time it made its second attempt. Slowly it was turning in what seemed to be a painful maneuver, at almost stall speed, and then it righted itself just before touching the ground at the beginning of the runway. A perfect landing, especially for a wounded bird.

At the first sounds of the siren indicating a landing emergency Sam and Maurice dropped everything and ran toward the landing strip. As the plane passed them by on the ground they both marveled how this thing had stayed up in the air, and how anyone could guide it to a safe landing.

The plane stopped and the pilot cut the engine but remained on board. Sam and Maurice and some of the ground crew ran toward the aircraft, and they could hear the siren of the ambulance racing behind them. If the crew was injured, a few seconds could mean the difference between life and death for the souls on board.

The bombardier emerged from the right side of the plane and walked toward them, seemingly unhurt, and then the left door opened and Harold stepped out of the cockpit, exactly as Sam and Maurice reached the plane.

"Son of a bitch," Harold cursed loudly under his mustache. Normally a jovial Canadian, Harold was angry and for good reason— he almost did not make it.

"What happened?" breathless Maurice called out over the noise of the sirens.

"Those damned Butterflies almost blew us out of the sky!" Harold was furious. "And we didn't even finish the mission. Instead of blowing up the Egyptians these things almost blew *us* up!"

"This damage was from the Butterflies? Not from ground fire?"

"You bet," Harold muttered. "Our own bombs tried to kill us."

The amount of military equipment purchased by the Israeli Air Force and its predecessor the Haganah from Czechoslovakia was substantial: The original ten Avias were augmented by some fifteen more. Then there were bomb racks and bombs for the B-17s, guns and ammunition for the planes, and all sorts of other armaments.

As a token of appreciation for all these purchases the Czechs threw in some "goodies," materiel left over by the Germans during WWII. Most prominent among them were crate upon crate of the Sprengbombe Dickwandig 2 kg, or SD2, Butterfly cluster bombs. These SD2 looked like tin cans, stuffed with explosives and shrapnel, packed ten to a case, and were used as anti-personnel grenades. Anyone within 300 feet of the exploding grenade would be either dead or injured.

They were ideal for the Israeli Air Force in its early primitive days. They did not need special planes equipped with bomb racks or special equipment to deliver a barrage of shrapnel to the enemy troops on the ground. All the pilot or bombardier had to do was fly below 2,000 feet and throw the upside down crate out the window or the door of the plane. The grenades would fall out of the case and extend their wings—hence the name Butterfly bombs—thus arming them. Depending on the type of fuse they were equipped with, these bombs would explode either after a time delay, were tampered with, or when they impacted with the ground.

Thus when a C-46 arrived in Israel carrying a load of these grenades, donated at no cost by the Czechs, it was a pleasant surprise.

But now, they became an unpleasant surprise.

"What happened?" Sam asked.

"The bombardier here followed the procedure," Harold said. "He opened the door and threw the case out, just as instructed, and those damned things exploded almost immediately, right under the tail section of the plane. There was no delay!"

Harold was clearly agitated, only his skill as a pilot with thousands of hours of experience flying in adverse conditions allowed him to bring this wreck of a plane back. And to top it off, neither he nor the bombardier had parachutes—those were too hard to come by, so had he not made a good landing they would certainly be dead.

Sam and Maurice walked around the plane. It was so damaged it was beyond repair, and would have to be scrapped.

"This Canadian is good," Maurice commented. "You need to be a great flyer to bring this thing back."

"He is one of the best. A solid bomber pilot with tons of experience," the squadron leader who had joined them agreed.

Harold was one of Sam's favorite Machalniks. This Canadian Jew hailing from Vancouver, British Columbia, had arrived sometime in the early days, mid-June or so. Unlike Maurice, he was not "conscripted" by the Haganah, but through some contacts in the Jewish Agency in Europe he volunteered his way to Israel to help with the war.

During WWII Harold was a pilot for the Canadian Air Force stationed first in England, then Scotland, and later Wales. He flew for the Bomber Command in Europe in search of unfriendly submarines or surface ships, namely German or Italian. He amassed thousands of hours in the air in all weather conditions, and on one of his missions in 1943 he intercepted and sunk a German U-boat for which he received the Distinguished Flying Cross commendation. After the war ended he joined with the Jewish Agency, and helped rescue and smuggle Jews across Eastern Europe. When Israel's War for Independence broke out he immediately signed up to join the Israeli Air Force in its infancy.

How ironic was it then when he boarded his first commercial flight en route to Israel: The flight was bumpy, with tremendous turbulence, and this veteran pilot sitting as a passenger in the cabin became sick. He was so embarrassed! His embarrassment must have shown because the flight attendant approached him and comforted him.

"It is all right sir," she said, "it happens to everyone on their first flight." He did not tell her he had logged more flight miles in his life than she had.

Now the experience of all those miles had saved his life.

Maurice and Sam investigated the incident and debriefed the bombardier: Did he do something wrong? Did he follow the instructions to the letter or was there some operational mistake here? At what altitude did he throw the crate out? Was there anything else that could have caused the mishap? Was he sure?

There was nothing wrong with the procedure he followed.

"These grenades must be defective," was Maurice's verdict.

"We can't assume by one incident there is something wrong with these things," Sam retorted. "It could have been a fluke."

"By the evidence, the entire content of the crate exploded at once." Maurice persisted. "This is dangerous stuff. We are lucky Harold could bring the plane back in one piece. These things can cause one of our planes to go down, and we will also lose some lives in the process."

"True, but at the same time we can't just throw them out without knowing what is going on," Sam retorted. "These things are extremely valuable to us. They are superb antipersonnel weapons. Maybe only one grenade was bad, and caused the entire crate to explode at once?"

"You are right of course, it is possible. They are great if they work right, and I would hate to lose them. When used properly, they are very effective against infantry and soft vehicles," Maurice said. "I saw them in action during WWII, and sadly they cost us quite a bit of casualties. We certainly need them in ground attacks against columns of the enemy."

"I think we must do another test before deciding," Sam said.

"The bombardier said the grenades exploded prematurely, immediately as soon as they fell out of the case and got armed. We can't risk another plane or another pilot," Maurice replied.

"You are right. These guys were lucky, but others may not be."

Maurice put his engineering cap on. "What if we rigged the crate to be trailing the plane some distance back before releasing the grenades? That won't put the plane or pilot in jeopardy."

"Moreover, he was flying at slow speed in a Piper Cub. We can use a Norseman instead. It is more robust plane, and can fly at 150 miles per hour. We can have a guy in the back control the case and release it rather than the pilot. That will reduce the risk too," Sam moved the idea forward, supporting the idea of another test run.

"I will draw up the release mechanism, and have the machinists fabricate it," Maurice said. "Tomorrow we will have a test run."

The test failed. Once again the grenades exploded upon arming, and although the plane's damage was minimal, the test confirmed the grenades were of no value as they were.

"This is really bad news," Sam said.

"Very much so. I was hoping the previous failure was a fluke," Maurice said. "Had this test succeeded then we could have an approach that won't endanger the pilot or plane. Now we are back to square one."

"It seems this batch of grenades is defective after all. The whole shipment is useless unless we can do something about it," was Sam's conclusion.

"Do what?" Maurice asked.

"We can throw the case with its cover, and let the grenades explode when they hit the ground. But that would defeat the purpose of these things, and limit the damage. Or," Sam paused, "we can try and disassemble one and see what the problem is."

"Are you nuts? You are not suggesting that seriously, are you?"

"I don't see another way. If we don't find out what is wrong, we have to chuck the whole shipment, and that would be painful."

"Not as painful as losing whoever is going to try to take them apart," Maurice said.

"We don't have to decide today," Sam said, "let's sleep on it."

"Good idea. Maybe we will come up with something."

The next morning Sam made a decision. He was not ready to share it with Maurice; he knew Maurice would give him hell for it and try and stop him, so he kept it to himself.

He quietly asked around the Israeli mechanics if any of them had ever dealt with these Butterfly bombs, and one of them actually confirmed he had.

"While I was a partisan in Czechoslovakia during WWII I saw one taken apart," he said.

"How are they inside? Are they easy to take apart?" Sam asked.

"These things have a very sophisticated and complicated mechanism inside, with lots of moving parts. Removing the detonator is very difficult, it is deep inside, but if you open them you can lock the detonator in place to not operate, making the device safe. A delicate operation but not very difficult."

Sam explained to the mechanic what the problem was and asked him if he would be willing to show him how to disarm the bomb. The Czech hesitantly agreed, so they walked to where the load of Butterflies was kept.

Sam gingerly retrieved one of the devices from one of the crates careful to not let the wings be released. They walked a distance away, and then he watched the mechanic very carefully take it apart and lock the detonator, thus rendering the bomb practically inert.

He was right, it was a delicate operation, but neither difficult, tricky, nor physically demanding.

With the detonator disabled, they examined the mechanism inside. It was rusted, and the gears were frozen in place. They cleaned some of the rust off, and using anti-rust gun oil lubricated the moving parts and loosened them. The mechanism seemed to work correctly. They took another grenade and also successfully rebuilt it.

The prudent course of action, Sam thought, was to clean and oil a whole case of these Butterflies, and run another experiment like the previous one that they ran, but Maurice would never agree to that. So the next day Sam bypassed him and went directly to Ezra.

"Good morning Ezra," he said.

"Good morning Sam. What's on your mind?"

Sam rarely approached Ezra unless it was something serious. Ezra had his hands full without being bothered with Sam's issues.

"We have a load of Butterfly grenades courtesy of the Czechs," he explained.

"Yeah, I know. What about them?"

"They are defective, WWII vintage that were not properly stored, and now they are rusted and they explode prematurely. They are supposed to be dropped from the plane and explode close to the ground, or on the ground."

"Yes, I am familiar with them. What's the problem?"

"They explode as soon as the wings are released, and are a danger to the plane and the crew."

"That is not good news. We can't afford to dump them; they could be useful in our support of ground operations. Can they be fixed?"

"That's why I am here. You should know I did not tell Maurice I was coming to see you, so he knows nothing otherwise he will cut off my balls."

"Why?"

"I took a close look at a couple of them yesterday. The mechanism is rusty and does not work right. It needs to be cleaned and oiled. One of my crew, a former Czech partisan took two of them apart, and we restored them to working condition." He paused.

"I want your authorization to take two volunteers and work on cleaning and oiling the rest to restore them to operational status."

"Are you nuts?" Ezra thought Sam was off the deep end.

"That is the only way."

"How would you do that?"

"The volunteers and I will go into the underground bunker, take them case by case, work on the grenades, and then put them back in place."

"You are crazy. This is so dangerous! If one of them detonates we won't even find your remains."

"I know, but it has to be done."

"This is a suicide mission. How about your wife and children?"

"That is a big concern of mine. You may not know this, but according to Jewish law if the husband disappears or is blown away, and there is no proof of death, the woman remains in limbo for seven years. *Aguna* is the term. She is not a widow, can't remarry, in limbo, and I definitely don't want that fate for my wife.

"On the way here I spoke with the camp chaplain Rabbi Goren and he confirmed that I am right. He said in a case like this when so much is at stake, the possibility of saving many lives by taking this risk, he can draw up divorce papers for me to sign, and if something went wrong she will become a divorcee just as if I had given her a *get*, and able to remarry."

Ezra remained still for a moment, digesting what Sam was telling him.

"Listen Sam, personally I don't want you to do that. This is insanely dangerous, and maybe I should, but I won't stop you from risking it. I understand you feel the urgency of restoring these grenades and making them usable, they can be so useful in saving many lives. So despite my objections I won't order you to not do this."

"Thank you, Ezra."

"May God be with you, Sam, and make sure I don't hear a loud bang from the bunker."

"You have my word for it," Sam faintly smiled.

Sam did not have much difficulty in getting two volunteers to join him in this most dangerous task. Aside from the inherent risk of one of these Butterflies exploding, it was not going to be easy to be cooped up in that underground bunker for as long as it took to get those Butterflies restored, but the volunteers came forward anyway—the former Czech partisan dragged one of his colleagues and they were ready and able to take it on.

On October 5, the Evening of Rosh Hashanah, the three of them entered the bunker. They took these grenades one by one, took them apart, disabled the detonators, and then cleaned the rust, oiled the grenades, restored the detonator, and placed them back in the crate. Initially ten minutes per grenade, later down to almost five, a crate of 100 in about three hours with all three working, and sweating, in the unventilated bunker.

When each case was done, they took it out, and retrieved another defective case into the bunker. In between cases they occasionally made a short trip to the mess hall where the cook had been ordered to be on duty around the clock to feed them. After the meal, and a quick cigarette, Sam and the other two went back into the hole.

They emerged for the final time three days later, and now that the job was done they could breathe a tremendous sigh of relief. Not all the grenades were salvageable, some were too far gone, but the majority of the cases were usable and back in service. And then it occurred to Sam that this was the first time since he left the Latvian army that he missed Rosh Hashanah services at the synagogue.

They slept for the next two days, and when Sam woke up Maurice was sitting on his own bunk staring at him. He was still pissed at the stubborn man who tricked him and bypassed him.

"You should not have done it," he finally said. "Had anything happened to you I would never have forgiven myself for the rest of my life."

He was silent for a moment then he continued.

"Think about it, what would I do here without you? I am not very effective on my own. I rely on you in so many ways that without you, you son of a bitch, I would be totally ineffective here." He paused. "But since you are still alive, it calls for a drink," he pulled out a bottle of cognac from his footlocker, and they each had a swig.

"L'chaim," Maurice raised the bottle.

"Cheers."

❖ ❖ ❖

There was no applause, no parade, no commendations or decorations for Sam or his crew, for this act of bravery. During wartime, especially when loss is not an option and victory is the only avenue to survival, these acts of heroism are taken as a matter of fact.

When the need arises, ordinary people can rise to the occasion and perform extraordinary feats.

Chapter 31

The continued stress of long hours under adverse living conditions and the demanding work was taking its toll on the crews at Ramat David, and friction was developing between some of the teams. Everyone's nerves were frayed, and misunderstandings started to affect the quality and speed of the assignments. Minor skirmishes between the English-speaking crowd and the non-English-speaking members, and sometimes even between the different nationalities of the Machalniks, were intensifying, and Sam felt something had to be done to reduce the tensions.

He discussed it with Maurice and their decision was to take the possible hit to productivity and let the men have some free time outside the base. Let them go to Haifa and blow off steam there. Haifa is a port city, and like most port cities around the world, it had entertainment venues designed for visiting sailors, and the men could find some enjoyment in that.

Sam arranged with Ezra to release one of the few trucks the base had to drive the men to Haifa and pick them up in the morning. He had heard stories from these men about their "activities" while on furloughs during WWII, so his only words of caution to the group before letting them leave the base were: "Make sure you are not brought back to the base under police escort, either military or civilian!"

Off they went to Haifa. To be fair, while Haifa had been known as the entertainment capital of Israel during the British Mandate, that role had somewhat diminished once the Brits left, but the men could still find places where they could get a stiff drink, chase some girls, and do whatever soldiers on leave do.

Without a single exception, all were at the collection point the next morning, and Sam could tell that though they were tired from the busy night, spiritually they were rejuvenated and ready to get back to work.

Over the next two weeks Sam ensured every person under Maurice's command, except Maurice and himself, had the opportunity to enjoy the entertainment offerings of Haifa. Tensions in the camp subsided sharply—their remedy worked, or so it seemed.

And occasionally the men who were off duty would stay after dinner in the mess hall, move the tables to the sides, form a circle in the middle of the space, and dance a dance they called the "Zumba." A few would start, quickly joined by others. They would put their arms on the shoulders of their neighbors within the circle, and move the circle counter-clockwise chanting a rhythmic "Zumba, Zumba, Zum-ba," "Zumba, Zumba, Zum-ba." Slowly at first, and more vigorously as time progressed, it was as if they would enter a trance. Soon others would join, and the noise level would increase, a frenzy of dancing, grown men jumping up and down in unison chanting "Zumba, Zumba, Zum-ba," at the top of their lungs.

But still some tension remained.

One late afternoon Sam was on his way to the spare-parts hut. As he passed by the latrines he heard some excited voices coming from the inside. The men inside were agitated and angry, forcefully so, and something in their voices made him stop and listen.

The men were speaking Russian, and Sam did not like what he was hearing. They were not concerned about being overheard— almost nobody in the camp except them spoke Russian so they thought they were "safe."

"I am going to get that son-of-a-bitch good-for-nothing major tonight," one of them said. "What he did to me is inexcusable."

"What are you going to do to him?" another asked.

"Kill him, what else? When he comes out to smoke his stinking pipe tonight, I am going to come from behind and slit his throat." He was dead serious.

"I am with you; I don't like this American," the third guy said.

"We need to get him away first, you don't want to kill him right in front of the hangar. I can help you grab him."

"But he's got that .45 on him, and it is loaded."

"We can take care of it too. I will come out to smoke a cigarette, then hit him over the head from behind with a heavy hammer. You Sasha will help me drag him away and Sergei will slit his throat. It will look like some Arab infiltrated the camp and slit his throat—it is their favorite thing to do to Jews."

"That American major is going to die tonight."

Sam quickly walked away. There was only one American major who smoked a pipe in the camp, and it was Maurice. He had to warn him.

"But wait," Sam thought, "if I warn him he will be ready for them, and he will shoot them on sight. There are only these three Georgians and one Czech who speak Russian, and as soon as they come near him he will shoot them. That won't be good. Maurice will be arrested, and the air force will be short three mechanics, and damned good ones too."

Tough decision, reminded him of the Latvian Air Force incident.

He continued the analysis. "If I confront them they will kill me without batting an eye. I 'spied' on them after all. I therefore must disrupt their plan without them knowing they had been discovered."

Then it came to him. Simple and effective.

It was already 6 o'clock, almost time for supper. He went to the mess hall and Maurice was not there, nor was he in their room. He finally found him on the way back from the hangar.

"Maurice," Sam said, "I need your help."

"Sure, Sam, what do you need?"

"I want to have the room all to myself tonight."

Sam had a mischievous smile on his face, and he winked at Maurice. "Do you think you can find somewhere to go?"

Maurice gave Sam a suspicious look. Sam was not the type to play around.

Sam did not give him time to think much. "Here are the keys to the Opel. Why don't you go and take the night off? Go to Haifa. Or better still, how about you take Ruth to Haifa, or Naharia, and have some fun off-base? If you decide to stay longer that's okay too, we'll manage here for a few days without you."

Maurice was mulling it over in his mind. A most tempting proposition: Get out of this hell hole for one night or more and go to Haifa with his girlfriend.

"I am not sure Ruth can take off tonight."

"Then go by yourself. I need the room all to myself," Sam insisted.

"Well, okay, if you need it, it is yours."

"Yeah, but I want you out of here, too. You have not had a day off since you got here. Go enjoy. I will cover for you if needed. I will tell Ezra you needed some time off, and there won't be an issue."

"Thanks, Sam."

"I owe you one," said Sam.

"I owe *you* one," Maurice replied, not knowing how much that 'one' was. He went to hunt for Ruth, and before too long they were heading out of the base in the Opel.

Sam turned around and walked into the base commander's office.

"Ezra," he said, "we have a minor problem on our hands."

"What is it, Sam?"

"Do you remember the three Georgian mechanics?"

"Sure, what about them?"

"I overheard them this afternoon plotting to kill Maurice."

"Kill Maurice?" Ezra asked incredulously.

"Yes."

"But why?"

"Presumably he insulted one of them, and you know how quick they are with the knife."

"Let me call the military police, I will have them arrested immediately."

"That is not a good course of action, I think."

"Why not?"

"If you arrest them, it is their word against mine, and they are three, I am one. Also, the air force loses three good mechanics until the investigation is over."

"So what do you suggest?"

"I lent Maurice my car, and under some cockamamie excuse I sent him to Haifa. He is out of the base, so he is safe. He took Ruth with him and he won't be back till morning.

"Tomorrow morning we must transfer those three goons out of here. They have it against Maurice, and nobody else, so we can send them to Ekron, or another base. This way they still can help with the war effort."

"Excellent idea, Sam. I will get on to it first thing in the morning and find them a new home."

Sam stepped out and went to have supper. "Thank God," he thought, "Issue resolved, and crisis averted."

Chapter 32

November, December, and January flew by, and Leah was getting accustomed to the feeling of angst and worry about Sam being in harm's way. Although she did not know the details, she knew what he was doing was quite dangerous and his life could be snuffed out without warning, but she had no choice but to accept it.

She was keeping Sam informed of how she and the children were doing, but not mentioning the income problems she encountered with Sam's partners. Bella was in third grade, Ofer in first, and they were doing fine, she wrote him, fine both physically and emotionally. The air raids had stopped, and with them, the Bofors anti-aircraft gun ceased thudding and shaking their home. From time to time the sirens were wailing, but those alerts ended up being false alarms. Since the downing of those two Egyptian bombers no new bombs fell on the city. Somehow the Jordanian Air Force "disappeared" too.

The days ground on and Sam missed Bella's eighth birthday and then Ofer's sixth birthday. He wished he could celebrate with them, but that was not possible. He sent them his love and wishes by letter promising to give them hugs and kisses when he would see them next time. Birthday gifts were not customary in Israel so knowing his busy schedule, those letters were more than the children expected.

On his end, Sam did not have much time or inclination to think about the dangers he faced day in and day out. There was a crisis almost every day, be it a plane coming in for landing with a bomb dangling under its wing, or dangerously expired ammunition that had to be handled and loaded onto an aircraft. Or it might have been an Avia coming in for an emergency landing with half the propeller shot up by its own gunfire due to its machinegun getting out of synchronization, or a DC-3 cargo-plane-converted-to-a-bomber returning with a partial load of bombs on board because of some mechanical malfunction.

Sam and his crews entered a routine of sorts, with a scheduled work day from early morning till late evening, or the overlapping equivalent night shift. Fifteen hours on duty, nine hours off. The mechanics' roles were growing with new arrivals, and the tools and facilities were improving as well, and slowly Ramat David was becoming self-sufficient in machining replacement parts for the aircrafts.

Nevertheless, neither Sam nor Maurice could take a long break, although on occasion they could go to nearby Haifa to get away from the constant tension of dealing with the unexpected. Tel Aviv was way too far: They would have had to drive through Haifa and then by the "Black Road" to Petach Tikva, then head to Tel Aviv via Ramat Gan. The Black Road was still a single-lane-in-each-direction blacktop, quite slow, and it could take four hours or more to travel the seventy five miles to their destination, especially if one was unfortunate enough to drive behind a truck or a tractor. There was an alternate shorter route, but it was not safe, with quite a few hostile Arab villages along it, and the military recommended not using it unless accompanied by an armored convoy.

Sam could not even take the time to visit his nephew Misha in Binyamina, a much closer destination, so he grudgingly accepted the notion that until the war was over he would not see any of his family.

But then around mid-morning on a cold damp January day, Herman showed up at the base looking for Sam. He was carrying a letter from Philip.

"How did Philip get to you?"

"Leah gave me the letter yesterday. She said Philip came to visit her yesterday morning, and he gave her the letter for you—he knew you were in the air force, but he was not sure which base you were at, and anyway, as you know he does not have a car. I looked for you last night but you were asleep."

"Are they okay?" Sam asked.

"Yes, she said they were all fine, not to worry. She said it is good news in the letter, but did not tell me what it was."

Sam quickly tore the envelope open. It contained one sheet of paper with five lines on it:

"Mulya,
Isaac arrived yesterday from Cyprus and he is in my home.
He is OK, but is weak. He is asking for you.
Is there any way you can come?
Philip."

"Thank you, Herman, you are an angel," Sam said. He dashed toward the base commander's office.

The door was open, and Sam barged in without fanfare.

Ezra looked up from the papers he was reading.

"What's up, Sam?"

"Ezra, I need a couple of days off. My brother was just released by the British from a D.P. camp, and he is in Ramat Gan. I haven't seen him for ten…"

Ezra raised his hand to silence Sam.

"There will be a Piper Cub heading for Sde Dov in Tel Aviv in fifteen minutes. Be on it!"

"How about my crews? What do I do about them?"

"You leave that to me. Go pack a bag. On your way to the plane pass through here and I will have some paperwork for you. And I will take care of Maurice if he needs help while you are gone."

Sam ran to his room. On the way he told Herman he is going to Tel Aviv for a couple of days to see his brother who survived the Holocaust and has just arrived in Israel. He would of course also see Leah and the children.

His bag packed, Sam headed back to the office with some minutes to spare.

"Here are your papers, Sam. When you get to Sde Dov you find Smoky, or whoever is running the place if he is gone, and give them these papers. Stay as long as you need. When you are able to return go back to Sde Dov and they will send you back up here."

"Thank you Ezra. I really appreciate it."

"Don't mention it. It's the least I could do. Now go."

He was on his way to the flight line. Harold came out of the air crew barracks and joined him.

"Where to?" Sam asked Harold.

"Sde Dov," Harold said. "I thought you knew; I am your chauffer." He chuckled.

"What do you mean?"

"I am your transportation to Sde Dov. Ezra assigned me to be your pilot."

"You mean he is sending a plane just for me?"

"Not completely. I have to pick up some parts too, but he is using that as an excuse to fly you over."

"Good old Ezra, at best I was hoping he will let me drive down to Tel Aviv, and he is flying me over. And even with all the pressure here is letting me stay there as long as I need. He is really being nice."

"That is Ezra. That is why everyone likes him a lot at the base," Harold said. "By the way, do I get a dinner for being your chauffer?"

"You bet."

They climbed into the plane.

Harold started the engine, got clearance to take off, and they were on their way. He guided the Piper Cub with ease, the weather was clear with no turbulence, so he could converse with Sam over the intercom.

"How are you holding up, Harold?"

"I am doing fine," was the reply. "It is very different flying a Piper Cub as a bomber, and not a real bomber like in WWII, but you do what you have to do."

"Yeah, I know," Sam responded. "There is not much we can do to make this a real fighting aircraft. Maurice and I tried hanging real bombs off the wings, but there is no member of the airframe strong enough to carry the load."

"Well, isn't it fun having the bombardier sit where you sit, and have him 'lap bomb' the Arab armies from 1,500 feet? He opens the door, and then drops the bombs that are lying on his lap. Not very accurate, but what else can we do with this paper-thin plane."

"I saw you guys sometimes collecting soda pop bottles in the canteen. What do you use them for?" Sam asked.

"Those are real fun," Harold smiled mischievously. "When we run out of bombs we drop those on the Arabs as well. They are very effective coming down from 1,500 feet. They explode when they hit the ground, make one hell of a bang, and spray glass shrapnel all over the place. Those damned Arabs are scared to hell of those," he laughed. "It is also some protection from them shooting at us with their rifles and making holes in the wings."

He did not mention that those bullets could actually kill someone if they hit the cockpit. Sam and his crew had welded a steel sheet under the cockpit as armor to protect the crew, but it was not effective against a .50 caliber machine gun.

The ride was short, so much shorter than four hours by car. Within minutes of landing Sam handed the papers to the base commander at Sde Dov, and in no time at all a Jeep appeared at the door.

"Just bring it back when you are ready to go back to base," were his instructions.

"I am going back to Ramat David," Harold said.

"Hey, wait a minute, how about the dinner I promised you?" Sam asked.

"Some other time. But I will hold you to it."

"Anytime, Harold, anytime." And there *would be* many opportunities for that later.

Sam saw the plane take off, jumped into the Jeep, and raced to Ramat Gan.

He ran up the four flights of stairs, and rang the bell. Philip opened the door and looked at his brother with tremendous surprise.

"Mulya," he exclaimed, "How did you get here so fast?"

"Never mind. Where is Isaac?"

"He is in father's bedroom, resting. Come into the living room, we need to talk."

"Why, what's up? He is not injured, is he?"

"Yes and no. Come into the living room and I will explain."

Sam followed his older brother to the living room. He was anxious to see Isaac but trusted Philip's judgment that they needed to talk first. He had not seen his brother for nearly ten traumatic years, so a few more minutes would not change anything.

"Isaac is not very well, both physically and emotionally." Philip said, "He spoke very little since he arrived."

"How did he get here in the first place?" Sam asked.

"He arrived from Cyprus by a government ship. Our government took the British government to court in Cyprus because the British did not want to let the Holocaust survivors leave for Israel—they were trying to pander to their Arab friends. The judge ordered them to release the survivors immediately as it was illegal for them to hold these poor souls one minute longer. The Israeli government had planes and ships standing by to bring them to Israel."

Sam had been so disconnected from what was going on in the world he knew nothing about this. Without a radio and without time to listen to the base radio he rarely ever heard the news beyond briefings about what was going on in the battlefields.

"When Isaac's ship docked in Haifa government people were waiting to help resettle the survivors with relatives if they had any, or in other places if they did not. Isaac had my address so they brought him here.

"He arrived two days ago and I immediately went to Leah yesterday to give her the news. I did not think you will be able to get here so soon, but now that you are here I have to tell you about Isaac's condition.

"Since Isaac arrived he has spoken very little. He eats very little and rests most of the time. He is still weak and only gets up to pray the three daily prayers—*Shacharit, Mincha,* and *Maariv.* All of a sudden he is very religious. He borrowed my *tefillin* and puts them on during his prayers.

"I guess he is still in shock, and is not ready to tell us what happened to him during the last nine years, but whatever it was it must have been horrific.

"Let me go and get him, but please Mulya, be aware he is not the same Isaac we once knew, not that vibrant assertive man we saw just before your wedding."

A minute or two later, time that seemed to Sam like an eternity, Philip came back into the living room followed by another person. Philip stepped aside, and the man and Sam gazed at each other for the longest time.

Sam could not believe his eyes. Was that Isaac? Could it be? He would never have recognized him in a crowd.

Isaac was a skeleton, a shadow of a man. He could not weigh an ounce more than eighty-five pounds! Although in the past he was 5'8", about an inch taller that Sam, he had shrunk and was now shorter than Sam by about an inch. His deep-set eyes, a family trademark, were even more sunken than before, and had very little life in them.

This was an apparition, a ghost, a wobbly remnant of a human being, Sam thought, and it was his brother!

Isaac uttered one word, and even his voice had changed. "Mulya," he said, acknowledging his brother with a faint smile.

Sam reached out and hugged his brother. His heart was torn and crying inside, but he tried to not let it show. Is this what became of the aristocrat, proud industrialist, man of the world, and a pillar of his community?

Sam wanted so much to ask him about what he had gone through since that fateful day when the Nazis had marched into Riga, but he remembered his brother's advice and kept the conversation to more mundane things.

"I am so glad you are here," Sam said the obvious.

"Me too," Isaac answered.

"Are you feeling well?" Sam asked.

"Yes. I am well."

"You look weak. I know that Manya and Philip will take good care of you, and will get you back on your feet in no time whatsoever."

"I am well," Isaac repeated.

It was obvious to Sam that Philip was right in his assessment. Isaac was not very talkative, and seemed more like in a daze.

"How did you get here from Cyprus? Was it by plane or ship?" Sam asked.

"By ship."

"Did it take long?"

"No, one day."

Sam quickly calculated in his head: The distance between Larnaca in Cyprus and Haifa was about 165 miles which is 140 knots; these ships normally sailed at around twelve knots which meant it took around twelve hours to make the trip; so one day for the whole process was not unreasonable.

"Were you comfortable on the ship?"

"Yes, everything worked fine. The sea was calm, not like the other times."

"The other times?" Sam saw an opening.

"Yes, the other times," Isaac would not go beyond.

"When did you go on a ship before?" Sam couldn't keep himself from asking more.

"Before, when we came to Cyprus."

"How did you get to Cyprus before?"

"By ship."

Sam did not want to push Isaac any further. It was clear Isaac was not going to share anything beyond what he had just said. He obviously was not ready for that, and Sam definitely was not going to force the issue.

Just then the bell rang, and Misha walked into the apartment—in those days people did not lock their doors, and Misha knew Philip would be there. Philip had left word with Misha's secretary at Elite he would be home.

Misha had already seen Isaac, but he did not expect Sam to be there.

"What a pleasant surprise, Mulya. How did they let you out?" Misha asked.

Sam explained.

"Yeah, I saw a military Jeep outside and wondered whose it was. That was nice of your commander although I am sure you deserve it. How long can you stay?"

"I need to get back as soon as I can, the war is not taking a break. I heard the United Nations is trying to force a truce, but we are still under pressure to regain the land we lost in the early days of combat. So unless I can be of help here, I am going home to see Leah and the children. I came directly here from Sde Dov and they don't even know I am in town. I will probably leave tomorrow back to Ramat David."

"I have a suggestion," Misha said. "I know it is difficult for you to come to Ramat Gan. Would it be easier for you to get to Binyamina?"

"Yes, most definitely. Binyamina is much closer."

"What I can do is take Isaac with me to my farm, let him recuperate there and I can take Philip with me whenever he wants to come and see Isaac. And when you are able to break away for a few hours you too can come there."

"That is a wonderful idea," Sam said, "but first let Isaac rest awhile here."

"That is fine." Misha agreed.

Isaac was watching them, and did not raise any objection.

The men hugged each other, and Sam and Misha said good-bye to Manya who had graciously stayed away in the kitchen the entire time, and walked down the stairs.

"Can I give you a ride back to Elite?" Sam asked.

"Thank you. What was your impression of Isaac?"

"I think he has not yet confronted his emotions and circumstances, and we need to be close to him when he does. Unfortunately, I can't get to Tel Aviv very often while the war is going on, so your idea of bringing him to Binyamina is a great one. The atmosphere in your home is calm and wholesome, and Rachel and your boys are wonderful. It may be a very healing environment for Isaac."

"You can drop me off here at the corner. Say hello to Leah."

A short time later Sam walked through the door of his home and Leah almost fainted at the wonderful surprise.

"Father is home, father is home!" the children circled him, holding hands, and dancing around while he was trying to hug Leah. They won, and he knelt and hugged them first—order must be preserved in the household, the children come first, right?

Chapter 33

Early the next morning Sam headed back to Sde Dov, and from there he took a ride on a cargo plane back to the base. The war was still on, and in full force.

The armistice agreement with Egypt signed in Rhodes on February 24, 1949 provided some serious relief to the Israeli Air Force. The B-17 bombers no longer had to travel the distance from Ramat David to Rafah, or Cairo, and could be used elsewhere to help support the ground war.

But the war did not end there, and the armistice agreements with the various Arab countries were still to be signed for the war to end.

Until then Sam remained substantially in Ramat David with short hops to next-door Nahalal to visit with Herman and Rosa, and occasional trips to Binyamina. Tel Aviv was still too far to reach on a short leave, and going to Binyamina provided Sam an opportunity to gently inquire about the events that befell Isaac from the time the Nazis entered Riga to Isaac's arrival in Israel. Slowly he assembled the pieces of a puzzle that, although incomplete, was almost impossible to contemplate, let alone face.

Hesitatingly and disjoint in the beginning, as time passed Isaac's descriptions became more fluid and vivid. Initially only the skeleton appeared, but slowly it grew to include some flesh, and finally the skin encased the body with texture and tone.

The story that unfolded was terribly sad and painfully horrific. It described death and destruction, hunger and disease, loss of property, life, and dignity—cruelty beyond comprehension.

Sam absorbed the story and empathized with it and before too long he could sense it, see it in his mind's eye, smell it, taste it, and feel as if he were an observer to the events. Still, he was totally aware he could never, without having God forbid truly experienced it, really descend to its bowels and become a full participant in this hell on earth. No one could.

It depressed him greatly to know his brother, his flesh and blood, had to go through such horror and be so altered by the events. Isaac was not the same as before in almost all respects. It was as if he were a totally different person, and now, after hearing his story Sam understood how, being put through this torture for so many years, this transformation could take place.

He did not love his brother any less. To the contrary their talks brought them closer together, almost like old times before Sam's departure from Riga. There was a difference though; he no longer was Isaac's little brother, lower in familial standing. Now they were both grown men, Isaac 57 years old and Sam 39, both mature adults having undergone life-altering experiences.

Driving back to the base after these talks, Sam always tried to push the conversations with Isaac aside and refocus his thoughts on the tasks ahead. The activities at the base were not as hectic as in the beginning of the war, but they required a higher degree of sophistication. The solutions were more complex, and were true engineering problems, and Maurice and Sam enjoyed those more than solving more mundane maintenance issues.

At the same time things were much better all around. Supplies were no longer dripping in sparingly, but were available as needed. Not lavishly, but as truly needed. The base started looking more like a regular military base with airmen and ground crews in uniform, organized, and better disciplined. Sam could not but marvel at how quickly this unruly collection of individuals had become a real air force with solid aircraft, fully serviced and armed, ready to do battle at a moment's notice.

The armistice agreements were incrementally signed with the warring Arab nations. Finally, on July 20, 1949 the Syrians signed their agreement and the hostilities, for now, stopped. For all intents and purposes it seemed the war was, in fact, over.

The war was over and both the air and ground crews at Ramat David Airfield could stand down from their hectic schedule. The incredible services these crews had contributed to the success of the battle were something to reckon with, an incredible sacrifice, and a sacrifice that was no longer needed.

It was time to take off the uniform, bid farewell and return home. For the Machalniks—the volunteers from overseas, like Maurice and Ruth, Maggie, Lou Lenart, Danny Kravits, Smoky Simon and the wonderful others, many of whom Sam rubbed shoulders with—it signaled an end to an adventure, time to start stepping off the stage and return to their homes overseas, while others remained and were embraced with open arms.

Al Schwimmer decided to make Israel his new home, and over time took on the establishment and growth of Bedek, what is today the renowned Israeli Aircraft Industries. Others accepted positions with the Israeli Air Force, and Harold and Danny Rosin decided to remain in Israel and became two of the earliest pilots for El Al, the new Israeli national airline. On one of the trips to Johannesburg that they flew Danny introduced Harold to his cousin Dina, and after a short three-month courtship Harold and Dina married and settled in Israel, and remained close friends with Leah and Sam for many years.

Maurice and Ruth returned to the United States, and also after a short courtship married and moved to the Los Angeles area in California. Maurice resumed his professional career, forming several successful companies servicing the aeronautic industry, while Ruth raised the family.

Sam was sad to see some dear friends go. The comradeship people develop during military service, especially in war time, is unparalleled in strength of bond, sometimes lasting a lifetime.

And Sam himself? He was only waiting for his discharge papers to return to his family, and civilian life.

Precisely two weeks after the end of the war he was summoned to air force headquarters in Tel Aviv to meet with Shimon, the deputy chief of the air force. This time he drove the distance in his trusted Opel in relative comfort. He enjoyed the opportunity to see the countryside south of Binyamina, which he had not seen for some twelve months.

He arrived at military headquarters at the Kiryah section of Tel Aviv, and after presenting his credentials was directed by a professional looking military police sentry to the headquarters of the air force.

Shimon was waiting for him, offered him a cup of Turkish coffee, and they sat across the desk from each other.

Shimon went straight to the point.

"Sam, we are heading toward a very challenging time in the service," he said, "and we need the most capable officers to help us become an elite world-class air force. We would like you to remain with us and be part of it.

"We saw you in action, and think you are the kind of asset we need. You have demonstrated to us you have both the people skills and the technical skills required for this position.

"We want you to play a central role in the development of the Israeli Air Force, the arm of the service that we think will be most critical to the survival of the country going forward. Surely, the other branches of the service are critical also, infantry, armor, artillery, and also the navy, but without air cover those are sitting ducks for any enemy aircraft. So the mission of the air force will be to not only protect the skies over Tel Aviv and Jerusalem, and Beersheba or Ashkelon, but give air support to all our troops on the ground, and also engage the enemies' air forces and ground forces where they live.

"You know how small the country is. If we are attacked there is not enough room to maneuver without incurring civilian casualties. We therefore must be able to take any armed conflict to the enemy, on its land and not ours. To do that we need an air force that can provide air cover for our troops far away from their bases and also protect our homes at the same time. We will need to be nothing but the best, most agile and flexible air force in the world. The prime minister has committed to giving us a priority over other branches of service in funding and budgets, to modernize the service with the latest and best aircraft and tools, but the budget is not unlimited. We will need to exercise best judgment on which aircraft to buy, what weapons, and what on-board systems we should get or develop. We will need someone with the experience and competence to guide the air force through that."

Shimon paused for effect, then continued.

"You, Sam, were chosen for the job. We want you to take over the position of chief technical officer of the air force with a rank of colonel," Shimon concluded.

Sam sat quietly absorbing what he had just heard.

"Thank you, that is very flattering," he finally said. "I know the importance of the next few years in solidifying the gains we have made over the past year and a half, and although you seem to be convinced, I am not sure *I* am the best person for this position."

He paused. "Don't misunderstand me please, Shimon, I appreciate the opportunity, but am concerned about staying in the military as a lifetime career. I have a wife and two children I have barely seen during the past fifteen months, as well as a business, and deep down I really want to get back to civilian life.

"If it is all right with you, I need to seriously think about it and consult with my wife on it—she is my life partner. I need two days to get back to you on that. Is that okay?"

Shimon could not hide his disappointment.

"Are you sure? I was hoping you would jump at the opportunity. After all, an opportunity like this doesn't come every day. But yes, I will wait for your response in two days."

He looked at his calendar. "Thursday at 3 p.m. here, captain?"

"Yes sir."

Sam noticed Shimon referred to him as "captain" rather than by his name, the informal way they had been communicating in the air force until now. Was it that Shimon was trying to stress the offer of two promotions at once, from captain skipping major directly to colonel? Possibly, Shimon was certainly that clever, and definitely sneaky enough to do that.

And why did Sam not accept the position on the spot? It really was a fabulous opportunity. True, the pay was not high and it might be tough, but it was consistent, regular, month after month. As a colonel he would receive a salary, which by itself was not enough to live on with two children in the house, but the other benefits of free medical care for the entire family, housing, a Jeep and driver at his disposal, and uniform, and more, all added up, and Leah was a master at managing with whatever she had. And in a few years he could retire from the air force, most probably at a higher rank too, a general, and go into the Foreign Service, something that might be interesting for the multi-lingual and multi-cultural person that he was.

Sam did not really need to "check in" with Leah: If he indeed wanted the job would she stand in his way? Or would she support him to the best of her abilities? If anything, she always encouraged him to make bold moves and take some risks, within reason of course. She was mostly fearless, trusting things would turn out well in the end, so she would not have discouraged him from any decision he made, and he knew it.

Nor did he need time to make the decision. Before leaving Shimon's office he had already made up his mind to refuse the offer. He had asked for the time because he did not want to give the impression he was rejecting it out of hand, and wanted to give himself the right to say "I gave it a lot of thought…"

But Sam was going to turn it down. He would consult with Leah of course, but unless she came up with an astounding reason why he should remain in the military, an unlikely event, he was planning to return to civilian life as soon as he was released from duty.

Leah left the decision up to him. They discussed it at length. Mostly he discussed it and she listened, serving as his sounding board while he rationalized why he would not take Shimon's offer. She asked him questions, but tried to not influence his decision too strongly—after all he would be the one on the "front line" of the consequences of the decision, and she would only be impacted by the side effects. Without coming out and saying it out loud, the decision was his, not hers, to make.

Sam did not realize it at the time, nor did he account for it for many years to come, but the reason he rejected the offer was that he did not have the self-confidence to take on the challenges of the job. He always undervalued himself, underestimated himself and his capabilities, and was never sure of his self-worth. Despite the fact that he had just received a fabulous compliment—the best compliment anyone could receive for his service to the country and accomplishments over the past fifteen months—and despite all his other bold achievements in life, he was unsure he would be able to rise to the occasion and face the challenge. The ghost of his father ever present, looming so large and shadowing everything else, ever critical, never reassuring and comforting, never bolstering his fragile self-image, never approving or commending, had left an indelible mark on his psyche and crushed his self-confidence. His father never told him how good he was, how capable, bright, and hard-working, the ingredients one needs to excel in life. In short, he was never encouraged by his father to go that extra mile, to reach for the stars, and accomplish the impossible.

Except that Sam did not see, not then and not for many years later, what was the real reason why he turned the offer down. He simply did not realize how damaged he had been by his harsh father whose approval he always sought, an approval that never came. He was totally oblivious to the true dynamics of his psyche.

Sam spent the next two days rationalizing and concocting a response to Shimon as to why he was willing to throw away this winning offer and opportunity and stay put at Coldomat with his two partners whom he considered losers.

And he was yet to find out the extent of their misdeeds.

Chapter 34

After taking off his uniform and returning to civilian life Sam spent a week with Leah and the children. He needed to unwind from one hectic environment before entering another. He knew once he went back to Coldomat there would be a lot of issues to contend with, and he wanted to take advantage of the fact that the children were out of school on their summer recess, so it was perfect timing all around for him to spend time relaxing with the family.

They went to the beach, although Sam and Ofer, both light skinned, could not stay too long under the hot sun. They also went to visit Leah's mother Pessia, and Philip and Manya, and one day they hopped into the Opel and made the trip to Binyamina. It had been a long time since the children saw their cousin Misha, and now they were going to get to know his children too—Misha and Rachel had three boys whose ages were close to Bella and Ofer's ages, and it would be fun to spend a day on a farm and away from Tel Aviv.

They would also see their uncle Isaac for the first time, so all in all this was going to be an adventure.

Riding in the back of the Opel on an outing was a lot different than riding in Herman's truck as they did along the same route a few months earlier. This time they could look out the windows and notice things they barely could see from the back of the truck then.

Passing through mostly rural areas this fifty-mile trip took almost two hours. In Binyamina they navigated through the side streets to Misha's farm.

While on the way Sam thought about Isaac's remarkable recovery, both physical and mental under the wonderful care of Misha and Rachel and the children. Physically, although still slim he had regained some weight, and mentally he was now alert, responsive and even somewhat talkative. However, he stayed away from discussions about the Holocaust in general and his horrific experiences in particular.

Sam had shared with Leah Isaac's current conditions, both physical and mental, to prepare her for seeing him again, after these eventful ten years since she saw him last. But he had not yet shared with her what Isaac had told him during his visits from Ramat David to Binyamina—he wanted Leah to see his brother first before being exposed to the horrific details of the past ten years in Isaac's life.

They soon arrived at Misha's and Rachel's farm. By Israeli standards it was a large farm, with a big house, a barn with some cows, a couple of horses, and chickens running around, and behind the barn were two fields, one with fruit trees and another one plowed, ready for fall seeding. All in all, it was very exciting for the children, and while they played in the yard with their newly discovered friends—their second cousins—the adults sat in the spacious kitchen and talked. At noon everyone gathered in the kitchen and Rachel served lunch. Afterward, the children ran back out to roam around in the neighborhood, and the adults remained in the comfortable kitchen and talked.

In all the times Sam had visited Misha, Rachel, and Isaac from Ramat David, it was dark by the time Sam arrived, and Sam had not recently seen the farm during the day. This time there was still plenty of daylight, so Misha and Rachel took Leah and Sam out to show them around while Isaac went to rest for a while.

The smells of the farm reminded Leah so much of her youth, and the Children's Village and kibbutzim where she had worked during the summer months. She used to enjoy the earthiness of farm life, although cleaning cow manure was never one of her favorite pastimes.

A few more hours passed, and it was time to gather the children, have dinner, say good-bye and head back to Tel Aviv. Bella and Ofer, exhausted from their running around chasing chickens or whatever, and the fresh air, huddled in the back seat and soon fell asleep.

"Sam, you told me you had been seeing Isaac while in Ramat David and he was getting better. If he is better now he must have looked like a ghost when you saw him the first time, because he still is not back to normal."

"I don't think he will ever return to what you would call 'normal,'" Sam replied. "He is forever changed, and I had to learn to accept him as a changed person. It was not easy in the beginning, he is my brother after all, and he is nothing like I remembered him from before the horrors he went through."

"You haven't told me anything about where he was and what had happened to him."

"I know, on purpose. It is hard to relate, and I wanted you to first see him before telling you his story. He told it to me in parts over several conversations toward my later visits to Binyamina, and even then it was not very detailed. I am sure he suffered a lot worse than what he described, but he is not willing, and probably never will be, to delve into it to any detail. I think he is simply refusing to relive the tragedy, and he will probably take it with him to his grave."

Sam paused, took a deep breath and then continued.

"What he told me was basically this: Six months after they returned to Riga from Palestine, Hitler attacked and occupied Poland. That made Latvia exposed because now all that separated them in Riga from the Germans was tiny Lithuania acting as a buffer zone, and that was scary for them—by that time they had already heard some about what the Germans were doing to the Jews who came under their occupation. The initial rumors about the German actions against the Jews were no longer just rumors, but had morphed into a consistent flow of news accounts of the systematic extermination of the Jews through 'labor camps.' Those labor camps were nothing but enormously efficient slaughter houses.

"Then in 1940, the Soviet Union occupied Latvia to the great relief of the Jews. They knew about the non-aggression pact that Ribbentrop and Molotov signed before the German blitz into Poland. Remember? Isaac had written about it in his letter from Riga."

"Yes, I remember," Leah confirmed.

"Now that Riga was under Soviet protection, the Jews once again felt mostly safe, despite the atrocities committed by the Soviet Union itself. Those were not directed specifically against Jews but against dissidents, and so long as one lay low they were not being rounded up and sent to Siberia, or worse.

"It was a terrible surprise and shock to them when the Nazis swept into Latvia in July of 1941. No one was prepared for it. Within a few days Riga was in German hands, and for most there was no time or opportunity to escape. During those days, Isaac had arranged for passage on a ship out of Riga, but in the last moments the ship developed engine trouble and could not sail.

"Since they could not make a run for it Isaac, Gita, and 13-year-old Marc went into hiding. They buried themselves in a small basement, with minimal provisions and in total darkness. They had enough provisions to last them some time, but not indefinitely. They hoped it was a temporary situation and the Soviets would counterattack and defeat the Germans before too long.

"The Soviets had no such intention. They could not care less about that little country called Latvia; they were busy protecting their own Russia, Ukraine, and Belorussia. They were totally unprepared, taken by surprise by the German onslaught, retreating, and they could not afford the distraction of defending Latvia.

"The Nazis were in Latvia to stay for a long time, long enough to exterminate practically the entire Jewish population of the country, and others they had assembled and transported from elsewhere.

"Isaac, Gita, and Marc stayed in the bunker for two months in conditions that were quickly deteriorating, both physically and emotionally. The sanitary conditions were not good—they could hardly wash up, and the stench was growing by the moment. They had to keep very quiet, could not speak in more than a whisper to not be overheard by anyone upstairs. The Germans were constantly sweeping the area, with the aid of Latvians who volunteered or were conscripted to rout out the Jews who might be hiding.

"Finally in mid-September someone sold them out, and the Germans came and ordered them out. It was a sunny day, bright, and they had just come from total darkness into blinding mid-day light. There were hundreds of Einsatzkommando troops outside, armed, frightening, shouting orders in German. Marc became terrified and started running. Gita went after him calling him to stop, and the Germans shot them both dead right in front of Isaac's eyes.

"Can you imagine that? Seeing your wife and son being gunned down in front of you?"

Leah remained still. She could not imagine the horror of such an event.

"They marched Isaac away, along with other able bodied men, and transported him to the 'labor camp' Dachau.

"Isaac was strong—you saw him when he was in Palestine he was in good shape—and despite the two months of hiding in the bunker he was still fit, so they assigned him to a work detail in a rifle factory outside the concentration camp.

"The conditions in the camp were horrible. People were dying everywhere, being starved to death with one bowl of soup and a slice of bread a day. There were no hot showers, latrines were overflowing. The stench in the barracks of the unwashed bodies of the living and the remnants of the dead was indescribable.

"Isaac felt he was slipping away.

"He wanted to live. He wanted to live long enough to avenge his wife and son and all the others dying around him. He wanted to see Germany defeated and the criminals hung or executed by firing squads. So he prayed."

"He prayed?" Leah asked in disbelief. "Isaac prayed?"

"Yes. He prayed. This agnostic, totally secular, assimilated former Jew, practically an atheist who had walked away from any religion, his own included, prayed to God to rescue him.

"He was not being a hypocrite. In his hour of total devastation he needed to feel there was someone, something, some higher power larger than he, a power that could help him survive—he knew by himself he was no match for these evil forces of the Nazi killing machine.

"It was not just death, it was also the tremendous humiliation, being treated like a rat, worse than an undesired animal, a flea, a cockroach, to be crushed without any reason other than that it existed.

"He was desperate and so he prayed. Imagine that! This declared, unabashed agnostic, prayed. He promised God that if God saved him, and kept him alive, he would return to his faith and be an observant Jew for the rest of his life, following all of God's commandments, not only to their letter but also to their spirit. He promised he would be devoted to God and would live his life from then on as a *Tsaddik*, a righteous person."

Sam paused for a moment to let the effects of that description take its course with Leah. Since the day Isaac had told him this Sam had been thinking about it, and feeling it emotionally, trying to understand the depth of desperation that Isaac, and all those with him in Dachau and elsewhere, must have been feeling.

Leah was silent, internalizing what Sam was describing, and then he continued.

"Then the next day, the very next day, Isaac was on his work detail outside the camp in the rifle factory. He described that he was keeping his head low to avoid attracting attention of the guards watching them. If you tripped, you were shot. If you looked a guard in the eyes, you were executed on the spot, so he was careful at where he was going. And then, just as they were getting near the factory gate something glittering on the ground caught his eye. Without stopping he leaned forward, picked it up, and stuffed it in his shoe.

"Only in the evening could he see what it was. It was a gold coin. A real gold coin that somehow was placed in his path, that none of the people walking in front of him saw. He took it as an omen, a sign of a miracle from God—his prayers were answered.

"With that coin he bribed one of the administrators of the camp for two spots in the kitchen detail, one for himself and another for our cousin Baruch who was with him in the camp.

"Being on the kitchen detail gave them each an additional bowl of soup a day, and on occasion a larger slice of bread. Soup was mostly water with something cooked inside, and this something extra and that slice of bread, is what saved their lives.

"Baruch and he suffered the next agonizing three years, but they survived the horrors of the camp.

"They were liberated by the Americans on April 29, 1945. Isaac remembers the date very vividly for more reasons than the liberation itself. On that day when the Americans came, only a small detachment of foot soldiers arrived, led by an American major. But on the next day, the last day of April Isaac remembers vividly, the rest of the American soldiers, the Seventh Army, with tanks and all, entered the camp.

"When the American soldiers saw the conditions of the survivors, it broke their hearts. Most of the survivors were down to sixty pounds, starving to death, skin wrapping bones. Out of the goodness of their hearts the soldiers shared with these living skeletons whatever they could, gave them all the rations they had. Whatever they had, they gave away. That is what the American people are all about.

"Baruch was one of those who got a can of food. Isaac begged him to not eat it all at once, but Baruch was so hungry that within a few minutes he finished a whole can of chopped cooked meat. He wolfed it down, but his body could not process the food, and he died in Isaac's arms only one day after being liberated. That's how Isaac remembers the date."

Sam paused again to gather his thoughts.

"And then what happened?" Leah asked.

"He languished in Dachau for a while longer. They were not permitted to leave the camp for quite some time—until the Allies could figure out what to do with those miserable souls, they remained prisoners. After a while he was transferred to the Displaced Persons camp in Italy, near Rome. From there we got the first letter from him, remember?"

"How could I forget? The relief you felt when you found out he had survived! You did not say much, but I could tell how much his survival meant to you."

"True.

"Without a doubt the conditions in the DP camp were so much better than in Dachau, not to compare. They received medical treatments, food, clothes, and shelter, but regardless, he was still behind a fence with nowhere to go.

"He was never going to go back to Riga. There was nothing left for him there except terribly sad memories. He did not think any of the family members survived there, and after nearly five years his business was certainly gone, and even if it were still there he did not want to have anything to do with it. He did not want to have to deal with the Latvians either—he had finally found out how truly anti-Semitic they really were. No matter how assimilated one had become, how much 'one of them' one pretended to be, that is all it was, a pretense, and the Latvians knew precisely who one really was, a hated and despised Jew. After all, didn't they betray him to the Nazis?

"So Isaac came to the conclusion there were only two places where he could go. For a while he thought maybe he could go to the United States where our sister Tanya was, but then he spoke no English, his riches gone, and anyway the Americans would probably not admit him. The United States government did not want to have anything to do with the refugees from the concentration camps in their midst; only a trickle of refugees made it in to the United States, and he did not think he had a chance.

"The only other place was Palestine where his father and brothers were. Other than that he was all alone, destitute and desperate, and without any moral, emotional, or physical support. So when the Haganah emissaries at the camp offered to bring him to Palestine, he felt relieved.

"And that started his next ordeal, making it to Palestine.

"Over the next two years the Haganah tried to get Isaac to Palestine twice, both unsuccessfully. The first time in 1946, the Haganah boat was intercepted and shadowed by a British frigate in international waters and ordered to turn back. Despite the urging of the Haganah emissaries on board, the Greek crew refused to try to run the blockade during the night, and turned back to Italy. Back to the DP camp Isaac went.

"The second time during 1947 was even more dramatic.

"Do you remember when the Haganah sabotaged the British radar installation north of Tel Aviv?"

"Sure I remember. You went on a mission that night and I was sure you had a hand in blowing it up," Leah confirmed.

"I did. My squad did. After giving the British an advance warning, to avoid casualties on their part, we blew it up.

"Do you also remember that two nights later I left and did not come back until morning, in the middle of the curfew? We were setting up buses blocking all the roads in Tel Aviv leading to the beach."

"How could I forget? The British were going berserk, with their machine guns and armored vehicles, shooting wildly and pushing the buses away trying to force their way to the beach because they thought a ship was coming aground and that was why the Haganah was blocking access to the coast line. One of the bullets even came through the window and spread glass on Bella's bed. I was so scared that night! I thought I may never see you again!"

"That was all a diversion. The British were duped. The ship was not supposed to come to Tel Aviv at all. It was going further north, to Netanya. That is why destroying the radar station north of Tel Aviv two nights earlier was so important, so it couldn't track the ship heading for Netanya.

"Sadly the ship wandered off course, too far north, and was detected by the British radar installation at Stella Maris, on top of Mount Carmel outside Haifa. They dispatched a frigate, intercepted the ship, and after being ignored for the longest time, by morning the British sailors finally boarded the vessel and forcefully diverted it to Haifa port."

"Sure, it was in the papers," Leah said. "The passengers were removed and moved to the holding camp in Atlit, right?"

"Exactly. Isaac was on that boat. He was one of those refugees put into Atlit. He and the others were so near—Misha lived only twenty miles away in Binyamina—and yet they were so far, in limbo, once again behind a barbed wire fence, with guards with guns.

"To add insult to injury after a short while the refugees were once again forced to re-board a ship and sail to yet another camp, this time near Nicosia in Cyprus."

"I remember that too. What a slap in the faces of the refugees who finally made it to Palestine to have to sail back to some other concentration camp."

"So later, when the emissaries told them once again they would be leaving the camp and finally going to the Promised Land, no one believed them. Everyone thought they were going to try and run the blockade again, and again they would be rebuffed by the damned British and end up somewhere in Europe in another concentration camp. They did not know about the ruling by the judge forbidding the British government from holding them even one more day.

"So the emissaries hoisted the flag of Israel in the center of the camp and told them they were no longer going to Palestine, they were now going to the State of Israel, and no damned British were going to stop them.

"Some boarded boats, others flew by planes, and within a few days all 29,000 refugees in that camp arrived in Israel.

"When they disembarked, they were met by representatives of the government who helped find their relatives if they had any, or if they did not have anyone, then the Government found temporary places for them to live. That is how Isaac ended up at Philip's home. He had the address with him, and the representative of the immigration department brought him there.

"Think of it, how horrible Isaac's life over the past ten years had been. He had gone through hell, lost his wife and son, saw them killed before his eyes, spent nearly eight years in concentration camps of one type or another, and was not even able to attend the funeral of his father who passed away while he was incarcerated in Cyprus, years after the war had ended."

"But he is alive, and safe from anything like that ever happening to him again," Leah said.

She turned in her seat and looked at her two children sleeping peacefully in the back seat of the car.

"God willing, never again," she said.

"Never again," Sam echoed, "never again."

Chapter 35

The next day the whole gang was sitting on the veranda at Café Stern in Tel Aviv enjoying a relaxed conversation over a cup of coffee. Leah's best friends Mira, Shifra, and Riva, were there, and so were their husbands. Mira and her husband were from Lithuania, Shifra and her husband were from Russia, and Riva and her husband were from Poland. But despite the fact they all were totally fluent in Russian, they preferred to speak in Hebrew, except when they were discussing something they did not want the children to understand. Needless to say the children understood their Russian quite well by that time, but never let on they knew what the grownups were talking about.

Seemingly on his way someplace, Dan walked past the veranda and spotted Sam sitting there, so he stopped to say hello to him, all as if by coincidence.

Sam had known Dan since the Haganah days. They both were squadron leaders and had met a few times during training in the sand dunes of Manshiya, but they had not seen each other for some time, so it was natural that Dan would want to catch up on old times.

After a word or two of idle talk Dan asked Sam if he would join him for a moment. He said he was running an errand and wanted to ask Sam something in private. Sam had no idea what it was all about, but since Dan asked him to join him for a private conversation he excused himself and they went walking south on Dizengoff Street.

They chatted for a few minutes, sharing stories of events since their last encounter some two years earlier. Dan told Sam he had been a scout company commander in the infantry for some months, and then was transferred to military intelligence at headquarters in Tel Aviv. He somehow seemed to know Sam had been in the air force, but Sam did not inquire how he knew that.

"I have to go see someone nearby. Do you mind coming with me? It won't take a minute, and then we will walk back to the café," Dan said.

"Sure, no problem."

At Keren Hakayemet Boulevard they turned right and walked another block and a half toward the beach. Sam knew the area very well: Not only was it close to his home, but it was on this boulevard that Sam had parked a bus across the roadway blocking the access to the beach on that night in 1947.

They must have reached their destination because Dan stopped in front of a small house.

"I want you to meet someone," Dan said, and without waiting for a reply started walking toward the entrance of the house.

Sam knew this place quite well. A nondescript one-level house, nothing fancy, situated on a small lot with a low brick fence surrounding it. His squadron in the Haganah had guarded this place a few times during the British mandate.

It was the residence of David Ben Gurion, the prime minister of the State of Israel, and the same man who on May 14 the previous year had read the Declaration of Independence of the State of Israel to the nation and the world.

There was a sentry on duty, and when he saw Dan he waived them through. He obviously knew Dan.

What were they doing here? Whom would they see?

They walked in. David Ben Gurion's wife Paula was scurrying about catering to the other people in the house. She said a hurried "shalom" to them and went on about her business carrying a heavy tray with tea cups on it. She clearly knew Dan, and Sam noticed that.

Dan poked his head into the living room and signaled a man sitting there to come forward. As soon as he saw Dan beckoning him the man got up and crossed the living room walking toward them. He was of medium height, somewhat heavyset and balding, but Sam did not recognize him.

"Come, let's go to the backyard," the man said. He did not introduce himself, did not even utter the customary "shalom" to them. He just breezed by them and headed to the backyard. Dan followed him and Sam brought up the rear.

There were a number of chairs in the backyard and Dan and the man made a circle with three of the chairs and sat down. No one was within earshot of their circle.

"Listen, Sam," the man said without wasting a second on amenities. He obviously knew who Sam was, although they had never introduced themselves to each other. Sam wondered about it for a second, but then he remembered how he was drafted to the Haganah years ago—they knew quite a bit about him then too.

"I will get directly to the point. We need you."

Sam did not need to ask who 'we' were. They were sitting in the backyard of the house of the prime minister of Israel, so it had something to do with the government, and the state. Could it be that Shimon sent reinforcements trying to convince him to take the position with the air force? That did not sound plausible, so it must be something else.

The man came to the point.

"I know you turned Shimon down on the job for the air force, and that opens up another opportunity.

"You are a master of more languages than we can count," the man continued. "You have perfect command of the critical languages that we need—English, French, German, Russian, and of course Hebrew. Yiddish and Latvian are of no use to us right now so they don't count, and I know you are pretty good with Arabic too, although you won't admit to it because you do not read and write the language well enough.

"On top of that you are a chameleon—you have the unusual and uncanny capability of blending in with a crowd. You look European, northern European, and you would not stand out among people in several of those countries. That is an asset.

"In addition, you are an engineer, mechanically minded, and technically capable. You know aviation, airplanes, weapons, and armament. Here and there, you spent nearly four years in military service, not to mention your Haganah service of over ten years, which together give you a basic understanding of military strategy and tactics. Finally, you are very adept with your hands, can fix anything."

"Is there anything this guy does not know about me?" Sam wondered. Clearly this man who did not introduce himself had done his homework. By now he knew the man was not trying to twist his arm about the job with Shimon.

He set his observations aside. "You said you needed me. In what capacity? To do what? What precisely do you need?" Sam asked. He was not argumentative or defensive, just curious to know what this was all about.

"You had lived for four years in France," the man continued. "Two of those years you lived in Lille, so you know that city quite well."

"That was some twenty years ago, it must have changed since then, the war and all," Sam observed.

"Never mind that," the man dismissed Sam's comment without fanfare. He took a deep breath and got to the point.

"We would like you to return to Lille, and set up shop over there."

"Set up shop? What kind of shop?"

"Whatever, some mechanic's shop, a refrigeration repair shop, a plumbing repair shop, something like that. We can work on the details with you later."

Sam was starting to understand.

"You want me to be an agent of the government, is that it?" Sam asked.

"You got it. You said it better than I could."

"You have to be clearer than that. What kind of agent? Do you need a procurement agent for the government, or an intelligence agent, a spy?"

"Right now it is more of the latter. Later, who knows?"

They were silent for a moment.

"Listen Sam, despite the vote in the United Nations for the partition of Palestine and the creation of a homeland for the Jews in Palestine, we still have quite a few countries in Europe that wish we did not exist. Britain abstained from the vote; only thirty-three countries voted for our existence, including the United States and the Soviet Union, but quite a few of them did so reluctantly. The Arabs are putting pressure on them and will continue to do so for years to come, and we need eyes and ears over there to be aware of what is going on. We need to have someone who can exert influence when the need arises. As you know the Jewish existence in Europe was decimated during the war, so we need to send someone from here who understands and can represent our interests well.

"We don't have many friends in the world, if any. Our best friend right now, the United States, is trying to hurt us badly in every way they can. We had known for a long time the U.S. State Department was anti-Semitic and now anti-Israeli, but we were hoping President Truman would be able to control them and force them to be less antagonistic toward us. But we are now of the opinion, and it is grounded in fact not just speculation, that Truman really does not like Jews, and rather than controlling the State Department, they are controlling him. The State Department had imposed an embargo in 1947 against us obtaining weapons to defend ourselves, but they did not impose the same embargo on the Arab countries that later attacked us. And even then those bastards stole our aircraft carrier that was fully paid for, and also put Charlie Winters in jail for getting you the three B-17s that you worked on.

"So, if that is what our best friend is doing to us, you can imagine what others are doing, mostly behind our backs. We need eyes and ears on the ground to help us there, tell us what is going on, and from time to time help influence the outcome.

"That's why we need you."

There was a long silence while Sam digested this appeal to his patriotism.

The man saw his hesitation. "If you don't like Lille for any reason, then choose another location, but it has to be on the northern part of the continent, somewhere where you will fit in easily, and I doubt you want to go to West Germany."

"Germany? Not now, not ever. They killed 123 of my cousins, my aunt, sister-in-law, nephew, and many more members of my family."

"Unfortunately you don't speak Dutch or Danish, those would be desirable locations for us too, but Lille or Paris are our first and second choices."

Sam sat quietly for a while, thinking about what he just heard. Could he do that what they were asking? Probably. Would he?

"I understand the need," Sam finally said. "I also understand the gravity of the situation Israel is in. We are in a serious predicament, but it is not quite a matter of life and death." He paused for a minute.

"I am a Zionist. I fought to come to Palestine, and then I fought to throw the British out and create a homeland for us, and then I fought to help save our country after its independence. Ever since I was a little boy all I wanted was to live here, in Zion, and in our own country. And now you are asking me to forsake my life's dream and go back to the Diaspora and live among the goyim, the anti-Semites whom I so deeply detest?

"You are asking me to risk my life for the country? That is not an issue with me. I have risked my life for this country before, and am willing to do so in a heartbeat again.

"But what you are also asking me to do is to uproot my family, take them out of here and bring them to the environment from which I ran away, and that I cannot do, and will not do."

"No Sam," the man was emphatic. "We are *not* asking you to uproot your family. As a practical matter you have to be free of all obligations, to move about as needed, be away as necessary, and your wife and children can't be there. They must remain here."

"And what happens if I get caught? What will you guys do for me then?"

There was a long silence, with only voices coming from the inside of the house.

"If you get caught," the man finally answered, "we do not know you. We can't afford to have an international incident, you understand."

The man stopped to allow the statement to sink in, then continued. "We will of course take care of your wife and children, but will disavow any knowledge of you or your activities."

He looked at Sam who clearly understood the seriousness of the discussion and its implications.

"Do you need more time to think about it, Sam? Take a couple of days to consider it. I can even give you authorization to discuss it with your wife, but no one else, of course. I must reiterate, from our perspective you are the best candidate for this job. In addition to all your other qualifications you have the right temperament, and we need all the help we can get. So think about it a day or two and then get back to Dan here, he'll tell you where to find him."

Even for Sam it was a bridge too far.

"I don't want to leave this yard without giving you a definite answer," Sam said, "and the answer is no. I am sorry, very sorry, but I simply cannot do that, go live with the anti-Semite murderers from whom I ran away. My heart is torn, I understand the need, but I have to refuse, and my answer is final."

He stood up from the chair. He was not going to bend, and did not want to leave an opening for them to try to coerce him. He drew the line in the sand right then and there.

"Shalom," he said.

He turned around and walked back through the house.

Dan stood up and followed him to the street. They walked back to where Leah and their friends were.

Partway down the block, Sam stopped, grabbed Dan by the arm and looked him straight in the eyes.

"Are you from the Mossad?" Sam asked the inevitable—was Dan now a member of the newly formed Israeli intelligence agency?

There was a long pause.

"Yes."

"Bless you. Good luck." He turned and they walked back to the café in silence.

Chapter 36

Sam's week of a relaxing vacation passed in a blink of an eye, and it was time to get back to work at Coldomat. Although Leah did not say anything other than assuring him his partners gave her money every week, Sam had a slight inkling, a sixth-sense feeling, that things were not well at the company, and his two partners had not been faithful to their word.

In his worst nightmares Sam could have never envisioned the utter devastation he walked into at the company. It took him less than an hour to realize the colossal destruction Meir and Yehuda had perpetrated on the company.

It was not incompetence, it was not just greed, and it was malicious. Most of the inventory of parts and tools Coldomat had accumulated over many years, painfully so, piece by piece, was gone, sold by these two partners.

Most of the old clients had deserted them, probably due to lack of proper attention and service, and no new clients appeared on the books during the entire time Sam was absent. They basically did not do anything, no service, no repairs, no new installations, nothing, during the fifteen months he was away. They abrogated their responsibility to maintain the business, took advantage of his being away, at a time when he was literally risking his life day in and day out to protect them and their families.

Sam knew he had a right to send them to hell right then and there. Prosecuting them for their actions was not a realistic option, but he knew he could dissolve the partnership on the spot, send them packing without any further discussions, and no compensation either—with the inventory gone, and the goodwill gone, what was there left to compensate them for?

Yet Sam did not do that. He was simply not ready for a confrontation with them, or anyone else for that matter. As far as he was concerned, what was done was done, they would have to live with their conscience. For him it was time to turn the page and move on.

But why? Did he not think he deserved better than that? If they were such scoundrels, as they proved to be, why did he not end the relationship with them on the spot? Was he afraid to take all that responsibility by himself? Was he afraid of failure?

If he were alone, running Coldomat without them, then he alone would be taking the responsibility for anything that happened, good or bad. Was he afraid then of success, or failure? This man who had taken greater risks in life than this one, all of a sudden was he fearful of taking one more decisive step? A man who, as a youth, took a train to a strange land without speaking the language and without any contacts whatsoever, and emerged after four years with all those university degrees; a man who came to another foreign land to start a new life; a man who smuggled weapons to save others' lives at the risk of his own; a man who took a senior role in the air force and risked his life on a daily basis; this man whose country believed in him enough to recruit him for intelligence work; yet this man would not take on and confront these two maliciously negligent useless bums and sever them from his life once and for all?

It could not be fear, so what was it in his non-confrontational character and temperament that held him back from addressing the matter aggressively, and resolve the issue decisively?

When Leah learned that evening why he came home so depressed and lost she was fit to be tied. And when he finally told her what the two "partners" had done to the company, its assets and goodwill, she was horrified, ready to go after them and hit them hard. But for the first time since they were married Sam forcefully stopped her from following her feisty nature. He put his foot down, and asked her to please not challenge them, curse them out, or otherwise inflict any pain on them.

That infuriated her even more: He is confrontational with her, forceful and unbending, yet he is cowering to those two good-for-nothings? Why can't he go after them with the same determination he is exercising with her?

Yet for the sake of a harmonious home, for the sake of the children, she acceded to his demand, but she never forgot.

At that time Sam did not know, and not until sometime later did he find out, that the revenues recorded in the books from the sale of the assets were not distributed equally, and that they had pocketed his share as well as theirs while giving Leah crumbs to live on. He later said that had he known at the time they were enriching themselves while she was struggling to stay afloat, he would have gone after them regardless, so fiercely protective was he of his wife and children.

But as it were, at the time he did not know. He believed that what was written in the books was true.

When tax time arrived a few months later Sam found out that not only did they cheat him and his wife, but by being a one-third owner of the company his tax burden was one third of the total, and he had to pay the income taxes on one third of the profits, money that he had never received.

These men stole him blind, and for reasons of his own he never did anything about it. Was it that he felt guilty about having left them to run the company while he was away? Maybe. Was it that he blamed himself for having accepted them as partners in the first place, knowing full well they were not worthy of his trust? Possibly. He never explained to Leah why he reacted the way he did, or more accurately did not react to their dishonesty.

On top of it all, had he wanted Shimon's offer back, he probably could have had it, and to hell with these two dishonest losers, but he did not go for that either.

In their lives together Leah and Sam had very few secrets. They were open and honest with each other, sometimes to a fault. But this time Sam just would not budge and would not explain or justify his inactions. It was what it was, he accepted it, and felt there was no further advantage in pursuing it. Something in his past must have triggered this bizarre behavior, and even many years later he could not confront that decision and analyze it or explain it, not even to himself.

Instead, he dove into rescuing the company from its demise, and he went after this mission with vengeance.

One of Sam's first orders of business was recovering the lost clientele—all those shopkeepers who had been their clients before the war. He did it the old fashioned way, by taking the time to visit them one by one, telling them the circumstances had been rough with him being gone for over fifteen months, and assuring them it shall never happen again, and promising they would be well serviced from here on out.

He also pursued new clients and business. Before too long he secured a contract with a couple of government institutions managing the refrigeration needs of old-age homes for the refugees and immigrants arriving every day. He was also able to obtain a small contract with the army to produce refrigerators for military units dispersed throughout the country. And with the economic conditions improving ever so slightly, he branched the business out to cover servicing of water coolers, although those were few and far between.

Bit by bit, drip by drip, work started coming in to the workshop too, and Meir was once again building commercial refrigerators of various shapes and sizes. At that point Sam thought of renaming the company from "Coldomat" to "The Phoenix," after the mythical bird that is reborn from the ashes of the fire, because that is precisely what he was able to do.

And in between the visits to those clients Sam was back to going out on the road almost every day, servicing clients wherever they were. Obviously there were no more trips to Beirut, Damascus, or Amman, or to Jenin, or Bethlehem—all areas now hostile to, and out of bounds for, Israelis. But the local client list was growing, and non-productive travel time was substantially reduced as compared to the "good old" pre-war days.

Somehow Sam was also able to enforce a savings and reserve policy for the company, and when the old Opel was finally deemed beyond repair, the company purchased its next vehicle, a 1937 Plymouth four-door sedan, a WWII relic. Compared to the small Opel this car offered a "luxurious" ride with its softer suspension, better seats, and a larger engine, so Sam's long hours on the road were spent in a bit more comfort than before.

Once again Sam was working terribly long hours. His work week started Sunday morning at 8 a.m. and lasted until 1 p.m. on Friday, with some time off for sleep. By the time he normally came home from work it was late into the evening, and he was simply exhausted and sleepy. And although he tried to inquire into his children' and Leah's day he rarely achieved much quality time with his family during the week.

And his partners? By 5 p.m. every day without exception they were at their favorite watering hole sipping a cup of tea. They surely had a free ride with Sam carrying the load and basically feeding three families with his toil. And all this while Sam's partners were nursing their investments in real estate and citrus groves, property purchased with their ill-gotten gains during the war.

❖   ❖   ❖

During that summer Sam's sister Tanya came to visit from the United States. Her husband Adolf had passed away a few years earlier, her two daughters were grown and married, and since all her other relatives were in Israel she boarded a flight to Lod airport and came to reunite with family, even if for two weeks only.

It was a real shock for Tanya, coming from the post-WWII prosperous United States where everything was in abundance, to see this new, impoverished country called Israel, with its scarcities and austerity. She was astounded to see how difficult life was, and how the population coped with the harsh and primitive conditions that still persisted.

Following years of occupation without any investment by the British, and a devastating war with its neighbors, the state of the country was grim, with so many needs and so few resources to address them. It was up to the government to create a string of miracles, difficult accomplishments all at the same time, with not much help from outside.

First were all the Jewish refugees that had to be rescued and gathered from the four corners of the world. There were the holocaust survivors, the displaced persons, still languishing in camps in Europe, and more urgently, refugees whose lives were still in danger, be it in Yemen, or Iraq, or Iran or the entire North Africa. They all had to be brought into the country, arriving with only the shirts on their backs, leaving all their possessions behind. They needed shelter, and food, and clothing, education, medical care, and all the other social services that most societies provide their citizens. Six hundred thousand Israelis had to absorb another one million refugees in very little time, and with limited financial resources consisting only of contributions from good souls, primarily Jewish citizens of the United States. It was a tough row to hoe.

By way of example, the Jewish population of Yemen was in danger from the authorities, and had to be surreptitiously air lifted from a remote desolate air strip in Yemen to Israel. The Yemeni Jewish tribes were gathered by undercover representatives of the Israeli government, and they walked hundreds of miles through the desert to the collection point where unmarked chartered planes were waiting, and all without attracting the attention of the authorities.

The planes had no seats to allow larger loads of human cargo in them, and these passengers, who had never seen an airplane, let alone flown in one, sat on the floor and lit a communal fire in the middle of the fuselage. It had to be quickly put out.

And while these people spoke Hebrew fluently, they were totally unfamiliar with modern-day living with the amenities their new country offered.

Equally important and urgent task was the building of the Israeli Defense Forces. The collection of disjoint units that had fought in the war had to be coalesced into a single real army, air force, navy, and other units. They needed to be unified, equipped, armed, and supported. Whatever weapons that could be purchased anywhere in the world, sometimes at exorbitant prices, were brought into the country despite the strict embargo imposed by the U.S. State Department and the U.N. The large WWII surplus of weapons, tanks, artillery pieces, ammunition, planes, and other war materiel dispersed all over the world were sifted through by Israeli government emissaries, and whatever could be purchased and transported found its final destination in this little country's army. Despite common belief, not a single round of ammunition was allowed to be shipped from the U.S. or by United States interests anywhere in the world to the struggling country trying to defend itself. Both Presidents Truman and Eisenhower supported this unconscionably unjustified embargo which lasted until John Foster Dulles's resignation in 1959.

And finally, there was a tremendous need to create a solid infrastructure in the country. In all its thirty years of mandate over Palestine the British did not invest in any improvements in the area. No roads or bridges of any significance were built, no industry was allowed to grow for fear by the British that such improvements would be used by the natives to cut their bonds and dislodge the British Empire from its dominion over the area.

To accomplish all these urgent goals the Israeli government imposed deep and painful measures of austerity throughout the country. Food importation, which required not only hard currency but also transportation resources and shipping from abroad, was strictly limited by the government to bare essentials. In the long term these limitations did have a positive effect of accelerating local food production, but in the short term rationing had to be imposed on the population. Even if one had the money to buy foodstuffs those were hard to find. Rationing coupon books were printed to ensure fair distribution of the meager food supplies available: one-quarter loaf of bread per person per day, four eggs per child per week and two for adult, one quart of milk per child per week and none per adult, one-quarter of a chicken per person per week. Vegetables were not rationed by the government, but the supply was limited and was based on a first-come-first-served policy. Except for fillet of Atlantic Cod, frozen into brick-like 2 lbs. packages, even fish was a rare commodity.

Grocery shelves emptied fast, so every morning before school, Bella and Ofer would alternate: One left the house first and joined the bread line at the grocery store while the other had breakfast. Then they would switch, and when both were ready for school, Leah replaced them in line to buy their allowable quota.

The impressive thing about Leah's household was that not once was the shortage of food in the country reflected on her dinner table. No matter how bare that tiny refrigerator Sam had built was, no matter how empty the pantry was, whoever showed up for a visit, unannounced and unplanned, was always welcome, and there was always enough food to feed them too. She was a master of making do with whatever was available, and it all was tasty despite the shortage of garlic, and onion, and other condiments.

"Please join us for supper," she invited the unexpected guest, be it one of the children's friends, or one of hers or Sam's acquaintances, and she would disappear into her small kitchen. Within a few minutes she would add something from here, or there, and whip up enough to accommodate another person or two at the table.

But it was tough on Leah, and only her ingenuity and craftsmanship ensured the family never suffered the pangs of hunger or want.

Tanya observed in awe this remarkable accomplishment of creating something from almost nothing, so when her trip was over and she returned to the United States she undertook to ship "care packages" to her brothers to make their lives a bit easier. From time to time she packed some canned goods and other non-perishables, and sent them to Leah and Sam to share with the others. Leah always examined the package carefully, and fairly divided its contents to be shared with her in-laws. Then she shared her own family's portion with Pessia to ensure her mother had also food on the table.

Beyond small personal packages all other imports were heavily taxed and discouraged to not clog the limited shipping and customs resources, and at the same time bring in some revenue to the slim coffers of the government. Of course there were some black-market activities going on. Some people tried to circumvent the rules and regulations and import goods under false pretenses, and the stories about illegal contraband were always circulating. One story told of a religious man who came from Jerusalem to release a crate of "Religious Artifacts" from customs, since religious artifacts could be imported duty free. When the crate was opened and inspected at the port it was found to contain hundreds and hundreds of bras, some black and some white.

"What is this?" the bewildered customs official asked the bearded man. "These are bras, not religious artifacts as it says in the manifest."

"To the contrary. These are religious artifacts," the man said. "We cut the bras and make two yarmulkes out of each one," was the man's response. It did not work and grudgingly he paid the duties.

Or the other man who showed up at the Haifa port to release a 100-pound sack declared as "Bird Food"—again a tax exempt item.

"What 'bird food?' It says here on the sack it is Brazilian coffee," said the customs official.

"This is bird food," insisted the man.

"This is Brazilian coffee. Birds don't eat coffee," exclaimed the inspector.

The man shrugged his shoulders. "If they want, they will eat. If they don't want, then they won't eat." He did not get away with it either.

One small skinny man, a Russian immigrant, used to walk up and down the main streets of Tel Aviv unabashedly calling out loud in Russian to the tenants in the apartment buildings around: "Чёрный базар! Чёрный базар!" "Black market! Black market!" openly offering his contraband wares.

In the sweltering heat of Tel Aviv summer days he wore a full-length wool coat, and on the inside was a treasure trove of sorts: Small gifts—lighters, pens, flashlights—or some small food stuffs—a can of anchovies or sardines, a small salami not guaranteed to be kosher, or a pack of American cigarettes.

Nobody knew his real name, in fact everyone referred to him as "Black Market" as if it were his given name, and he had everything available. You could order something special from him—a bottle of brandy, or a pair of silk stockings, anything, and a few days later he would show up with it, take his premium price and continue on his merry way.

By and large Leah and her friends avoided this man's services, but on the occasion of their anniversary in 1950 Leah wanted to surprise Sam with something special: She bent her own rules and ordered two raw steaks from him, something even the butcher hadn't seen in ages. As promised, the very next day he delivered two very expensive cuts of beef. Leah who kept a kosher home brought the cherished meat upstairs, soaked it for a half-hour, salted it, and let it stand for the traditional one hour on the salting board to make it kosher. Then she went on with other chores in the house, dreaming about the surprise awaiting Sam for dinner.

It was a warm day, and the windows to the kitchen were open. When she returned an hour later the salting board was bare, with the meat gone! On the ledge of the building next door she saw two ravens feasting on recently koshered uncooked steaks.

If it were not so sad it would have been very funny, but poor Leah had paid a large sum of money she had saved, penny by penny, over a long period of time. She splurged one time to celebrate with her family, but had absolutely no intention of feeding ravens with those steaks. Alas, the steaks were gone, and the ravens were enjoying themselves, probably sneering at the poor lady who served them such a fabulous, albeit salty, meal. There was nothing to do but chuckle at the loss, and a loss it was.

The hand-me-down clothes continued, and so did the one-size-too-small open-toe shoes, but this time it was not because Leah and Sam could not afford it, it was simply because clothing and shoes were not readily available. It was not poverty as much as empty stores with no local manufacturing and a supply line stretched thin with more urgent needs.

Laundry was done by hand, running it back and forth on a scrubbing board, then carried up to the roof to hang out to dry on clothes lines set there, and then ironed by hand. Since there was no gas supply to the buildings, and electricity was extremely expensive powered by imported oil, cooking was done on one of two kerosene devices: One was a kerosene lamp with a larger wick, the other was a burner acting as cooktop. It took forever to warm up the food, or even boil water for a cup of Turkish coffee.

Leah's sewing machine was working overtime, reusing any piece of material that could be adapted to the need. An old bedsheet became a Sabbath shirt; an old shirt became a bra; an old drape became a slip cover for the couch. Socks were mended; old towels became rags to wash the floor with. Serious consideration was given before throwing out anything that had outlived its usefulness in one function, lest there may be another use for it in "another life."

And then one day an unforgettable event happened. Harold, now a captain for El Al, the fledgling Israeli airline, arrived from one of his flights to Cyprus and brought Leah a most cherished gift, a dream come true—a large wooden basket full of regular yellow onions!

Regular yellow onions normally are hardly a cause for a celebration, but Leah had not seen any for the past two years. For her it was like manna from heaven. Harold had brought her and her three friends with whom she shared this bonanza immense delight, and immediately after using each onion Leah put the roots in water to try to maybe grow a new onion from the old one.

There is a Yiddish saying:

"ו ען פרידזך אן עורם מאן? ווען ער געפינגדס וואס ער הוט ׃ רי ורן"

"When is a pauper happy? When he finds what he had previously lost." That was the type of happiness the three ladies and their families felt.

Onions, simple yellow onions, long-lost friends.

Chapter 37

Sam woke up much earlier than usual that morning and headed into the shower.

"Why are you up before dawn?" Leah woke up as well, and followed him into the bathroom.

"I have to go to Eilat today. We received a requisition from the army to install a water cooler in Eilat. There is nothing much there, just a garrison where the Jordanian Um Rashrash police station used to be. It is beastly hot there, with no civilization around, and the soldiers have nothing cold to drink."

"How are you getting there?" she asked.

"A military Jeep will drive me."

"How long does it take to drive to Eilat?"

"About seven or eight hours, depending on how the roads are, and how fast the convoy will move."

"Convoy?" she was surprised.

"Yes. It is too dangerous to travel alone so the army is sending a convoy with a security detail to protect us from an attack by those Jordanian or Egyptian terrorists, *Fedayeen*. They also are sending a couple of mechanics in a spare Jeep just in case we have a mechanical breakdown, and some supplies for the soldiers there."

"Do you think you will be back tonight?"

"Not likely. By the time we get there it will be late afternoon, and we cannot travel at night. Too dangerous, the *Fedayeen* can set up an ambush."

"I will pack you a spare shirt then."

"Thanks."

Some habits are hard to break so Sam put on his usual clothes that he normally dressed in for a work day: Khaki shorts and short-sleeve shirt, long woolen socks and military boots, and a beret to cover his head. Typical British military-style outfit worn in hot climates, all but the proverbial cork hat the British colonial forces used in tropical climates.

The Jeep was waiting for him downstairs and they drove off. They stopped at Coldomat's shop, picked up his tools and loaded the water cooler into the back of the Jeep. As the sun came up over the hills to the east they met with the convoy outside Tel Aviv and they headed south through Beersheba and on to Eilat.

The road took them from Beersheba southeast, past the Small Crater and down the Scorpion Pass. The pass was a narrow steep twisted road in poor physical condition, with extreme drop-offs of hundreds of feet and no guardrail, making travel slow and dangerous. The supply truck could not negotiate the turns in the road in one pass, and had to back up and then proceed at every twist of the serpentine. At the bottom, the road carried them along the Arava Valley to their destination several hours further south. Throughout the journey, and especially down the Scorpion Pass, every person, particularly the security detail, was extremely vigilant to anything unusual or any motion along the sides of the road. Traveling this slowly because of the road conditions made them a superb target for any Arab infiltrators sitting in ambush.

The Jeep was an open vehicle, so Sam was sitting in the sun all day. They arrived by late afternoon and he went to work without delay. Installing the water cooler was not too difficult for him, he had all the tools and parts necessary to hook it up to the water supply. Electric power was provided by a small generator that could be run as long as a couple of hours each day, depending on the available fuel supply.

In the meantime, while Sam was working, the others unloaded the supply vehicle. When he was done and the cooler produced its first cold drink they congregated around a camp fire, ate military K rations and then called it a night. They slept on the ground next to the vehicles, and were guarded by their security detail. It was not comfortable sleeping on the ground, and there was always that danger of a scorpion seeking the warmth of the human bodies. Fortunately, no one was stung that night—a yellow scorpion's poison is most painful and is sometimes even deadly.

By early morning, with mission accomplished they all boarded the vehicles and headed back north. Climbing up the Serpent Pass was much more difficult than descending it, and although now empty, the supply truck was laboring up the hill. It took a long time to negotiate the twists in the road, and by the time they exited the top of the rise, Sam realized he was in deep trouble. His legs, from mid-thigh to mid-calf were burnt from the exposure to the sun as were his arms and forehead. He should have worn long-legged pants, a long-sleeve shirt, and a hat on the trip, but it had not occurred to him the sun would be as ferocious as it was.

He tried to cover the exposed part of his legs with the old shirt he had worn the day before, but by then it was too late. Blisters started to appear in the exposed areas, and he was in serious pain. Nothing could touch the blistering skin, not even the light fabric of the shirt, without making that pain worse.

By the time he arrived back home in the evening Sam was in agony, with serious burns on his arms and legs. Dr. Landau came to Sam's rescue, riding his bicycle of course. Experienced in burns since his days in the Kaiser Wilhelm's army during WWI, he treated the wounds as best he could, but Sam was disabled for several more days.

He never wore shorts outside the house again.

❖　❖　❖

Another year passed, and summer arrived. The children were out of school ready to freely roam about the city, visit their friends, join in youth-group activities, and complete their summer homework assignments. Every summer the students in Israeli schools were given a booklet of exercises to complete during their time off from school, practicing the material studied during the year and writing some book reports as well.

Summer in Tel Aviv could be quite hot, with temperatures rising to the mid-to high-nineties and sometimes even beyond 100°F. Living in a fourth-floor apartment of a concrete building could be quite unpleasant on days such as those, with the sun baking the black tar-covered roof and heating the inside of the apartment like an oven. So one morning every spring, early enough when the roof was still cool, Leah, Sam, and the children would take on a fun family project: They would haul bucket upon bucket of whitewash onto the roof, and with big brushes spread it over the black tar. The whitewash would reflect the rays of the sun and help reduce the discomfort of the residents of the apartment below. Part of the fun for the kids was getting themselves and their clothes all messed up with whitewash—nothing that won't come off in the laundry and shower though.

Like most of Israel at the time, there was no air conditioning in their home and since the apartment faced east, away from the sea, there was not much of a cooling breeze coming off the Mediterranean either. Worse, living only three blocks from the sea they suffered the high humidity of coastal regions, causing people to sweat and feel uncomfortable as if the temperature were even higher than it really was.

The exception to this high humidity heat was a *khamsin*. Instead of the breeze coming over the Mediterranean, thus cooling off some, but gaining humidity, on occasion the air flow shifted south over North Africa and then came up travelling over land up to Tel Aviv and beyond. This flow over the Sahara Desert could raise temperatures to as high as 110^{0}F or beyond, but the humidity level would drop dramatically to single-digit percentages. It felt then like being in a baking oven for the next few days.

For some curious reason that no one had ever adequately explained, *khamsins* in Tel Aviv always lasted an odd number of days. If you entered the second or forth or sixth day of this suffocating heat wave you knew you had two more days of it to endure. Then after an odd number of days, in early evening around 7:00 p.m. or so, it was as if you could hear a loud bang, and the direction of the air would change, and a much cooler breeze would appear from the Mediterranean and you knew the *khamsin* "broke."

To cool the interior of the home during those *khamsin* days, Leah's remedy was to hang wet bedsheets inside the rooms. By evaporation, the bedsheets cooled the air in the apartment to a more livable temperature, at the cost of raising the level of humidity. Either way everyone would sweat a lot.

The only other escape from the suffocating heat was a little black Westinghouse fan Sam brought from the shop one day. It had belonged to one of his clients, and when it prematurely "died," Sam resuscitated it and made it work as new, but the client did not want it back. Instead, it noisily pushed the hot air around the apartment, providing the sensation of some airflow. Better than nothing.

Going to the beach was not an option. The sea around Tel Aviv was contaminated and the health ministry forbade swimming in the otherwise inviting cool water. To enjoy the Mediterranean one had to travel some ten miles out of town and it was not something Sam and

Leah could do during the week. During the short weekends there was always something else to do so dipping in the sea was not as common a relief as they would have liked it to be.

So they took showers, cold showers. Once, twice, three times a day, to chill the body some. Although there was a hot water heater, and one could really scrub the grime and dirt accumulated during the day off the body, the shower was always concluded with a long burst of cold water from the tap. Fortunately in Tel Aviv there was no shortage of running water. Jerusalem was a different story, with its water scarcity, but it was regularly cooler there because of its higher elevation.

That summer Bella was away at camp, and from time to time Ofer joined Sam at his work. He roamed around the shop exploring the piles of magnificent pieces of metal, tools, and junk, all fascinating things for a technically inclined boy with a vivid imagination. But most of all Ofer enjoyed it when he could accompany Sam on service calls away from Tel Aviv. They would ride together in the old gray Plymouth for an hour or two to the customer. Once there, Sam would climb up on top of a large commercial refrigerator, on purpose leaving his tools on the floor below. His little helper could then climb up the ladder and hand him the tools he needed. Thus the boy learned the different tools, their purposes, and also about refrigeration and electricity, much as his father had learned while working in the railroad yard in Nantes so many years before.

It was fun for the boy learning all these new things, and after several trips Sam even allowed Ofer to tighten some screws, or add some refrigerant to the system, always under close supervision of course. Afterward, when the job was done, they would hop back in the car and head to another client. In between clients they could stop at some mom-and-pop restaurant for a home cooked meal, thus making the event a father-son outing.

Alas, those outings were the only occasions where father and son really connected. Sam was not much of a sports enthusiast and almost never invited either of his children to a ball game. Although soccer was a favorite sport in the country and seats to games were inexpensive or even free, Sam rarely took the children to a ball game, or any similar activity during Ofer's entire childhood—only when Sam's friends cajoled him to join them and their children did Sam invite Ofer to tag along. Initiating an outing with his children was not in the man's vocabulary, and regrettably nor were concerts, opera, or other cultural events.

Sam was kind to Bella and Ofer, and concerned about them, and always willing to help them when they needed. But he was battling the legacy of his father and the poor parenting example the old man had provided. And while he had a somewhat closer rapport with Bella, he never learned how to relate to either of his children during their childhood years. He loved them, there was no doubt about it, was willing to sacrifice for them, but he did not know how to show them that they were in the center of his world, or close to it.

Part V

THE NEXT
GENERATION

Chapter 38

Time went by and Bella's Bat Mitzvah date was fast approaching so Leah took the challenge on with gusto. She had a lot of work to do: All the preparations for the occasion fell on her shoulders and had to be accomplished within a limited budget too. Bar and Bat Mitzvahs in Israel at the time were "friends and family occasions," without extravaganza or opulence. The guests would congregate at the home of the boy or girl on a Saturday mid-day or early afternoon, enjoy a light lunch, and joyously celebrate the event. No ballrooms, no outings to special venues, no catering, no fanfare. Down to earth and simple joy of getting together and celebrating the transition of a person from child to Jewish adult.

And Bat Mitzvahs were even lower-key affairs than Bar Mitzvahs, basically a glorified birthday party which in turn were very rare, almost nonexistent. Following Orthodox Judaism, which was the only form of Judaism practiced in Israel in 1952, girls did not participate in, let alone lead, the services in the synagogue. The celebration was limited to a gathering, normally on a Saturday afternoon, focused on the friends of the celebrant, without adults except the parents of the celebrant, and those were present only to supervise the group of young teenagers enjoying themselves with some food, games, sweets, and cake.

Leah's sister Ida came to help, primarily providing moral support more than anything else. She was not a renowned chef, not even a good cook, or otherwise especially gifted in any of the normal homemaking crafts. Neither was she terribly organized and disciplined but she could give Leah some opinion or advice here and there, and lend a hand in some menial task. Her makeup was that of a free-spirited artist, having been a classical dancer for quite a few years, dancing in theatres and cabarets all over Europe before WWII, and in the Casino in Haifa until the British left and the Casino closed.

Her other forte was music, and she played piano fairly well although not perfectly. But most of all, her most wonderful attribute was her heart of gold, warm and giving, always ready to help anyone in need. Not having had any children of her own she deeply loved Bella and Ofer, and her only other nephew, Nahum's son, whom she absolutely adored.

So when Bella was having her Bat Mitzvah Ida was there to help. She ran to the grocery store to fetch some missing ingredient in the cooking and baking, washed the pots and pans, watched over the flame on the newly purchased gas cooktop replacing the old kerosene burner, but most importantly she kept Leah company. The two sisters were extremely attached and devoted to each other, very close in their souls, and got along extremely well in every instance, except when one would bring the other some gift.

Gift *giving* was something both enjoyed tremendously, but gift *receiving* was something totally different, and a cause célèbre for a war of the worlds:

"Why did you get me this?" the recipient would ask.

"For your birthday," (or anniversary, or holiday, or ….,) the other would reply.

"Who needs it? Who needs this thing?

"I don't want it! What do I need it for?

"Why did you spend so much money?

"You wasted all this money, and now it will sit in the closet (or wherever) and is of no use to me."

And it would go on and on. To their dying day neither knew how to graciously accept gifts, even the smallest of gifts. But help, assistance, moral support, caring—anything that did not impoverish the other by one broken penny, those were another thing altogether, and always welcome and cherished.

Pessia also came to watch over the preparations, so Bella's Bat Mitzvah afforded the three women, mother and two daughters, the opportunity to busily interact and enjoy each other's company.

Leah hunted around and found some material and sewed a new dress for Bella for the occasion, a cute artistic piece based on her own unique design. Ida and Pessia gathered around Leah sitting at the old manual Singer sewing machine, a machine probably older than Pessia, and gave their advice on how to cut the material and how to sew it, as if Leah did not know how to do that on her own. It became a community affair, a joyous one, with each feeling good about her contribution to the creation.

As was expected, with competent Leah at the helm everything was ready on time, and all of Bella's friends and classmates gathered on the roof that Sabbath afternoon, all dressed in their Sabbath clothes ready to celebrate the occasion. Nothing elaborate by any means, a home-cooked lunch, and games for entertainment; and since September in Tel Aviv could be quite hot and muggy, a lot of soda water and lemonade were on hand for refreshments. Luckily the weather cooperated and it was a sunny comfortable day to be out-doors, and everyone had a marvelous time. Bella and her friends en-joyed themselves, and Sam, who normally stayed away from such events, interrupted his Saturday afternoon nap to come up onto the roof for a few moments to share in the birthday cake and bless his daughter on the occasion of her Bat Mitzvah.

A week later came the High Holidays in quick succession: Rosh Hashanah, Yom Kippur, and Succoth, and when those passed the school year entered into high gear. Bella was now in eighth grade and was preparing to graduate elementary school and head for high school.

Which high school would she attend weighed heavily on her mind. Which high school a student would attend was determined by a combination of two factors: The student's grades, and a demanding entrance exam. While not a straight-A student, Bella's grades were mostly good, B and B+, so it would be up to the entrance exam re-sults to qualify her for the top high school in Tel Aviv at the time, Municipal High School 'A'. That was the school she so badly wanted to attend.

Typical Bella, she dove into preparing for the exam with deter-mination. She wanted so much to prove to herself and to her parents she was worthy, so she studied hard. In the end she felt good about her performance—she knew she had done well in the tests.

How devastated was she when the results came in and she was notified by the detestable homeroom teacher Ms. Finkelbrand, in front of all her classmates, that she had not "made the grade" and would therefore be relegated to a second tier school.

On top of the actual fact of her failure—confirming her feelings of inadequacy—the ugly manner in which the announcement was made was more than the young girl could bear. She kept her composure in school but when she arrived home she broke down into hysterical sobbing. The defeat, the embarrassment, the rejection, the feelings of failure and disappointment, were too much for her to handle. Worse still, she felt she had let her parents down, especially her mother who was normally very critical of her and now could point to yet another event by which the girl supposedly proved herself to be unworthy.

Ever since Bella was born Leah had some resentment toward her, and was not always kind to the girl, her own daughter. Was that because she was not ready to raise a child when she became pregnant with Bella so soon after getting married to Sam, not having had time to establish and enjoy the union with him all by themselves? Or maybe it was the difficulty of the pregnancy combined with the harassment she endured from her father-in-law, harassment leading her to issue an ultimatum to the love of her life? Or maybe because a child, any child, prematurely "clipped her wings" and curtailed her freedom? Whatever the reason, Leah was very hard on her daughter and treated her harshly, always critical and demanding, from the time Bella was a baby on.

And it was not justified by any means. Bella was a model child, never complaining. To the contrary she was very responsible and independent, so responsible in fact that shortly after Ofer was born, Leah felt quite comfortable letting this little girl become his surrogate mother, taking care of the baby and watching over him. She even trusted the little girl with the safety pins used to change the baby's cloth diapers.

So while Leah never abused the child, she was not terribly affectionate toward her, very demanding of perfection, always critical, and not forgiving by any measure.

However, while she herself was harsh on Bella, she would never allow anyone else to mistreat or harm her daughter. She was not the type of mother to sit idly by in the face of her child's deep anguish. Like a tigress she was fiercely protective of her cubs.

Early the very next morning after Bella's humiliating experience in class Leah went to the school and met with the principal.

"There must be some mistake," she told him. "Bella studied so hard for the entrance exam, and came back feeling good about the test."

"I am really sorry for Bella's anguish," he responded sympathetically. "While it would not be the first time a student misjudged the quality of his or her test results, I know Bella, and she is as solid as a rock. Unlike other students she had never complained about a grade being wrong, or her work being misjudged, so I take her complaint seriously.

"I can assure you neither I nor anyone else in the school had anything to do with the scoring and the creation of the list of those who qualified for Municipal High School 'A'."

"I understand," Leah said, although she did not quite believe him.

"It was done solely by the department of education, and not by us. That said, I promise you I will investigate and let you know what I find," the man said.

"How long do you think it will take to find out?" Leah asked.

"It might take some time, probably a week or two. My first step will be to find out who handled the results, and then file a protest and have them go through all the test results and investigate Bella's particular test to make sure she was treated fairly in the scoring."

"I am not asking you to do anything more than your best. The girl is devastated, especially since all her close friends from this school are on the list, and for once I feel she did well on the test and deserves to join them."

"I will do my best, I will," he promised.

He did not get back directly to Leah or Sam, but two weeks later a letter arrived from the ministry of education. It was cryptic saying:

"Our investigation of the test scores of your daughter Bella shows her grade was inadvertently mixed up with that of another student with a similar name. With the error corrected she has been placed on the list of students qualified for attendance at Municipal High School 'A' next year.

We regret this error and wish her success in her future."

What a relief it was for Bella! What a vindication! She was not as dumb as her homeroom teacher had tried to portray her on every occasion all these years!

Not two weeks later, and one week before the end of the school year, the homeroom teacher beckoned Bella to approach her desk.

"You know, Bella, you are not going to Municipal High School 'A' after all." She said gleefully.

"What do you mean?" Bella was shocked.

"We had to add a more deserving student to the list, so you were taken off."

"You can't do that! You have no right," Bella was angry, and the gloves came off. "I don't know why, but all these years you have been coming after me for anything you could, trying to hurt me in any way possible, but I won't let you do that this time. I will not allow you to do that."

And with that she stormed out of the room.

A few minutes later she was home, and her mother heard the news.

"For five years my homeroom teacher Ms. Finkelbrand has been coming after me," Bella sobbed. "I don't know why she hates me so much. She has been insulting me and embarrassing me in front of the class at every opportunity she had."

"Why didn't you tell me about it all this time?"

"I didn't want to bother you with it. I didn't tell you or father about it because you have a lot of other issues to deal with, but now this horrible woman is trying to cause me real harm by not letting me go to the same high school with all my friends who are going to that school."

Within a blink of an eye Leah was out the door on the way back to school, with Bella in tow.

"What is going on here?" she burst into the principal's office. "I demand to know what is going on here, and why this horrible mean woman is after my daughter. This is unacceptable, and will not be tolerated any longer."

"What happened, Mrs. Gielan?" the shocked principal asked.

"I just found out that for the past five years this old spinster has been tormenting Bella, going after her in a most vicious way. But despite all her efforts she has not broken the girl's spirit. Bella took it on the chin all these years and never even complained to me about it."

"This time it is different," Leah was furious and it showed. "This time she is trying to harm my daughter and her future, and I will not allow that to happen."

She told him what Ms. Finkelbrand had done, removing Bella from the list to insert another student who did not previously qualify.

"She cannot do that," the principal said quietly. He was clearly trying to defuse the situation. "She doesn't have the authority, and you can ignore her. Bella will be going to Municipal High School 'A' with all her friends. You have my word for it."

And he kept his word. To the great delight of Leah and Sam, Bella was admitted to the best high school in Tel Aviv. It was a tremendous honor to be a student at that school, and finally Bella could believe she deserved the credit—she had worked so hard to achieve it.

The teachers at that particular school were renowned university professors who immigrated to Palestine, or later Israel, and despite their credentials could not find a seat on a university faculty—there were simply not enough universities to accommodate all these superb professors, so they taught high school instead. Municipal high school "A" was the primary repository for all these fabulous teachers in Tel Aviv. The discipline was uncompromised, students wore blue school uniforms, strict attendance was enforced, and teachers were held in awe and treated with respect. All in all, it was an institute of academic excellence.

For a long while Bella did not recognize the tremendous achievement of being selected to attend the school—280 teenagers, the best and brightest of the entire Tel Aviv metropolitan area were chosen, without regard to the parents' station in life, income, or "connections." Despite being crowded into classes of forty-plus students each, thanks to the unwavering discipline, the quality of instruction was kept at very high standards. Thus that school produced the next leadership of the country in every field, from science to the humanities, from arts to finance, every conceivable profession except, interestingly enough, politics.

So although Bella intellectually understood the significance of her being among the select few, emotionally she did not translate it to: "I deserve it, I am bright, worked hard for it, and earned this trophy." From her early days of the Rex incident, followed by years of uncompromising treatment by her mother which her father was not aware of, and culminating in nearly five years of abusive dislike by her homeroom teacher, Bella's self-confidence and self-worth were seriously impacted.

Leah and Sam were just not very attuned to the psychological makeup and needs of their children. They had everyday worries of survival to contend with, and it was hard enough to provide for the physical needs of their children—shelter, and food, and clothing, and safety. And while they knew about Bella's lack of self-confidence they did not seize the golden opportunity to help her overcome her insecurities. They did not stress to Bella the tremendous recognition she received due to her own achievements, being accepted to the most demanding and prestigious high school in the country, and the great honor and trust the department of education placed in her and her ability to thrive in that environment. So while her physical comfort was assured in the home, she did not receive the moral support and encouragement all children need.

To the contrary, some years later when Ofer was in high school too, they sometimes compared her unfavorably to Ofer who was spending his afternoons gazing out the window rather than studying as he should have been, and his school grades were slipping.

"If you would just study as hard as Bella does, you could make all A's," they admonished him on numerous occasions, even while Bella was within earshot. Bella was really studying hard yet her grades were still more in the 'B' domain—the girl had always had difficulties taking exams. Leah and Sam were trying to encourage Ofer to address his studies more seriously, but what Bella heard instead was she was not as smart and bright as her younger sibling.

Bella's departure from the elementary school they had attended together was a tremendous loss for Ofer. He liked to be near her, felt safe with her around, and her classmates always treated him with affection and kindness—they were a nice and friendly group. On top of that, entering seventh grade he "inherited" Bella's homeroom teacher, that mean and nasty old woman who had tormented Bella when she was her student, and now decided to go after him instead.

Fortunately for Ofer he did not have to suffer long. Just about that time, Leah and Sam put every penny they had, money Leah had saved over the years with tremendous difficulty, as a down payment on an apartment. They moved to a nicer building a bit further north in Tel Aviv, more of a residential neighborhood and away from the noise of a main street. Shortly after the move Ofer transferred to the local neighborhood school, and he did not have to endure the wrath of Ms. Finkelbrand anymore.

And anyway, within the month, Ms. Finkelbrand was relieved of her duties as a teacher of that school.

Chapter 39

Ofer's new school, a mere block and a half away from the new home, was a true school building and not an old converted apartment building like the previous one was, and it even had a nice playground for the students. All in all, it was a much better environment, although from an academic point of view not any less demanding than its predecessor. Both schools made no distinction between the sexes: all students attended classes in woodworking and metal shop, as well as sewing, needlepoint, and knitting. Everyone was required to complete the same identical strenuous academic program; no elective easy-grade courses, or other "light weight" studies.

The family's new apartment was also on the fourth floor, a few blocks further than the sea, this time facing west toward the Mediterranean, and that made the apartment much cooler than the old one. The breeze coming off the sea was always welcome in the summer evenings after a hot day, and the balcony was often used to entertain friends who would drop by for a cup of coffee—unannounced of course, as was the custom.

Every day when the children arrived home from school Leah was there to greet them. Whenever Sam was in town and not on a service call he, too, came home for lunch. Since schools did not offer lunch the family had their midday meal together.

Life in Israel in those days was quite informal. Leah and Sam had a phone, but not many other people did—so few in fact, that Leah and Sam's phone number consisted of only four digits! Only 9,990 phones in the entire Tel Aviv metropolitan area, and Sam was lucky to qualify for one, while other people had to wait months or longer to be connected to the antiquated system. There was no television so people socialized more, visiting each other after dinner, and, typical of southern Mediterranean countries, that meant after nine o'clock. Having dinner in a restaurant was uncommon, and bars and nightclubs were few and far between, patronized mostly by foreign visitors. Alcohol was not a great attraction for adults, let alone teenagers, and drug addiction was practically unheard of except for very few hashish smokers in the narrow streets of old Jaffa. All in all, a wholesome healthy life—that was the environment in which Leah and Sam raised their children. The children were free to roam the city in utmost safety, roller skate or ride the single bicycle they shared. They spent their afternoons and summers visiting friends or attending after-school activities that mostly did not require parents' supervision or attention, and they stayed out of trouble. Their most mischievous prank was pulling a fake home-made snake across the path of people walking on the sidewalk, watching their reaction and giggling if anyone was ever startled by it.

As part of the high school curriculum, every student in Israel was required to take part in the Gadnah, or Youth Brigades. Being that the threat to Israel was constant from the surrounding hostile governments—always inciting their populations against the Jewish State, promising to annihilate it at the first opportunity, and sending terrorist infiltrators into Jewish communities to cause mayhem and bloodshed—the population in Israel was taught ways by which they could defend themselves should the need arise. Thus, these Youth Brigades offered the high school students a platform for paramilitary training. During an hour or two a week, added to the school day, the students were taught basic skills in hand-to-hand combat, similar training to what their parents' generation received during the Haganah days: How to defend oneself with a bitter orange tree branch made into a fighting stick, how to shoot a rifle, a little bit of Judo, and other courses as the time allowed.

And in the afternoons, as extracurricular activities, students could join one of the "professional" groups of the Gadnah and receive training in aeronautics, naval studies, sharpshooting, scouting, and more.

Finally, each school year the students were required to spend two weeks of National Service in a kibbutz acting as extra hands during harvest season. In the winter months it might be picking tomatoes in Ein Gedi near the Dead Sea, and during the summer it might be picking fruit in Manara in the northern Galilee. Other times it might be milking sheep at Harel on the way to Jerusalem. Wherever there was a need, that's where these youngsters were sent to. That, in addition to some two- or three-day hiking trips around the countryside at least once a year. So by the time high school was over the students had been exposed to more than just the intense academic classroom and homework experiences.

All this in addition to the extremely rigorous and demanding school schedule. In high school Bella attended a six-day school week: Sunday through Thursday she had classes from 8 a.m. to 2:30 p.m. and 8 a.m. to 1 p.m. on Fridays. Classes were fifty minutes each with a ten-minute break in between, with only a half hour break mid-morning, and since no lunch was served in the school there was no lunch break either. A very demanding and grueling schedule for teenagers.

Since Ofer was still in grade school his schedule was somewhat less hectic, with six days a week classes from 8 a.m. to 1 p.m. with the same mid-morning break. So every day when Ofer arrived home, and while waiting for Bella to return from her school, he tended to his homework. Sam normally also arrived around the same time, and took a nap until Bella returned from school, then they all had a family lunch after which he returned to his work while the younger generation was free to do their homework or go out and meet their neighborhood friends or undertake their extracurricular activities.

Before too long Ofer's Bar Mitzvah was approaching, and Sam assumed the role of teacher/Rabbi in earnest. Relying on his years of religious studies at the yeshiva in Riga and Ofer's Bible and Hebrew studies in school, Sam was able to teach the boy the prayers and blessings and prepare him for his part in the service. And when the day arrived, Ofer was more than ready, at least insofar as the services were concerned, to step into Jewish adulthood. From all other aspects he was still a boy of thirteen, with all the trappings of that age.

The service was almost identical to Sam's own Bar Mitzvah in Riga so many years earlier. Tradition ruled: The same structure, format, and procedure, the same prayers and service, albeit in a better pronounced Hebrew. Like father like son, this time too the Bar Mitzvah boy did not disappoint his teacher and performed his portion of the service extremely well to the delight of his family and friends. Then the smaller crowd of well-wishers came to the house for a short celebration over a buffet lunch.

Soon Passover arrived, and with it the traditional Seder at Pessia's home. Everybody, every member of the family was there, each arriving with their own Passover dishes and table settings because Pessia did not have a service for thirty-two or so. The dining room table was extended into the adjacent living room, then extended again into the hallway, and soon there was space enough for everyone to participate in the joyous occasion. There were quite a few youngsters lending their voices to the singing of the traditional melodies for the text of the Haggadah.

By the time services were over, the last piece of the *Afikoman* consumed, the table cleared and the house restored to its normal state, it was quite late and everyone was exhausted. So no wonder when Sam woke Ofer up the next morning to go to the synagogue with him for prayers, the boy, now young man, rebelled.

"I don't want to go to the synagogue," sleepy Ofer said.

"Wake up, get dressed, and come with me," was Sam's stern reply. He was not letting the boy off the hook.

"I don't want to. I don't care for it."

"I am not interested in your commentary." Sam was relentless. "You will come with me. Now get up."

Reluctantly but obediently the boy rose from his bed, washed up and put on his Sabbath clothes. He grabbed a piece of Matzah with some jelly on it, and hurriedly wolfed it down with some milk.

On the way to the synagogue he was still smarting about being forced to attend services. He repeated his assertion, now even more forcefully, that he does not want to go to synagogue with his father anymore.

"I am not interested in religion," he stated. "I had my Bar Mitzvah, and now I am considered a Jewish adult, and I don't care to spend my free days in the synagogue."

"Listen to me, young man," Sam was gently forceful, not overbearing. "I know you are not interested in it, and would rather spend the time sleeping till afternoon and then going visiting with your friends. I understand. I was a boy your age once too, and felt the same way you do." He paused.

"You are only 13, and know very little about the religion and the philosophy behind it."

"I know quite a bit and am not interested in it." Ofer objected.

Sam looked at him for a moment.

"When I was your age I was already attending the yeshiva, and knew a lot more than you do now, but even then I did not know much. I kept going with my father for services every Friday night and every Saturday morning and evening. I am not asking you to spend your weekends in the synagogue, Ofer. I am not asking you to go except to accompany me when I go, which is only on holidays."

"But I really don't want to go, I don't care for religion," Ofer continued to argue.

"When you reach 18 and will be on your own, you can make your own decision whether you want to follow the religion or not, and if so, how closely. I can't and won't force you to follow in my footsteps, or anyone else's for that matter. It will be your decision to make, yours alone. But it is my responsibility to make sure that when that time comes for you to make the decision, you will make it based on knowledge, and not ignorance.

"Until then you will join me to the synagogue, and I will teach you as much as I can so that you will make your decision based on knowledge, not ignorance."

He won the argument by decree.

❖ ❖ ❖

Only a few months later Ofer graduated from elementary school and, to the relief of his parents, he followed in Bella's footsteps and was admitted to the same high caliber municipal high school she attended. Once again the siblings studied in the same school and could keep a watchful eye on each other.

Beyond the obvious, attending the same school had some other benefits for the children: Firstly, they knew the same teachers and could share stories, anecdotes, and gossip about them, and events at the school. Secondly, on most mornings Sam could drop the children off at school on his way to work, saving them a lengthy ride in a city bus with many stops, not to mention the bus fare as well. Whenever possible, they also waited for each other after school was out, and rode home together in that lengthy public bus route, although when their schedules were different they made their way home separately.

All was going well for a while. But then, within a few weeks of the start of the school year, world events took center stage and once again the existence of the State of Israel and its citizens was put in jeopardy.

❖ ❖ ❖

A few months earlier, in July 1956, in violation of international treaties, the Egyptian President Gamal Abdel Nasser had nationalized the Suez Canal and closed the straits of Tiran at the southernmost tip of the Red Sea, disrupting world shipping through the canal and choking off Israel's access to the Far East. While this was an expensive nuisance to European trade with India and Japan, forcing their shipping to go around the Horn of Africa, for the Jewish State it was a devastating blow, sealing off the use of Eilat as a viable port. Both Israel and Europe were not going to let it stand, and the winds of war were once again blowing over the region.

Very quietly in September 1956, Israel started mobilizing the reserves. There were no announcements, no calls to arms. It was done extremely discreetly, but over a period of a few weeks, eerily people started disappearing from the streets of the cities, noticeably so.

Sam knew something was brewing because some of his acquaintances and friends were called out of their homes in the middle of the night, but to his chagrin no one came for him. The government even conscripted Coldomat's Jeep, a 4-wheel-drive vehicle so much in demand by the army, but did not ask Sam, a former captain in the Israeli Air Force, still young at 46, to take part in defending the country in the inevitable upcoming hostilities.

Sam was not called up for reserve duty, not recruited for service of any kind, and he was very distraught about it. He felt rejected, useless, an excess vintage technical officer, former captain in the air force, now discarded. Surely he understood that during the seven years since he had left the Israeli Air Force it had undergone an incredible transformation: What had been then a ragtag collection of misfit aircrafts, all propeller driven, mostly civilian ones of different make and origin, had been replaced by French and British jet fighter planes—since the United States' embargo of military equipment against Israel was still in full force, the Israeli Air Force had to seek airplanes from other sources. France offered Israel their Dassault Ouragan fighter jets and Fouga Magister training planes, to augment the British made Gloster Meteor which Israel had acquired some time earlier. They all were substantially inferior to the top of the line planes supplied to Egypt by the Soviet Union, but were the only planes Israel could get.

Sam realized that had he stayed in the air force these past seven years and not turned down Shimon's offer to undertake the role of chief technical officer, the combination of his technical knowledge and absolute command of French could have been so instrumental in the discussions and negotiations with France. Alas, he had made the decision then and had to live with the consequences.

It was not the first time nor probably the last time he felt the pangs of regret for not remaining in the military. It would have been so exciting to stay with the mission of forming a first-class air force, and he actually did enjoy the discipline and structure of military life. Was his sacrifice really necessary? Was it truly a sacrifice that he made for his family, or was there some other reason why he turned the position down? His doubts as to the wisdom of his choice returned, yet he never voiced them to anyone, Leah included, and possibly himself as well.

By mid-October, war was no longer in doubt, and if it were to happen, it would happen soon—Israel could not sustain having its entire productive workforce taken out of the economy for long. Practically every able-bodied man from 20 to 50 years of age had been taken away from their normal occupation, fitted with the uniform and equipment of a fighting force, and sent out to sit and wait should hostilities begin. In addition, the resource-poor Israeli Defense Forces had to "borrow" vehicles to transport these reservists and their supplies, feed the units and tend to their needs, all bearing a heavy toll on the coffers of the country.

The civilian population was preparing for the almost certainty of suffering heavy casualties. It was anticipated that the Soviet-equipped and-trained Egyptian Air Force which had been supplied with the best front-line Mig 15 fighter jets and Ilyushin Il-28 bombers would inflict heavy casualties on the civilian population, just as they had tried to do eight years earlier when they bombed and strafed the open defenseless cities of Tel Aviv and Haifa. And although the air defense system had since been upgraded, and relied on Radar installations rather than rooftop observers, it still was quite ineffective against a first-rate air force. That, of course, unless the Israeli Air Force could divert some of its meager resources to defend the cities at the cost of protecting the ground troops embroiled in the fighting.

One bright October morning all the students of Municipal High School 'A' were summoned to an assembly on the school grounds. The bald-headed heavy-set school master addressed the assembly.

"As you know, once again we are facing the possibility of a war," He said. "The Egyptians President Nasser, with the help of his Soviet ally, are taunting the western world. He nationalized the Suez Canal, making it difficult for the Europeans to continue trading with the Far East.

"For us, he closed the straits of Tiran and promised to sink any ship coming from Eilat through there. We cannot allow him to do that, because Eilat is a very important port for us and we do not have many other ports to use.

"He also poured a large military force into the Sinai, threatening to cut Israel in half, and take the Negev. He always wanted to create a land bridge to Jordan and Saudi Arabia, and that would accomplish that.

"So war is almost inevitable, and soon.

"We do not have an air raid shelter in the school, definitely not for all 1,200 of you plus your teachers. We do not want to close the school, because we don't know when the war will start, and how long it will last, so we decided to dig trenches in the yard for protection.

"You will be given shovels, and we will dig trenches all around the school yard, and use the sand and fill sandbags to put in front of the windows for protection. Your homeroom teachers will tell you where and how to dig."

Preparations for possible carnage.

Students and teachers dug the trenches and filled the sand bags. In the empty field beyond the school grounds heavy tractors were digging a large hole in the ground to serve as a mass grave for anticipated bombing casualties. In that section of Tel Aviv alone the projected estimate was 50,000 dead.

But then, when the Sinai Campaign began on October 29, 1956 the hard work and investment of the population, and its well-wishers from abroad, paid off. That wonderful, modernized, disciplined Israeli Air Force prevented the anticipated carnage, and not a single Egyptian plane landed a single blow on Tel Aviv or any other city.

Israel dealt a quick and decisive defeat to the Egyptians. Following good military principles, the IDF brought the battle to Egyptian territory, into the Sinai, and away from Israeli civilian centers. Despite its inferiority in both number and quality of equipment the air force attacked and decimated the Egyptian Air Force and followed it by hammering the Egyptian ground forces. Within eight days the Israeli Army took over the Gaza Strip, occupied all of the Sinai, and reopened the Straits of Tiran.

Seeing Israel's unqualified success, British and French forces invaded Egypt proper and were equally successful in reopening the Suez Canal.

Unfortunately, the misguided United States State Department convinced President Dwight D. Eisenhower to intervene, or better still interfere, and force a premature ceasefire which kept the Egyptian President Nasser in power. By his own admission Nasser was twenty-four hours away of resigning his presidency, and Eisenhower's actions gave him a reprieve and he stayed in power, and his Soviet benefactors maintained their supremacy and influence in the region.

One hundred twenty days later, Eisenhower added insult to injury, and under threat of sanctions forced Israel to retreat and return the entire expanse of the Sinai Peninsula, an excellent buffer zone, to Egyptian rule, with nothing in return. Nasser's only "punishment" for his belligerence was his agreement to allow a small lightly armed United Nations peace keeping force in the Sinai. In essence Eisenhower handed Nasser a gift for his aggression, rewarding him for his bad behavior, and resulting in continuous mayhem and turmoil in the Middle East for years to come. A golden opportunity to crush Soviet influence in the Middle East was squandered, Nasser retained his power, and being emboldened by the U.S. actions, did not feel the need to negotiate peace with the Jewish State.

What a colossal blunder.

Chapter 40

With the 1956 Sinai Campaign over, things were getting noticeably better all around, both for the family, and the country as a whole. The economic climate was slowly but surely improving. The Israeli currency was stabilizing somewhat, and that translated to better times at Coldomat as well. Customer loyalty was rising and, by word of mouth and through referrals, the client base was growing. The business was making more money—not much more, but in a more consistent way. Gone were the days when Sam would come home on a Friday with empty or nearly empty pockets. The old '37 Plymouth was replaced by a '52 Dodge, the Jeep was restored after the war and returned to service, and one more vehicle was purchased for use by the technicians who responded to service calls outside of Tel Aviv.

The only "fly in the ointment" was Sam's pain in the calves of both legs. Mildly at first, but with increased frequency and intensity as time progressed, Sam was having difficulty walking either fast or long distances. On those occasions when Leah and he went strolling on the promenade by the beach, near where they had first met, he would find an excuse to stop from time to time and pretend to be looking at one thing or another, faking it, trying to not alarm Leah who was always concerned about his health.

But Leah was no fool and very observant, and after a while she challenged him, and he finally told her about the pain in his legs.

"Go see Doctor Landau," she suggested.

"It is not bad enough to go see a doctor," he retorted, "and anyway it will probably go away after a while. I have flat feet, and that causes the calf muscle pain, but there is nothing they can do for that."

She decided not to argue, and dropped the subject for the time being.

Seeing Dr. Landau was not a difficult task. You did not need an appointment, you walked into his office anytime, day or night, and he would see you mostly right away—that was the type of doctor that he was. It was not expensive either, Dr. Landau charged the equivalent of a couple of dollars, and if you could not pay even that, then he would see you for free. "I charge only what I need," he used to say. "Why take the money from the people to give it to income tax? Better let the people keep their money."

But for some reason Sam refused to go.

Was it that he was afraid of bad news, or was it just part of his male "macho" psychological makeup to avoid doctors? He suffered in silence for some time longer, but the pain did not abate.

Leah noticed the deteriorating condition. By then he could barely walk a city block without finding an excuse to stop and gaze into a shop's window pretending he was interested in the merchandise, or worse, find a bench to sit on, to "observe the people passing by." Her concern could not be dismissed any longer, and she pestered Sam repeatedly to go see Dr. Landau.

"What does he know?" Sam retorted, defensively. "He is very old, and probably not up to date on all the medical advancements. He does not read English and most new medical developments are published in American trade journals."

Leah gave him a disgruntled look. All of a sudden Sam had become an expert in medical technology publications? She would have none of that.

"I don't know why you refuse, but if you don't want to see Doctor Landau, then go see some other doctor. But do go," she insisted.

"All right, I will go," he promised, and he finally did. Through some referral he found a medical clinic that claimed to specialize in treating leg pains, and went to have them check him over.

After several visits and some tests and examinations, they concluded that it was not Sam's flat feet that were causing him discomfort. Their diagnosis was that he had blockage in his blood vessels in both legs causing him the pain and impairment in walking. Their recommendation was for him to undergo this "special treatment over an extended period of time, using their super sophisticated and advanced massage machine designed specifically for conditions such as this."

For several-months-turned-into-a-year Sam went to the clinic twice a week to undergo treatment with this "revolutionary" special machine, costing a king's ransom. In addition, they prescribed him some medication that made him drowsy, and impaired his level of alertness and ability to concentrate.

Leah who was increasingly worried by his deteriorating condition continued insisting that he go see Doctor Landau.

Doctor Landau, an orthopedic surgeon, had been a medical officer in the Kaiser Wilhelm's army during World War I. He must have been born in 1888 at the latest to have been past medical school already by 1914, so in 1958 he was already in his mid-70s at least. A bachelor, never having been married, he escaped the Nazis during WWII into Switzerland and somehow made his way to Palestine where he went into private practice as a general practitioner. His office was the room at the end of the long hallway in his ground-floor apartment on one of the main streets of Tel Aviv.

Despite his advanced age Dr. Landau was in good physical shape and sharp of mind. In all the years Leah and Sam and all their friends were treated by the good doctor, his diagnoses were always crisp and accurate, and his treatments very effective. He even made house calls, riding his bicycle to his patients when they could not come to his home office, as he had done when Sam had those burns on his legs.

He never minced words, told people the unadulterated truth, in a blunt fashion so typical of this no-nonsense man who had seen real misery during his military service in WW I. One time when Leah's friend Mira came to him with some aches and pains, something she did fairly frequently, he got exasperated by her complaints.

"*Ja, ja,*" he told her in a dismissive tone. "*Das is gar nichts.* This is nothing. Why don't you ever come to see me with a *substantial* disease?"

So when Sam finally made it to see Doctor Landau, the doctor was sitting in his office behind his big desk. He watched Sam walk down the long corridor to his office.

"*Ja, ja,*" he greeted Sam in German even before Sam could open his mouth to say 'Hello.' "You have intermittent claudication of your arteries in both legs."

"How did you know?" Sam was stunned.

Dr. Landau looked at him quizzically, as if saying "Why are you asking me this stupid question?"

Instead he said, "You give me five minutes, and I will tell you exactly where in your legs your veins are clogged."

He rose from his chair and came around the desk, motioning to Sam to sit on a chair by the wall. He told Sam to raise the right pant leg to the knee, and put his stethoscope in various places around the leg. He listened intently to the sound of the blood flowing through the arteries.

Within two minutes he located the spot on the right leg, then took two more minutes to do the same in the left leg. No special machines, nothing but his stethoscope, his ear, and so many years of experience.

He then rose to his feet and went back around the desk.

"Listen, Sam," he said in German. "You have blockages in both legs, and they are severe and serious."

He paused for a moment, observing Sam's expression of bewilderment: In less than five minutes the doctor told him what the other guys took months to diagnose.

Noticing Sam's skepticism but not knowing the background he continued: "If you don't trust me, then you can go to one of those fancy clinics that claim to specialize in this, pay them a king's ransom for their fancy machines, and medications, but nothing is going to help."

Sam was not ready to admit to having done just that, being fleeced by those "experts" for the past year.

"I can prescribe you some medication that might help the pain, but it won't cure your arteries. The blockage is too long, and an operation is not worth the risk."

Then Doctor Landau delivered the coup de grace. "Listen to me carefully," he said in a very serious tone. "If you do not stop smoking we will chop off one leg, and then the other."

He said it just that bluntly, that forcefully, that harshly. He used the crudest way to describe it. He did not say "amputate" or "remove," he did not couch it by "you will lose..." He said "chop off," and that was as unambiguous as it could get.

Sam sat motionless for a moment, absorbing what he had just heard while the doctor scribbled something on his prescription pad.

"Thank you doctor," Sam finally said rising to his feet. He pulled a couple of bills out of his wallet and placed them on the doctor's desk and picked up the prescription. Then he reached into his other pocket, pulled out a pack of cigarettes and a lighter, put them on the side table, and walked out.

He never smoked another cigarette in his life.

Chapter 41

Bella graduated high school with solid grades, and after a brief delay of a few weeks headed into the Israeli army. Every girl at 18 was required to perform a two-year compulsory service stint in the Israeli Defense Forces, the IDF, unless she received one of three dispensations: Rooted in the political blackmail by the religious parties in the coalition government she could be released from the obligation if she declared that she was Ultraorthodox, or she could get married and thus receive an honorable discharge, or she could get a deferment by being admitted to a university for undergraduate studies and join the equivalent of the ROTC which meant that she would be studying during the year, do military service during the summer recess, and then have to commit to remain in the service for four years rather than the required two, but commissioned as an officer.

Bella decided against all three options. She was determined to honorably perform her compulsory military service and then pursue her education, in that order.

She spent two months at boot camp where the recruits, who were gathered from all walks of life and all corners of Israel, with various backgrounds, were brought into strict and unified discipline. During those initial two months they were taught basic fighting skills including weapons handling, infantry tactics, and some first aid, along with undergoing strenuous physical training, thus bringing everyone into shape and into the cohesive structure of a military unit. But most importantly, during those months at boot camp the young recruits, and this applied to male as well as female recruits, learned for the first time to be independent of their parental home, make their own decisions albeit while being supervised, cope with harsh and difficult circumstances, and mostly grow up in a hurry—no organization is as powerfully effective as the military in getting young teenagers become self-sufficient adults in no time whatsoever.

During those months of boot camp the army also observed the recruits' character and behavior. While being pushed to the limits of their endurance, the recruits were tested, both physically and psychologically, and their strengths and weaknesses were determined. Using these results the IDF then decided where they would serve the country best, in which unit and in what capacity they would be most effective for the duration of their service. Once basic training was over the recruits would then receive additional training specific to the military profession assigned to them by the IDF.

Bella was assigned the role of analyst in the psychology department of the IDF, helping evaluate recruits and their capabilities. At least initially, she was to grade the various multiple-choice tests that recruits had taken during their induction period, a function nowadays performed by machines—a very boring and mind-numbing but necessary task.

She was stationed in a camp on the outskirts of Tel Aviv, within a free half-hour bus ride from home, and thus could come home almost every night, except when it was her turn to be on guard duty or if some emergency arose.

Sam was very proud of his daughter serving in the army. For him it was far beyond her contributing to the country. Through her he was observing how mature the country was becoming, and while in civilian life corruption of all sorts still existed, and not everyone shared his fierce fervor for the country, the IDF was considered as clean, moral, and efficient a military organization as any in the world.

Leah also appreciated Bella's activities in the military and was also gratified that Bella was taking her task, albeit mundane, in earnest. As always the girl was trying to do her best, and God forbid that she should embarrass her parents by not performing her duties perfectly. Not that Bella was a perfectionist, but her mother, Rex, and Ms. Finkelbrand were always in the background of her psyche, making her complete each and every task that she undertook with tenacity and dedication, resulting in a job extremely well-done.

Before long, her chain of command in the IDF recognized her solid performance, and as soon as possible they reassigned her to a different more substantial role within the same unit. This time she was trained as a vocational analyst, assessing military personnel under stressful circumstances, and exploring ways by which their effectiveness could be increased under adverse conditions. Rising in rank to Sargent she became a true member of the psychology department—

guided by professional psychologists and sociologists she was sent to different and diverse environments to view and assess the requirements of specific professions within the military, and the ways by which individuals should be tested, qualified, and trained for those military vocations. From pilots to submariners, from artillery to armor, from Delta Force troops to infantry, she would join a unit during training exercises, and document the conditions and stresses, physical as well as psychological, that these military personnel were subjected to, in order to help select and prepare those troops better for their military responsibilities.

This job offered Bella a rich and exciting venue from which to observe the various military professions, and it guided her toward an area that she was keen on—the psychology of individuals, and what made them tick. In essence it inadvertently propelled her toward her eventual professional life as a clinical psychologist.

Sam and Leah encouraged Bella to spend dinnertime with them and tell them about her experiences and the things she observed—without revealing any military secrets of course. She could not tell them, for example, the physical locations she visited. When she had to spend time in a submarine, she could not tell them where the submarine traveled, or how deep it dove, or any specifics about the crew, but she could relate some general observations, knowing full well that nothing she ever told them would be repeated outside their dining room.

For Sam and Leah, it was extremely heartwarming to learn how far the IDF had progressed since the days that they themselves were involved in the security of the country, during the Haganah and the War of Independence. From being a militia staffed by civilians, in less than ten years it had become a top-notch disciplined military force, second to none, and they were proud that their daughter, and soon also their son, were part of its heritage.

Chapter 42

The phone rang in the middle of the night. Even before Sam's head was raised from the pillow he was wide awake and quickly walked over to the hallway telephone.

Sam's older sister Tanya was on the other end, frantic.

"Mulya, I have to leave the United States, and quickly," she said.

"I see. What happened?"

"I worked out a plea bargain with the prosecutors, and the judge accepted it just now. I am free but I have certain conditions to meet and I don't have much time to deal with them." She paused for a minute. "I am calling you from my friend Tilly's house. I can't call you from home, my phone is tapped, and I think the mail I receive is being intercepted also, so be discreet. If I don't want to be on the street or in jail, I have to quickly set my affairs in order and leave the country."

"Where are you planning to go?"

"I want to go to Israel. I thought a lot about it and that would be the best. I can explain later. Right now I need for you to come here and help me with the arrangements. You can tell me what to take from here, and what to dispose of."

"I see."

"Can you please come as soon as possible?"

"Sure, as soon as I can get a visa to the United States. I have no idea how long that will take, but I read in the papers that the American embassy is giving people a lot of trouble to obtain a visa. For how long should I ask?"

"I think that it will take a month to make all the arrangements. I will need to ship some of my belongings, which means packing, dealing with international shippers or freight forwarders and creating a shipment. I also will need to furnish a home in Israel, so I will need Leah to help me with selecting the décor."

"I will start on the visa for both of us first thing in the morning. Our passports are current so that is no problem. I don't know if I can be absent from work for a whole month, but I will do my best, and I am sure Leah will be able to stay there as long as is required."

"That is great, I really appreciate it. When I know that you have the visas I'll get you the tickets."

"That will be fine."

"I will call you again in a week or so. What time is it there?"

"Midnight."

"It is 5 p.m. here, so it is a seven hour difference. I will call you earlier next time."

"Sounds good."

She hung up. He put the handset on the cradle. Leah was standing right by him.

"It was Tanya," he said.

"Yeah, I understood that. What did she say?"

"She needs us to come to the United States and help her immigrate to Israel."

"I see."

Sam described Tanya's part of the conversation, the part that Leah could not hear. Leah listened without interrupting.

"At least it seems that there is a resolution to the problem. It sure had been long enough, and I am glad for her that it is over," Leah said.

"It won't be over until she is out of the United States, I think."

"You go to work as usual tomorrow. I will go to the American embassy and get the visa applications."

It was an ordeal that started several years earlier when Tanya, a successful obstetrician and gynecologist in New York was swept up in a sting operation, as a doctor willing to perform an abortion for an undercover police woman. At the time, abortions were illegal in the State of New York and in a politically charged environment Tanya was arrested and charged with a felony, with tremendous publicity of a "famous NY doctor caught…" and her picture plastered on the front page of *The New York Times*.

Over time it became obvious that her arrest had been more of a public exhibition motivated by the political aspirations of an over-zealous district attorney, and that the testimony of the police woman alone was not enough to convict her of the charge. The DA could file other charges, but by that time his incentive was gone—he had been reelected and was no longer seeking the publicity, so he negotiated a plea bargain with Tanya's attorneys.

In a subsequent letter to Sam Tanya explained that she had been ready to retire anyway for some time, so when the DA offered her to plead guilty to a lesser misdemeanor charge and agree to surrender her medical license and never practice medicine in the United States again, it was not a difficult decision for her to make—she had other activities she was eager to pursue. She could easily also sustain the fine, thus avoiding a showcase trial and possible jail time. This settlement gave her peace of mind and also the return of her passport that had been confiscated to avoid her fleeing the country before conclusion of the case.

"Now I find that the case is actually not concluded. Since they were unable to throw me in jail for the alleged crime, the Internal Revenue Service is after me for supposed tax evasion, which is not true," she wrote in a letter following their phone call.

"I know that they are pursuing some action, and it won't be long before they come for me again. That is why I need to do whatever I need to do, quickly. My lawyer tells me that once I am out of the country, they will not pursue me, and leave me alone. I have some money in a Swiss bank account, money that will last me for quite a few years in comfort, and if I move fast and sell this townhouse I can probably get that money out of the country as well.

"That is why I hope you can get the visa quickly and come and give me a hand. I have put the townhouse on the market already, and will rent it back until it is time to leave."

Less than a month later Leah and Sam received their visas and headed to New York. What helped expedite the process was the fact that they were leaving their children behind—Bella in the army and Ofer in high school—hence were not a risk of coming to the United States for a never-ending visit as others had done.

Ofer took over as the homemaker. Coming home from school early afternoons he would do the grocery shopping, and prepare dinner for Bella and himself, and enjoyed her companionship.

A week after their departure two of Leah's girlfriends came visiting, primarily to check up on their friend's children. They wanted to make sure that the children survived well in the absence of their mother, the homemaker, and had food in the house. Instead, they were received with coffee and cake that Ofer had baked for the occasion, assuring them that the household was being run well. Two weeks later Sam returned, leaving Leah in New York to help Tanya with her final purchases, and he too was impressed by how smoothly the house was running in his wife's absence. She had taught the children well, he concluded.

Leah arrived a few weeks later. She flew together with Tanya via London where Tanya's daughter Beata was living at the time. Tanya remained in England for a few weeks while Leah continued on her way back home.

But Leah's work in helping Tanya settle was by no means done, and in her wildest dreams Leah could not imagine how this experience helping Tanya settle in the country will become an invaluable asset to her years later.

The first order of business was finding a suitable apartment for Tanya in Tel Aviv, and that meant spending days on end trotting from one building to the next exploring recommendations of the real estate agent. Good modern apartments were hard to come by, especially one suitable for a person accustomed to a four-floor luxury townhouse on East 64th street in New York, elevator and all. But Leah's persistence and perseverance finally paid off, and she located a two-bedroom apartment for Tanya on the fourth floor of a nice modern elevator building in a new section of town. It was well situated and in close proximity to a cultural hub: The Mann Auditorium—a newly built spectacular concert hall–the Helena Rubinstein Pavilion of Contemporary Art, and the renowned Habima theatre. And although Tanya would be driving her little car, the apartment was also near a main thoroughfare with ample public transportation and a taxi stand across the street.

Next, it was releasing Tanya's goods from customs. It took weeks of discussions with customs officials at the port, no easy feat by any measure. Bureaucracy, inherited from the British rule and local Middle Eastern culture, were difficult to shake off. Although "*Baksheesh*"—bribing officials, as was the custom prior to the establishment of the State of Israel, had been substantially eradicated by the new country, dealing with officials of the government was still a difficult issue. Typical of Middle Eastern and Southern Mediterranean countries, a capricious lack of adherence to rules was the norm, and "come back tomorrow" was normally the way to defer government work.

Relentlessly Leah battled these clerks at the port, and finally was able to release Tanya's containers of household goods that as a "Newcomer" she was entitled to bring to the country duty free. Sometimes it came down to haggling over some household item—is it permitted or not to be imported tax free?

And then, negotiating with movers to physically extract the container from the port. Once the furniture was in the apartment, Tanya insisted that Leah help her decorate her home. Moreover, Tanya spoke no Hebrew and had only a few acquaintances, mostly through her past work at Women International Zionist Organization and Hadassah, people she had never met before but had corresponded with. So it fell on Leah to help her with every aspect of daily life. There were documents to get translated, and notarized, registration at the interior ministry to obtain an identity card, contracts to sign, and other bureaucratic procedures to follow.

It took some time for the new immigrant to settle in the country, and Sam and Leah were always there to help her in learning the ropes, driving her around to run her errands, and otherwise softening the trauma of relocating from the comforts of the orderly and organized United States to this mostly still-primitive country of Israel.

Only years later did Leah realize how important the experience of Tanya's immigration to Israel would be for her in helping others engage the same process.

Chapter 43

Saturdays were the only weekend day in Israel where the daily obligations of work or school were not in effect. Work and school stopped midday Friday and resumed Sunday morning, so the day-and-a-half of free time each week were dedicated either to religious or to leisure activities. For years, ever since Sam's father moved out back to Ramat Gan in 1940, and even before that when he had Haganah duty, Sam no longer attended synagogue on the Sabbath, so Leah and Sam could enjoy a pleasant day with their children free of pressing obligations or commitments.

Saturday mornings were habitually dedicated to visiting Pessia in Tel Aviv, Aunt Dora who, once her parents died had moved back to the old converted chicken coop in Ramat Gan, or the "clan" in Binyamina—Isaac and his new family, and Misha, Rachel, and their children, or driving up to the beach in Herzliya. Although the Tel Aviv beach had been cleaned up and restored, and swimming was allowed, habits are hard to break, so the family preferred to drive north the ten miles to enjoy the less crowded venue of Herzliya.

It was an unspoken rule that although the parents enjoyed the company of their children during those outings, they did not force participation by the younger generation. They were free to do whatever they liked as long as they were home during lunchtime: By 2 p.m. all would congregate at home to have a Shabbat meal together. As time passed however, even that rule was somewhat relaxed allowing Bella, on occasion, to join her friends on out-of-town all-day excursions.

On this particular Saturday morning in early spring of 1959 Bella preferred to join her friends at the beach while Sam, Leah, and Ofer made their monthly pilgrimage to visit Aunt Dora in Ramat Gan. Visiting Aunt Dora was somewhat of an adventure for Ofer, especially in the late winter and early spring when he could climb the trees in the orchard and pick bushel upon bushel of oranges, lemons, mandarins, and grapefruit for all to enjoy.

The adults sat on her veranda and chatted about events happening in the country. Despite the fact that Dora was no longer very mobile, and most of her friends lived in Tel Aviv and rarely if ever came to visit, she was well versed in current affairs. She was well read, albeit not as well read as her brother Motya, the book publisher.

Motya was home, and soon came down from his perch on the second floor of his townhouse.

"I saw your car, so I knew you were down here," he said. "You did not come up looking for me," he complained.

"We did not know you were home," Leah retorted. "You travel constantly to Jerusalem, or Haifa, or elsewhere, so we did not think that you were home."

This ladies' man in his seventies had girlfriends in practically every major town in Israel, and he would "do his rounds" visiting them on weekends. He even had a mistress who was married at the time, and he still found the courage and chutzpah to stay at her home and sleep with her whenever her husband was out of the house.

"I wanted to speak with you," he said, "so before you head back home please come on upstairs for a few minutes."

It was obvious that he did not want to speak in front of his sister Dora, and they wondered why. A bit later, after having tasted some of Dora's new creation—a chopped liver imitation made out of eggplants, which actually tasted very good, they climbed up the stairs to his home.

"I have a proposition for you," he started, and immediately Sam and Leah went on the alert. A proposition from Motya was surely something that would benefit *him*, and may not be advantageous for them.

"Like what?" Leah asked. In dealing with Motya she always took the lead. Firstly, he was her uncle and not Sam's, so it was her responsibility to keep him in check. Secondly, in temperament she was much better equipped to handle the old miser and his shenanigans— Sam was too much of a gentleman for this old fox, while Leah could probably out maneuver him with her wits.

"We are family and should take care of each other" he started.

Leah and Sam glanced at each other, knowing that "the uncle" as he was normally referred to, was cooking up some story with this opening.

"We are not getting any younger, and you are renting an apartment in Tel Aviv. Dora is living in the chicken coop downstairs, and it is not good for her health."

"We are not renting. We own our apartment in Tel Aviv," Leah retorted.

"I stand corrected then, but that is not the point. No one knows how long Dora is going to live, but it would be better for her if she had more comfort than that musty and moldy old apartment downstairs. And when she dies, since she has no husband or children, her estate, which is one-half of this entire orchard, valuable property, will go to her heirs.

"She had four brothers—myself, your late father Chaim, and your uncles Uri and Morris in the United States, so each will receive one quarter of her estate. Since your father is dead his share will go to his children, so Nahum, Ida, and you will each receive one third of his share, or one twelfth of her estate."

He had clearly spent much thought on this proposition to get to that level of detail.

"As the trustee for the estate of both of us, I had already sold off some parcels of land and am holding her money in trust, a trust from which she is getting a monthly stipend to live on. You know about those sales, Leah, you helped me record the deeds in the land registry."

Leah nodded. She had negotiated some of the terms of the sales, and one land swap with the municipality, and knew also that not all his dealings were on the up and up. She also suspected that as "trustee" he was dipping into the proceeds as "management fees," but she had not yet caught him with his hand in the cookie jar.

"I say why wait until after Dora is gone for you to get your share?" Here came the bait. "Why not take advantage of the money and use it now, and later we can do the accounting and subtract it from your portion of the inheritance?"

"That is very kind of you," Leah said, waiting for the other shoe to drop, and it was not long before it did.

"I am working long hours and travel a lot, and Dora is here by herself with no one to take care of her. I am now being sent overseas at the invitation of other governments," he boasted, "and when I am not here, there is no one Dora can rely on. She does not have a phone to call for help if she needs."

"So?"

"What I am suggesting is that instead of your future inheritance you take one-half of the lot next door, and Dora will take one-half of the lot, and you can build a two-family home on it. That way if she needs anything you are close by."

Leah was on to him and his mischief and treachery. Her uncle was trying to trade a one-twelfth share of Dora's entire future estate for one-half of a small lot, a small fraction of her fortune. Sam and Leah would then lose a substantial amount of money, money that would somehow flow into his own pockets.

For a split second Leah was tempted to confront him and for once really give him "a piece of her mind," but then she thought better of it.

"Interesting concept," she replied. "I would not mind moving here from Tel Aviv, it has become too noisy with the buses running up and down the street. What do you say, Sam?"

She gave Sam a look and he got the drift. He, too, smelled a rat here.

"Something worth considering," he said. "Leah and I need to talk about it some, and then see if it is something we want to pursue."

"Okay," Motya said, not realizing that Leah and Sam understood his deceit. "Take your time, there is no urgency."

They bid him farewell. Back in the car they were silent for a few moments, mulling it over.

In principle, moving out of their neighborhood was not an issue. Having to climb four flights of stairs every time, especially when laden with groceries, was getting tiresome. The locale of the proposed lot was almost perfect, on a side street from Petah Tikva Road, a main artery to the center of Tel Aviv, only two miles from the beach, with much public transportation in all directions, yet a quiet residential neighborhood.

But Motya's scheme was clear. Not only was he trying to offload the responsibility of taking care of his aging sister to his niece and nephew, so that he could go gallivanting around free of any obligation, he was also trying to steal a substantial amount of money from them in the process.

And what would he do with this money when he has no children to leave an inheritance to? Why would he stoop to cheat his own kin? For what purpose?

Leah and Sam discussed his offer over the next week, and formed a strategy. They verified that Motya would be home the next Saturday, and drove up to visit him.

"We want to be up front with you," Leah opened the conversation. "We don't mind taking care of Dora for you, to allow you to be free of obligations, which is really what you are after."

She called him out, eliminating any notion that he may have had about being able to pull the wool over their eyes. Once she clarified to him that his deception would not work with them, she addressed the actual proposal.

"In principle we are open to the idea of building a two family house with Dora. Which lot do you have in mind?"

"The one in the back of this one, on Zvi Street. Let me show you precisely."

They went downstairs and walked around the property, seeing the boundaries of the lot. It was an eighth-of-an-acre lot, large enough to build a two-family home on it with two apartments side by side, even with the strict zoning laws of Ramat Gan.

Not wanting to continue the conversation and give him an opportunity to try any of his mischief Leah led them back toward the car.

"It is certainly something to think about," she said, and then she called his bluff. "I will get an appraiser to assess the value of the lot this week, and we will record that amount in dollars against my share in the inheritance," Leah said.

Motya opened his mouth to speak, but he was boxed in. Leah did not leave him any options. She outmaneuvered him, and he now realized it. Thinking ahead she figured that by the time Dora passed away and her estate was probated, that lot would be much more expensive in dollars than its current value, so basically she got it at a bargain-basement price. A befitting turn of events to counter Motya's original plan.

❖ ❖ ❖

Over the next year Leah and Sam built their portion of the two family house. To be precise, it was Leah who built it, and Sam observed. The architect and general contractor was Leah herself: With some help from Ofer she designed the layout of the apartment, and then consulted a structural engineer for the calculations of the foundations, instructing him to size it for a four-story building, as limited by the zoning laws for the area. When the time comes, she explained to Sam, they can sell the air rights to build the other three floors to a developer. She then carried the plans to city hall and fought with the city engineers and administrators for all the permits, and negotiated all the services—electricity, water, sewer, garbage collection, street lighting, and telephone, the whole long list.

By the time she was done Leah was recognized in the municipality as a force to be reckoned with, not taking "no" or "come back tomorrow" for an answer, dealing with a bureaucratic nightmare and winning. When she would walk into the office all the officials would duck, urgently leave for a bathroom break, or accommodate her, whichever was more expeditious to get her out of their hair.

As Bella ended her first year of military service and Ofer entered his senior year in high school Leah embarked on constructing the house. Not an easy task under normal circumstances, it was more difficult for a woman, especially one with barely a high school education and not much support from her husband. Not that Sam did not appreciate her achievements, but he did not encourage them either. It was as if her success would detract from his standing and his own accomplishments. Were his own insecurities, unfounded as they were, causing him to be threatened by her feat?

And it continued to be a feat. She hired the construction crews, found the best sources for materials, negotiated all pricing, purchased the materials, arranged shipping of the supplies, and maintained the budget. From daybreak to nightfall she spent her days at the site supervising the workers and ensuring that their workmanship did not falter. Her standards were very high, and the construction had to be impeccable.

She even ensured that the only trees removed from the lot were those growing directly within the footprint of the new structure, and even those had to be delicately removed and replanted elsewhere on the property. By law no fruit trees could be cut down without a permit and a harsh penalty, and Leah was conscientious of the value of these trees to the country—the orange, grapefruit, or lemon trees, and especially that old mulberry tree in front of the property that her grandfather had planted with his own hands so many years earlier.

Slowly but surely Leah's and Sam's new home was taking shape, while Dora's section remained empty. Maybe out of some premonition, and despite urgings from all, Dora delayed work on her part, and before Sam's and Leah's section was complete one night she peacefully passed away in her sleep.

For Sam and Leah, there was no turning back at that point, and the construction proceeded. The two-family house reverted to a single family home with the only difference being the basement air raid shelter, required by law for a multi-unit apartment building but not for a single unit home, and it could therefore now be filled with gravel to avoid rats or other undesirable creatures taking residence in the space.

Even before the house was completed, changes were occurring in the family. Bella was honorably discharged from her military service, passed the entrance exams to the university with distinction, and headed to Jerusalem to study sociology at The Hebrew University. Once again Bella proved herself and her tenacity—admission was extremely competitive due to the large number of applicants for the small number of seats available.

Almost at the same time that Bella left the IDF, Ofer was drafted. There was never any doubt in his mind as to what role he would play in the military—he was going to be a pilot in the Israeli Air Force, carrying on the tradition of his father's service. Alas, he failed the physical exams, and after a mere two weeks was rejected by the air force academy and returned to the general pool for another assignment within the military.

Ofer called home to let his parents know how distraught he was that he had not been accepted to flight training, and instead he was going to volunteer to the paratroopers, then the most difficult and dangerous branch of the military.

Sam was proud of his son and his choice, but horrified Leah sprang into action—she was going to stop him from his youthful foolish notion. All of a sudden she forgot about her own volunteering for difficult and dangerous assignments in the Haganah, and all the sacrifices she herself was willing to make for the country, risking her own life. But when it came to her children, and especially her son, she was not going to allow him to take unnecessary risks and join this dangerous unit of the IDF.

She hailed Bella out of the university to exercise her connections at the camp, and have one of her former colleagues intercept Ofer on his way and stop him from stepping forward and volunteering to the paratrooper brigade. And when the new recruit was ordered to return to his barracks to await his reassignment, by a sergeant no less, he obeyed the order.

The result of Leah's intervention was that Ofer was assigned to the armored corps, one of the most difficult branches of service, and for the next two and a half years of compulsory service, plus another nine months of regular service, and further reserve duty till age 55 Ofer was to wear the black beret of that branch of the service. As they say, the black beret signifies the black life of a member of the armored corps, and it was a tough life for sure. But to Ofer, if it were not the paratroopers, at least it was another combat unit and not an administrative desk job someplace in the IDF. He proudly wore the uniform and the black beret adorned with a red background underneath the insignia of the armored corps, signifying his belonging to a combat unit.

Thus neither Bella nor Ofer were nearby during the completion of the construction of the new family home: Bella at the university in Jerusalem, and Ofer somewhere in the military, undergoing training as a tank crew member.

At long last, the new home was finished. Leah and Sam sold their apartment in Tel Aviv and moved to their new location, next door to where both of their children were born and where Motya still lived in the townhouse, now famous for its pink color, near the Elite Junction at the entrance to Ramat Gan.

Chapter 44

A few months after moving into the new home in Ramat Gan Sam finally walked out on his partners in Coldomat. For years Leah had been badgering him, to no avail, to sell his share in the company and leave. She repeatedly told him how she deeply disliked, disrespected, and despised, the two leaches he had for partners and wanted Sam to rid himself of them. For years his brother-in-law Nahum had been trying to recruit him, urging him to come and take a senior leadership position within his set of Amcor companies, and for years Sam had declined.

Now all of a sudden, abruptly and without any explanation, Sam set aside his previous reservations and accepted Nahum's offer.

It was never clear what precisely triggered his actions, what was the straw that broke the camel's back. All those years of hard work that he had devoted to the company—acquiescing to so much inequity with his partners, carrying the bulk of the load and not being appropriately compensated for it—and then one day it finally came to a head, and for some reason he was willing to walk away from it all, literally with nothing but the shirt on his back.

He walked away not receiving anything for his share in the company, its inventory, goodwill, or other property. The thing that he was not willing to do to his partners all these years, having them walk away with nothing, always expecting to have to buy their share from them, he now accepted for himself. He signed over his shares in the company for nothing, not even a broken penny. One more time the two charlatans swindled him, convincing him that his share in the company was worth less than one third of the taxes owed, and that he was lucky to get away without owing them money. But, since Yehuda was managing the books, and Sam suspected probably cooking them too, it would have been difficult for Sam to prove a case in court, so Sam walked out with nothing.

Leah was furious. "How could you allow these two blood-suckers, these two losers, to swindle you out of your share of the equity? It is so unfair!"

Sam's only defense was that it was nearly impossible for him to prove that the books were cooked, and that any action on his part would only perpetuate a very aggravating situation. After a while her fury was replaced by the understanding that further protest was futile if not harmful to his health, and she yielded to the notion that he would finally be free from these two leeches and charlatans, and the aggravation constantly gnawing in him for being so used, and that was a good thing. After all, she had been pestering him to escape Coldomat for years, ever since she recognized his partners' collusion and theft during the War of Independence.

Normally, despite Sam's tremendous experience and competences, it would have been difficult for him to get a job at age 50 in Israel. The social benefits of an employee commence when the person initially enters the work force, after military service or later after graduation from the university. Similar to European social standards and unlike the United States', benefits are carried from job to job; at 50 he would qualify for a salary commensurate with twenty-six years of service, an annual vacation of five weeks, and more benefits, making the hiring of a younger engineer more attractive to the manager or business owner. But Nahum recognized Sam's extraordinary qualifications and personality traits, and appreciated his professionalism and competence, far exceeding in value the additional burden of hiring the more senior engineer. There was also the matter of trust and loyalty that Nahum would enjoy from his brother-in-law whom he liked very much, loyalty that would be difficult to find in other recruits, and loyalty so needed in the politically charged environment of Amcor.

Thus Sam became an employee of the Amcor family of thirteen companies, the leading manufacturer of household appliances in the country, with a long list of products—refrigerators and air conditioners, stoves, cook tops, dishwashers, mixers and food processors, washers, water coolers, radios, toys and teaching aids, even solar hot water systems for home use—all products either internally designed or adapted from foreign licensed products. Interestingly, the only product of common household appliances that Amcor did *not* produce, and for good reasons, were clothes dryers: The high cost of energy and the abundance of sunshine preempted the viability of that product in the local economy and a climate of 300 sunny days a year.

Sam's joining as chief engineer of one of the companies, Amnur, enabled the Amcor conglomerate to branch out to yet another area: the design and production of commercial refrigerators and freezing rooms, areas where Sam's unique expertise was unrivaled. With Israel's growing population these products were in high enough demand to warrant establishing a full-fledged manufacturing production line

For Sam, this change in employment had serious ramifications, both physical and psychological. He no longer had to worry about meeting payroll every week, thus being directly responsible for the well-being of his employees and their families, a burden he could now set aside. He also became immune to the ups and downs of a small business, from feast to famine, as he had experienced for twenty-five years at Coldomat. Instead, he had a somewhat lesser salary than the draw from his own company, but it was consistent, week after week, predictably so. He also could take the yearly vacation he was due, something that as a business owner he had been reluctant to do. And finally, there was a pension plan and social security to guarantee him and Leah a dignified existence past his anticipated retirement fifteen years hence.

The downside of this change was the need to acknowledge some level of failure. He had fought for the dream of making Coldomat a leading force in its field, and that dream did not come true, and surely he felt some responsibility for that. Along with it was the tinge of glamour of being a business owner and the hope that when the business grew and flourished he would be able to someday sell the business and retire with a substantial bundle of money, and an estate that he could leave for his children.

But Sam never complained, never felt the victim. Instead, he accepted his new station in life as a challenge. He was tasked with building and leading a division within Amcor Enterprises, and he met that challenge head-on, with vigor and intention of success. And as time passed, it became clear he had risen to the challenge and had made Amcor the leader in this domain as well.

The only major drawback was the fact that the production site for this division, where his office was, was in Beth Shemesh, part way to Jerusalem and some distance from Ramat Gan. Sam had to become an early riser, and be out of the house by 6:00 a.m. to be at the plant before opening at 7:00 a.m. His commute back was equally long, returning at 5:30 p.m. without the benefit of the lunchtime siesta he had been accustomed to in recent years at Coldomat, where the office was a mere ten-minute drive from home.

Regardless, Sam never complained. The only thing that somewhat bothered him was Amcor's politically charged environment: Amcor was being run by two disjoint partner groups, two cliques you may add, with two competitive co-presidents, and he belonged to one of these cliques—the one led by Nahum. Moreover, even within Nahum's team there was resentment that he had been brought in to a senior executive position, "substantially," they said "because of his personal relationship with the president—Nahum, and probably not because of his capabilities and competences." For Sam the internal squabbles were nothing but a destructive distraction that made him angry, sad, and distraught, all at the same time.

"Why don't you talk to Nahum about these resentments?" Leah suggested.

"I'll deal with it," he responded. "I don't want to take advantage of our family relationship to Nahum to help resolve these issues. I am a big boy and will handle it myself, my way."

"But don't you think it will be good for Nahum to know what is going on with his underlings and subordinates?"

"Sure, but that will be done at the right opportunity. I don't also want to come across as the sniveling weakling running to the boss for cover every time there is some issue."

"You'll be doing him a favor alerting him to what's going on behind his back."

"True. I'll find the right opportunity and occasion."

Leah accepted his view without further discussion.

Sam handled the issues himself, in a calming manner, and after a while no one challenged his authority anymore, or tried to disrespect or denigrate his contribution or success. When people got to know him they realized he was a "regular guy," nice, considerate and conscientious, honest and decent, a man they could relate to and could trust with their issues.

And they did. Before too long his employees and coworkers learned to rely on his acquired wisdom and sophistication, and consulted with him on personal as well as professional matters. He quickly became their "Rabbi," their counselor, their sounding board, their elder, a person who would neither lead them astray nor violate their trust. And Sam accepted this role without any reservations; it was a role consistent with his personality, much more so than the purely technical chief engineer role he officially assumed.

Whenever Sam and Nahum got together socially, Sam avoided "talking shop" with him, feeling it was not appropriate. True, from time to time Nahum would ask him "So, how is it going at the plant?" and Sam would give him a brief factual rundown in a sentence or two, but other than that Sam kept the business life separate from the family life.

There was, however, one incident where Sam did approach Nahum, in a formal way, at his office.

"Nahum, a situation is developing where the possibility of a strike is quite high."

"What is the issue?"

"The plant manager is mistreating some of the employees in an openly hostile and disrespectful way, in front of others, and the employees have raised a complaint with the union. This is bound to get to a boiling point if nothing is done quickly. There is talk of a strike. I have a committed schedule of product deliveries and I can't jeopardize it due to a strike." He described to Nahum the grievances of the employees in adequate details.

Without hesitation Nahum picked up the telephone, called the plant, and asked the receptionist to put the plant manager on the line.

Sam sat quietly, as if he weren't there.

"Yair," Nahum said into the mouthpiece, "I need you here tomorrow morning at eight o'clock in my office."

He listened for a moment.

"Cancel it," he said. "Be here at eight sharp."

He hung up, not giving Yair an opportunity to ask questions or object.

"I don't need to hear the whole story from the employees," he told Sam. "I trust what you tell me as if I myself was there and saw it with my own eyes. Yair is history.

"As you know it is tough to fire anyone in Israel, even in management, but he will have to go, whatever it costs. I can't and don't want to afford the damage of a strike because of some jerk. I have heard rumors about him from some others, but decided to let it ride because of the difficulty and costs associated with firing him. But when *you* tell me what you just did, that changes everything. He is gone effective tomorrow at 8:01.

"It will be tough to find a replacement. Do you think you could take over for him for a while?"

"I would rather not," Sam replied. "I won't feel comfortable about it. As the Bible says 'you have murdered and now you shall inherit?' I don't want to do that. Ask the head of research and development to take over the other aspects of the plant management. I will manage my division without Yair."

"Fair enough. You are right. Won't look good. Someone will figure it out that your visit today here was related to this dismissal. The head of R&D is an excellent choice."

Chapter 45

Based out of an armored corps location not far from Ashkelon, Ofer spent three months of strenuous basic training in the armored corps boot camp as an infantry soldier. Similar to what his sister endured during her initial phases in the IDF, he was introduced to basic military skills of weapons handling, map reading and navigating, unit tactics in both offense and defense, and lying in ambush during the nights.

There was so much new stuff to learn and absorb, so many unfamiliar situations and conditions to contend with, all under strict military discipline and induced stress and fatigue due to lack of sleep–the standing orders required "lights out" by 10:30 p.m., but there were no standing orders when wakeup time was, and so the sleep time could be as short as the company sergeant determined it to be, for all intents and purposes even down to a few minutes.

And the stress was not only mental, it was physical as well. Long forced marches with a heavy backpack and carrying a heavy weapon followed by the storming of a hill or two while using live ammunition, simulating real-life infantry fighting conditions.

Added to that there were also the other duties of course, such as guard duty at the base camp every few nights, kitchen assignments, cleaning the latrines, and other chores, not to forget the occasional extra drills as punishment for failure to meet expectations or regulations.

The main effect of this stress was that these eighteen-year-olds, with varied backgrounds, upbringings, and personalities, grew up in a hurry, learning to be self-sufficient and mature, responsible for themselves and each other, all within the framework of a cohesive military unit and discipline.

At the conclusion of this boot camp, the unit was assembled at the parade grounds, dressed in 'A' uniforms, for the graduation ceremony.

"You have successfully passed your basic infantry training," the battalion commanding officer announced. "Welcome to battalion 82 of the 7th brigade of the IDF armored corps.

"The next step in your training to become tank crew members will be a driving course. Before handing you an expensive tank to drive, the IDF prefers that you practice on less expensive trucks.

"At the conclusion of that course, which will take approximately two months at a camp near Haifa, those of you who pass the final test will receive a driver license. You will return to this camp, will be assigned your primary role within the tank, and proceed to be trained as tank crew members.

"That training will last over 4 months. And while each of you will be assigned a designated role within the tank, each of you will be trained in all roles: Driver, gunner, and a combined role as canon loader and signals specialist. In addition, consistent with IDF forward thinking, as tank crew members you will also be provided some training at the next level, as tank commanders, although to be so certified required another three months of a specific training course.

"See you in two months. Good Luck."

The battalion sergeant major dismissed the parade.

❖   ❖   ❖

The driving course near Haifa was a tremendous departure from the experiences of the previous three months in the IDF. The days started at 7 a.m. not at dawn like before, and no calisthenics or morning parade. After washing up, breakfast was served at the dining hall, and the first classes commenced at 8 a.m. and ended at 5 p.m.— a normal day at the office. The only other assignment the students were responsible for was guard duty every few nights, and the guard positions were well lit within the barbed wire fence of the camp.

The first month of the course consisted of classroom study and practice of the mechanics of the Dodge 2-ton truck, and the rules of the road including all the road signs. The second month consisted of actual driving practices: A half dozen students would be alternating driving these manual-transmission trucks in the streets of Haifa, negotiating heavy traffic and the hilly terrain, as well as driving on the interurban road leading toward Tel Aviv. The course concluded with a final driving test, at the end of which those who passed received their driving license.

The two months passed in a blink of an eye, and it was time for Ofer and his co-recruits to return to the base camp of the 82nd battalion for tank crew-member training.

Initially, most of the training was conducted in classroom studies as well, covering technical aspects of the various roles within the tank. Then, for the next three months, the hands-on portion of the training commenced, including over two months of drills in the sand dunes of the Negev desert, out of a home-base in Ttze'elim south of Beersheba.

As Ofer described it to his parents—once the training course concluded and he finally received his weekend pass—the life of a tank crew member was hard, under harsh conditions.

"The day would start before dawn. We would check the engine oil, before starting the engine of this powerful metal beast. By first light we have already dispersed the tanks from their tight night formation and covered them with a camouflage net. Then the food truck would show up and deliver a "hot breakfast," which, by the time it arrived was totally cold, and included a fair portion of dust and sand.

"After that is when the actual work would begin: long hours of training continuing almost non-stop till way after dark, in the suffocating heat and dust clouds of the Negev. We would be constantly moving and occasionally shooting at targets strewn among the sand dunes. Finally, at around 10 p.m., we would stop, gather the tanks in a closed circle in a night formation. Then, while the infantry unit training with us would clean their weapons and go to sleep, we, the tank crews, would start performing the daily maintenance of the tank—cleaning the piles of dust accumulated all day, oiling all the hinges, cleaning the machine guns, brushing the barrel of the cannon, re-arming the weapons, changing the oil-filled air filters, and refueling the thirsty tank, all that and more, in preparation for a 2 a.m. inspection.

"Assuming we passed the inspection we would then try and find a place to sleep. A preferred location was on top of the engine compartment, which was still emitting some warmth, or even inside the tank, but there is no room for four people or even two to stretch inside. And if all else failed, we would then dig a trench in the sand near the tank, in a place that no vehicle might run us over, and try and sleep on the ground. And sometimes we still had guard duty to perform too.

"During the days we would be enduring the baking heat of the desert, with temperatures reaching of 125 ^{0}F in the shade. The steel of the tank would get so hot that you could fry an egg on it, and you had to be careful not to touch it with your bare hands. Then, typical of desert climate, at night the temperature would drop to 35 ^{0}F, making it very difficult to sleep while covered with one thin blanket, if at all. And by first light, we would start the cycle all over again.

"We were so tired that we would take cat naps at every opportunity. As soon as the tank stopped somewhere, the driver would be immediately asleep. When we needed to move again the commander would have to remove the tank antennae and hit the driver over the head to wake him up. And as soon as we started moving, the gunner would close his eyes, and when he had to shoot the commander would kick him to wake him up.

"In this state of stupor we had to perform our drills, like robots, without thinking or hesitating.

"And on top of that, for days on end we could not take our shoes off, even at night–being near the border with Egypt we were constantly on alert, ready to move at a moment's notice.

"We were breathing all the dust you could imagine; getting terribly dirty with a mixture of oil and dust baked in the desert's heat during the day; changing work clothes only when the supply truck arrived once a week; water was scarce–we had one canteen a day per person to wash our faces brush our teeth and shave, and a tanker truck would show up once a couple of weeks offering us the luxury of a cold shower from a fire hose; and food-wise, we were eating mostly cold K-rations sprinkled with sand.

"But we practiced and drilled, and drilled some more. Every action within the tank must become a second nature, automatic, instantaneous—in combat, the reaction to an event must be immediate, and in the confusion and stress of battle one cannot stop and think what to do next. A split second delay while thinking may be the difference between life and death, so everything has to be reflexive, drilled over and over again, till it became second nature. Every event type—tank hit, engine compartment fire, enemy spotted, canon misfire, crew member injured, loss of a track, and any other conceivable occurrence must be drilled, and drilled some more, making the training exhausting, long, and difficult.

"The armored corps makes sure that the tank crews are trained as best as humanly possible, so that they will be prepared for any conditions they may encounter in battle, and come through it alive."

❖ ❖ ❖

The next step in Ofer's armored corps training was a Tank Commander course lasting three months. This time the course was conducted at the armor school proper, but instead of the newer British Centurion Matk IV tanks that Ofer was familiar with, the IDF was using substantially inferior tanks, the older American made WWII M1 relics. Their rationale was that it didn't make a difference in quality of commanders graduating the course, while exposing the students to a wider variety of weapons within the IDF arsenal, and also preserving the more valuable Centurions for potential conflict with the Arabs.

This course was substantially less taxing to the students, and concentrated on more of the tactical and strategic aspects of tank warfare, and the making of the correct command decisions and leadership roles as tank commanders.

Once he graduated, and was qualified as a tank commander, Ofer declined the opportunity to proceed to officers' course which would have required him to sign up for 2 additional years of regular service. Instead he was offered a position as instructor in the signals department of the armor school, where he remained for the duration of his service, rising in rank and responsibilities, becoming chief instructor.

Signal operations are critical within the armored corps. Crew members must communicate with each other within the tank via intercom; tanks depend heavily on ability to communicate via radio with other tanks within their unit, and also other units and their military command; and when stationary, radio silence may be invoked which implies running telephone cables and operating a switchboard. Tank crew members therefore have to be trained in operating intercom, radio, and even telephone equipment, as well as communication protocols, ciphers and coded messaging, semaphore operations, and more.

As chief instructor for the school, all training at all levels, from tank crew members all the way to senior command officers, were

Ofer's responsibilities. He was charged with restructuring the training, rewriting all the instruction manuals for the courses, preparing all the visual aids, teaching the other instructors in the new teaching materials, and providing personal training to senior armor corps officers, and also visiting foreign generals, this time conducted in English.

And when the IDF broadcast radio crew came to produce a report about the school, it was Ofer's role to represent the school and conduct a demonstration lecture to the visiting reporters.

Chapter 46

Bella finished her freshman year at the university with very high grades, and came home to enjoy her summer in Ramat Gan. The course load at The Hebrew University was quite high, and very intense, following a rigorous program that crammed into one year material normally covered over two years at universities in the United States. Just as in high school, there were no electives, no easy courses, and the standards were very demanding with many contact hours and a substantial amount of study and required reading for after-school hours.

So the nearly three-month summer vacation was very well earned, and Bella and her two friends enjoyed the relaxation of not having any obligations, school or otherwise. They spent time meeting their former high school friends, going to the beach, attending cultural events, and partying—all the things they could not do during the school year. And when the summer came to an end, Bella and her two closest friends packed their school bags and headed back to Jerusalem to start the sophomore year at The Hebrew University.

As she did in her freshman year Bella refused to spend her weekends alone on campus in Jerusalem. She made the bus ride to Ramat Gan every mid-day Friday, and returned to school on Sunday morning before classes resumed. And from time to time, once every several weeks, Ofer would hitchhike a ride, and also arrive for a weekend furlough from the army. Thus the whole family could spend some quality time together in a warm and friendly atmosphere.

Whenever Bella or Ofer arrived home for the weekend, they could not escape the traditional family Friday night dinner and the Saturday Shabbat lunch. They would share their experiences with their parents, and the conversation would flow and cover the events within the family, the country, and the world.

On this particular Friday, April 14, 1961 Bella returned from Jerusalem at her usual time. Normally upon arrival she would poke her head into her parents' bedroom to say 'hi'—they would be resting but awake, but this Friday she was in no mood to socialize with anyone, her parents included. She went directly into her room and closed the door. Sam and Leah felt that something was wrong, but they decided to not investigate and let her tell them what was bothering her on her own terms.

A couple of hours later Leah called Bella for dinner, and she came to the dining room and sat down in her usual place. She sat through the Friday night Kiddush, and quietly recited "amen" at the appropriate places, but unlike other weekends she did not share her experiences during that week with her parents. She seemed subdued, perturbed, and finally Leah asked her what was wrong.

"Nothing is wrong," Bella said, "I am just very disturbed by the events of this week."

"What events? What happened this week?" Sam asked.

"The trial." Bella responded.

She did not need to specify which trial it was. Everyone in Israel and elsewhere knew that the trial of Adolf Eichmann, the Nazi SS lieutenant colonel, the architect of the "Final Solution for the annihilation of the Jewish people," had commenced that week in Jerusalem.

When WWII ended with the defeat of Germany, the Allies captured many of Hitler's most prominent politicians, military, and judicial leaders, and in the famous Nuremberg Trials military tribunals in 1945 and 1946 tried twenty-four of them, and twenty were convicted to be executed or imprisoned for many years to come. Among the convicted were Martin Bormann, Wilhelm Frick, Alfred Jodl, Rudolf Hess, Herman Goring, Albert Speer, and other well-known Nazi leaders who had a senior role in the Third Reich killing machine.

But, in the confusion following the end of the war, quite a few Nazis, including some of the top echelon, succeeded in evading capture by the Allies. Using pre-staged resources and logistics, thousands of them escaped to various places, primarily to Latin America. They established colonies deep in the jungles of Argentina where they were protected by Juan Peron, and also in Paraguay, and Brazil.

After its establishment, the government of Israel issued a call to locate and bring to justice the Nazi perpetrators of the Holocaust. With the aid of the Simon Wiesenthal Center some were identified and their prosecution was handed to the local authorities, primarily in

Germany and Austria, but other Nazi leaders evaded capture, most notably Adolf Eichmann and Joseph Mengele.

After years of search, the Mossad, the Israeli Intelligence Service, with assistance from several others, finally located Adolf Eichmann in Buenos Aires, hiding among the population as Ricardo Klement. On May 11, 1960, in a daring operation the Mossad abducted him, and within a few days whisked him out of Argentina for trial in Israel. The State of Israel charged him with crimes against the Jewish people, and crimes against humanity.

"What about the trial?" Leah asked.

"I was there. I skipped classes this week and spent my days at the trial."

"You were? How did you get in? I heard on the news so many people wanted to attend the trial there was a long line, and you got it?" Sam asked.

"Yes, my friend and I waited for hours, since very early morning, and we got seats. We were in the fifth row, so close to the glass cage where this monster was sitting we could see every move he made, every twitch of his face."

"We heard portions of the trial on the radio, but it must have been something else to be there in person." Leah said.

"Yes, it was, a devastating experience, so depressing! The prosecutor was very good, laid out the case against him in great detail. As you know they did not charge him with murder, because they could not tie him to personally having killed anyone—he did not personally shoot anyone," Bella said.

"Anyway, there is no death penalty in Israel, except for crimes against humanity and crimes against the Jewish people," Sam said, "and I think they want to exact a death penalty on him."

"That is what he was charged with. Crimes against the Jewish People, and crimes against humanity. I think that the prosecutor wants him convicted and executed," Bella concurred.

"If anyone deserves that punishment, he does," Sam said.

"I watched him during these days, and I don't think he really thinks he had done anything awful at all. I got the impression that he thinks he was obeying orders, was doing what he was told, and therefore he should be declared not guilty, and to me, that is the most depressing part of the experience. How can someone perpetrate such atrocities, be the mastermind of a mass killing of six million Jews, and so many others, and still think he is innocent, just obeying orders?"

"And he seems to be an educated man, an otherwise cultured person," Leah commented.

"His mannerism during the days I was there, that is what really bothered me," Bella said.

"I have said that before, and say it again. It is not just the Germans or Austrians. Many others took part in the Holocaust. The Ukrainians, Latvians, Lithuanians, Romanians, all of the other countries had Nazi collaborators, but it was the Germans that astonished me most. Germans, those illustrious people, cultured, sophisticated, and educated, the nation that brought us the world's greatest philosophers like Goethe, and Engels, and Marx, and Schiller, and so many others, if they can perpetrate such atrocities then *any other nation on earth* can descend to this level of inhumanity and depravity as they did."

"I guess you are right, Sam, no people is immune from this curse. That is why we must preserve this homeland of ours, our safe haven," Leah said.

They finished their dinner in pensive silence.

❖ ❖ ❖

Sometimes events happen that seem coincidental.

At the conclusion of each several-weeks course at the signal school of the armored corps, Ofer always led a final exercise to ensure that all the students could actually practice what they had learned in class. They were divided into groups, each staffing a specially-equipped WW II half-track armored personnel carrier vehicle.

They set out after dark, each vehicle heading in a different direction, following specific routes, with designated "radio rendezvous" points at specific times. Once a vehicle reached each rendezvous point it was to establish communications with all others, thus ensuring that the students knew how to operate the equipment in an optimal manner, even with ever growing distances and increased radio interferences.

On this night of May 31, 1962, Ofer followed the prescribed route. He had led these training exercises quite a few times before, his armored personnel carrier always following the same specific route.

All went according to plan for the first few designated stops. However, when his vehicle reached the Ramla rural intersection at 11:45 p.m. he found the road blocked by a police car parked across it—a roadblock.

He ordered his driver to stop and exited the vehicle to check what the roadblock was all about. Two police officers emerged from the darkness, and Ofer noticed that they were armed with pistols. This was very unusual—normally police officers in Israel at that time were unarmed. Maybe there was a breakout from the Ramla prison up the road?

"Good evening, officers," Ofer greeted the policemen. "What's going on?"

"Good evening sir," the officer nearer to Ofer answered. "I am sorry, but you can't proceed on this road. The road is closed to traffic."

"Why, is there some problem ahead?"

"We don't know, sir, we were ordered to block the road and divert all traffic," the officer said.

"All we know is that this road is not passable until around 00:30," the other police officer volunteered.

"I am on a military training exercise and must be further down this road by fifteen minutes after midnight."

"I am sorry, sir. I am afraid you will have to either wait here, or find an alternate route."

Ofer went back to his armored personnel carrier and consulted the map. His destination was less than 10 miles ahead, but according to the map if he selected an alternate route he wouldn't make it there in time, and then the entire timetable would be seriously off.

He weighed the alternatives. They had said that the roadblock would be lifted at 12:30 a.m. so if he remained in place, using the current location as the rendezvous point, a slight improvisation, he could still catch up to the next rendezvous point in time.

"And you don't know why?" Ofer asked.

"No sir, we have no information."

Ofer did not believe them. In the headlights of the vehicle he noticed that by their insignia they were not regular police, but belonged to the Prison Unit of the Israeli police. He also noticed something peculiar about the lighting of the Ramla prison a bit further up ahead.

"This is strange. Something must be going on at the prison."

"We are sorry, we don't know anything more, sir."

"I understand," Ofer said. "I checked the map and if we take another route we can't make our next stop in time, so we will wait here."

"That would be great," The older officer was enthused, and did not explain further.

Ofer ordered his driver to park the armored vehicle across the road next to the police car, and put a magazine into the Uzi but not load a round into the chamber—if the policemen were armed it meant they were considering the possibility of needing to use their side arms, so better be prepared. He further ordered the driver to stand guard in the vehicle, providing additional firepower to the two officers' pistols. He then instructed his students to commence the setting up of the antennas and begin preparing for establishing the communications from that spot. Thus he was proceeding with the exercise, modified to meet the unexpected circumstances while providing additional support to the two police officers manning the roadblock.

They waited.

At fourteen minutes after midnight the police radio woke up with a short message.

The policemen acknowledged the message and came forward.

"Thank you so much for your help, sir. To be honest we were not comfortable being here just the two of us in the dead of night blocking the road, so we are so glad you stopped," said the younger officer. "Now we can tell you why you and the others were stopped from going through."

"Why was that?" Ofer asked.

"Adolf Eichmann was just executed," the officer responded.

"Adolf Eichmann is dead?"

"His execution was scheduled for midnight this night. According to the radio message we just received he was hanged six minutes late, at 12:06 a.m. June 1. We were sent here to block the road to ensure that there will be no disturbance during the execution. The architect of the 'Final Solution of the Jewish People' is dead."

The older officer unbuttoned and rolled up his sleeve, and his partner shone a flashlight on his arm. There was no mistake, the tattooed serial number from a concentration camp was clearly visible.

"Tonight I avenged my family that perished in Auschwitz," he said.

Ofer thought about his uncle Isaac who had lived through hell for this moment. How he would feel in the morning when he wakes up to the news that the Jewish People avenged, in a small way, the atrocities committed against them, and Eichmann was dead.

What a remarkable coincidence—Bella was at the beginning of the trial, and Ofer was there for the execution.

Chapter 47

As in every year at The Hebrew University, at the end of her sophomore school year Bella faced the period of final exams. She arrived home for the study period preparing for the exams, and in her usual dedicated manner, she dove right into it. She studied mostly with her two best friends who lived nearby, but on occasion she locked herself in her room and concentrated on the task at hand, alone.

One particular Saturday evening Bella was deep in her studies. Leah and Sam had gone to the airport to pick up their friends Yaffa and Tzvi who had returned from a trip overseas. She heard them when they came to the apartment, and heard the voices of their friends as well, but she was too engrossed in her work to be distracted by getting out of her room to greet them as she otherwise would have done.

Leah knocked on the door and poked her head into Bella's room.

"Come and say hello," she urged Bella.

"I am studying a difficult passage," Bella responded, "and I don't want to break right now."

"You should come out just for a minute to say hello," Leah insisted.

"Maybe later." Bella was not to be distracted.

Leah left, only to return a few minutes later.

"Why don't you come and say hello? It is not good manners, you know."

"I told you, I am studying something difficult, and don't want to break my concentration."

"Take a break. You have been at it for a long time. Take a break and feel refreshed."

"Why are you insisting? You know I don't particularly care for Tzvi with his crude humor. Yaffa is all right, but Tzvi turns my stomach."

"It is not polite, they were overseas for a long time, and they know you are home."

"Are they leaving already?"

"No."

"So later," she would not budge.

Fifteen minutes later Leah was back. Evidently she was determined and relentless, and Bella did not understand the urgency that she should stop her studies and go see her parents' friends. After all she saw them at least once a month when they would show up for the Friday night card playing group, and frequently a few times in between.

"Oh, okay." Reluctantly she rose from her desk and followed her mother into the living room.

Yaffa and Tzvi were there on the couch, having some coffee and cake. Sam was sitting in one of the armchairs, deep in conversation in English with a young man sitting in the other armchair.

"Hi Yaffa, Tzvi," Bella greeted the couple. "How was your flight?"

At the sound of her voice Sam and the young man stopped their conversation and turned toward her.

"It was fine, thanks," Yaffa answered. "We stopped for two days in Paris, so it was a short flight from there."

Bella walked around the coffee table and sat on the chair opposite her father and the stranger.

"This is Leon," Yaffa introduced the young man. "He is from the United States, here for the summer. He came to visit us just as we arrived from the airport, so we brought him here with us."

Leon acknowledged Bella with a faint smile and a "Hi." Sam who was not impolite but clueless resumed the unrelenting conversation with the young man.

Bella looked at the stranger and sized him up. He surely was handsome, in his mid-20s, and seemed well mannered, and although she could not quite make out the conversation between him and her father on the other side of the coffee table, it did not seem frivolous. They were both so engrossed, it seemed as if they were solving world problems.

After a little while she stood up and excused herself to return to her studies. Leon rose to his feet with the typical American "Nice meeting you."

"Leon is all by himself in the country and does not know any young folks. Would you mind showing him around a bit?" Yaffa was direct, in English.

"Sure, will be glad to," Bella replied also in English.

Leon pulled a small black notebook from his pocket. "Could you please write your phone number in my *pinkas*?" he asked. He used the Hebrew word for a pocket notebook, and was obviously proud of it, but the rest of the sentence was spoken in English.

Bella scribbled her name and phone number on a blank page. "I have finals this coming week. After that I will be free."

"I will give you a call," he said.

After the weekend Bella left for Jerusalem, aced her tests and came back to Ramat Gan to enjoy the summer.

Two weeks passed and Leon had not called. Bella shrugged it off and decided to forget him. It was not atypical for Israelis to promise to call and not mean it, and Bella assumed that American young men were no different. Anyway, she had a fairly busy social life without this guy, and she did not cherish being saddled with playing tour guide or nursemaid to him.

The next time Bella saw her, Yaffa asked her about Leon.

"Have you shown him around?"

"No, he has not called me since we met here last time."

"I wonder why. As far as I know he did not know anyone else in the country, and when I spoke to him later that evening he was quite enthused about meeting you and having someone local to show him around."

"Well, probably he was not *that* enthused, or he met some other people and they are keeping him entertained. How did you meet him anyway?"

"A friend of mine from Hadassah in the United States had sent me a letter introducing him. She wrote that she knows his mother, and that he is a medical student from New York and is coming to Israel to do a summer internship at Tel Hashomer hospital. She said that he did not have any contacts in Israel, so she gave him my name and address and hoped I didn't mind."

"He did not call so it must be that he is not interested in me acting as his guide. Just as well." Bella dismissed the whole affair.

A few days passed, and then one evening the phone rang. Sam answered the phone.

"Hello, this is Leon. How are you?"

"Hi, Leon, we are fine, how about yourself?"

"I am fine, thank you. I wanted to call you earlier, but I had lost my *pinkas* and lost your phone number."

"Oh, I see. So how did you get our phone number to call?" Sam asked.

"I wrote my mother, and her friend gave my mother Yaffa's address and phone number and she sent it to me, and Yaffa finally gave me yours just now."

"You went to all this trouble?"

"Yes, I wanted to thank you for your hospitality. I also enjoyed our conversation when we met last time."

"You are welcome. It was our pleasure to meet you. I enjoyed our conversation as well."

Then Leon came to the point. "May I please speak to Bella?"

"Sure, let me call her to the phone."

They made plans to get together Friday evening and for Bella to show him the sights. Leon was staying at the dormitory near the hospital but getting back there at night would be an expensive cab ride, and no buses were running on Friday night, so Bella invited him to stay the weekend at her parents' home in Ramat Gan—Ofer was not coming home from the army that weekend, so his room was available and Leon was welcome to it. He gladly accepted.

Through the remainder of the summer Leon came to Ramat Gan whenever he could, to spent time with Bella. Sometimes she could drive him back to the dormitory using Sam's company car, and that made it easier on them. They went visiting various places in and around Tel Aviv and made some trips out of town as well. It was obvious that the two had hit it off well, and were getting attached to each other.

Sadly, the short summer was coming to an end, and Leon was about to leave for another year at Albert Einstein School of Medicine in New York. But before leaving, Leon decided to take a major life altering step.

Leah was in the kitchen preparing the Sabbath lunch. Leon and Sam were sitting in the living room and Bella and Leah joined them for the conversation.

Leon went directly to the point.

"Bella and I are in love with each other, and we decided that we want to get married," he said. "We are asking for your blessing."

Sam remained silent for a few moments, absorbing the impact of this statement, and sorting out how he felt about it. He was not surprised. Being observant of human nature he could see their relationship developing over the summer, and therefore he was somewhat prepared for this possibility. He liked Leon—cultured, well-educated and mannered, and a decent human being, gentle and bright, and void of the gruffness so typical of the Israeli youth of the time. Although Bella had never dated any of those "boorish" bad-mannered Israelis, and always attracted more refined suitors, Leon stood head and shoulders above even the best of them.

Judging by what he had observed Leon would make Bella very happy. As it were, during this summer he could see how her general attitude had become so much more positive, she was in good spirits, and her time spent with Leon had brought an aura about her he had never seen around his daughter before.

So accepting Leon as a future son-in-law was not difficult for Sam, and neither would it be for Leah—after all she was the propellant that got the match going in the first place. And if the couple were determined, then all would be well. Beyond that, Israel could use the talents of a promising young doctor, so it was good from every respect.

"Of course you have my blessing," Sam finally said. "I think you will be a fine couple together."

"Mazal Tov," Leah chimed in.

"This calls for a drink. Would you like some cognac?" Sam asked Leon, the women did not like the stuff, he knew.

"Most certainly, for the occasion."

Sam reached for his "stash" of really good liqueur. Other times he would offer his guests some local brandy, 777 or Stock 84, but this time he served his best—a very expensive bottle of Courvoisier V.S.O.P reserved for special occasions.

They raised their snifters with the traditional *L'chaim.*

Sam was pensive.

"So what are your plans?" The practical Leah. "Have you thought how you would make it work with you studying in New York, and Bella with two more years at the university in Jerusalem?"

"We have not thought it out in detail, but in general we thought that I will return to Israel next summer, we will get married, and then we will both go back to the United States till I finished medical school."

Sam was deep in thought. What he had just heard did not please him. First, they are thinking of separating for nine months or so, and for a couple in love, as they were, such a separation would be hard to endure. More importantly, do they really know each other that well to make such a serious commitment for life, and on the basis of a two-month courtship, and a lopsided one at that?

He did not want to douse their fire with even one drop of water, but he had to express his words of caution. He took a deep breath, bracing himself for what he had to say, fully aware of the ramifications, especially for himself.

"You guys know each other for a couple of months only, and under uneven circumstances," he said. "You, Bella, have the advantage of being on your home turf, in familiar surroundings and the comfort and support of your family and friends, while you, Leon, are out of your normal element, vulnerable, in unfamiliar circumstances and void of your normal support structure."

He paused.

"I am not trying to dissuade you, but I think that even if you are convinced about your love for each other on such a short acquaintance, you guys need to see the other side of each other before making this deep commitment. Bella, you need to see Leon in his familiar surroundings while Leon, you need to spend time with Bella out of her home environment."

"How can we accomplish that?" Leon asked.

Sam was hesitant in his response, as if weighing if he should utter the words or not. If they agree with his plan, it would be very painful for him.

"I think the only reasonable way would be for Bella to travel to the United States, to New York, and continue your courtship there. Of course, this depends on Bella's ability to transfer her credits to some university in New York. I will not agree for her to sacrifice her education at this point. She must finish her studies toward the BA degree that she is pursuing."

At the personal level, verbalizing these thoughts and making this proposal were difficult for Sam, actions that cut directly through his heart. His attachment to his daughter had been deep, and the bond between the two was very strong. In his limited capacity as a parent, his devotion to his Bella was far greater than to any one else in his family, his wife and his son included. Ever since his father died, and even before that, Bella was the centerpiece of his universe, the light in his heart. Being away from her for who knows how long was going to be extremely painful, and he was fully cognizant of it at that time. She had not even agreed to the idea, and he was already missing her as if they had been separated for months.

Sam knew very well that if Bella traveled to the United States the financial burden will be enormous. First is the legal restriction of access to hard currency of $150 per year meaning that money for her college tuition and living expenses, as meager as they might be, would have to be purchased in the black market. Then there is the issue of cash flow, meaning there would not be an extra coin left in their bank account, and definitely not enough to go visit her in the United States.

So if Leon and Bella accepted his perfectly reasonable and logical idea then he would have to get accustomed to the separation from his daughter, possibly for years, and that would be extremely painful for him.

But he knew it was the right thing to do. No chivalry, no gallantry, it was simply the correct solution to Leon and Bella's desire to create a home together, and possibly add a new generation to the family.

Was he hoping in his heart of hearts that they would not agree to his proposal and would stick with their original idea? Not Sam. He was too honorable a man to count on anyone's misfortune, and definitely not his daughter's, for his own personal gain. He always was willing to sacrifice for his family, and he made the offer, and would stand by it no matter what.

Sam and Leah knew that sending Bella to the United States would place her out of their ability to protect and support her, morally as well as physically. If she needed help, they would not be there even in an emergency, and that weighed on their minds. Leah, who until now had been observing the interchange without much comment stepped forward with a suggestion.

"We have very good friends in Great Neck on Long Island, the Koppelmans," she said. "I will ask them if Bella can stay with them, at least initially, and that will take a load off my mind."

And so, over the next few months, the plan was slowly but systematically—as was Sam's style—put into effect. Based on her credentials from The Hebrew University in Jerusalem Bella was admitted to Stern College at Yeshiva University, and in mid-winter she arrived in New York to resume her studies in the spring semester of her junior year.

Seeing Bella off at Lod Airport on her way to the United States in the winter of 1963 was even more painful for Sam than saying good-bye to Isaac at Riga's port so many years earlier when Sam embarked on his journey to the Promised Land. Although he had a few months to get accustomed to the idea that she would soon be leaving, he still had tremendous pain in his chest seeing her go.

With tremendous pride he watched her climbing the stairs to the departure gate; he was so proud how she had grown to be such a fine young lady, pretty and well-groomed, with impeccable manners and poise. He wished he could come out and tell her in words how much she meant to him, but that was just not something he knew how to do.

But then Bella knew, even without the spoken words. She knew how devoted her father was to her, how proud he was of her, and how he would miss her, and, despite their problems in the past, so would her mother.

Driving back from the airport and entering the empty house, Sam and Leah felt a deep void, a void they would never fill. But life goes on, despite our losses, especially when they are for a positive new adventure, and part of the natural progression of life.

So with Bella overseas and Ofer in the military, Sam and Leah became for the first time physically remote from their children, and the communication between the close-knit foursome was now replaced by aerogrammes, letters, and postcards.

But this situation would be temporary, only for a while. They were sure—no, absolutely certain—that Bella's bond to her country and friends was so strong that as soon as Leon finished medical school they would come back to Israel. Bella was a Sabra, born and raised in the country and Sam and Leah knew she would find living abroad without the closeness of the family and friends an alien existence, something she would not want to endure. And after all, Leon, being a doctor would be welcomed with open arms, able to find a suitable position with a hospital in Israel, let alone open a private practice.

That conviction was what allowed Sam to make his offer in the first place. Neither he nor Leah would ever encourage their children to permanently leave the country they so loved, the homeland for the

Jews, the country that they fought for, the homeland they helped create and build.

But life sometimes takes strange and unpredictable turns.

Chapter 48

Since no training was performed at the signal school of the armored corps during the Sabbath, Ofer was able to leave for home on Friday afternoons and return to the base by 8:00 a.m. Sunday. Sometimes during the week when not on duty he could also hitchhike his way to Ramat Gan and back, some thirty miles each way, so long as he was at his station in the base before 8 a.m. So Sam and Leah were retaining the notion of one of their children coming home at least for the weekends if not more often than that.

As the last months of service were coming to a close, Ofer had to decide what he wanted to do during the nine-month gap between the end of his two and a half years' compulsory military service and beginning of college. He had decided that he wanted to study mechanical engineering at the Technion in Haifa, and he knew he would need to pass rigorous entrance exams to qualify for the limited seats available. Studying required a clear mind, which suggested a not too stressful environment, but Ofer dismissed the idea of staying idle through those nine months. The question was what employment he could find that would leverage his limited professional experience while earning him some income and yet allowing him to study and prepare for college.

He elected to sign up for a year of regular army service, continuing in his previous assignment at the base. But since the school year was scheduled to start after only nine months and not a full year, he obtained a waiver in the contract that would release him from the one-year term after nine months, but only upon being admitted to a university.

Sam and Leah fully supported his decision, even if from patriotic reasons—in their eyes being regular army was an indication of commitment to the country and its security. Moreover, being regular army he could come home every night with transportation being provided by the military, and the parents liked having him around—he livened up their otherwise mundane existence around the dinner table.

Not that Leah and Sam had that much idle time either. After all Leah had a wedding to prepare, practically single-handedly. Bella and Leon would be arriving in June for a short trip during which time they planned to get married in Tel Aviv, so it was up to her to make all the arrangements.

Beyond Sam and Ofer providing Leah minimal advice she could count very little on either for help. Sam woke up at 5:30 a.m. to wash up, have a quick cup of coffee, and head out to the plant, and by that time Ofer was already at the bus stop waiting for his military transport to take him to his own job. Sam normally returned around 6 p.m., too late to be of much help, and Ofer arrived even later than that, and after a quick shower and dinner headed to his studies with friends.

So without much fanfare Leah made all the arrangements: She booked the wedding venue, ordered the flowers, the meals, the band, the Rabbi, everything. She even ordered the wedding dress, one that Bella hated but when faced with her mother's insistence—an insistence for which Bella never really forgave her—she gave in and despondently ended up wearing that dress.

Sam and Leah wrote the text of the wedding invitations themselves and sent them to the printer. They started with a list of over 600 family members and friends, but because of budget constraints had to pare it down to around 150 guests at the Sheraton Hotel in Tel Aviv on a Tuesday in mid-June, 1963.

As the date approached, Leah and Sam sat down and addressed the invitations themselves. They expected most of the family and friends in Israel to attend, but they also sent invitations, more as courtesy announcements, to their friends and relatives abroad.

"I don't know why we are spending money on postage for these people," Sam commented one night. "They are not going to come anyway: Harold in Vancouver in Canada with his family, your uncles and cousins from Sea Gate in Brooklyn, Maurice and Ruth in California, the Koppelmans on Long Island, and the rest, they all have their lives and are not about to drop everything and come running because Bella is getting married!"

"But at least they will know," was Leah's response. "We always got notices from them about events in their families. Maurice and

Ruth sent us a letter after getting married and moving to California, and then when their children were born, Harold and Dina wrote about their children, so let's send them ours anyway."

"All right. That is true. We'll send them just to let them know."

June arrived, and a week before the wedding the bride and groom arrived as well, together with Leon's father. Leon's mother could not make the trip for health reasons, so his father represented the groom's entourage.

Obtaining the marriage license was quite difficult for the couple, faced with a hostile Rabbinical Court. They demanded all kinds of assurances: that Leon was not already married, that Bella was still single as well, and had not been intimate with him prior to the marriage, and more. They gave the poor couple such a hard time that Sam was drawn into a rabbinical discussion with them and lambasted them for the difficulties they were giving the couple simply because they came from overseas to get married in Israel. When the Rabbis of the court heard that he was a graduate of the yeshiva in Riga, and a learned Jew, and when faced with a certificate from a recognized and respected Rabbi in New York who testified that he knew the couple and blessed their union, the Rabbis relented and on Friday before the wedding issued the marriage license. What a relief it was!

Tuesday evening all was ready. Sam dressed up in his best suit, and Leah had prepared a pretty dress for herself. Even Ofer was dressed in a suit, where he got it from nobody knew, but he was properly attired, tie and all. Two hours before the designated time they set out to the venue, a mere ten-minute drive from Ramat Gan.

There were two main entrances to the ballroom, one from the lobby of the hotel, and one from the parking lot, so Leah made the executive decision about the greeting parties: Ida who knew all the invitees, together with Leon and his dad, would man the post at the main outside entrance and Sam and Ofer would man the interior hotel entry to the ballroom. Bella and two of her friends were already upstairs in the bridal suite, and Leah was floating around to take care of any last minute issues as well as helping Bella prepare for the event. Thus everyone had their marching orders, and they proceeded to their respective spots, waiting for the guests to arrive.

Sam was beaming, in a sort of a euphoric trance. As each guest passed through the doorway Sam greeted them with a broad smile affixed to his face. He extended a warm handshake to them, clasping their hand in both of his and uttering his welcoming speech in Hebrew: "Shalom, I am so glad you could come."

He clearly was "not there." Physically he definitely was, but emotionally and mentally he was somewhere else, over the clouds, in an ecstatic mindset no one had ever seen him in before or since. Glowing with utter elation and joy he was going through the motions in indescribable exuberance.

He performed that same welcoming ritual with about a dozen couples, all friends or family, he was in no position to tell, and then he turned to the next couple in line and greeted them in much the same way.

He froze in mid-sentence, stunned, and did not move for what seemed like an eternity.

"Maurice! What are you doing here?" he exclaimed in English with the sincerest astonishment in his voice.

For a moment there was silence.

"Well, that is some chutzpah!" Maurice never missed a beat in an admonishing tone. "You sent us an invitation, we come ten thousand miles to your daughter's wedding, and you ask us what we are doing here? Nice way to treat your guests!"

For a second, Sam was speechless. "Son of a gun, you never responded to the invite!" was all Sam could exclaim to justify his surprised question.

And then came the embrace, the jumping up and down with joy. It was a sight to behold: Two grown men in their fifties hugging each other and dancing in a circle like the loving long lost friends that they were, comrades in arms who have not seen each other for fifteen years, chanting "Zumba, Zumba, Zum-ba." And soon Ruth, beautifully clad in an evening gown fit for the occasion, was dragged into the circle as well.

They danced for a long moment and then Sam dashed off with them, leaving Ofer to man the post while he ran looking for Leah to share his happiness at being reunited with Maurice and Ruth after so many years. He also wanted to make sure that two additional settings were arranged at the head table for his VIP guests.

Now Sam had two reasons to celebrate that night.

❖   ❖   ❖

For their honeymoon the couple, accompanied by Leon's father, took a short trip to Tiberias and the Galilee, and soon afterward packed their bags and left to establish a new home for themselves in New York.

Sam had always said "I want my daughter to get married as early as possible and my son as late as possible," although he never really explained his reasoning for saying so. Now he had to face the reality that his daughter, his beloved daughter, having fulfilled her part of his wish, would be so far away from him. Besides the personal anguish about her not being close to him and him not being able to see her and spend time with her frequently, there was also the patriotic aspect, the Zionist aspect that he had to negotiate.

His daughter had emigrated from the country, and it dawned on him that there were no assurances whatsoever that she would ever return to live in Israel, the homeland for the Jews he helped create. Despite that, he never said a word to her about returning to resettle in Israel. He was deeply saddened by it, and tried his very best to hide his dismay, but it weighed heavily on him. He also felt somewhat guilty for having enabled this situation with his original suggestion for Bella to travel to New York. Had he not proposed it, she probably would have remained in the country, and he was fairly certain Leon would have come back to Israel and continued the courtship here rather than overseas. Alas, he felt he had done the right moral thing to not stand in their way, and let the chips fall as they did.

The only person who perceived his discomfort was his trusted life partner and companion Leah. Initially he did not mention anything to her, but he could not hide it from her either—she knew him all too well. No other person, not Ofer, Ida, or Nahum, detected it, so successful was he in suppressing his feelings and keeping them in the shadows.

And when Maurice and Ruth left and returned to the United States some two weeks later, Sam's discomfort bordered on depression, and for some time he was barely functional. The attachment he had always felt to his daughter now became a negative force in his life, and despite that, he was not too eager for it to subside. Was he supposed to be punished for his supportive actions? Was he supposed to mentally flog himself for having the moral compass to propose the right thing, even at his own peril and sacrifice?

He finally shared his anguish with Leah. As they did frequently, after dinner and clearing the table, they sat down and had long conversations about what was happening in the world, the country, and personally with them. But while Sam had an excellent capacity to understand others, and uncover what made them tick, he had difficulty understanding himself, so when he finally spoke with Leah about his feelings, it was a strenuous effort requiring Leah to exercise her innate ability and closeness to him to really understand his anguish.

Otherwise he bore it quite well, and although inside he was hurt and crying, he carried on with his life as normal. But something had changed within him. He became a bit more subdued, a bit more serious, and a bit more anxious for any mail that looked anything like an airmail letter or aerogramme from the United States.

And then came Barak.

❖   ❖   ❖

For years Sam had told Leah in no uncertain terms that he did not want to have a dog. Sure, he loved animals, and dogs in particular, but despite the fact that Leah absolutely adored them, he did not want the responsibility of owning one. Maybe he never got over the Rex affair? So when one evening after dinner he asked Leah if she had any leftovers of their dinner she was curious.

"The wife of one of the foremen at the plant walked out on him leaving him to take care of their three little children," he explained. "He also has a dog, a beautiful German Shepherd that he is no longer able to care for all by himself. Since the dog could not stay alone in their tiny apartment all day long, he brought the dog to the plant and tied him up by the gate to be a guard dog."

"Who takes care of the dog at the plant?"

"Some workers bring the dog food from time to time, and there is a water bowl for him, but nobody can do any more than that. He is a very big dog, and people live in tiny apartments there. You know Beth Shemesh is a rather poor town, mostly new immigrants who don't have much.

"So if we have some leftovers I will take it to give to the animal."

"Let me put something together for you," Leah said.

Going forward she started cooking a bit more food than for the three of them, so there would always be some leftovers for the animal.

September arrived, and with it Rosh Hashanah. Because Jewish holidays go by the Jewish lunar calendar, they do not happen on the same day of the week each year. That particular year, the holiday landed on Thursday and Friday, and the plant therefore was closed from Wednesday mid-day until Sunday morning.

Sam arrived home on Wednesday at lunchtime with a big dog in tow.

"A dog?" Leah thought to herself. "That is not a dog! It is the size of a pony! This beast is immense! A beautiful male German Shepherd bigger than anyone had ever seen!"

"I could not leave the animal at the plant," Sam said apologetically. "Because of the holiday followed by the Shabbat, nobody could come and bring him food for the three days when the plant will be closed. I just could not bear the thought that this dog will be starving until then, with no food and water. It could die."

"I understand," was Leah's response. "You know I absolutely love dogs, so it is no problem at all." She calmly let the dog sniff her, then felt safe to pet it on its huge head.

"It is only for the holiday, after that I can take him back to the factory," Sam said.

Leah smiled. "Yeah, right," her sarcasm was unmistakable. "Anyway, we certainly can keep him until then. What's his name?"

"Barak. Lightning. He is house broken and very friendly. His owner told me that he is docile and loves people and other animals, but I suspect that he was mistreated when he was a puppy."

"Why do you think that?"

"When you pet him did you notice? As soon as you reached for his head he folded his left ear, as if he is afraid of something."

"I noticed that," Leah said after confirming Sam's observation once again. "He does not do that with his right one, only his left ear."

"Who knows what he endured as a puppy, with little children around the house. Without meaning to be so, unsupervised children can sometimes be vicious to a dog, poke a finger in its eyes or pull its tail."

Sam let Barak off the leash, and the dog did what dogs do when they are introduced to a new place—he went around the apartment investigating his new turf, respectfully, without leaving his mark the way some male dogs do to declare their ownership over the territory. Obviously this dog had been trained.

"How old is he?"

"About two years old. His previous owner was not sure himself."

Leah softly chuckled to herself at hearing "his previous owner." It seemed as if Sam had just become "his current owner." Was that a "Freudian slip?"

She went to the closet, pulled out an old remnant of a rug and laid it up on the landing outside the door, and guided the dog to his new bed. That way he would be able to go out onto the yard whenever nature called, and she did not need to cater to him too much. The yard was fenced and the dog could spend most of his time outside and come in only at night, so it was no bother. The landing was also under roof, so the dog was protected from an occasional and infrequent rain.

But Leah's love for animals was strong, and from time to time she would step outside and hug this gentle monster whose tongue felt like a wet rag to her face.

By Saturday she had bonded with the animal.

"Do you really need to take him back to the plant?" Leah asked. "Check with his owner and maybe he could stay with us a little longer. After all Yom Kippur and Sukkot are coming, and Simchat Torah, and you don't want to have to drive him back and forth," she suggested to Sam.

It was not a hard sell she found out. In the three days of the holiday, some of which Sam had spent in the synagogue, and the Sabbath, he too, became attached to this big dog always welcoming him at the top of the stairs, tail wagging.

The holiday and Sabbath passed, and the dog stayed.

For Sam, the dog was a form of therapy, providing a calming effect to his painful separation from his daughter, now commencing her last year of studies toward her bachelor's degree in the United States. Slowly but surely it dawned on him that his daughter would not be coming back to Israel so soon, not even for a visit. He realized that the young couple was struggling financially, as most interns at hospitals do, with long shifts for almost no pay, and they certainly could not afford to make the trip. Nor could he afford to underwrite such a trip with his reasonable, yet not extravagant, after-tax income. Even Leah's magic could not prevail this time.

Added to his financial woes was the fact that Ofer was admitted to the Technion in Haifa to commence his studies in mechanical engineering. So now Ofer would need some financial assistance to cover living expenses away from home. Tuition was not an issue—it was substantially subsidized by the government and required only a token participation by the students and their families, but food and lodging were up to each individual student.

Without ever verbalizing his sadness over seeing any possibility of a reunion with his daughter fade beyond the horizon, Sam concentrated on the positive aspects: His son had worked hard and had overcome the tremendous odds and the high ratio of applicants to those admitted, and was now a student in this fabulous university, a mark of achievement bar none. He was determined to make whatever sacrifices, financial or otherwise, to provide for his son's expenses while studying in Haifa—books and fees, room, board, and other incidental expenses.

Ofer had been caught in a "Catch 22" tug-of-war between the Technion and the military: Ofer had signed a one-year contract with the IDF with a provision that he would be released early upon being admitted to a university. Now the two institutions were at an impasse: The Technion would not admit Ofer and assign one of the few precious available seats to him unless and until the military released him from his service contract, and the military refused to release Ofer from the contract unless and until he was officially admitted to the Technion.

After much discussions and pleadings, the Technion offered a compromise solution to the deadlock: Instead of admitting Ofer for a normal four year course of study during the days, they would admit him to the Evening Division. This way even if the IDF did not honor their commitment, he could still commence his studies, albeit with a very long commute for the first three months of the freshman year. Upon hearing that he had been admitted to the Technion the IDF released him from the contract, but by now Ofer was firmly in the Evening Division and would have to study his freshman year spread across two years.

Within the first two months of arriving in Haifa, Ofer got his solid footing, and established his routine. Being in the Evening Division his school hours ran Sunday through Thursday from 6:00 p.m. to 10:00 p.m., and during the days Ofer prepared his homework and studied in the library. Once settled though, Ofer realized he had some free time on his hands, and sought to find a job to fill those hours. He soon landed a job as a technician with a household products company, visiting clients and repairing their refrigerators, air conditioners, washing machines and the like, all the products that the company serviced.

It was a job, not a career. It offered him, the mechanical engineering student, the same insights his father gained many years earlier in Nantes while repairing railroad cars, and that was how to *not* design products in a way that makes them more difficult to service. And it provided him a paycheck.

Sam and Leah were apprehensive about him taking on this obligation of a day-job but Sam was proud that the outings where Ofer used to join him on the road years earlier paid off, and Ofer could now put those experiences and lessons learned to good use.

What Ofer did not know at the time, but learned later, was that he got the job through an intervention by his mother with his uncle Nahum who arranged this position for him in Haifa. Once again, Leah's long arm reached out to influence his life.

A month later Ofer received his first paycheck. As he had done every week since arriving in Haifa, he came home for the weekend. At Friday dinner he told his parents about his week, and then proudly showed them his pay stub.

"I want to talk to you about this," he said to his parents.

"That's very nice. I am so glad," Leah said. "You should put it in the bank, and have some savings to use as you please."

"That's not what I had in mind," Ofer said. "I know that my schooling is a financial burden on you, and I don't think it is fair. Now that I am working and earning money, I can cover my expenses. I want to pay for my schooling myself."

The ensuing silence was deafening, as if Ofer had just dropped a bomb in the middle of the table.

Sam and Leah gazed at each other, uttering no sound for the longest time.

"No," Sam finally replied. "You put the money in the bank as your mother said. We will pay for your schooling and expenses."

"But why?" Ofer inquired. "I want to help a bit."

There was another pregnant silence.

"No, Ofer, you put the money in the bank. We will pay for your schooling."

"But why?" Ofer repeated his question.

"Listen to me, young man," the voice was quiet yet bore the strength that comes from the inside of one's soul.

Sam was angry, really angry, Ofer could tell. In his nearly twenty-one years of life Ofer had never seen such a reaction as he witnessed in his father's features just then. This moon-round gentle light-complexioned face with those soft blue eyes had turned red with a fierce look of deep anger.

"You will put your money away. *We* will pay for your education" Sam repeated slowly, emphasizing every word and barely hiding his anger. "It is not our *duty* to pay for your education. It is our *privilege*, and you are not going to take it away from us."

They were quiet for a minute. Ofer was stunned into silence, and Sam was collecting his thoughts. And then Sam continued, speaking slowly and deliberately, stressing every word:

"They can take everything away from you. Everything, even your dignity. But there is one thing that they cannot take away from you, and that is your knowledge, your education. And I am going to make damned sure that you get the best education that you can get."

He had used the word "they." "*They* can take from you." He did not say "you may lose everything." He actually meant someone else, an external human force, coming to get you and everything you have, and Ofer understood it perfectly well. It was not a persecution complex speaking, it was reality of the post Holocaust era, post pogroms, and centuries of rampant anti-Semitism coupled with the fourteen Arab states surrounding Israel, and their allies, all bent on the destruction of the Jewish state and annihilation of the Jewish people.

For the longest time Ofer sat frozen in his place. He understood perfectly well where his father was coming from, and had no retort. The image of Isaac came to his mind, and he knew why his father was so forceful. There have been countless "they" over the years, generation after generation, century after century, and those "they" will continue to exist and torment the Jews wherever they are.

Slowly calm came back to Sam's face as they sat in silence for a few moments longer.

"It is not our duty, it is our privilege," he repeated, "and you are not going to take it away from us."

Chapter 49

Leah's mother Pessia passed away the following spring, in April 1964. Some months earlier she fell and broke her leg, and had been bedridden for the longest time while she slowly healed. Since she could not tend to herself in her own home Leah and Sam brought her to their home, settled her in Bella's old room, and tried to make her as comfortable as possible.

Alas, for the duration Pessia made Leah's life miserable, really miserable. She was demanding, not pleasant, and her worst character attributes erupted, mostly hurtful to Leah who was tending to her every whim. Her greatest displeasure was that she wanted to go home to her own bed and her own kitchen and her own neighbors, so when she recuperated from her physical ailment Sam and Leah reluctantly accommodated her and brought her to her home on Bograshov Street. It was quite inconvenient because they now had to travel to her home almost every day to take care of all her needs, and make sure she was as comfortable as possible, but that is what children in a civilized society do for their aging parents, and Leah and Sam respected that tradition.

Leah's sister Ida could not help during the week—she was working long hours, traveling an hour by bus to the factory far outside Tel Aviv then an hour back, and neither could Nahum—he had a large company to run with frequent trips overseas, and his wife did not drive a car and was not terribly inclined to go out of her way to take care of her mother-in-law who had never cared much for her in the first place.

Over a period of time Pessia's mental condition deteriorated into severe dementia, and then one morning when Leah arrived to check up on her mother she found her peacefully asleep, the eternal sleep.

The funeral was large, primarily friends of the bereaved and neighbors, as well as a large contingent of members of the synagogue across the street. Those who used her home as a *Shtibbel*—a place of prayer for the overflow crowd during the holidays—came to follow her in her last journey. She was interred in the old Trumpeldor cemetery of Tel Aviv, in a plot reserved for her next to her late husband Yitzhak who had died some twenty-three years earlier.

As is customary in Judaism Ida, Leah, and Nahum sat *shiva* at the deceased's home, and there was a constant flow of visitors coming to console the bereaved, as well as the traditional minyan for the three daily prayers of *Shacharit, Mincha* and *Maariv.* Pessia had been an orthodox religious Jewish woman, and her children honored her departure by conducting a strictly orthodox bereavement.

During the long seven days, the three of them discussed erecting the stone on Pessia's grave as soon as was possible. By Sephardic tradition followed in Israel, you may erect the tombstone at thirty days from death, or any time after eleven months, but not in between. None of them wanted to leave the grave unmarked for the eleven months, so they agreed to make the effort to erect the stone at thirty days.

The only hitch was obtaining the permit from the Chevra Kadisha—the caretakers of funerals and cemeteries. It is a volunteer nonprofit organization that ensures that the deceased receives a decent burial, at no cost, and that their graves are maintained according to the strictest of religious Halacha laws.

The threesome decided that since Leah was not occupied by a scheduled job, she would go and obtain the permit from Chevra Kadisha. And so, a few days after the week of mourning was over, she set out to the cemetery to meet with the caretakers there and get the necessary permission.

She walked into the little office at the cemetery, her head covered with a kerchief as befitting a married woman.

"Shalom. I am Leah, the daughter of Pessia Ostrovsky," she introduced herself to the man sitting behind the desk. He was clad in the traditional white shirt and black coat, his head covered by a black wide-brimmed hat, and sporting a long black beard. "He must be hot in that outfit," Leah thought.

"Oh yes," the man said. "Pessia Ostrovsky. She was a dear righteous woman. I hope the funeral and burial were to your satisfaction."

"Yes, thank you, I am sure Pessia would have approved."

"So how can I help you?" he asked.

"We want to put a stone on her grave at thirty days, and need your permission."

"Sure, that should be no problem."

He turned to the side and hollered to someone in the other room. "Zalman, bring me the file of Pessia Ostrovsky."

Not a moment later, a hand appeared through the opening in the wall carrying a binder. It was thick, about two inches thick, full of papers to its brim. The man set it in front of him and leafed through the first few pages.

Leah gazed at the binder in disbelief. What in the world could be in there to make it so thick?

"There is no problem getting you the permit," he confirmed. "Everything seems to be in order."

"Good. I am glad," Leah said, a bit stymied. She wondered what could possibly be not in order to prevent them from putting the tombstone on the grave.

"There is just the minor issue of the fee."

"Fee?" Leah asked surprised.

"Yes. The fee helps us cover the costs of managing the cemetery."

"How much is the fee?"

"Let's see," he said, again leafing through several pages in the folder "It will be 30,000 liras."

"30,000 liras? What? That's not possible! There must be some mistake here." She was stunned.

She had expected several hundreds of liras, maybe a thousand, but 30,000? That's like $30,000. That was just for the permit, not the stone itself, which would probably be some 500 liras or even less.

"There is no mistake here," he said calmly. He looked at the paper again and repeated: "30,000."

"The permit for erecting a tombstone is 30,000 liras?"

"Yes, we charge according to what you can pay."

"I can't pay this kind of fee! I don't have this kind of money!" She stated emphatically.

He looked at her for a second, and then he looked back at the papers.

"Yeah, of course, we know," he said in a reassuring voice. "We know that you don't have this kind of money. We know you do not work; you have two children, one a student overseas and one a student at the Technion. Your husband is the chief engineer of Amnur, and he has a good salary, but it is just a salary of an engineer, and you do not have many investments. You own your apartment in Ramat Gan, but you have a mortgage on it still."

He turned a few pages in his folder. "We also know that your sister Ida is a poor soul, a divorcee, has no children, is a secretary at Amron in Herzliya earning 600 liras a month, lives in a rented apartment in Tel Aviv, and does not have this kind of money either."

He paused for a second, flipping through another page, and then another.

"But then there is your brother Nahum. He is an industrialist. He has all these companies and factories. He is rich. *He* can pay the 30,000 liras."

Leah was shocked. How did they know all this information about the entire family? This man had better intelligence on the family than the Mossad did. He probably knew everything about everyone since the day they first arrived in the country by either birth or immigration. What an unbelievable intelligence service!

From the man's mannerism she concluded that this "case" was routine, nothing unusual, standard procedure. A stiff fee, but as he said they charge according to the ability of the family to pay, and there was no argument that Nahum could afford it. The impressive thing was the thickness of the dossier with all the details in it.

She concluded there was no sense bargaining or negotiating with this man.

Nahum paid, and they erected the stone on the thirtieth day.

Chapter 50

In an effort to expand the offerings of commercial refrigerators Sam realized it would be tremendously advantageous to obtain know-how from a reputable manufacturer of such products. After some research Sam came upon one such company in Philadelphia. According to the trade magazine *Refrigeration Week*, Fogel Refrigeration, an established American company with a stellar reputation, seemed to have precisely the product line that he was interested in.

Over a period of several months he corresponded with the company, and he was pleased to find out that Fogel Refrigeration was open to a licensing arrangement with Amnur. They would gladly meet with a representative of the Israeli company, and, subject to successful negotiations, they would share as much of their expertise and know-how as was necessary.

Visiting Fogel in Philadelphia would offer Sam a special treat: He could stop in New York and visit with Bella and Leon for a few days before their imminent departure to Illinois. The Vietnam War was in full swing and rather than being drafted, Leon had volunteered to join the United States Air Force as a medical doctor, thus reducing the likelihood of being sent overseas to the war zone. Instead, the couple would shortly be relocated to Chanute Air Force Base near Chicago, so this would be perfect timing for Sam to travel to the United States.

Sam scheduled the trip to Philadelphia during the spring of 1965. His mission was to learn as much as he could about the Fogel line of refrigerators, and see if their products could be adapted to Israeli conditions. If suitable, he was authorized to agree to reasonable royalty payments for each refrigerator produced based upon the American company's design.

Prior to this trip to the United States Sam had unsuccessfully tried to establish similar relationships with suppliers in Holland,

Germany, and France. He visited their plants and found that while they did have the technology and designs he was seeking, their fear of retribution from the Arab countries for dealing with Israel was serious enough to prevent them from reaching an amicable arrangement. The Arab boycott was still in full swing!

Under pressure of the Arab boycott against Israel, Nahum's agreement with the American company Philco had been cancelled several years earlier, so Sam did not hold much hope of reaching an agreement with this American company either, but it still was worth the effort and expense to try.

He rode the train from New York to Philadelphia, took a taxi and was impressed that the company name was all he needed to give the taxi driver—seemingly the company was so well known that no address was necessary.

He introduced himself at the reception area and within a minute or two a somewhat balding man about his age came through a side door and introduced himself.

"Hello Sam, I am Bill."

"Nice meeting you, Bill."

"I am glad you could make the trip and come visit us. Let's go into the conference room and chat for a while, then I will give you a tour of the factory, and then we can sit and talk business."

Bill led the way.

"How much time do you have?" he asked.

"I am free all day. I am taking the train back to New York this evening," Sam explained

"Why don't you stay in Philadelphia a bit longer? It is a wonderful city. We can take you out to dinner in one of our famous restaurants in town and show you around some, and tomorrow we can tour the city during daylight hours."

"Thank you, that is very kind of you, but my daughter and son-in-law are in Manhattan and I would like to spend as much time with them as I could. They are moving to Illinois soon and getting there would be much more difficult for me."

"I understand. Maybe next time," Bill said.

They entered the conference room. Sam looked around. Not a large room, with pictures of the company products lining the walls.

"Who are we meeting with here?" Sam asked.

"No one in particular. I put everyone in standby mode, as I didn't know where this discussion will take us. From the correspondence and our research, we were not sure what precisely you needed, so I did not schedule anyone at a specific time or in a particular order. We are flexible."

"Thanks, that is great," Sam said.

They sat down.

"Can you tell me a bit about the company?" Sam wanted to get to understand the company and the hierarchy.

"Sure. Fogel Refrigeration is a private company, we have been in business since 1899, and are quite successful, with a solid reputation. But you probably know all of that, so let me go into the organization.

"I am William Fogel, the president of the company," Bill said. "You have been corresponding with Joel, our business development VP, who reports directly to me, and he will be joining us later."

So now Sam realized that not only was Bill the President of the company, he was also the owner of the company.

They chatted for a while, and then Bill offered to escort Sam through the plant. They toured the manufacturing area, extremely impressive and impeccable, well organized and functional, and then they returned to the conference room. Bill called Joel to join them there.

Over lunch served in the conference room Bill and Joel, reviewed the various products Fogel was manufacturing for various business needs. There were glossy pictures, and Sam was truly impressed with the thoughtfulness of the offerings and concluded that many of them would be a wonderful addition to the current product line of Amnur.

Then the conversation turned to the business side, and the three discussed the terms of any licensing agreement between the two companies. Despite his amicable mannerism and exhibited friendliness toward Sam, Bill, aided and abetted by Joel, was driving a hard bargain, demanding tough provisions and heavy fees, far more than Sam felt were reasonable for Amnur, and Sam was beginning to wonder if his trip were not in vain.

"I am not sure I can agree to your terms," despondent Sam finally responded to the latest set of demands. "We are not a wealthy company. We live and operate in a country that is not wealthy either, has a limited-size market, and imposes substantial tariffs on almost everything. Fuel and all raw materials are all imported and hence very expensive; labor is also expensive since almost every male employee and some female employees have military reserve duty of thirty-five days every year, and by law the employer has to cover the Reservist's pay.

"Your designs are fascinating and exciting, but they call for a very sophisticated production line, which will require a substantial capital investment as well, and as much as I like them I don't think we can afford such an investment. And on top of that you are asking for hefty royalties that we cannot pay. We cannot sell these units and make a profit under these terms."

Bill Fogel and Joel exchanged glances, then Bill looked at Sam and smiled.

"I know, Sam. Nothing that you have told us is news to us," he said. "Before you arrived we had done some research, spoke with the Israeli consulate in New York, did some calculations, and have come to the same conclusions."

He paused for a moment, and looked Sam in the eyes.

"These are our terms for everyone," he stated without fanfare, then after a pause he continued. "Everyone *else* that is."

Bill leaned forward in his chair.

"Sam, I am a Jew, and have a great affinity for Israel. For some time now I have been eager to start an association with a reliable Israeli company, and when Joel brought me your correspondence I thought we may have finally found a partner to our liking.

"This morning you confirmed my thinking. I like you Sam, and believe that you are sincere in your interest in our products. I tested your resolve, and liked what I saw. You demonstrated the kind of personality that I can trust and will enjoy associating with.

"So forget all of our discussion and negotiations so far. Those terms do not apply to you, and Amnur."

He picked up his cup of coffee, took a sip, set the cup down, and then continued.

"I will now make you a proposition that will be more to your liking," he said with a sly smile.

"I will provide you with all the know-how that you need to establish a production line of our products similar to what you saw in the factory earlier. I will provide you with all the design drawings; I will provide you with a complete detailed bill of materials down to the last screw; I could also provide you with a "starter-kit" of sample parts, but those will not be useful to you because they are fabricated according to the American measurement standards of inches, and you use the metric system.

"As to the production facilities, I will connect you with the suppliers of the equipment necessary to produce the refrigerators, including the toughest part–the polyurethane insulation machine. Through my connections you will not be charged a penny for that equipment, you will only have to commit to purchasing supplies from these companies, and they are trustworthy, and fair.

"I will guide you in every way you need, and I will even send our chief engineer to help you start the production line. In essence it is a package deal and the only thing you will have to do is to convert our designs and drawings from our system to yours. And to avoid any misconceptions you will not be required to put our logo on your products, you can put your own. That will also make it your products."

He took another sip of his coffee, then continued.

"And best of all, I will not charge you a single penny for all that. Not a single penny."

Sam sat there speechless, stunned. He would be getting all this handed to him on a silver platter for free? Then it occurred to him that even with all that, the royalty payments were oppressively high.

"What about the licensing fees that we discussed?"

"Forget that. As I said, forget all our earlier discussions."

Now Sam was bewildered.

"We will charge you a licensing fee of $1 per year," Bill Fogel smiled.

"One dollar?" Sam asked in utter astonishment.

"Yes. One United States dollar. That $1 will make it an official business transaction, and the contract a valid contract."

"And how about royalties?" Sam asked.

"No royalties."

"Are you serious?" Sam wanted verification.

"I could not be more serious than that."

"But why? Does that make good business sense for you?"

"Listen Sam, we are an established profitable family-owned business. We are quite successful. Charging you licensing fees or royalties will not make a dent in either our top or bottom lines, but for you it will make all the difference in the world.

"I always wanted to do something good for Israel beyond buying Israeli bonds, and you just gave me a tremendous opportunity to do that. I am grateful to you for coming here to see me, and helping me find a way to help the State of Israel in some little way.

"Furthermore, I know that some of these refrigerators will end up in military camps of the IDF and that gives me the good feeling that in some small way I have improved the lot of the soldiers defending the country.

"I appreciate it very much," was all Sam could utter.

They sat there for a minute, reflecting on what had just transpired.

"Would you like some more coffee, or something else to drink?"

"No, thank you."

"It is now 3:30 p.m. I think you still have time before the train back to New York. Tell me more about Israel, the situation there, and your life."

Sam described the conditions in the country, a country of mostly immigrants from all corners of the world. He spoke about the cities, and how Tel Aviv was growing by leaps and bounds.

"Do you live in Tel Aviv?" Bill asked

"No, I live in Ramat Gan, which is adjacent to Tel Aviv. The factory is in Beth Shemesh which is about an hour drive, half way to Jerusalem."

"And your family, how about your family?"

Sam briefly described his family.

"Were you born in Israel?"

"Oh, no. I was born in Latvia. I came to Palestine during the British Mandate in 1934."

"You were born in Latvia? No kidding. Where in Latvia?"

"From Riga, the capital of Latvia."

"That is something!" Bill exclaimed. He reached for the phone on the conference table. "Suzie, ask Rob to join us in the conference room."

He hung up, and turned to Sam with a sneaky smile on his face. "Our chief engineer is from Latvia, also from Riga. I am sure you guys have something in common to talk about."

For the first few moments, conversing in Latvian was difficult for Sam. Except for a rare short conversation with his brother Isaac he had not practiced the language for over thirty years now. But after a few hesitant sentences he was back into the groove and he and Rob had a pleasant conversation in their native language. Needless to say, from that moment on, any and all doors were opened to him, and he received the most dedicated cooperation one could hope for from a supplier, especially one who is asking for nothing in return.

When Sam returned to Israel loaded with blueprints and bills of materials and a commitment for a licensing agreement at no cost, he was greeted by all as a hero. Even his detractors, as there always are in a business enterprise—those who are jealous of one's success, or those who wished they had been appointed to the role, or those who had other motives to not belong to Sam's fan club—all agreed that he had concluded his excursion with excellent results.

For his part, Sam reported his tremendous achievements in the United States in a factual manner, not crediting himself with any contribution toward its success—that was his humble nature to not boast about his accomplishments. He took the events in stride, and set aside the importance of his successes.

And his achievements went far beyond the original goal of expanding the line of commercial refrigerators. With the assistance of Fogel Refrigeration Sam established contacts with the suppliers of the machinery producing the polyurethane insulation for the refrigerators, and those machines opened up the opportunity to enter into several new marketplaces and other product offerings.

The IDF, now using these new refrigerators somehow got wind of this new polyurethane insulation capability of Amnur, and inquired if Sam and his team could design and build low-cost, resilient, modular freezer rooms, to be delivered to their bases and, more importantly, to remote outposts, some of which were difficult to supply on a regular basis. Having such units would enable the army to reduce the frequency of supply deliveries under adverse conditions, thus simplifying the logistic complexity while improving the lot of the troops.

Sam and his engineering team set out to design and deliver the units to the military according to their specifications, and those far exceeded the expectations. Because of the special properties of polyurethane they were lighter, stronger, and able to withstand adverse weather conditions, including sandstorms that are not an uncommon phenomenon in the Negev desert.

One thing led to another, and Sam came to realize that if his team could build modular freezer rooms in expandable configurations, why couldn't the same basic designs apply to prefabricated housing, with air conditioning units instead of freezing units? Only minimal changes would be required, and a whole new production line would help reduce the pressure on construction of housing units for the newcomers to the country.

Thus this innovative and inventive thinking not only improved the company's bottom line, but also became a valuable tool for the government's efforts to resettle newcomers who were arriving from all over the world. No more *Maabarot*—the tent cities of the early 1950s, nor the *Shikunim*—the vertical housing complexes of one-size-fits-all of the late 1950s. These new prefabricated units were homes, could take different shapes and sizes, and were more pleasant to the eye as well.

Although Sam's standing in the company became firmer, he felt his achievements were nothing out of the ordinary, just the application of his faculties for which he was receiving a monthly pay check, and that's that. At least outwardly there was no change in his demeanor—he remained the same humble guy who still could not realize his immense contribution to more than his immediate family.

Did he acknowledge his value to himself? Probably not, again the remnants of the imprint left on him by his father. Yes, he was pleased and felt that he was accomplishing "something," although he would not appreciate the value of this "something" to the homeland for years to come.

Chapter 51

During the two years since Sam had brought Barak home with him, the dog proved to be a very easy animal to care for. Although his official post was on the landing outside the front door, watching, barking at, and scaring every pedestrian passing by, the door was always kept ajar allowing him to come in and out at will. He was substantially healthy and except for the yearly checkup, and a huge amount of food that he consumed, specially cooked for him, he was no trouble at all.

Whenever Ofer was in town he spent time with Barak, training him with all the normal obedience tricks and establishing the discipline that was necessary to keep such a large powerful animal in check, without fear of it hurting anyone, intentionally or by mistake. And it was important that Barak was well trained as to whom to allow entry into the property and whom to scare away. Not that he would bite anyone, but just his size and growl were enough to keep undesirables out of the yard. At the same time the dog allowed the mail carrier and the water and electricity meter readers unfettered access to the mailbox and meters respectively. He would give them a dirty look, warning them to not stray off their mission, but then allow them to go about their business unhindered.

It was clear that Barak suffered from a hearing problem in the left "folding" ear. To compensate for that deficiency Barak had developed exceptional eyesight and was able to discern and identify objects at far greater distance than most dogs are able to do. His sense of smell was also enhanced, probably for the same reason.

After a Friday night out, Ofer and his friends normally met around 2 a.m. at a specific eatery in Tel Aviv and wolfed down a sandwich or two. This particular kiosk offered a Mediterranean delight—a pita sandwich stuffed with a slice of charcoal grilled meat, some salad and pickles, all smothered in Tahini sauce.

After a few outings to this place, Ofer noticed that the owners of the eatery who were tending to the customers from behind the counter, would cut off and throw away the bones from the meat before serving, so he requested some of those bones to bring home for the dog.

What a delight was it for the animal! He would sense Ofer's arrival and smell the delicious addition to his normal diet. It was a weekly celebration for him. He would pounce on the bones and attack them in gluttonous fervor. And for Ofer, bribing the dog that way allowed him to sneak into the house without being licked to death by this loving creature.

Leah would be reading in bed, next to Sam who was sound asleep with his back toward her. She had a small table lamp and she covered the shade to minimize the light in the room so Sam would not be disturbed, but it was sufficient for her to read unimpeded till dawn. When Ofer would show up in the doorway to the bedroom she would rise and join him in the dining room. Just as the bond between Bella and her father was incredibly strong, so was the bond between these two, and they normally chatted until all hours of the night.

On one such occasions Leah complained.

"You bring bones for the dog, but you don't bring your old tired mother anything," she gently and fancifully reproached her son.

"I didn't know you would like the stuff," Ofer retorted.

"You know I love pork chops," she said.

"Pork chops? I know you eat *treyf* outside of home, but you keep a kosher home! How is that going to work bringing you a pork chop sandwich home?"

From the beginning Sam had insisted that Leah keep a kosher home, to ensure that any observant person, including his father, Pessia, and later his orthodox brother Isaac would be able to have a meal at their home. Sam was by no means a fanatic, and did not carry kashrut to extremes, but in Sam's and Leah's home there were two sets of dishes, pots and pans, and cutlery for everyday use, one for dairy products and one for meat, and also two such sets for Passover. As for Leah who had to deal with keeping kosher, she could not care less for it, yet out of respect for Sam's wishes she made sure to keep the four sets separate and uncontaminated. She bought only kosher foods and although there was only one refrigerator, and one sink, she did keep two dish rags that were kept on either side of the sink, one with a blue ribbon and the other with red, showing their purpose—dairy and meat respectively.

"So long as I eat the pork chop in a pita sandwich it won't contaminate anything."

"But what about dad?"

"He does not care what I eat, so long as the house is kept reasonably kosher. Anyway he is sleeping and will not care."

"Okay."

Without fail, the very next Friday night Ofer arrived home with bones for the dog, and a sandwich for his mother. He came into his parents' bedroom gingerly, careful to not wake his father or startle his mother, and then he handed her the sandwich.

The gourmet delight was wrapped in wax paper to keep the Tahini sauce from dripping. Sam was sleeping with his back to her, snoring gently, so Leah carefully unwrapped the sandwich. As hard as she tried to not disturb him, the crackling noise of the paper woke Sam up. He raised his head off the pillow and briefly looked over his shoulder.

"If you want to eat pork, eat pork," he reproached the two, "but don't make so much damned noise with the paper."

Typical Sam—lenient, accommodating, not overbearing, non-imposing, that was his makeup. While he himself would not eat pork or other *treyf* food, not even outside the home, he did not impose his wishes on others. "Live and let live" was the essence of his being, in such contrast to his late father's manner and outlook.

So from that day on, there were two souls eagerly waiting Ofer's arrival from his Friday night outings with his friends, and Ofer accommodated them both with an appropriate gift-pack for each.

Alas, not for long. There was something wrong with Barak and he began showing some signs of discomfort. Every once in a while he would wake up from a deep sleep and would growl as if he saw a threat. He would snarl. His upper lip would be raised, exposing his fangs and front teeth, a scary sight to behold. And then, as quickly as this behavior came unexpectedly, it would disappear, and the animal would return to its normal loving self. Was he getting obsessed by something?

As time progressed over a period of several months, the frequency and fierceness of these episodes grew to the point that the family became alarmed. It was obvious that during these episodes the dog was reacting to something that distressed him, but no one could tell what it was. They resolved to seek help from a veterinarian, and after a few more episodes Sam took an afternoon off and Leah and he drove the animal to be examined.

The veterinarian had no definitive answer. He needed to run a battery of tests on the animal to give a more accurate diagnosis, but when those proved all negative he finally suggested an X-ray of the dog.

His findings were devastating to the family. The dog had developed a brain tumor under that folding left ear, and the only remedy he could propose was to perform brain surgery to save the animal.

"I am reluctant to take it on," he admitted. "It is not a simple operation, and from what I can tell by the X-ray, this is more complicated than I feel comfortable with. Moreover, if I try to perform the surgery, the likelihood of success is about half at best, and I would be devastated to have such a beautiful animal die on my operating table."

"What is the solution then?" Leah asked.

"I don't know. It is also a very expensive surgery, with a long recovery time in an animal hospital, and I don't know any vet in private practice who has the wherewithal and the competence to do it."

"Is there anyone who *can* perform the surgery?"

"The only place I know where this dog has a fighting chance is with the police or border patrol Canine Units. They have the best veterinarians anywhere, and the facilities to handle such a case."

"How can we get them to save the dog?"

"I don't know. Call them and find out. They are located in Beit Dagon."

Sam knew the place, he passed it every day on his way to the plant, so a few days later he stopped and inquired about what they could do for the animal. They scheduled a time for them to come and meet with Leah and him, and take a look at Barak.

A few days later, two officers from the police K-9 unit arrived. During the weekend before the police arrival, Barak had a very serious episode at the end of which he latched his fangs into Ofer's arm and left a deep gash. He did not really want to hurt Ofer, whom he loved more than anyone else, but he simply needed to bite into something, anything, and Ofer's arm happened to be nearby.

The officers, both veterinary doctors, examined the dog, tested and observed him for a long time, viewed the X-ray, and then produced their verdict.

"The tumor is pressing on vital parts of the brain and is causing him these episodes of pain and anguish. If you do not have him operated on he will suffer an agonizing death within probably several months to a year. We believe that we can successfully perform the operation and save his life, but by law we can treat only our dogs, dogs that belong to the department.

"We need dogs like Barak in the department to help with various security duties. He seems to have very acute eyesight and an excellent sensitive nose, and the hearing issue may be related to the tumor. We would love having a dog like him in the department. Such a dog could be an enormous asset to us, if he can be cured of course."

"What are you suggesting?"

"If you give us the dog we give you our solemn oath that we will operate on him, and try to save his life. He will remain with us, and we will re-train him for our needs. The only caveat is that you will not be able to ever know what happened to him, nor see him, or have any contact with him—without that, we cannot break the bond and ensure that the dog is truly 'ours' with no outside allegiance."

"Why can't we know what happened to him?" Leah asked.

"Because if you know where he is, the temptation will be great to go see him, and that will defeat our efforts to estrange him from you."

Leah and Sam sat quietly internalizing what they just heard. They would have to give Barak up for him to be saved. But then they would lose him in any case, either now or within some months while he needlessly suffered. And if the police are able to save the dog then they, Leah and Sam, have indirectly helped the country's security through his service.

Painful as it was, the decision was clear.

"Could you please come back Sunday to pick him up? We want our son Ofer to be able to say good-bye to him before you take him away, and Ofer won't be in Ramat Gan till the weekend."

"Sure, no problem. We will be back Sunday evening."

The days through the weekend were somber for the family, a close member would be departing soon, never to be seen again, but he would remain alive—somewhere.

On Sunday night the two officers were back. Leah and Sam gave them all the dog paraphernalia, hugged their dog one last time, and stood at the door watching their beloved animal follow the two officers.

Partway down the stairs the sergeant turned around to face the two.

"I know this must be painful—the dog has been with you almost two years and is obviously loved, but it is the right decision on many fronts. Think about the good that this dog will bring to the country and its security."

And with that he turned and followed his colleague to the car.

❖ ❖ ❖

A year passed and a few months followed. Leah, Sam, and Ofer missed the dog, and often wondered about whether the police veterinarians were able to save him, but there was no word from the police about the animal.

Then one Friday, an article appeared in the Sabbath edition of the evening newspaper about a kibbutz in the north of the country, not too far from the Sea of Galilee, being shelled by the Syrians on a regular basis, and suffering attempted infiltrations by Arab terrorists.

The article described the life of the members of the kibbutz, and how they were coping with these threats. Embedded in the article was a picture of a member of the kibbutz petting his dog Barak, the guard dog of the kibbutz, and when Sam and Leah saw the picture tears came to their eyes. The pain of loss of this dog surfaced once again.

There was no doubt. This was Sam's and Leah's old Barak, folded left ear and dimple in the left cheek. This was their dog, the dog Sam had rescued from starvation at the plant, the dog that was always at the top of the stairs welcoming them when they arrived home, wagging his tail and extending his wet tongue, so happy to see them.

So the police veterinarians had been successful after all!

Chapter 52

Sam was in the kitchen preparing his cup of "mud" coffee. He put a heaping spoon of finely ground "Turkish" coffee and a spoon of sugar into a cup, and then poured boiling hot water from the old trusted aluminum kettle that Leah and he had owned since their wedding. He briskly mixed this concoction and then headed to the bathroom to shave while the grounds sank to the bottom and the coffee cooled down some. He would drink it on his way out the door.

As he passed the telephone in the hallway on his way to shave, the phone rang, startling him. He glanced at his watch. It read 5:35 in the morning.

He wondered who would be calling this early, Ofer was in Haifa, having left the previous morning for a couple of days, and he was due to return tonight. But why would he call? Maybe it was Bella? She was in Illinois and there it was 8:35 in the evening, but she never called, it was so damned expensive. Most probably it was a coworker, who needed a ride to the plant.

All these thoughts passed through his head in the briefest of a millisecond. He rushed to pick the handset up from the cradle of the ugly black desk phone, considerate of Leah who was still sleeping. She always read until the wee hours of the morning, and then slept late, so he did not want her to wake up.

"Hello," he said softly to the receiver.

"Sorry to call so early, Aba," Ofer was on the line. "Everything is fine, but I wanted to let you know that I will not be coming home tonight as planned, and did not want you and mother to worry.

"I got called out last night, mobilized, and we are on the way south. The bus stopped for gas in Herzliya so I am using the phone here. We will be re-boarding in a minute. I hope to be home for the weekend, but who knows."

Sam glanced at the calendar hanging on the wall, scribbled all over with Leah's handwriting reminding her of birthdays, anniversaries, and other events happening in their lives. It was Wednesday, May 17, 1967 he confirmed. Two days earlier they had celebrated Israel's nineteenth Independence Day, and that was why it was a short school week for Ofer.

"I understand," Sam said.

"I will let you know. I have to go. Others are waiting for the phone. Shalom."

"Be safe, my son," Sam said.

"Thanks, Aba." There was a click and the line went dead.

"Who was it?" Leah was at the end of the corridor.

"It was Ofer. He was called to reserve duty."

"For how long?"

"He didn't know, but they are heading south, probably to the base. He said he won't be home tonight, but maybe this is a drill and then he will be free by the weekend."

He glanced at his watch.

"I've got to go, or I'll be late to the office."

He gave Leah a kiss and she headed back to bed. A few moments later having quickly shaved, he emerged from the bathroom. Leah's night table lamp was on, so he surmised she did not go back to sleep.

"A mother," he mused. He drank his coffee and headed out the door.

On his way to Beth Shemesh he did not notice anything unusual. Normal traffic, like most other days. Some soldiers in uniform carrying their side arms were standing at the regular bus stops. As was common practice in Israel, and as he did almost every day, he filled his car with soldier-hitchhikers. An ordinary day, no sign of high alert; even his passengers did not exhibit any tension and carried on as on any normal day. It must be that Ofer was called as part of the periodic reserve call-out drills.

The weekend arrived and there was no sign of Ofer. Leah and Sam sat down for the traditional Friday night meal, and somehow Sam's Kiddush over the wine seemed to be sung with deeper emotion than normal. By that time Sam was getting the feeling that something was brewing in the country. More and more reservists were sprinkled among the regular soldiers in the bus stops on the road. There were tank transporters—those behemoth flatbed trucks with camouflaged tanks on them, and other military convoys heading in different directions.

On Saturday morning Sam broke with his normal routine and went to the synagogue for prayers, something he had not done since his father had passed away almost twenty years earlier. He was worried for the safety of his son—should hostilities break out, Ofer would be front and center in the thick of it. He was a signals officer of a tank battalion, and would be tasked with ensuring their communications were functioning properly, especially when in combat and under fire.

And it was clear that hostilities could break out at any moment. That same Saturday the saber rattling Egyptian President Gamal Abdel Nasser, the one that Eisenhower foolishly "rescued" in 1956, expelled the United Nations Emergency Force from Gaza and the Sinai. Upon the first call to vacate, the entire U.N. force stationed in the Gaza and Sinai to ensure it remained demilitarized caved in. Without objection or protest, they abandoned their mission and hastily left the area, thus making it easier for Nasser to advance an enormous army into the Sinai, threatening the south of Israel.

Embolden by his ability to bully the world with impunity, on the following Tuesday, Nasser once again, as he had done in 1956, announced the closure of the Tiran straits at the southern tip of the Red Sea to Israeli shipping. He belligerently poured an army 80,000 strong into the Sinai Peninsula, supported by 500 battle tanks and top notch Russian supplied military equipment, threatening the obliteration of the State of Israel, and no one in the international community spoke up or protested. They cowered to this tyrant and his Soviet masters.

Leah called Sam later that day to tell him they had received a postcard from Ofer. Unlike a regular postcard, this one was a plain white card with no picture on it, the military's notion of a correspondence instrument. On one side were Ofer's name and military post office designation which meant nothing as to where he was physically located, and on the other side he had scribbled that he was fine, had everything he needed, but did not know when he would be back home.

He did not mention his location, the conditions there, or what he saw or heard—these things would be a violation of the secrecy and security of his unit, and would probably have landed him in hot water with the military censor. But at least he was well, to the great relief of his parents.

Another week passed and then another, and the tension on the borders was mounting. By then it had become obvious that there had been a massive deployment of the reserves in Israel, and almost the entire economy came to a screeching halt. Even civilian trucks that normally would carry goods to the market vanished from the streets, conscripted by the army to provide logistics support and supplies to the troops now amassed along all the borders with Egypt, Jordan, Syria, and even Lebanon.

How long could this small country hold out with its economy shut down and its entire workforce in uniform and at the borders?

On Saturday morning June 3, Leah and Sam woke up to the phone ringing by Sam's bedside.

"Shalom Aba," Ofer was on a crackling line, "Can you meet me at Netivot Junction at 11 o'clock?"

Sam glanced at his watch. It was ten minutes past 8 a.m., and the trip to Netivot should not take more than an hour and a half, probably less since the roads had been empty in the last week.

"Sure."

"Meet me at the gas station there. If you don't mind, can you please bring me my binoculars, my sun glasses, and the camera?"

"Do you need anything else?"

"No, I don't think so. I have everything I need, except maybe a couple of pairs of my underwear. These army-supplied boxer shorts drive me nuts with their front opening, you know what I mean."

"Yeah, I understand," Sam chuckled.

"See you at 11."

"Okay."

Leah and Sam arrived twenty minutes early to the Netivot junction. Over a cup of coffee, they sat patiently waiting for Ofer to arrive.

In typical military punctuality at 11:00 a.m. sharp a dusty gray-colored open civilian jeep arrived, and Ofer jumped out. He was tanned and looked fit and relaxed, an Uzi sub-machine gun slung over his shoulder, and a military radio on his back.

"Pick me up here at 11:50 sharp," he told the driver. "Stay by the radio, and if there is any change I will contact you." The Jeep turned back, and Ofer dusted off his uniform and entered the coffee shop.

After the greetings and the warm hugs, they sat for a while talking. Sam looked at his son, a young man in the ill-fitting military garb, and there was a slight tinge of jealousy in his eyes. He wished he could join his son to guard and protect the country, but at 57 he was no longer in the reserves. The truth was he felt somewhat discarded.

"Tell us everything, from the beginning," Leah had to get the details. "How did they call you? You were in Haifa, and still they knew?"

"Sure, I had given them the Haifa address as an emergency contact during weekdays."

"How did they call you?" Leah insisted.

"There was a knock on the door around 2 a.m. A tall man in his thirties was at the door carrying a clipboard. I immediately knew he was from the military calling me for a reserve duty readiness drill. Normally they have me sign the roster and let me go, or at worst expect me to appear in the gathering point before discharging me.

"He told me: 'I suggest you take a toothbrush with you. There are buses waiting downtown.'

"So I figured that it must be a real reserve call-out exercise. They would probably take me and others to the camp, maybe even issue us the standard gear, go through the motions and test the process to its end, all but actually dispatching us out to an assigned destination.

"Sure enough a civilian bus was quietly waiting at the central square, trying to not attract too much attention. Within minutes we headed south, in the dark of night. I called you from the gas station when the bus stopped to refuel. Then they brought us to our camp, and issued our gear.

"Wednesday night after dark we headed out toward the border and have been here since."

They discussed the situation with Egypt. Netivot would be a logical jumping point for Ofer's unit into the northern Sinai, so Egypt was front and center in everyone's mind at the table.

"Last week we had a visit by the division commander. He came to give us a pep talk and brief us on the forces on both sides of the borders. You probably read some of this in the papers. The Egyptians have thrown their best units into the conflict zone," Ofer said. "They have some 500 tanks facing us, and some of their stuff is top notch. They have Russian equipment, very simple, but robust. They have T34s, T54s, T55s, and even Stalin 3s, all tanks that have diesel engines, and have speed and long range.

"Against that, we have about 150 tanks on this side of the border. Our equipment is more sophisticated but we are gasoline powered tanks, which means shorter range. Some of our tanks are Sherman M1s, leftover relics from WWII, others are British Centurion tanks which are much better. We are better trained and organized than the Egyptians, and above all we are determined that we simply cannot fail. If we fail, the country is gone."

Ofer looked into his parents' faces and he realized that he was scaring them and making them even more worried than they already were. It was all true, but he should have kept this information to himself. Now if hostilities break out, which they almost certainly would, his parents would be worried sick for him and his unit. He had to reverse that impression and give them something that would make them less anxious, not more.

He glanced at his watch; the Jeep would be heading out to pick him up in a few minutes.

"Do you have some time to spare?" he asked.

"Sure." Sam answered. "Why are you asking?"

"I was given one hour and have to go back to the unit by 12. But there we can spend some more time together. I would like you to come with me."

"How are we going to get there? I have the Peugeot 404, not a Jeep with 4-wheel drive."

"You are one of the best drivers I know. You will make it." Ofer reached for the radio and told the Jeep driver to stand down.

Reluctantly and hesitatingly at first, Sam put the Peugeot in gear, and headed down the powdery sand road toward the campsite. The car and Sam worked in unison for the next three miles to reach their destination. If he had not been such an excellent driver, they probably would have gotten stuck in the deep sand.

They climbed up the rise to the plateau and there was Ofer's unit spread out over a large area, each tank under a camouflage net—an impressive sight.

"This is my battalion. We have our tanks and all the support vehicles. I have my signals truck which has a repair shop for broken radios and telephones, and a civilian refrigerated milk truck where we keep the spare parts. I also have my own command car that I and some of my guys run around in."

He did not tell them where he was supposed to run with that command car, or that it was meant to carry him and his signalmen to tanks during battle to fix their communication equipment. An unarmored vehicle "soft target," but he had already scared them enough.

They sat down and chatted with some of Ofer's signalmen, a fine bunch of jovial types. Men of all stripes and professions mingled in a cohesive unit, including one of Ofer's professors in the Technion who was now his subordinate signalman. What impressed Sam and Leah was the positive mood of the members of Ofer's company: While apprehensive about the prospect of an impending war, they were more anxious to get it over with.

Ofer then took his parents for the grand tour, which included the climbing up on one of the tanks to look inside. For Engineer Sam, the tank was an impressive piece of machinery, one that bolstered feelings of safety and respect for the metal beast and its fire power.

A while later they walked back to the green Peugeot, now white with a coating of dust.

"It is going to start either tomorrow or Monday at the latest. There is no question about that," Ofer said quietly.

Then he added: "You saw that we are well prepared and well equipped, so don't worry. You met some of the guys here, and you saw that their morale is high, and they are ready to defend the country. They are anxious to get it over with."

With that they hugged, and teary-eyed the parents left their child to face the unknown.

He did not tell them the not-so-good parts. His unit had good ammunition for the tanks, but was very weak in the small arms and small-arms ammunition departments. Some of the tank crews were issued automatic long rifles. What do you do with a long rifle inside a tank? There is no place to keep it; it would be in the way. Some of his troops received Mauser 1898 bolt action rifles, WWI weapons, and everyone was limited to fifty rounds of ammunition. That is about a five-second burst with an Uzi sub machine gun.

When the division commander came visiting the unit a week earlier, one of the soldiers asked him: "What can we do with fifty rounds of ammunition?" The Commander replied: "Fifty rounds are enough to kill fifty of the enemy."

"Yeah, right!" quipped one of the soldiers.

Ofer also did not say, but it was perfectly understood by all his fellow soldiers that it all depended on air cover. If a pilot in an enemy jet spots you riding in your beautiful and powerful tank, and decides to take you out, there is nothing to stop him from blowing you to pieces. Survival depended on air cover provided by the Israeli Air Force, that same air force that his father had helped seed and build less than twenty years earlier.

Chapter 53

The Six Day War started Monday morning with the Israeli Air Force obliterating the Egyptian Air Force, thus being able to provide total air cover to the Israeli armor engaging the enemy in the Sinai.

It was a tremendous relief for all of Israel, especially for those who had friends or family in the thick of things in the Sinai that the mighty Egyptian Air Force, equipped with the best Soviet armament, was no longer a threat to the Israeli ground forces. Sam and Leah had no doubt Ofer was somewhere in the Sinai engaging the Egyptian superior forces, superior in both numbers and equipment.

By ten o'clock that day of June 5, Jordan entered the fray as well, followed closely by Syria. Sam and Leah were glued to the radio at every opportunity, constantly listening to news from the fronts. While there was continuous influx of reporting, not much of it was from the front itself. The notion of "embedded journalists" was not developed, and the communication capabilities from the front were practically non-existent, so it was the Israeli Defense Forces radio that provided updates through the military spokesman rather than independent "on the scene" reporters.

A few days passed, and there was no word from Ofer, but nonetheless day after day Leah ran down to the mailbox whenever she thought the letter carrier was in the neighborhood.

To their great relief, Friday's mail finally brought a military postcard from Ofer. It was stamped Wednesday, and on it he wrote that he was fine although tired, not having slept since Monday morning when the hostilities broke out. But he was alive, uninjured, and in good spirits.

He did not mention where he was in the combat zone. At the bottom of the card Ofer noted that the son of Yehuda, Sam's former Coldomat partner, a tank commander in his battalion, was injured and was evacuated to a hospital, and although his injuries were not life threatening they were serious.

Leah called Sam at the plant and read to him Ofer's card. When Sam returned from work that afternoon he reached out to Yehuda, with whom he had not had any contact since departing Coldomat. Despite his resentment and dislike of his former partner, this was the time to show his genuine support and well wishes for Yehuda's son's speedy recovery. The young man, a promising tennis star, would never play tennis again.

Over the weekend Bella called from the United States, and Leah and Sam updated her on whatever news they had. She was mostly concerned about her brother, but also about how her parents were managing.

A few more days passed with no news from Ofer. Wednesday was the holiday of Shavuot, and as was his custom, Sam went to the synagogue for the morning prayers. Leah was deeply asleep having read some romantic novel most of the night.

Someone startled her by touching her arm. For a moment she did not recognize the man dressed in green, covered in dust, over-grown hair and unshaven, an Uzi submachine gun and an AK-47 assault rifle slung over his shoulders, leaning over her. And then the sleepiness was torn away from her.

She jumped out of the bed crying out loud "Ofer," and she reached out and hugged the young man in a way she had never hugged him before. Tears were streaming down her cheeks, and she clung to him for the longest time. Then she let go, took half a step back and looked at him.

He looked tired, more like exhausted, and was dusty, but otherwise he was well, with all his limbs intact. He was tanned she noticed, probably from the desert sun.

"Aba is in the synagogue. He should be back at one o'clock. What time is it?" She asked.

"Eleven thirty."

"I will go bring him home."

"No need, he will come back soon enough. I have been on the road for nearly twenty hours, awake since yesterday morning. I am tired and need a shower."

"How did you get home? On Shavuot there are no buses running, and you probably didn't have any money on you for a cab."

"They drove us through the Sinai overnight, and brought us to Beersheba, and then let us loose. I hitched a ride with some guy to the outskirts of Tel Aviv, and there a taxi driver offered to take me home for free, which was very nice of him."

"Are you hungry? Do you want to eat something?"

"No, thank you. I need a shower."

He could not keep his eyes open. Right after a good scrub in the hot shower he fell onto his bed. He was fast asleep even before his head hit the pillow, and stayed motionless for the longest time. He did not hear his father come home and missed the holiday lunch with his parents.

When Sam woke up the next morning, Ofer was gone. For a moment Sam wasn't even sure if his son had really been there the day before, but the unmistakable signs were there—a ruffled bed, the camera and binoculars on the desk.

On the kitchen counter was a note saying:

"Aba,

Sorry I missed you.

Heading back to camp to return the equipment to the emergency stores.

May be back for Shabbat.

Ofer."

He did. Friday evening he returned, this time without the military hardware. He was once again a civilian ready to go about his normal studies as a junior in mechanical engineering at the Technion.

Leah and Sam were hoping Ofer would tell them about the events of the war and his experiences, but their son was not accommodating. He was not willing to talk about it. He did not refuse; he just clammed up and would not discuss those ten days, the days between their meeting in Netivot, and his return at Shavuot. The impact was probably just too harsh on him to relive it so soon. He needed time.

It wasn't that he would not talk at all. They spoke about the political landscape, the international ramifications, any and all subjects that came up in the conversation, but the time period from the beginning of hostilities to their end were a sealed book inside his head, and he was not going to open it, at least not yet.

Over the weekend Ofer spoke to some of his friends from the Technion by phone, and was told that his class suffered a casualty in the war. Months later the details of this loss were made public: Returning from a bombing run over Egypt his classmate's damaged jet strayed over a restricted area, and did not respond to warnings—the pilot was probably unconscious, or maybe even dead, from wounds suffered when his plane was hit. The area ground commanding officer could not take a chance that the plane might crash in a security zone, so to protect a critical installation he gave the order to shoot it down. An Israeli plane was intentionally shot down by an Israeli missile.

The second piece of information Ofer received was that during his long absence, gradually many of the students of his class were called up. Despite that, the school continued the academic year as if no one had been mobilized into the reserves, and the school was not making any concessions to those who had been called up, despite being a majority of the student body. That meant that having missed over a month of classes Ofer and others faced imminent exams within the month of July, with no accommodation to those who had been out of school because of the war: As normal, if students were not ready for the final exams at the beginning of the summer then they could take them in the fall, but that was that.

No give. The veterans were on their own. No breaks.

So Ofer studied hard, trying to catch up as best he could, and his parents did everything they could do to help him out. Since Ofer preferred to study with a group of friends, there was always food in the house to feed his classmates who came to study together. And in the end, they all passed their finals with flying colors thus thumbing their noses at the unforgiving Technion.

❖ ❖ ❖

During that summer between junior and senior years Ofer was hired as an engineer to work in the research and development department of Amcor. He thus could put to practical use the material he had studied during the previous four years, and also bring some new thinking to the engineering of new products for the Amcor conglomerate. He spent his days in the headquarters of the company in Tel Aviv, and his nights at his parents' home in Ramat Gan.

One evening Leah and Sam were out visiting some friends and Ofer was on his way out the door to meet with his own friends when the phone rang.

"Hello, may I please speak with Philip?" the caller asked in English.

"Philip? There is no Philip here, you may have dialed the wrong number," Ofer replied.

"I am looking for Philip Glickman," the man said.

Ofer was further stymied—Philip and Isaac had both changed their names from Glickman to Gilan at the same time Sam did during 1948. Different spelling in Latin letters but same in Hebrew.

"Oh, I see. He does not live here, he lives in Rehovot. May I ask who is calling?" Ofer asked.

"I am sorry, I should have introduced myself. I am his cousin Percy Glickman from South Africa."

Ofer did not recognize the name. If that man was Philip's cousin, then by default he was Sam's cousin as well, and Ofer had no notion that his father had any relatives in South Africa, and he never had heard that name before.

"May I ask how you got this number for Philip Glickman?" he asked.

"Sure, I contacted the Division for Locating Relatives of the Israeli Government and they gave me this number."

During the Holocaust most people lost contact with friends and relatives, and when Israel was established the Ministry of the Interior created a division to facilitate the reconnection between people and their relatives.

"Oh, I see. That explains it. I am Ofer, Shmuel Glickman's son," he used Sam's Hebrew former name. "They gave you this number because Philip does not have a phone."

"You are Mulya's son? That's great, I finally made contact with kin. I came to Israel a couple of weeks ago looking for family, and it seems I finally found my relatives."

"I think you did."

"May I speak to Mulya?"

"He is not home right now, but I can leave him a message. Where can he reach you?"

"I am staying at Dan Hotel in Tel Aviv," Percy said.

"As soon as I see him I will ask him to call you."

Sam was delighted at the news.

So out of 128, six cousins, not five, escaped Hitler and the Nazis.

Chapter 54

Bella reported her great news: Firstly, her husband Leon completed his two years of service in the U.S. Air Force; secondly she completed her studies and graduated with a master's degree from New York University; and finally, and most importantly she said, Leon was offered a position as a resident at Mount Sinai Hospital in New York so they were heading back to the great City.

Sam was elated, and Leah was very pleased that Leon's military service was complete without him having to spend time in a war zone. With the Vietnam War raging on, and not progressing very well for the United States, a tour in Vietnam could be extremely unpleasant for both the military person and his family. By having volunteered for the air force Leon had all but ensured that he would not be heading to the war zone. But in these matters there are no guarantees, and he could still have received marching orders to the front regardless. Now, to everyone's relief, he was free and clear having been honorably discharged from the service.

The other effect of his wise decision to enlist the way he did was that he now qualified for the benefits of the G.I. Bill and those would supplement the meager income that a resident doctor at Mount Sinai received for the many hours of duty. It would also assist Bella in pursuing a doctorate degree, something she felt compelled to do for several reasons.

"It is really great that Bella and Leon will be in New York," Sam told Leah. "Now the time difference between them and us will shrink by one hour to only seven hours during most of the year."

"I am not sure it will make such a big difference," Leah objected. "We don't normally call them that often. Nor do they call very often either. It is so damned expensive."

"You are right, I guess."

"Back to the aerogrammes and air mail my friend," she chided him.

Sam's handwriting was meticulous, easy to read, well-formed letters in straight lines, and his language was flowing and flawless. Leah's handwriting on the other hand had a somewhat more of a disheveled look, although her Hebrew was as elegant as Sam's. Despite being so well read her English required a bit more polish.

So over the next few years the communications with their daughter was conducted over regular air mail.

Bella and Leon rented an apartment in a high rise only two blocks away from Mount Sinai hospital at the edge of Spanish Harlem in Manhattan. The neighborhood was not considered the safest around, so soon they were joined by a German Shepherd aptly named Magen, shield or protector in Hebrew, and the dog undertook the role of bodyguard and companion to Bella on those long thirty-six-hour shifts that Leon had to endure at the hospital.

The ensuing months entered a routine for Leah and Sam. Ofer stayed with them during the summer, and when school resumed Ofer reduced his hours at his job from full time to part time, and was shuttling between his school in Haifa, his job in Tel Aviv, and home in Ramat Gan.

When the winter arrived, Ofer declared his interest in pursuing his graduate studies in business administration in the United States, and neither Sam nor Leah could argue much against it, despite the fact that if accepted, Ofer would also be far from them, thus leaving them as true empty nesters.

With his credentials of a soon-to-be graduate of the Technion with high grades and nearly 350 credits towards a bachelor's degree—practically three times as many as an equivalent American student would accumulate—Ofer had no difficulty in being admitted to some very prestigious schools: Columbia University, Wharton, New York University, and MIT. Because Columbia University had a reputation in Israel as an excellent institute he chose Columbia University in New York City, not too far from Bella and Leon's home.

During the summer that year Bella and Leon came to Israel for vacation and what a joy it was for Leah and Sam. Sam took some time off from work so they could travel around the country and spend as much time together as was possible.

And Ofer? During that year he was mobilized for an extraordinary number of days of military reserve duty. From the time he was called to the war in May 1967 and the time he left the country in August 1968 Ofer spent 105 days in uniform, protecting the western border with Egypt in the Sinai and also performing garrison duty in the Gaza Strip. It may have been this reserve duty that loosened his mental block and he finally was able to tell his parents and sister and brother-in-law about those ten days that he kept bottled up within him.

"Monday when the hostilities broke, we saw our air force fly over us on the way to Egypt. They were flying in formations of four going in, and coming back in groups of only three, typical of the 'missing man formation' normally flown if one was shot down. That broke our hearts. We did not know that this was an intentional tactic, to keep planes over the targets while others went to get rearmed and refueled, and not because they were shot down.

"At mid-morning we moved out, but in the direction of Jerusalem, to help against any Jordanian aggression, but then they turned us around and we headed towards Nitzana. That's when our scouts came back from Beersheba holding up a newspaper announcing the total destruction of the Egyptian Air Force, an immense relief to our troops.

"At midnight we crossed into the Sinai, and into the battle.

"By mid-morning we were in a convoy on the road to Abu Ageila, and there was a traffic jam at an intersection, so we were stopped on the road when we were targeted by mortar fire. My men and I were sitting in an open Dodge Power Wagon, with nowhere to go: We could not get off the road, the entire area had been mined by the Egyptians, the road forward and back was plugged, and so we were sitting ducks. One of the shells landed very close by and one of my men was wounded by shrapnel, and had to be evacuated. Fortunately his wound was not life threatening, and someone got the mortar to stop shooting, but it shook us up that this was no drill, it was real war, and we all could get maimed or killed.

"Soon thereafter we passed the intersection, and started chasing after the tanks of the battalion while shells were flying all over.

"It was scary, because we had an unarmored vehicle driving openly between the fighting tanks to ensure their radios were working, and thus were an easy target for the Egyptians. My crew and I stopped only for a few minutes at a time, whenever we could, to pick up some weapons and ammunition—the crew on my vehicle had only bolt-action rifles from WWI and I had an Uzi, and that was clearly not enough to defend ourselves. So whenever we saw an abandoned Egyptian troop carrier, not too far from the road, we carefully walked there to see what weapons we might find. Carefully, mindful of land mines, and possible booby traps—you take the pin out of a hand grenade, and carefully wedge it between the door and the door post of the vehicle; if someone opens the door, then boom, the grenade goes off.

"The guys found Karl Gustav submachine guns with loads of ammo, which was also usable in the Uzi. I picked up a Kalashnikov assault rifle, the famous AK-47, ammunition, and a Guryunov machine gun with its belts of ammo, which I installed in the vehicle.

"We continued like that, non-stop, with our battalion leap frogging with another battalion where one takes the lead while the other one rearms, then they switch. We moved like that non-stop until Wednesday night when our tank battalion took a break near a place called Jabal Libni.

"That was the place where we lost our scout team–the Egyptians had put a flat-bed truck across the road, and our scouts, driving without lights in a dark moonless night, crashed into it with their Jeep, and they all died. From where we were parked all we saw was the flash of the flames, and then heard the sounds of the crash. Was aweful.

"When the tanks stopped on Wednesday for the night was the only time when my company could get to work on the tanks in earnest, testing and repairing the radio and intercom systems, while not being under fire.

"Thursday morning we moved again towards the Mitleh Pass, and that was where the true horror of the war was evident in the carnage of the Egyptian convoys that were trying to escape our advance. Bless our air force, they decimated these columns of Egyptian tanks, trucks, artillery and other vehicles.

"We had to drive in between these carcasses of the Nasser's military might, and it was a most unpleasant experience. The sight and smell of the dead, the burning vehicles, the blown up tanks, are horrific memories that will remain with me for the rest of my life. Thinking about those poor souls that perished, and the pain of loss borne by their families—parents, siblings, and other members—makes you feel devastatingly sad.

"Friday afternoon we were stopped at the exit from the pass. The road climbs up a hill, and then comes down on the other side to a low level plateau all the way to the Suez Canal. A sole Egyptian Stalin 3 tank was sitting smug some 4 kilometers away and anytime one of our tanks tried to exit the pass, the Stalin would shoot. Our tanks did not have the range to hit it so we waited until morning when the air force was scheduled to come and take care of him. But when first light arrived, he was no longer there. Must have crossed the canal during the night.

"While we waited, we were taking small arms fire from the hills of the pass, remnants of the Egyptian Army which was dug in along the road. That's where the AK-47 became really useful returning fire at longer range than the Uzi's capabilities.

"One of my guys took a bullet to his neck. We tried to stop the bleeding, and called the doctor by radio, but the doctor and medics were too far back to arrive in time and save him. I held him and talked to him pleading with him to stay with me, but he died literally in my arms. What a devastating feeling of helplessness, anger and sadness.

"The next morning we proceeded towards the Suez Canal. It was slow going. As I said, the road was full of carcasses of Egyptian military vehicles, so the tanks simply got off the road went ahead, but the soft civilian trucks were getting stuck in the deep sand, so I found an abandoned Egyptian troop carrier with a winch in the front, and with that I could get the trucks towed out. That took a couple of hours of hard work in the oppressive heat.

"During that entire time, Egyptian foot soldiers were passing us by, naked except for their skivvies, walking barefoot in the hot sun. The temperature was 120 degrees in the shade, so the sand must have been scorching their feet. They were begging for water, crying 'moya, moya.' Although the Egyptian Army had placed three supply depots along the route with food and water and fuel, the senior officers did not tell the soldiers where these depots were, for fear that they would use that information to run away. Can you believe that?

So we shared with them as much water as we could—we had very little ourselves, meager rations being parachuted to us once every couple of days, but we shared it with these poor souls. No hatred, just pity and compassion. Later, when we got to the Suez Canal we saw some of them floating in the water, having been shot by their own machine guns from the other side. No wonder, Nasser did not want 80,000 defeated soldiers coming back and possibly causing turmoil in the country.

"Anyway, we detained the officers, and let the soldiers go on. How could we tell who was an officer and who was regular recruit you ask? I told you they had no uniform, no rank, and were naked except for their underwear. Well, if their underwear was made of silk, then he was an officer, and if made from cotton, a regular soldier. Can you appreciate that? Officers belonged to the aristocracy, regular soldiers belonged to the proletariat.

"On the way we also captured an Egyptian general, sitting in his air-conditioned trailer with none of his officers or troops around, except for his valet. We took him with us as POW, and later, when we got to Ras Sudr on the Gulf of Suez which was our final destination, we asked him why he stayed behind when he saw us advancing in the Sinai. His answer was very surprising. 'My officers were telling me over the radio that they are advancing towards Tel Aviv, and their radio signals were fading away, so I believed them.' 'But you saw us advancing towards you, and still you believed them? Their signals were fading because they were running away towards Cairo and you saw us coming but still stayed behind because you belkieved them?' And he is an educated man, speaks English fluently, a general, a graduate of the Sandhurst British Military Academy. It is unreal!"

In his description of those days, Ofer did not paint the complete picture of the terrible things he saw and was exposed to. Like many other soldiers before him, he could not convey the horrible events, scenes and smells, and emotions one records in battle, not the least of which is fear of injury or death. But by then Sam and Leah had seen quite a few pictures of the remnants of the battlefields, and could understand why Ofer had difficulties sharing those with them earlier.

Chapter 55

When the summer ended, Ofer left for his studies in the United States and Leah's and Sam's home felt truly empty. Returning home after delivering Ofer to his flight, they finally realized that from now on they were just the two of them at home with both their children far, far away.

Then early in January Bella and Leon's family grew with the joyous arrival of Ron, Leah's and Sam's first grandchild.

"We should try and make a trip to visit the children in the United States as soon as is practical," Leah suggested.

"It will have to wait until spring," Sam responded. "Winter in New York can be pretty cold, and you know you don't suffer the cold very well."

He put it on her, totally circumventing the truth that he also did not tolerate the cold well–while the condition of his clogged arteries had not worsened over the years, it had not improved much either, and the cold weather made his legs cramp painfully. In addition, his new Russian lady-doctor diagnosed him with the beginning of Angina and that, too, would be exacerbated in cold weather.

"Spring sounds good, anyway neither of us has heavy clothes for the winter in New York. Let's start planning something," Leah said.

"Let me see. Maybe I can finagle a business trip to Philadelphia while we are there. We can stay in New York and I can make a couple of day trips to Philadelphia—it is only an hour and a half by train from New York."

So the hoping and planning took center stage and somewhat overshadowed and mended the hole in their hearts. After all, this was the first time in twenty-eight years that neither of their children was "home."

When the spring arrived they made the trip to New York to visit with their children. They stayed with Bella and Leon at their small apartment. Ofer had a room at International House, and had no place to accommodate them, but they were more comfortable at their daughter's place anyway. Since Ofer was carrying a full-time load at school, and was working as an engineer during second shift in a plant in New Jersey, his days were full from early in the morning to after midnight every weekday, but he could break away from his studies during the weekend and see his parents.

Sam and Leah stayed in New York for a few weeks, and not until almost the end of their trip did they venture to International House to see where and how their son lived. It was really surprising to Ofer that his parents were not curious enough to make the two-mile trip to see their son's quarters and the environment where he spent his limited free time. He wanted them to meet some of the people he associated with, and the unique atmosphere in this multi-cultural interesting dormitory where 500 graduate students from all over the world resided. Even so, their visit was short, just a "look around," as if they were anxious to get out of there as fast as possible. Ofer was hurt and puzzled by that lack of interest, but he decided not to raise this issue with them—that is what they elected to do, so be it.

Having "recharged their batteries" spending time with Bella, and as time permitted with Ofer, Leon, and the baby, Leah and Sam boarded the long flight back to Israel, not knowing when they would have another chance to see their children again.

And over the next months there were major events in their children's lives. Leon completed his residency at the hospital, and Bella and he decided to move to northern California; Bella became pregnant with their second child; during her seventh month of pregnancy she flew back to New York to successfully defend her thesis for her doctorate in psychology at New York University and receive her degree; Ofer concluded his studies, came to Israel for a short visit, and returned to the United States to work and pay back his student loans; and Bella delivered her second child Adam.

All of these events were wonderful news for Sam and Leah, with the major exception of Ofer's return to the United States. They realized that he would not return to Israel in the foreseeable future, and possibly remain in the United States for a few more years, and that saddened them deeply.

Especially for Sam, this was a very painful experience to see his son negate his own valiant battles to escape the Diaspora. He had sacrificed so much to come to this land of the desert, the land of Israel, and now both his children abandoned it and were seeking to make a life back in the same Diaspora he escaped from, back into a minority existence in a foreign land, back where a Jew may not be as welcome as in his own homeland.

After all, he repeated his dire reasoning, if the illustriously cultured people of Germany—the people who brought us Nietzsche and Hegel and Kant and Bach and Wagner and so many other cultural gems—if they could perpetrate such horrific atrocities on the Jews, then there was no other nation on earth, not even the United States, that was immune to that kind of hatred, and they too could rise against the Jews someday.

For him and Leah there was no other place to live than the State of Israel, despite its rough edges and the less-than-perfect life. Their Zionism was ingrained deeply in their very existence, and it was therefore a tough pill to swallow that their children did not quite share their feelings, at least not to the same level of dedication. Especially since both were Sabras, born and raised in Israel, had served in the military, defended the country, and, despite trying to assimilate in a new country would forever be Israelis, accent and all.

❖   ❖   ❖

Upon returning from his visit to Israel, Ofer was laid off from the company he had been working at, and with the help of an introduction by Leon, he landed a job as an engineer with the telecommunications giant AT&T in New York City. Although the pay was not extravagant by any means, it enabled him to live comfortably in the city and start paying back his student loans. A significant advantage of his new position was the subsidy for phone service that all employees enjoyed, that allowed Ofer to keep in close connection with his sister in California and his parents in Israel. Telephone calls from Israel were still an expensive proposition, but Ofer could call from time to time, and relay messages to Bella who was further away by three hours. The main communication mechanism remained however the cassette tape shipped via the postal service back and forth. Leah and Sam would record the events of their lives, about trips they took within the country, vacationing in Tiberias or The Dead Sea or Eilat, and social or cultural events they attended, including concerts of the renowned Israeli Philharmonic Orchestra at the Mann Auditorium where they had season subscriptions, plays at the

Habima theatre, and other venues mostly in and around Tel Aviv. Ofer received these cassettes from his parents, and after previewing them forwarded the recordings to Bella. Bella and Leon recorded messages of their own and sent the cassettes to the parents in Israel, and Ofer did the same independently from New York.

In one of the recordings during the summer of 1971 Sam told his children of his upcoming business trip to Europe. Over a ten-day period, he was scheduled to visit business associates in Paris, Amsterdam, Rotterdam, and Munich. And since the schedule was quite sparse, in between meetings he would be sightseeing, visiting museums, and enjoying a leisurely pseudo-vacation.

On Saturday morning Ofer called from the States. Leah picked up the extension and after their greetings she listened in on the conversation between Ofer and Sam.

"If you are going to Europe, how about coming to the United States for a few days when you are done with the business there?" Ofer asked.

Sam took a moment to respond. "I can't do that. I have some meetings in the country scheduled right after my last meeting in Munich, and anyway Rosh Hashanah starts on the nineteenth, so I want to be back home by then."

"Can you compress your schedule some and finish your business meetings in a few days and come here after that? I'd love for you to come."

"I can't, there is no way I can."

"I wanted to spend some time with you," Ofer insisted. "As I told you in our last conversation we have a strike of the AT&T unions here, and we, in management, have to work in place of the union folks to keep the telephone service going. I am working fifteen to eighteen hours every day, thirteen out of every fourteen days, raking in a lot of overtime pay, but I can take a couple of days off to spend with you. Can you come?"

"I'm sorry, son, I simply can't. It took such pains to schedule all these meetings, and I can't very well ask them to change the schedule now."

There was silence on the other side of the line.

"If you won't come here, then I will come to Europe instead," Ofer finally said.

"You would?"

"I will. It is a shame to leave all that money of the strike on the table, overtime and all, but I will come. What is your schedule like? When and where will you be staying?"

"Hang on, I will get my itinerary."

Sam left the phone and came back a moment later.

"My first stop is Paris. I will be arriving in mid-afternoon of the fourth. My last meeting is in Munich on the fifteenth and from there I am flying back here."

"I will meet you in Paris then, and we can travel together for a few days."

"That'll be wonderful," Sam was truly happy. And so was Ofer— that would be the first time since he grew up that he would be spending serious time with his father, alone, one on one, leisurely, without external pressures. It would be a golden opportunity for them to reset their relationship, as two adults, and less so as father and son, and without the presence of Leah hovering over the two of them.

To be sure, they confirmed the schedule a couple of weeks later in late August when all the preparations were in place.

"I checked the flights, and there is an Icelandic Air from New York to Luxembourg leaving Friday night. There I will rent a car and drive to Paris. We can drive everywhere we need so long as I return the car to the same place, and that's why I chose Luxembourg."

"That was smart. Sounds good to me. Will be fun to drive around Europe rather than go by train as I originally planned."

"I will meet you at your hotel on the fourth at 8 p.m. sharp."

"Excellent."

Sam arrived on schedule, and checked into the hotel. It was still only 6 p.m., and he had two hours or more to wait for Ofer to arrive. He was anxious that Ofer's long flight, followed by a long drive, would go without a hitch because if there were a delay or some other difficulty, Ofer would be hard pressed to communicate his progress to him. There was a telephone in the hotel, but not in the room, so he went downstairs and advised the desk clerk that he would be in the TV room waiting for his son.

He really appreciated Ofer's desire to spend the time with him on this trip. What other 29-year-old son would drop everything, including a very lucrative income stream, to embark on this type of vacation with his dad? Not many, he assumed.

There is a saying in Yiddish for what Ofer was about to do:

"פֿון אלע ארבעט אין בוד אראַין", "from all the work and into the bathhouse," meaning you drop everything and go gallivanting leaving all the work behind. Sam was thrilled that his son wanted so much to enjoy his company that he was willing to make the sacrifice for it. Hopefully his employer would not penalize him for deserting in the midst of the strike crisis.

Sam became so engrossed in watching the French TV news that he did not notice the time. There was a tap on his shoulder and the desk clerk was standing behind him. He jumped out of his seat and looked at his watch. It was 8:15 p.m.

"*Monsieur, votre fils est arrivé*—your son has arrived."

Sam stepped out of the darkened room. In the hallway was Ofer with his hands placed on his waist in a reproaching gesture.

"I travel nearly 4,000 miles by plane, and then 250 miles by car, and I am late by fifteen minutes and you can't wait for me?" Ofer said with the biggest smile on his face. He was so happy to see the roundish smiling face of his father coming toward him.

After big hugs, Ofer dropped the luggage in the room. They chatted for a while, then they realized they were both hungry.

"Where do you want to eat?" Sam asked.

"It would be nice to have a real French meal, but I don't know any place like that anymore. Last time I was in Paris was six years ago, and it seemed to have changed a lot," Ofer said.

"I know exactly what you mean. What you are looking for is a small restaurant where the owner is the chef, and his wife serves the tables, and it is an authentic French country cuisine."

"Exactly."

"That would be delightful. I wish I knew of a place like that, but I don't. I have been to Paris more recently than you have, but haven't come across any place like that," Sam replied.

"Who could we ask?"

"If anyone knows about a place like that it would be a taxi driver," Sam suggested.

"Makes sense."

"But not just any taxi driver. We need to find an old timer."

They walked up the line of taxis on Champs Elise avenue until they spotted one. Exercising his fluent French Sam asked the driver.

"I know exactly what you are looking for Messieurs," he responded. "Pity, but they no longer exist in Paris. For that you need to travel outside the city." Then he thought for a moment. "I know a place not too far from here that is not exactly what you want, but is a close second."

"That would be nice," and they climbed into the taxi.

Once underway, the driver asked Sam. "May I ask what town you are from? You are obviously not a tourist, but also not a Parisian, but I can't quite nail it which French town you come from."

Sam chuckled, and was not about to correct the French taxi driver. "I lived some time in Nantes and some time in Lille, so my pronunciation is a mix of both."

"Ah, that explains it." They drove a couple of minutes and reached their destination.

The driver was right, the restaurant was nearby, and also a close second. The food was solid, tasty, and plentiful, good country style cooking, and the two savored every bit of it.

They spent the next nine wonderful days together driving through the countryside from Paris to Calais where they took the ferry to England. Ofer was now driving on the left side of the road in a left-steering car, but with Sam's excellent navigation they were able to find Tanya's daughter Beata's house in the English countryside. They had a very pleasant visit with her and then continued back to the mainland through Belgium to Sam's next business appointment in Rotterdam. From there the route took them to Amsterdam where they spent a few days, and then continued to Frankfurt where they spent a day in a park with Ofer's friend. And then it was time for each to go their separate ways—Sam by train to Munich, Ofer to Luxembourg and home to the U.S. and back to strike assignment at the company.

Such a delightful experience they both had, an opportunity to bond as two adults who enjoyed each other's company, not hindered by the father-son relationship or the ever presence of Leah's looming shadow. They shared a hotel room, ate delightful meals at out-of-the-way places, got along perfectly, and spoke endlessly. For the first time in his life Sam really exposed more of his inner thoughts and some of his life experiences, more than he had ever done before.

And there were some fun moments as well. At a hotel in Rotterdam Sam attempted to sew a button on a jacket, but not very successfully so, and when he realized he was not doing such a terrific job he enlisted Ofer to use his grade school "home economics" training and assist in the effort. And the next day Ofer watched Sam conduct a business meeting with Dutch industrialists, leveraging his language skills as well as his natural ability to successfully interact with strangers and quickly size them up.

During the many hours together, Sam and Ofer discussed many topics. Ofer was curious about his father's childhood, growing up in Latvia, his experiences studying in France, and his life before Ofer was born and even after. And Sam was equally inquisitive about Ofer's life in the United States, and how he perceived it going forward, both professionally and socially. And while he never directly raised the question which was on his mind, when will Ofer return to Israel and settle there, it was obvious that that was the thrust of his inquiry. He still has not come to terms with the possibility that Ofer will remain in the USA beyond the necessary. Not his and Leah's son, no.

Ofer told Sam that he still has to pay back his student loans, and until he does that he could not consider leaving the United States. Socially, he said, he made some friends, and he had an active social life, he was dating some girls, but was not attached. He is not making any plans for the future at the moment, just taking life one day at a time,

When the time came to say good-bye they hugged, and Sam took another look at Ofer, no longer a youth, but a mature full grown man of 29, independent and successful in his own right, and Sam felt proud for how his son had turned out.

"You have no idea how I appreciate your coming here," he said to Ofer. "I know it must have been hard to leave in the middle of the union strike, drop everything, and come clear across the ocean to spend these ten days with me. But I must tell you also how much I enjoyed every minute of it. It was an unforgettable trip and I must thank you for it."

"It was a marvelous experience for me as well, spending all this time with you, just the two of us. I learned so much about who you are as a person, and I understand why after all these years mother is still so much in love with you."

"Have a safe trip home." Did Sam have a tear in his eyes?

"Yeah, you too. Give my love to mom."

Chapter 56

The Yom Kippur War in October 1973 came as a total shock to the country. True, there had been some signs of danger on both the Syrian and Egyptian fronts, but with a colossal failure of the military intelligence apparatus, the country was not at all on the alert for potential hostile action by the enemy. Partly fueled by the feeling of invincibility that emanated from the decisive victory of the Six Day War six years earlier, and partly the result of misreading the signs of preparations on both fronts by Syria and Egypt, Israel was caught unprepared for a major offensive by those two armies.

By and large, the surprise was a failure of communication between the local commanders on the ground and the headquarters of the military. Several weeks prior to the outbreak of hostilities, local commanders of both fronts raised concerns about signs of movement on the other side of the skirmish line, but the high command dismissed those, and reassured the local commanders that nothing would happen. Obviously they were wrong.

On the Egyptian front, military intelligence misinterpreted the Egyptian adoption of a Russian military structure incorporating a Water Battalion in an infantry division: It made sense for the Russian military operating potentially over long distances to have a unit specialized in water supply, presumably for the troops, but the Israeli military intelligence attributed the Egyptian adoption of such a unit as stupidity of copying the inappropriate Russian structure. Those Water Battalions became instrumental in breaching the levees along the Suez Canal as crossing points for the Egyptian armor. Equally, the military intelligence dismissed the appearance of tall towers on the west side of the Suez Canal, thinking those were observation towers, not realizing their potential use as launching pads for anti-tank missiles.

The second failure was the strategy adopted by the Israeli army of establishing fixed fire bases—the Bar Lev line along the Suez Canal—which proved to be as disastrous an idea as the Maginot line of the French in WWII, especially for an army that was built on mobility and fire power. The Bar Lev line was no match for the Egyptian armor and was easily overrun, causing severe Israeli casualties.

Things were not going well for the country. Once the Egyptians pierced through the levees on the Israeli side of the Suez Canal with their water cannons, they crossed with their armor and advanced rapidly in the Sinai, inflicting heavy losses to the Israeli front line troops. They easily breached the defensive line, and, with missiles fired from the observation towers, decimated the Israeli armor that was rushing, in open space, to support the forward bases.

Within the first day or so the Egyptian army had moved some six miles into the Sinai, obliterating the Israeli defenses, and then they stopped. Luckily for Israel, the battle plans of Egypt did not include a deeper penetration into the Sinai, otherwise they could have easily taken all of the Sinai and even driven into Israel proper—there was no opposing force in readiness to stop them.

The Syrians were similarly successful in pushing some of their armor down from the Golan Heights toward the Sea of Galilee. The Israeli force on the Golan, although minimally reinforced just before the war, was no match for the solid wall of Syrian armor advancing. Equally miraculously the Syrians also stopped their advance, fearing an Israeli trap that was not really there. Had they continued their advance they could have reached the outskirts of Haifa with no military unit or ground force to confront them and stop them.

The only saving grace for Israel was the timing of the attack. On Yom Kippur nothing moves in Israel—all the roads are empty, in deference to the holiest day in the Jewish calendar. Most people are either at home, or at their synagogues, so when the attack started there was minimal interference as the regular army and reservists rushed to their bases, and from there to the front.

Leah and Sam, now ages 59 and 63, were immensely worried. The news from the front was getting worse by the hour, but there was nothing they could do to help. They stayed glued to the radio waiting breathlessly for the hourly chime of the news, twenty-four hours a day.

They tried to contact their children in the United States but it was impossible to get a line. All the circuits were busy, and after a while they gave up. Hopefully, they reasoned, either Bella or Ofer would call from the United States.

But the days passed, and by then a week, and there was no communication from the children.

"They may be having the same difficulties we are having in making a phone call," Leah suggested.

"Quite possibly. Whenever I try I can get a dial tone, but when I dial '19' for an international line I get the busy signal. There may not be enough circuits going overseas. I heard that our transatlantic calls are routed through France, and those French may also be playing games. Who knows? That bastard De Gaulle had imposed an arms embargo on us, and for all I know the French may be trying to cause us damage in other ways as well."

"By blocking our phones?"

"Would not surprise me at all. You know, Leah, the circuits are shared with the government as well, and if the French SOBs can cause mischief to the Israeli government and disturb the contact with the embassies abroad, they might do that just for spite."

"I don't know if they will go to that length to cause us grief."

"Neither do I, but I am just raising a plausible explanation for our terrible international telephone service these days. Before the war everything was fine."

Sam was obviously speculating, but a plausible theory nonetheless.

There was still no word from the children on Saturday, and the news from the front was still relentlessly pessimistic. The counter offensive was developing, gaining momentum, but no major advances were reported on either side. Sometime during the week Sam had called Itzik, one of Ofer's friends from the armored corps. His wife answered and told Sam that Itzik had gone to his base immediately on Yom Kippur, and she has not heard from him since.

Sunday afternoon, eight days into the war, they finally heard from Ofer. Sam answered the phone.

"Hello?"

"Shalom Aba. Are you guys okay?"

"Yes, we are fine. No need to worry about us."

"I am glad. I was worried. I tried to call from the United States but could not get a line, and neither could Bella."

"Where are you calling from then?" Sam asked.

"I am at Ben Gurion Airport. I called the Israeli consulate in New York all week, and the embassy in Washington, and they finally got their act together and put me on a flight. We are heading to the base to get equipped."

There was a moment of silence. Sam knew that his son was not in active reserves, and did not have to come for the war, yet here he was, arriving to help save his country in its moment of crisis.

"I knew you would come to help with the war," Sam finally said with pride and respect in his voice. "I knew you would come. I just did not know when."

❖ ❖ ❖

Later that same night Leah and Sam were sitting in the living room of the darkened apartment watching the news on TV when the doorbell rang. Without hesitation Leah headed for the door, and all Sam could hear was her delighted scream "Ofer," so he rushed to the hallway as well.

In the dim light of the doorway stood Ofer, still in civilian clothes and carrying his small suitcase.

"They let us out till morning," he said, "they were totally unprepared for us."

"Didn't they know you were coming?" Sam asked.

"Yes, but the chaos is immense."

They sat down in the dining room.

"You want to eat something?"

"Yeah, I have not eaten anything all day. The breakfast on the plane was spoiled too, and there was no food at the base. Total mess."

Leah rushed to the kitchen to bring some food.

"So after the airport, where did you go?" Sam asked.

"They took us to the base of the school of armor, where I was stationed during my time in the army. There aren't any reserve units based out of it, so there were no supplies for us, no emergency stores, no boots, no uniforms, no weapons, just a bunch of decrepit tanks belonging to the school.

"Nowhere to sleep, no cots or sleeping bags, no mess kits, no towels, nothing, and nowhere to put away our suitcases—can't stash them in a tank. Plus, most of us had foreign documents, passports, driver licenses, and the like, which would be bad if we had to take with us to the front.

"So being the highest rank on the bus I went to the camp commander. He said nothing will be done till morning, so I convinced him to let us go get our reserve duty stuff which we have at home, dispose of the suitcases, and be back in the morning. He gave us a truck to bring us to Tel Aviv, and it dropped me off at the Elite intersection. It will pick me up at 0500 at the same spot."

"Tell us from the beginning. How did you get to come back to Israel in the first place? Did they call you for reserve duty?" Leah wanted the details.

"No, they didn't. Bella called me on Yom Kippur morning to tell me that there was war in Israel. I immediately called the consulate in New York to register with them should they need me. Technically I did not have to register; I have been overseas for over five years already so I was taken off the rolls of active reserves, but I suspected that I may be needed, so I called.

"There was no answer. The consulate was closed for Yom Kippur. Nor was there anyone on Sunday either—a normal weekend routine, war or no war. Astonishing. From Monday through Wednesday I called and called and called, several times a day trying to reach someone knowledgeable at the New York consulate, but no luck there—nobody knew anything. So Wednesday I called the embassy in Washington DC, thinking maybe they knew something. They told me to call the consulate in New York, they knew nothing. Total chaos.

"Wednesday afternoon I finally got through and registered. The girl I spoke with asked me some questions including what my military profession had been, but when I told her I was a signals officer in armored corps, to my amazement she did not know what it was. She told me that if they need me they will call me. I could tell she did not know what she was doing. Total confusion, total disarray at the consulate, no direction, no one knew what was going on.

"I called again twice on Thursday, then Friday morning. The person on the other end of the line was more aware of what was going on, but told me: 'Don't buy a ticket, and don't pack your suitcase. If we need you we will call you, and we will give you a ticket.' Like saying 'relax.'

"When I came back from lunch not an hour later there were two frantic messages to immediately call the consulate. I called back the number they left. The man who answered the phone asked me: 'Is tomorrow evening too early for you to fly to Israel?' I asked him: 'Tomorrow? How about tonight?' and his answer was: 'El Al does not fly on Friday. Tomorrow 9 p.m. is the earliest flight out.'

"I was shocked. Can you imagine that? Not even war would make them fly on the Sabbath? But I confirmed to him that I will be at JFK for the flight.

"I went to my boss and asked for a three weeks leave of absence. I figured it will be over within two to three weeks, like it was in '56 and '67. My boss had me sign five separate forms, each good for one month. 'Five months?' I asked. 'If you come back earlier, I will tear those up,' He said. 'You should also be assured that regardless of how long you will be gone, your job is secure and will be waiting for you for when you return.' That was very nice of him, he acted like a prince.

"At the airport they gave me a one-way ticket. 'If you need the return portion, we will give it to you at that time,' they said. Very re-assuring. They were probably thinking that I might not make it back, in which case why buy me the return ticket?"

Now Sam and Leah knew exactly how Ofer got to Ben Gurion Airport Sunday afternoon, to hear his father say those proud words: "I knew you would come, I just did not know when."

❖　❖　❖

When Leah and Sam woke up the next morning, Ofer was already gone.

They did not hear from him for some time, and all the while the fighting was raging on, on both the Egyptian and Syrian fronts. The Jordanians decided to sit this one out, thus allowing the IDF to concentrate on the two main opponents, although just in case the Jordanians changed their minds, the IDF did dispatch armored units to take positions along that border as well.

After twelve more days of intense fighting, a ceasefire was declared on the 25th of October. A day later, Leah and Sam received a military postcard from Ofer saying he was fine, all in one piece, but had no idea when he would be allowed to return home and back to the United States. By now overseas communications had been restored, and they promptly relayed the information to Bella in California who was worried for her brother and his well-being.

It took another month or so for Ofer to arrive for a short weekend at home. Naturally Sam and Leah were overjoyed at the surprise visit.

"We are stationed about six miles east of Ismailia, at a place in the Sinai called the Chinese Farm," he told them, "and they arranged for us a flight from Fayed airport in that part of Egypt that was overtaken by Israel shortly before the ceasefire. Nothing fancy, sitting on the cargo door floor of an air force C-130 Hercules, hoping that the door does not open by mistake in mid-flight," Ofer chuckled.

"The Chinese Farm?"

"Yes. It has nothing to do with China or the Chinese. It is a civilian agricultural community that Nasser built years ago, before the Six Days War, but it was never occupied. It has some Japanese water pumps there, so someone thought that the writing was Chinese, hence the name."

Sam brought a map of the Sinai and Egypt.

"How did you get from the Chinese Farm in the Sinai, to Fayed which is in Egypt proper? It is quite a distance!"

"My friend Moshe and I found a damaged Egyptian military Mercedes Unimog truck and rebuilt it, and that became our transportation. Without it we could not have made it here and back in time."

"How long can you stay?"

"We have to be back Sunday morning. We have a flight back from Ben Gurion Airport to Fayed. My commanding officer will send the Mercedes to pick us up."

"How many is 'us?'"

"One member from each crew. Every week one member from each tank will get a weekend pass. In an emergency we can operate with one crew member missing—we all know all roles within the tank."

"What is your role?"

"They made me a tank platoon commander, commanding 3 tanks."

"A platoon commander? But you have not been on reserve duty since 1968!"

"True, very true, and I have not been a crew member of a tank since late 1961. But when I arrived at Ben Gurion Airport from the United States, they asked me what my military profession was. I told them I was a signals officer in a tank battalion, and they asked if I was certified as a tank commander. I told them that I was, so they said 'good, now you are a tank platoon commander,' and that was that."

"Wow," Leah exclaimed.

"I can tell you that the whole time till hostilities stopped I was scared out of my wits. Not so much for me, but for the other members of the platoon. One small mistake and they may get killed. Remember? I mentioned it several times before: Being in armor means you are so well drilled that you don't have to think about what to do next, it is automatic. But I was totally rusty—I have not had any practice drills for twelve years."

"That is some responsibility," Sam acknowledged, "I guess they were short of tank commanders."

"I guess so. And they were short of everything else. My tank was in terrible shape, veering constantly left while driving. Comes out that at the beginning of the war it had been sent to the Golan Heights, driving through east Jerusalem in a show of force for the local Arab population to remain out of the conflict. It lost its brakes, crashed into a house there, and killed a little girl. It took them several days before they could extricate it from the neighborhood and send it back to the base, but they didn't have time to fix it.

"Then, the canon has two shock absorbers filled with oil, one on each side, to suppress the recoil when you fire. The shock absorber on the left side of this tank was empty, had no hydraulic oil, and had we fired it before adding the oil it would have killed everyone except maybe the driver.

"And we were missing other stuff, like hand grenades, smoke grenades, and small arms ammunition. We had to break into some emergency store to find these things and arm the tank.

"As I said, this was scraping the bottom of the barrel."

"Wow, so sad," Sam said.

"Well, we are so relieved that you are okay, and that you came through without incident to your unit," Leah chimed in.

"Yeah, so am I. A couple of kilometers south of the Chinese Farm we saw some horrific stuff that happened to another battalion, battalion 14 with their M48 or M60 tanks. They were so devastated we could not even tell which model they were."

"What happened there?"

"Ariel Sharon struck again."

"What do you mean?"

"Just as he did in 1956 in the Mitleh pass, he let his irresponsibility and arrogance overtake proper military judgement. In '56. he didn't wait for the armor to arrive in the morning, and so he made his paratroopers storm the hills 3 times that night, up and down, against heavily fortified Egyptian positions, getting a lot of his unit killed. That was why he was set aside and had no role in the Six Day War.

"Here, showing his bluster, he was determined to arrack the Egyptians even though his force wasn't ready. So he sent a company of engineers to hold the bridges over the Suez Canal for 24 hours without being able to resupply them or send reinforcements, and they came under heavy fire. When he finally was ready to attack he sent Battalion 14 to push the Egyptians further north so he could open a gap and send his main force across and into Egypt proper.

"When the Egyptians saw the tanks approaching, they withdrew their armor and artillery, but left their infantry, well dug-in, with Sagger antitank missiles. Sharon thought that they were fleeing, so he ordered the tanks to pursue them, and the Egyptians ambushed the Israeli battalion and destroyed it.

"We saw the carnage. Tanks with their turrets blown away, tanks with six or seven holes of hits from all different directions, heartbreaking stuff.   Out of fifty tank crew members only 2 survived. All for his ego."

They were silent for a few moments.

Leah recovered first.

"So sad. I had heard about the '56 events from your friend Tammy whose brother was killed there, but I didn't quite believe it was Sharon's recklessness and ego. Now I am sure it was."

She paused for a minute, then changed the subject.

"Now go call your sister, she is very worried about you," was her directive.

It was still early morning in California. Leon answered the phone, and Bella came on the line right after. They too were relieved that Ofer was in one piece, and seemingly well, a marked difference from when he returned after the Six Days War.

"How long will you be staying there?" Leon Asked.

"I have no idea when the military will release us to go home. Our entire unit is people like myself who came from abroad to help in the war. My entire crew is three medical students from Bologna University in Italy, so medically I am covered. I offered to trade one of them for a life insurance guy, but there were no takers," he chuckled.

"That's funny," Leon said.

"So you are the next generation of Machalnik," Bella chided him. "When the army does finally release you, make sure you come to visit us in California."

"Sounds good."

They hung up.

"Maybe you want to take a hot shower, you have been travelling all this distance."

"But I took one this morning," Ofer retorted.

"You took a hot shower? Where? In the middle of the desert?"

"Yes. Long story, but my friend Moshe and I built a hot shower for our troops in the middle of the desert, and we shower almost every day."

"That's amazing. We want to hear the details," Sam said.

"Not much to it. Once we had the Mercedes rebuilt, which became sort of my personal vehicle, I could drive around a bit while maintaining radio contact with the company. So I went to look at the central facilities of the Chinese Farm to satisfy my curiosity. There was a water pumping station which, like the rest of the settlement was never finished or used. There I found a large water tank and hoses, and some other stuff, and that gave me the idea.

"We have a technical group of mechanics as part of the company, and they have a vehicle with a crane on it, so I asked them to bring their crane and hoist the water tank onto the roof of the structure nearest to where we spent the days. Come to think of it I never accounted for this heavy weight of the tank, plus water, plus one or two guys, on that roof. But then Moshe, who is a structural engineer, was comfortable with it, so I trusted him. He was right."

"Then how did you get the water up on the roof? Was there a water supply pipe?" Sam asked.

"That was the next step. Schlepping water up onto the roof in 5 gallon containers was not a good solution. Instead, we found a wrecked Egyptian amphibious vehicle, and it had an evacuation pump with a hose, like they have in boats. Every day our water tanker truck comes and brings us water, so we drop the pump into the water tank, hook it to the truck's battery, and we fill our water tank in a few minutes."

"But the water is cold. How could you heat the water?" again the engineer Sam was showing his methodical thinking.

"We scavenged some more and found an Egyptian field kitchen which had diesel fuel burners, so we 'borrowed' one. Our tanks are gasoline powered, so I arranged with the fuel truck to bring us a 50 gallon barrel of diesel fuel, and we were all set. Now every morning one of us climbs up on the roof–we also found a ladder–and lights the burner for about an hour, and there you have it, a hot shower for the troops, in the middle of the desert."

"Unbelievable," Sam was impressed.

"Let me make some coffee," Leah suggested, "and then you must tell us everything that happened since you left."

While the coffee was brewing, Ofer decided to take a hot shower after all, to get the grime from the trip off, and change into civilian clothes he had brought with him from the U.S.

"Once we arrived at the Chinese farm we got settled into a routine: Before first light we move the tanks and scatter them to within a few hundred yards, cover them with a camouflage net, and are done for the day. Since we don't drive around with the tanks, or shoot, the tanks remain clean, and the weapons oiled and we don't even have to check the engine oil, or do any maintenance. So we are left with nothing to do all day. Then before dark each crew removes and folds the net of their tank, and we gather the tanks into a circle. We sleep inside the circle with some lookouts on guard duty on top of the turrets, while the rest go to sleep.

"Very quickly I realized that this lack of activity and the ensuing boredom are our worst enemy. It is very debilitating to not have anything to do all day. It leads to a vegetating state and a downward spiral of wanting to do even less than the bare minimum. I decided I had to find something to do, or go nuts.

"Moshe arrived at the same conclusion independently, so we teamed up and undertook "projects" to improve the conditions, projects like the shower.

"We needed some shelter from the sun, so the two of us collected truck arches from some Egyptian vehicles. We planted them in the ground, covered them with a spare camouflage net, and had a space, cool and shaded, with the definite advantage of protecting us from the horrible big flies that attacked us otherwise.

"But to carry these arches from where they were to our central location we could not use the Mercedes–it was designed to carry troops, not construction stuff. So the next project was to rebuild a damaged Russian Gorky 2-ton truck, and with some work, we were able to restore it and use it to schlep things around.

"Then we asked the supply truck to bring us some board games, and some books, and daily papers, and the guys could keep themselves entertained.

"Next, we wanted to improve the sleeping conditions. Sleeping on the sand in sleeping bags is not ideal, especially with scorpions around seeking warmth during the night. Again, we scouted the area and found, in one of the structures there, brand new, never used, military cots and mattresses that fitted them. So now the guys no longer had to sleep on the sand but we were still exposed to the elements.

"When building the Chinese Farm the Egyptians used concrete for the walls. We found the frames of construction lumber they used as forms for the cement, and used those as walls. We built a corral like structure, and covered it with some more arches, and tarpulines we stripped from two damaged trucks.

"When the tanks gather in the evening they surround this 'barn', and then we can bring electric power from the tanks and portable lights, so we can see what we are doing, and even lie in bed and read at night.

"That made our lives much better all around, but we were still eating cold food. The supply truck would bring canned goods, and some fresh vegetables, and we had those small gasoline cooking stoves that each tank has, but those weren't sufficient to cook for some 50 guys, so the last project, so far, was to build an outdoors grill and wood burning stove to cook on. We brought some pots and pans from the Egyptian field kitchen—we washed them thoroughly of course, and built a pantry, found a large table and benches, and we are now all set in the food department."

"That is incredible, the resourcefulness and ingenuity of your crews" Leah was impressed.

"Not quite the crews. Sorry to boast, but it was only Moshe and myself that drove these 'life improving projects.' We had very little participation by the rest of the group."

"How come? Why would they not help? After all, it was for their benefit too, no?"

"Yes, but they fell into that downward spiral of mental decline that Moshe and I realized was possible, and were afraid of.

"When you fall into that state of mind, then doing anything, the smallest thing, becomes a very difficult undertaking. You don't want to do anything, regardless of its value or worthiness.

"Every morning it is a chore to convince one of the guys to go up and light the burner of the water heater; it is almost impossible to get anyone to come help unload the truck that brought food supplies; and when the other supply truck shows up with a change of work clothes, all the men have to do is to take off their dirty clothes and pile them up on the back of the truck, and pick a clean set to put on. Too much trouble. Even a call of nature is considered a difficult annoyance, because one has to walk a short distance away carrying a roll of toilet paper, with the boot dig a small hole in the sand and later 'cover his tracks.' Too much work!

"Here is an example: One day, I went on my bathroom break, and while so 'occupied,' out of nowhere a wild goose flew by and landed about 100 yards away. Quietly I loaded my Uzi and shot it with one bullet to the neck.

"When I brought the dead goose back to our camp, it was difficult to find a couple of volunteers to pluck its feathers so that our designated 'chef' could prepare a delicious lunch of wild goose roast, a lunch like no other we had had in the desert.

"What a treat it was, although truthfully, the meat was a bit tough."

❖ ❖ ❖

Ofer spent the next few months on the outskirts of the Chinese Farm. Once a month he would come to Ramat Gan for a short weekend, and on his way back to the desert he always carried with him some "goodies" for the guys, to make the life there a bit more palatable.

Finally, at the end of winter, the mission was complete and he was discharged. Leah and Sam drove Ofer to the airport for his return flight to the United States. He survived the war, and the long four months of service after the war ended, and as promised the army issued him the ticket back to the United States. Five months to the day after he left his job he was warmly greeted by his boss and coworkers.

For Sam and Leah Ofer's departure and return to the United States was a sad event. Deep down they had hoped that his long stay, breathing the air of the country and its environment, speaking the language, seeing familiar places—all those things—would restore his attachment to his native land and make him wish to remain in the warmth of all the things he had grown up with.

But they never uttered a word to him about it, never tried to cajole him to remain, and never tried to make him feel guilty for "abandoning" the place where he was born, the homeland for all Jews. They never openly faulted him for emigrating and choosing to live so far away from them. Still, there must have been some residual resentment and definitely sadness at the confirmation that their children would, at least for the foreseeable future, be so far away from them, living in a foreign land.

Their consolation was that they were financially more comfortable by now, and although Sam was still working full-time they nonetheless would be able to travel from time to time to visit their children overseas.

And deep in their heart of hearts was the hope that when Ofer recovered from the absence of these five months with bills piling up, he might, just might, come to the conclusion that the Diaspora was not the place for him and he would return to his own country, the one he had grown up in and had now twice fought for.

Chapter 57

When Sam reached 65, the customary retirement age in Israel, he did not want to quit his job. Over the years he had been too busy trying to make a living and had not developed a specific hobby that he could occupy himself with. Moreover, the income he was making through his employment was sufficiently strong to entice him to continue working full blast. Thus he was ready to remain a full-time employee of the company.

However, as Nahum explained to him, allowing him to remain working as the salaried chief engineer of Amnur would create a precedence, affecting the retirement of other employees in the future. Instead, they worked out an arrangement whereby Sam would convert his status to that of an independent contractor while retaining some of the other benefits of a full-time employee: He would maintain his position, the company car, and a few other perks, but he would no longer contribute to the pension fund, and his length of service would not be officially extended for Social Security benefit purposes. They worked out a financial arrangement that basically kept Sam's income comparable to that which he had before, assuming of course that he continued working the same customary forty-five hours a week as before.

What this arrangement allowed him to do was opt to take extended vacations beyond the normal five weeks per year that he, and all the other longest-working individuals, were entitled to.

And so early April of 1975 Leah and Sam embarked on an amazing adventure the likes of which most people could only dream of. They flew to New York where they were met by Ofer, who brought them to his home for a couple of days of rest and adjustment, before heading out on a trip throughout the United States, by car.

With the help of the Automobile Club of America Ofer had mapped out a trip starting in New York via a southern route, over a three-week period to Santa Cruz, California where Bella and Leon and their children lived. From there, the route extended through the northern part of the United States all the way to Quebec in Canada, and then back to New York—a 12,000 mile and six-week journey visiting most of the key states and their attractions.

Sam and Ofer shared in the driving, and Leah sat in the back seat navigating with the aid of the maps and books provided by the AAA and also chronicling the trip in a notebook. They stayed at motels along the way, ate in diners for breakfast and restaurants for dinner. For lunch they enjoyed sandwiches Leah prepared from bread, cold cuts, and fresh vegetables that they kept in a cooler sharing the back seat with her. Their luggage was kept out of sight in the trunk whose latch was reinforced by a special "Rube Goldberg" lock, a masterpiece of innovation and invention, a joint effort of two renowned engineers, namely Sam and Ofer.

The planned route was designed for them to cover long distances during two long days of sightseeing, and then spending a third day relaxing at a destination city that held some interesting attraction: exploring Underground Atlanta in Georgia, visiting relatives in Birmingham Alabama, and so on. They visited all the tourist attractions along the way: The Smokey Mountains, the vast ranches of Texas, Bryce Canyon, the Petrified Forest, Grand Canyon, Zion National Park, and of course Las Vegas to name a few. They even crossed the border into Tijuana before heading north through Los Angeles where they were reunited with their dear old friends Maurice and Ruth, to Santa Cruz.

After a day or so in Santa Cruz, Ofer bid them farewell, and flew back to New York while they spent three wonderful weeks with Bella, Leon, and their three boys. At the end of that enjoyable visit Ofer returned and they continued their exploration, this time of the northern states of the United States and the southeastern part of Canada. And while in Toronto they visited Leah's friend Mira's daughter who had immigrated to Canada years earlier, at just about the same time Ofer went to the U.S., and also Ofer's friend from the Yom Kippur War, Moshe and his family.

There were many places that they could not visit during this trip—the United States is vast, with so many places to see, that it would take much longer than six weeks to visit it all. They did however achieve their goal of seeing the broad range of terrain, and the lifestyles of the people. No longer was the poverty in Mississippi an abstract concept, no longer was the size of Texas, the flatness of the Plains or the immense size of the Grand Canyon a mere intellectual understanding; they saw those with their own eyes, and were tremendously impressed by it all.

Being cooped up in a small car for six weeks could give rise to conflicts and disagreements, but during the entire trip, everyone was on their best behavior and not once did friction rise between the travelers; the three, different personalities and all, were able to pass the time without one single discord. During the long hours in the car they had endless conversation about anything that came to mind, and occasionally even listened to the radio to stay current on world events.

When they returned to New York, Ofer went back to work, and Sam took advantage of the fact that Philadelphia was only about a two-hour drive away, and he went to visit his good friend Bill Fogel and his Latvian chief engineer. Were they ever so happy to see Sam! They treated him to a lavish lunch, shared some new designs they had been working on, and Sam took those back with him a few days later when he and Leah returned to Israel.

Beyond the deep impressions that the United States and the people they met along the way had left on them, Sam and Leah were most grateful to Ofer for making this unique opportunity possible. They appreciated him taking the time off from work, making all the preparations and even tuning the dual carburetors engine of the car to perfection. They considered the trip an unqualified success.

Getting back to work after such a long absence was a bit taxing for Sam. There was a stack of memos to read, trade magazines to leaf through, and quite a few issues to resolve, issues that surfaced while he was away. His leadership team was so happy to see him back; they all commented how they missed him during his absence, both at the professional and the personal levels.

A few days later Sam visited the company headquarters in Tel Aviv where he met with Nahum and the leadership of the Research and Development Department. He shared with them the new designs he had brought from Fogel, and they all agreed it was a good starting point for a new line of products to be offered, primarily to their institutional clients.

Sam wasted no time and went to work modifying the U.S. designs that were based on American standard measurements, to a new product line based on the metric system used in Israel. Along the way there were other adjustments to be made to adapt the products to the somewhat different conditions of the country.

Once the new line of products was ready, at least on paper, Sam joined the marketing team in validating their design with a sampling of the client base. Although it was not the custom in Israel of the time to show up with a set of glossy brochures under your arm to solicit client opinion and advice, Sam adopted the American "focus group" approach, and that proved to be a terrific boon to Amnur, both in obtaining valuable comments from these clients, and also as a positive public relations step.

Chapter 58

Sam held on to the phone handset a moment longer, and heard the click of Leah's hanging up the extension in the bedroom. By the time he returned the handset to the cradle of the old-fashioned black desk phone, Leah came around the corner in the hallway. She stopped and looked at Sam, her face showing her anguish.

"He is not coming back, is he?" She asked rhetorically.

"No, I think not. Not ever." His voice showed his deep pain.

Sam turned and went to the dining room and sat in his usual seat at the head of the table. He sat there for the longest time, looking lost, letting the hurt sink in.

Leah stood motionless at the tail of the table for the longest time. Sam finally looked up at her.

"Remember what Nahum had said to him before Ofer left for the United States for graduate school?" Sam asked. "Remember what he said when Ofer asked him for help with financing his schooling? Nahum turned him down. He did not want Ofer to go!"

He took a deep breath, then continued.

"Nahum was so astute! He predicted that if Ofer left, he will never come back to live in Israel. He predicted Ofer will find a girl there in the United States, with no roots in Israel, probably not even Jewish, and they will start a home and raise a family there, never to return to our homeland."

"He was right, I guess. It is coming to pass." Leah said softly.

They did not utter another word to each other for a long time. Leah turned to her chores preparing the table for the Shabbat mid-day meal. Sam rose and went to the cabinet in the living room, pulled out his bottle of 777 brandy and poured himself a stiff drink. He then sank into one of the living room armchairs, slowly sipping the drink.

Leah came and joined him on the other armchair.

"I had no idea that he was seriously dating anyone," she said, a bewildered tone to her voice.

"Nor did I. When we traveled with him earlier this year throughout the United States he never mentioned any girlfriend, did he?"

"No, he did not. He did not explain the rush either, why he is planning to get married all of a sudden, and we don't even know the girl. Shouldn't he have brought her to meet us before jumping in? Isn't that the custom?"

"I can understand not bringing the girl to Israel now, he already took six weeks off this year, probably could not take any more vacation. But he has not said anything until today when he dropped the bomb on us."

"Well, there may be a reason. He said something about just going before the judge in City Hall like Bella did before coming here for the religious wedding."

"Yes, but we knew Leon before they got married. Remember, Leon asked for our blessing?"

"Sure, I remember," she said

They sat for another minute in silence, digesting the news.

They had fought so hard, sacrificed so much to build a home in Israel, helped create the country for their children and grandchildren to live in, and now both of their children have left and gone back to the Diaspora, among the goyim, forsaking their own country and homeland.

Where did they go wrong? How could it happen?

They stayed silent, stunned, for a few more minutes.

"Come, let's go eat," Leah finally said softly.

Chapter 59

With both their children now settled in a foreign land, Sam and Leah continued their lives in Israel totally devoted to the country they helped build and defend. They were fiercely proud of the accomplishments of this nation, the third State of Israel, and continued contributing to its success by undertaking various volunteering efforts and charity.

Beyond that, Sam was preoccupied at work with the intermittent flow of immigrants from the Soviet Union into the country. Quite a few were engineers who had been educated and gained experience in the communist bloc. The technology employed there did not rise to the level of sophistication and modernization of the West: Materials engineering science in the Soviet Union was not advanced at all, and consequently their manufacturing processes were antiquated compared to the norms in Israel. A total retraining was necessary to update them and bring them in line with modern standards. So leveraging his absolute command of the Russian language, Sam volunteered to absorb as many of these engineers as he could and provide them "on-the-job training" to enable them to be integrated into Israeli industry.

Sam soon realized that technology difference between Israeli and Soviet industries was merely one component of the adjustment these Russian immigrants had to make to meld into the culture. He shared with Leah his observations about these newcomers and their difficulty in adaptation to the country. She offered to help his new recruits in whatever way she could, and he relayed her offer to them. Thus Sam became a courier of Russian documents that needed to be translated to Hebrew, something she gladly did, not knowing that she would be doing much more of that in the not-too-distant future.

Aside from this new endeavor, life for Sam and Leah returned to normal, tense and intense but by and large uneventful. Out of habit formed over the years the radio was on at all times while they were awake, and whenever not occupied by something specific, they would stop normal activities on the hour, most hours, and listen to the headlines of the no-nonsense-news of Kol Israel, the Voice of Israel, the national radio station.

Ofer and his bride came to Israel for a visit during two successive summers. First in 1976 after their orthodox wedding in New York, officiated by two orthodox Rabbis according to the strictest of Halacha law, and then a year later again. Most impressive to Ofer's wife was the experience of Yom Kippur, when the entire country stopped, and except for an occasional ambulance, no cars were on the roads; all commercial establishments were closed, and no bus or train service operated—a unique and unforgettable sight not found anywhere else in the world.

And during those two years significant events were happening in the country. In late 1977, with the support of the United States, the Egyptian president Anwar Sadat took the unprecedented step of being the first Arab leader to officially recognize the State of Israel, and on November 19 of that year he came to Jerusalem and made a speech before the Israeli parliament, the Knesset. That opened the door to a historic agreement between Israel and Egypt, sponsored by the United States under the leadership of President Jimmy Carter, ending hostilities and establishing peace between the two countries.

Egypt-Israel Peace Treaty, signed by the Israeli Prime Minister Menachem Begin and the Egyptian President Anwar Sadat in March of 1979, included the mutual recognition of each country by its former adversary, the opening of the Suez Canal to Israeli shipping and the return of Israel to its 1967 border with Egypt, with the notable exception of the Gaza Strip.

The Gaza strip, a narrow 140 square miles area, was occupied by Egypt during the Israel war of independence in 1948. It was annexed by, and became part of, Egypt from 1949, and its population was 100 percent Arab. During the six day war, as part of the Sinai campaign, it was occupied by Israel.

Sadat did not want the Gaza Strip back, considering it an alien tract of land, densely populated and poor. Begin did not want it within Israeli borders either, considering that the population was totally Arab, with Egyptian passports. Unfortunately, Jimmy Carter, who later proved in statement and deed to be no friend to Israel, did not support the Israeli position. And so, Gaza remained within the borders of Israel per the agreement, and that has since proved to be a colossal mistake of U.S. foreign policy. The Gaza Strip became a launching pad of terrorism attacking Israeli civilians, even after Israel withdrew from the area in 2005, and offered the Gaza Strip total autonomy.

But at least one Arab country had signed a peace treaty with Israel, ending hostilities and reducing the likelihood of yet another conflict like the Yom Kippur war threatening the existence of the country—it was recognized that Israel could not be overrun by its remaining enemies without the participation of the mighty Egyptian military.

❖ ❖ ❖

Leah was now in her mid-60s and Sam reaching 70, their health was still holding up more or less—more for Leah who had never been sick a day in her life, and less for Sam, who had the blood circulation issue in his legs, and a high blood pressure that was hardly under control using the medications available in those days. Then, at one of his visits to his trusted new doctor, a Russian immigrant, his blood pressure was way up, and whether by design or not the doctor left the blood pressure cuff on his arm while they chatted, in Russian of course. A few minutes later, she took another reading and his blood pressure was only a bit higher than normal. She then realized that he had a fluctuating blood pressure, not just an elevated one, and that was tougher to control.

In addition to Sam's long hours at the office and the long commute, he and Leah had also an active social life with their friends who habitually dropped in for a coffee and cake. Amazingly, both Bella's and Ofer's friends would also show up from time to time for a pleasant visit with their friend's parents. Even Bella's old boyfriends and Ofer's girlfriends would ring the bell, mostly unannounced, to enjoy a nice evening with the two old folks. They knew that they would always be welcome, and there would always be a good cup of coffee and some goodies: baked cookies, or a cake, and of course some delicious cold fruit that Israel is renowned for. And if they only gave Leah an excuse, the table would immediately be laden with all sorts of other foods—the refrigerator was always stocked with home-cooked delights.

Friday nights was the "clan's" get together in a rotation. Between six and eight couples would show up at the designated home and enjoy a lively conversation, some good card games on multiple tables, and needless to say, as is customary in traditional Jewish homes, food.

And so the summer passed, and fall arrived, and the days were getting shorter. Sam would leave home before first light, and return after dark, take a short nap and be ready to stay up late answering letters, paying bills, fixing what needed attention in the apartment, watching some TV, and mostly sitting with Leah around the dining room table or on the balcony, and having wonderful long conversations about any subject whatsoever. Nothing was taboo, not religion—Sam was much more into that than Leah, not politics—he was much further to the left than she was, and of course anything associated with the children, and grandchildren.

Sam continued his work at Amnur, reducing his professional activities to three days a week as a consultant to the enterprise. Leah liked his presence at home on those days when he was not at his job or at his volunteer roles. After all those hectic years of the past, they enjoyed each other's company during the days.

Time passed and the population of Israel grew, both organically and through Jewish immigration. Sam and Leah realized that the need for their personal contribution had substantially diminished, and was mostly taken over by the younger generation. Without resentment of not being so dramatically needed, the couple settled into a different style of life. Not being bound to a strict work schedule, every so often Sam and Leah would travel around the country, and would be amazed by, and proud of, how it had developed, and, with true investment in infrastructure by the government, it flourished and turned into a modern society with all the amenities, albeit and some of the ills, of an advanced democratic nation.

On occasion, Sam and Leah enjoyed coming to visit their children and grandchildren in the United States, spending a couple of months at a time visiting Bella and her family in California, and less time in New Jersey where Ofer had settled down with his wife and two children, never explaining to their children this imbalance. Although Ofer's wife always treated Sam and Leah with utmost respect and hospitality, deep down they unfairly blamed her for Ofer's decision to remain in the United States and not return to Israel. Still carrying the old-fashioned notion of their generation—the wife follows her husband, they did not hold Bella to the same standard, and did not resent her remaining in the United States with her husband and their three sons. But the undercurrent of their feelings toward Ofer and his wife was different. They blamed Ofer's wife, but held Ofer blameless in that matter, and the resentment that they held against her also affected their relationship with the grandchildren—Bella's three boys and Ofer's girl and boy.

Unwarranted as it may have been, Sam and Leah caused a rift in the family and this lopsided treatment of the grandchildren was not lost on anyone.

❖   ❖   ❖

At 5 a.m. one morning Leah woke up from a deep sleep. The windows to her bedroom were open and she distinctly heard the sound of a chainsaw outside. She peered out of the window to see a cherry-picker truck with the boom hoisted, and a workman with a chainsaw aiming for the branches of the tree in front of the apartment.

"Stop!" she screamed at him at the top of her lungs. "Don't touch that tree. It is protected property."

The chainsaw noise stopped. "I was told to take this tree down, it interferes with the power and telephone cables," the man called back.

She rushed out of the house in her nightgown pushing the workmen out of the way, and stood in front of the tree screaming at the astonished workers.

"Don't you dare touch this tree!" she bellowed at them, "This tree is as old as I am. My grandfather planted it with his own hands in 1918. It is a fruit-bearing tree, and no one will touch it!"

The supervisor came forward.

"Lady, we have orders to cut it down. It is interfering with us building the sidewalk. This tree is in public property, and it does not belong to you, and I was told to cut it down."

"It is on *my* property, and is *my* property and you are not going to cut it down. I won't let you. You do not have the right."

"We have a work order here," the foreman said.

"I don't care if you have a work order, you will not harm this tree. It is illegal for you to cut it down, and I will call the police and have you arrested if you try." She was vehement.

"It was not our idea, we are just workmen for the municipality," the foreman objected, shirking the responsibility for the decision. "If you have a problem, it is with the mayor, and not with us."

"I will talk to him, don't worry, but in the meantime you better disappear from here. Don't dare touch the tree. Go away. Scoot!"

She stayed in front of the tree until they loaded their truck and drove away. Sam had watched the entire event from the window of the apartment, and now headed to the shower and work.

As soon as the offices of the municipality opened at 8:00 a.m. she was there. She barged into the mayor's office unannounced and against the futile objections of his receptionist who rose to block her way.

"I did not ask for your permission, girl, so sit quietly and shut up," she told the poor secretary. "I am here to see the mayor, and you will not interfere."

The poor girl sat back down, and Leah passed by her and into the mayor's office.

"By whose authority are you cutting down the tree that my grandfather planted?" she asked him. Just like that, without first introducing herself, direct and to the point. "You send your crew like thieves in the night to cut the tree!"

"What tree?" the perplexed mayor asked.

"My tree, the old mulberry tree on my property."

"I don't know anything about that, madam," his voice trailed, visibly on the defensive.

"Then let me tell you," she was relentless. She described the situation in a few brief sentences. "Be aware that it is illegal for you to cut a fruit bearing tree, and I will prosecute you like anyone else. You will not touch that tree. You will order your men to cease and desist."

"I see," he said. "I will look into it."

She knew the drill, promise to 'look into it' and in the meantime the tree gets cut down.

"Right now. Not later or tomorrow. Pick up the phone right now or I am on my way to the police and the court next door. I don't think you want to be slapped with an injunction, especially in front of news reporters, do you?" She knew how to intimidate a politician.

"Okay, okay," he calmed her down. "Please sit down and we will clear up the matter quickly. We will work it out somehow." A true politician.

Then it was his turn to surprise her. "Would you like a cup of coffee, or tea?" he asked defusing the situation with a bit of kindness.

"Thank you. Black coffee will be nice." She had run out of the house before her traditional mandatory morning caffeine boost.

The mayor got on the phone, and a few minutes later the coffee arrived followed by the city engineer. The mayor explained the situation to him.

"Mr. Mayor, we are expanding the street, and through eminent domain we have taken six feet off the properties along the street. This tree must be outside the property now, and we need it down to put the sidewalk in place."

"Please go with this lady, take a look at the tree, and find a solution to her issue. Make sure the tree does not come down."

They traveled by car to her home, and he observed the situation first hand. When the city expanded the street the tree now was half on Leah and Sam's property, half on the city property, and that interfered with the retaining wall and the sidewalk they planned to lay down.

He promised her that no harm would come to the tree until a resolution is reached.

Two days later, another crew showed up at the house. This time they rang the bell, introduced themselves properly, and asked her to come down with them so they could tell her their plans concerning the cherished tree.

"Although it is partly in the public domain now we decided to build a semi-circle wall around it and reattach it to your property. No one is going to hurt this tree, and as proof I have a letter here from the Mayor himself attesting to it."

He handed her a few sheets, copies of the letter. Each said:

"This tree belongs to Mrs. Gielan.

It is on private property.

It is protected by law and my authority.

It will not be harmed except to be carefully pruned to avoid hazards to power lines.

Signed,
Uri Amit, Mayor
Ramat Gan
24 June 1984"

They built the retaining wall around the tree, and except for the annual pruning nobody touched that tree after that. The old mulberry tree still stands in front of 7 Zvi St in Ramat Gan.

❖ ❖ ❖

Out of the blue, one morning in May 1985 Ofer received a call from a colleague at AT&T International Advisory Services for whom he was providing consulting services.

"We have a short-term assignment in Israel that we were hoping that you could help us with. Are you free to go to Israel and assist us?"

"Go to Israel? Sure, would love to. What is it all about?" Ofer asked.

"We are having 'call completion' problems with various communities in Israel, and it is because the telephone network in the country is not working well. Calls from the US and elsewhere are reaching the telephone system in Israel, and then are getting rejected because of circuits within the country that are overloaded. This is costing us money because these calls back up the trans-Atlantic cables with non-revenue-producing traffic—if the call does not complete to the Israeli subscriber we can't charge for it, and the caller tries again and again tying up our circuits. Putting another cable across the Atlantic is very expensive."

"How are you planning to fix the problem, and how can I help?" Ofer asked.

"We are sending a representative to Israel to meet with the Israeli telephone company Bezeq and offer them our help in diagnosing the problems on their end. We are willing to invest some $300,000 to help them improve their internal network, and need someone who can help our representative communicate with them and convince them to accept the offer, no strings attached. They are quite suspicious of us coming and offering them a $300,000 gift. So we need someone who speaks the language, and moreover, knows how to deal with Israeli businessmen.

"This will be a short, one day on site trip, leaving this Wednesday, arriving Thursday afternoon."

"You got it, I'll gladly help you, and the country."

Preparing for the imminent trip Ofer realized his Israeli passport had expired. The consulate in New York required two weeks to renew it, so he would have to renew it upon arrival in Israel, a process that would take a couple of days.

Ofer and his AT&T colleague arrived in Israel late Thursday and at the airport they were met by representatives of Bezeq, who brought them to Jerusalem for a dinner meeting with Bezeq leadership in Jerusalem.

Friday morning, prior to the meeting with Bezeq in Tel Aviv Ofer arranged to get his passport renewed. "It will be ready on Tuesday," they promised, "guaranteed."

The meeting with the president of Bezeq and some of his engineers, conducted in English, was initially not proceeding well: Bezeq representatives were suspicious of the offer, questioning AT&T's motives–why would that company be willing to invest such a large sum of money with no perceived gain? So Ofer, with his colleague's agreement, turned to Hebrew and explained and convinced them that truly no strings were attached, and it was a win-win solution for both parties.

Bezeq accepted the generous offer. Over lunch they discussed the steps going forward. Mission accomplished, the AT&T colleague departed for the airport, and Ofer continued to his parents' home in Ramat Gan.

Ofer spent five glorious days in Israel while his passport was being renewed. Those days were reminiscent of the time Ofer was in the Technion and would come home for the weekends and holidays—he stayed in his old room, slept in his old bed, ate the same familiar home-cooked meals, and in all respects it was a feeling of reliving good times. He also met with his old friends, and on Shavuot that happened on Sunday he joined his father for the services at the synagogue.

As promised, he received his updated passport on Tuesday midday, and that night, Ofer's last night before boarding the plane early in the morning, Leah, Sam, and Ofer sat in the balcony and talked until late.

At midnight, Leah bid them good-night and went to sleep for a couple of hours, but Sam remained with Ofer to continue the conversation.

They had a heart-to-heart talk covering all the issues that over the recent years had tarnished their relationship. Primarily, Sam expressed his sadness about Ofer's emigration out of the country, his marriage to a non-Israeli girl which he regarded as the reason why Ofer never came back to resettle in the country.

Ofer rejected placing the blame on his wife; it was not her fault they had not come to resettle in Israel. He further expressed his sadness that because of that resentment, his parents never accepted his wife and children as belonging to the family. He also explained to Sam the circumstances of the birth of the children and why it was that Leah and Sam were not encouraged to come and assist in the initial adjustment period after the births, and finally why Ofer had not brought his family to Israel to visit in recent years.

In this long conversation that night they were smoothing the wrinkles of their relationship, addressing pain that had festered in both of them for quite a few years, and by the time dawn rose over the neighborhood, they felt closer than they had ever felt. All the hurt on both sides was gone.

On the way to the airport, Sam and Leah started planning a trip to the U.S. in July, and this time they would stay with Ofer and his family for a long time before heading to see Bella and her family. They parted with the tremendous hope of reuniting in a few weeks in the United States.

Alas, that was not to be. Sam never made the trip.

With the limited medications available in those days the doctors were unable to control his blood pressure, and barely two weeks after saying the warmest good-bye to Ofer at Ben Gurion Airport Sam suffered a massive cerebral hemorrhage. Leah rushed him to the hospital, but the doctors' efforts to save his life failed, and on Monday, the 17th of June, the 28th of Sivan by the Jewish calendar, Sam passed away at the age of 75.

The funeral procession was large. Hundreds of people came to show their respects to this gentle and kind man who had touched so many lives in a positive way during his time on earth. With both her children by her side, Leah, with incredible internal strength and tremendous dignity, despite a broken heart of a true love lost, she led the long line of people following the body to its final resting place.

The epitaph carved into the tombstone reads:

"Samuel Gielan

איש ישר ובר לבב אהוב על הבריות

An honest man, pure of heart, loved by all
1910-1985

Part VI

AGAIN LEAH

Chapter 60

Leah remained in Israel. She would not hear of leaving the country and emigrating to be nearer to her children and grandchildren. Despite not having been born in the country, her love for Israel was almost as deep as the love one has for a child. She still had the fighting spirit in her, and her desire to continue contributing to the welfare of the country was unabated, and she exercised it fully. Now at age 71, widowed, and with no obligation to care for anyone, she looked for some way she could still be a contributing member of the society. She thought of volunteering in a hospital, or another such institution, but despite her vigor and good health, she was not received with open arms—Israel is a youth-minded society, and, being in one's 70s people think one is more likely to be a burden than a help, so the reception was tepid at best. She checked some non-government charitable organizations, but was unimpressed by their work and bureaucracies.

It was a rough period in the country, with frequent terrorist attacks. Buses were a common target of bombings by Arabs coming from the West Bank and Gaza, areas taken from Jordan and Egypt during the 1967 war, and any place where people congregated was a potential target for mayhem. The country needed watchful eyes for unattended packages, and infiltration by terrorists hostile to the existence of the country.

Leah thought of the fact that she had been a squadron leader in the Haganah, an experience she cherished and service she was proud of. She even had participated in some covert operations in her time, and definitely knew how to shoot a gun, take it apart and reassemble it, so maybe she could put that experience to some use, and once again help protect the citizens of the country?

Leah headed for the Ramat Gan police station. There she hoped to find out how to join the Civil Defense unit as an Auxiliary Police.

When this little, barely 5' tall lady in her seventies approached the desk, she was not sure that they would not laugh her off as too old, or too small, or too feeble, or dismiss her for some other reason. To her amazement she was treated with respect, admiration, and gratitude, and within a short time she was embraced to the ranks of those who patrolled the city and helped maintain the peace.

The Civil Defense department gave Leah a short course in handling a more modern weapon than the ones she used during the Haganah days, arranged for a couple of afternoons at the shooting range where she could practice using the weapon, assigned her to a series of classes about anti-terrorism vigilance, and law and order from a policeman's point of view—how to deal with domestic issues, traffic stops, and the like—all the tools necessary for one to act as a full-fledged member of the Auxiliary Police.

They assigned Leah a male partner, and together the two of them would walk the streets of Ramat Gan, or wherever else directed, late at night, looking for anything suspicious or out of the ordinary: A package left unattended, something unusual by the gas tanks feeding apartments with liquid natural gas, a disturbance, someone climbing a water pipe on the side of a building—anything that is not as it should be.

They carried their weapons loaded, but were instructed to not use them unless attacked first, something that certainly could happen in a city where terrorists were trying to harm the civilian population. They were also advised that while they had the authority to detain any person on any reasonable suspicion, they could not arrest them officially but had to hold them until the regular police patrol arrived to take the situation over from them. They carried radios and could call Dispatch whenever they encountered anything beyond ordinary circumstances.

And at a time when buses were exploding as a result of bombs left behind by terrorists, injuring and maiming passengers, Leah and her partner were also conducting surprise inspections of buses passing by ensuring no strange packages were left unattended under the seats. They also secured public places such as parks, checked inside garbage receptacles for potential bombs, and inspected movie theaters in between shows, adding two more pairs of eyes to the ever vigilant population at large.

"If you see something, do not touch it. Just get everyone away and radio Dispatch," were the orders.

Leah enjoyed these nights out, three or four times a week, in company of another team member, always male. Beyond doing something she felt good about—helping protect the citizenry of her city, this was sort of her "date out with a nice man," and although not a flirt, she always did like the company of men.

The only problem she encountered was returning home by herself at a very late hour of the night. The duo would drop the weapons off at the police station and then part ways, each heading to his or her own home. A shift could sometimes run late until around one or two in the morning, and then she had to walk a somewhat darkened and empty street, and cut through the back yard of Motya's house to get to the back of her own home. She could take another route, but that would be much longer on an equally darkened street. She took that in stride though, and when once she felt that a man was following her a bit too closely for her comfort, she turned around facing him, swinging that heavy flashlight she was carrying, as if threatening him to not come any closer. The "gentleman" made a hasty retreat and never showed up again.

After some time, the police equipped them with a van to enable Leah and her partner explore and protect a much larger area of the city, and also assist in traffic management. The police van, with its blinking blue light on top also served as a calming effect of police presence on the population.

"No longer foot patrols," Leah lamented. "Now I will have less exercise to keep my weight down. I kind of enjoyed walking the streets, getting to know the neighborhood and its stray cats."

There was no doubt that these foot patrols were helpful, and in a couple of cases they even led to a de-escalation of a domestic dispute between neighbors or a couple. The mere sight of these Civil Defense personnel, dressed in civilian clothes but with a distinguishing armband, and carrying a weapon on their shoulders, made the warring parties lower the tensions and let cooler heads prevail. The net effect was that it released the regular police to perform their real duties and address the more serious issues of the city.

Leah kept the routine of Civil Defense for almost a decade and a half to age 85, come rain or shine, never failing to show up for her appointed rounds.

Chapter 61

During that time, in 1989, the Soviet Union under Mikhail Gorbachev lifted emigration restrictions, and the borders of Russia and its satellite countries opened in earnest for the first time since the end of WWII. People were allowed to leave, even if in moderation, although they had to leave most of their belongings behind. The initial trickle increased, and in 1990 and 1991 the flood gates opened, and a very large immigration wave from the former Soviet Union ensued. Nearly one million people arrived in Israel under the Law of Return, which provides a homeland to any Jew, from wherever they come, with whatever culture or heritage, so long as they could demonstrate a matrilineal or patrilineal Jewish descendancy, or be married to someone who was thus qualified.

Within a few days of the first arrivals in the country Leah realized she could be of tremendous help to these folks in their new country. She was fluent in Russian, and despite having left the Ukraine at age 10, some sixty-five years earlier, she could read and write the language like a native.

So Leah gathered her Russian speaking friends and they volunteered to 'meet-and-greet' these immigrants upon their arrival at Ben Gurion Airport and help them with their first steps in the country. They guided them through the process at the airport where they were offered the initial help, and were registered, documenting their status and what they needed, and that, in addition to her Civil Defense duty and nightly patrols.

These immigrants came into the country with practically nothing more than the clothes on their backs. Like in previous immigration waves from other countries—the Holocaust survivors in the late 1940s, Yemen and Iraq in 1950, all the other Arab countries during the rest of the 1950s—these people also came carrying very little, with no resources, riches, belongings, or even mundane household goods. All these items were needed by them, and in very short order.

Unlike in the 1950s, Israel did not establish transit settlements, *maabarot*, but tried to immediately house the immigrants in regular rental housing units although those were in woefully short supply. The newcomers were dispersed in the country wherever there were apartments, and, wherever these souls ended up they needed all the things that make a modern life livable. Each immigrant needed a bed, and a mattress, and bedsheets, and pillows and blankets, and pots and pans, and dishes and utensils, and clothes, and everything else you can think of that is used by a family unit.

Somehow these items needed to be found, procured, transported and made available to these immigrants, who on top of all their other difficulties of not speaking the language, not knowing the rules and laws, not ready for the bureaucracy and the navigation within it, and not understanding the democratic culture so alien to people who came from a totalitarian regime, aside from all of those handicaps they had very limited financial resources as well. The Israeli government generously gave these immigrants a stipend, around $800 each to start their lives all over again—a tough row to hoe.

Within a few days of observing the process at the airport, Leah understood that the needed assistance was so much larger and wider than just the meet-and-greet that she and her friends were providing.

Without hesitation she jumped into action. She had an idea that could help these immigrants in more ways than was already provided.

She started collecting household items from her friends, acquaintances, neighbors, anyone whom she came in contact with. Before too long her apartment was full of donated goods. She spread the word among the immigrants and soon her apartment became a place where immigrants could come and rummage through the items offered for a few pennies. She was running out of space, her apartment was becoming unlivable, and she realized that she needed some official support to make her efforts successful at a much larger scale.

One morning in 1991, she walked into the municipality of Ramat Gan. She had previously had some dealings with the city, including the tree incident some seven years earlier, and some of the clerks knew her, and knew she was fierce to deal with, a tough negotiator, a person who did not take "no" for an answer. As soon as she walked in, a few workers "took their morning coffee break" and disappeared from their desks.

This time however, she was not interested in any of them. Her dealings were with a much higher authority.

"Shalom, Edna. Please tell the mayor that I am here to see him," she told the executive secretary.

"Shalom Mrs. Gielan," Edna said. "How are you these days?" Not waiting for an answer continued, "He is in conference all day today and will not be able to see you. His schedule is full."

"Don't brush me off, young lady," Leah said, still in a friendly tone. "I know he is an important man, and thinks of himself even more important than he really is, but just tell him I am here to see him on a matter important to *him*."

"I am sorry, he can't see you today. He has meetings back to back all day."

"That's fine, I have time and I will wait for him. At some point he has to come out of his office."

"He will come out only when it is time to go home at 5 p.m. Is it an urgent matter? Maybe you could come some other day? Let me check his calendar, see when he will be available to see you."

She consulted the calendar on the desk, flipping the pages, one then another. "He has an opening next Thursday at 2:30 in the afternoon."

"I am going to see him today, Edna, not next Thursday or any other day."

"But he is busy all day today."

"Then I will wait for him until he becomes 'unbusy.' At some point he has to go to the bathroom, no?"

Edna looked at Leah with amusement, admiring her determination. This lady surely fit her reputation in the office of not giving up easily. In the past she had negotiated some tough land swap deals with the city and finally got what she wanted. And how about the old tree story? Everybody in the office knew about that tree.

Edna realized this feisty lady well known for her accomplishments in the city was not leaving.

"I am going to sit here quietly and wait for him, even if it takes the whole day," Leah said resolutely. Then she pulled a book from her purse and sat down in the ante room, waiting for him to come out.

It was a different mayor this time she realized, not the ones she had dealt with over the years. But she knew of him, and his reputation as a politician and all the implications of the title. He would certainly be interested in what she has to propose to him, it might improve his political image with the population.

She waited, and waited, and waited some more. At ten minutes past noon his door opened, and out he came.

She rose to her feet and blocked his way.

"Mr. Bar, Zvi, I am Leah Gielan, and you want to hear what I have to say."

He looked her over for a second. She clearly caught him off guard.

"I don't have time," he regained his composure. "I am going out to get a sandwich and then I have a meeting in twenty minutes."

"Then I will walk with you, and we will talk." She was adamant, and her tone was commanding. She was telling him, not asking his permission.

They walked down the stairs of City Hall and onto the street, then made a right turn toward a small food shop at the corner.

"Here it is in a nutshell," Leah said. "I am going to help you become an even more loved and admired mayor than you already are," she said seriously.

She got his attention. "How?"

"I want you to lend me the warehouse you have empty right now on Jabotinsky Street. It belongs to the municipality, so you control it, so there should be no issue in you lending it to me."

"What do you want with a warehouse?"

"The Russians are coming in droves, and they have nothing. I want to have a warehouse where they can come and get whatever they need, things that people will donate, and we will sell for pennies."

"Like what things?"

"Anything that people can donate. Let them empty their attics of the unnecessary stuff. I have two sets of Pesach dishes for eighteen people; I have pots and pans that I will never use; I have clothes of my late husband. Everyone has that kind of stuff. I am sure you do too. Let's donate that to the Russians."

He bought a sandwich and paid for it and they headed back toward City Hall.

"And how are you going to collect the stuff?"

"I have contacts and they have trucks. I have lived in this country since 1924, and I have many friends who can help. Some of my Russian friends from previous immigration waves are willing to come and sort the stuff. In a couple of weeks I collected enough goods in my apartment that I can't move in it, and my son wants to send stuff from the United States. I even arranged tax exemption status from customs for the goods that will be arriving from overseas, and we have planes going to pick up the American soldiers returning from the Gulf War, you know, Kuwait and Iraq. They are flying empty from the United States, large Boeing 747s, and they can bring the goods to the country on the way. All is ready, all thought out, I just need a warehouse. The Zvi Bar Warehouse courtesy of Ramat Gan Mayor Zvi Bar." That last sentence really got his attention.

They passed by Edna at her desk.

"Cancel my next appointment, this is more important," he ordered Edna. "Come in and let's finish the discussion," he said to Leah.

Half an hour later Leah came out of his office. At the door she turned back toward the mayor.

"Oh, and one more thing I want from you, Zvi. I am going to draw a few signs in Russians for the newcomers, telling them that there is help, and giving them my phone number where they can call and get help in whatever matter they need. What I want from you is to post these signs in the right places throughout City Hall. You will be doing a great mitzvah, and get the credit for really supporting the immigrants."

She made the signs, he posted them throughout City Hall, and Leah's phone rang day and night. She helped the immigrants with anything they needed, be it to translate documents, navigate the bureaucracy, obtain official assistance, and anything else they needed her guidance with. And the need was so great that she barely slept for weeks on end.

Over the next several months Leah ran the distribution center from that warehouse in Ramat Gan. She made sure every item was priced at a few pennies—being given things for free is not as respectable to the recipient as buying it, and she was conscientious enough to ensure that the immigrants retained their dignity. And in the corner of the warehouse Leah set up a little office where she, and her other Russian speaking friends, Mira, Shifra, and Riva, and the rest—all who had been in the country for a while and knew the environment—would take turns to help translate documents, explain procedures, provide guidance, negotiate with the bureaucracy, and render whatever other assistance as necessary.

Soon after the first wave of immigrants were settled they were encouraged to come and help their brethren, the next wave of newcomers.

Not many people knew much about Leah and her good deeds and accomplishments—it was not advertised in the media. But everyone knew about the wonderful Mayor Zvi Bar and his generosity toward the Russian immigrants.

And all that while she was still carrying on her duties as a Civil Defense Auxiliary Police.

Chapter 62

On Leah's 86th birthday she received a plaque and commendation from headquarters of the Civil Defense for her fourteen years of unqualified dedication and help to the local police and the country. She hung that plaque next to her Certificate of Appreciation for her Haganah service years earlier.

But age was finally catching up with her. All her friends had left this earth, and except for one nephew, Nahum's son, and one niece, Isaac's daughter from his new family, who came to visit from time to time, by and large she was leading a very lonely existence. She became concerned that if she tripped on an uneven sidewalk when returning alone late at night from duty with Civil Defense she could hurt herself and would have no one to help her or take care of her, so she decided to stop that activity.

The Russian immigration wave subsided, and those who came in the first waves were able to carry on her work and help the new arrivals, so no longer did she need to run the warehouse, or render the other assistance to the newcomers. And when she stopped that activity, she felt she had no further purpose to her life and could not do anything worthwhile for others in the society. Her life of contributing to others was over, and if so why linger around? What good was her life? What was its purpose? Maybe it is time to go?

She stopped taking care of herself, and in a sense was waiting for her end. With her children so far away, she saw no purpose in her continued existence.

Bella received a frantic call from the nephew saying that her mother, that tiny tower of strength was withering away, and would probably not last but a few more weeks, and Bella and Leon would not hear of it. They dropped everything and came to Israel, and within two weeks took Leah and some of her belongings and memorabilia and brought her to the United States to live with them. She tried to resist, object, and argue, but Bella and Leon stood firm, and would not succumb to her protestations. Finally, understanding that she could no longer stay by herself, and Bella would not consider hiring unsupervised help for her, she grudgingly acquiesced.

Over the years, she had spent some time visiting Bella in Santa Cruz, and since Bella and Leon belonged to the Temple there she had made some friends in the community. So she was not a complete stranger, and was very much liked and admired by those who knew her. They would come and take her on outings, and Bella also arranged for her to belong to a group of elderly people who met once or twice a week and sometimes also went on outings. And whenever Ofer could, he made a trip to spend as many days as possible with her as well.

But both Bella and Leon worked full time, and most of the days during the week Leah remained in the big suburban house by herself and was unhappy and lonely. Her eyesight was getting weaker as well, and she was no longer able to read until all hours of the night, or even during the day.

Even having a boyfriend at age 91 was not enough to kindle that light within her, and she was truly withering away. She missed her old apartment in Ramat Gan, the atmosphere of the country, but mostly Sam and her friends who had long passed away.

"I am of no use to anyone. I cannot do anything for anyone else, so why should I hang around?" she said to Bella on many occasions. In consideration to her children and grandchildren all of whom lived in the United States she chose to not be buried next to her Sam in Israel, but rather purchased a plot at the local Jewish cemetery.

She passed away on the 20th of October 2008, *Hoshana Rabbah* by the Jewish calendar, and is interred in the small Jewish cemetery in Santa Cruz California. She was 94 Years old.

The epitaph carved into her tombstone reads:

"Leah Gielan
אשת חיי
Woman of Valor
1914-2008
R.I.P"

❖　❖　❖

Leah and Sam are gone, and so are most of their contemporaries, those who actively pursued the creation of a homeland for the Jews in their ancestral land. They fought so hard, risked so much, sacrificed so much and in the end they prevailed. They established and nurtured the State of Israel.

They themselves are gone, but their legacy continues in that tiny country, a beacon of light and enlightenment for the entire world. That seed of primitive existence in the desolate desert of Eretz Israel years ago has now sprouted to become an advanced and highly developed and modern society, offering a welcoming place for all Jews who wish to return to their roots.

And the others, those who wish to remain within other societies in the Diaspora, they know that they will never again be mistreated with nowhere to turn. No more will they be expelled—like their ancestors were from England, France, Belgium, Austria, Spain, Portugal, Poland, and other places, or exterminated in Europe during the Holocaust—without a homeland waiting to take them in. Just as the Iraqi Jews streamed into Israel in 1950, the Yemeni Jews in 1952, the million or so Jewish refugees from the Arab countries, the Ethiopian Jews in 1984 and 1991, and the large Russian immigration in 1990-1991, all oppressed Jews will now have a place to go.

Thanks to the tremendous spirit and sacrifice of Sam and Leah and countless other ordinary people, the modern state of Israel offers Jews all over the world a homeland, a haven, a safe harbor, and a tremendous measure of pride.

We thank them all.

Gratitude

Leah and Sam never considered their contributions and sacrifices toward the creation of a homeland for the Jews to be anything remarkable deserving commendation or praise. They regarded their efforts as a part of normal life, and rarely, if ever, mentioned the risks they took in any other light than ordinary.

They were not alone, so many other ordinary people have risen to the occasion and performed extraordinary feats with bravery and humility, and some even made the ultimate sacrifice in the process.

This book originated as a project for our family, to document Sam and Leah's actions and achievements for their grandchildren who, because of circumstances, barely knew them and their accomplishments. But as I continued documenting their life's events, the story grew to include others who played a significant role in creating the State of Israel, and the content morphed from being a family oriented project into possibly having a wider audience.

Five people played a critical role in getting this book written and published, and I want to thank them for their participation in this endeavor.

My sister Offra, without whose encouragement and support I would not have had the will, and could not have dedicated the time needed, to research some of the events covered in the book and document others from memory. During many discussions she also contributed a great amount of her own knowledge, filling in the gaps in my recollection of events.

My phenomenal editor, Janis Leibs Dworkis, who tirelessly worked on the manuscript with care and caring, and a lot of heart and understanding. Her direction was irreplaceable, and I was very fortunate to have had her dedication and help. Only after she read the original manuscript did she realize the coincidence—her father, Jerome S. Leibs was the unnamed U.S. Army major mentioned in the book who liberated Dachau concentration camp where Isaac was being held during the Holocaust.

My daughter Michelle, who was the one who recommended Janis as the editor of the book and then proceeded to underwrite the editing and production of a manuscript, making it fit to print. My deepest gratitude to you, Mich. You helped make a dream come true.

My son David, so talented, who designed and created the cover and jacket of the book.

And lastly, my dear late friend Walter J. (Skip) Collins who passed away prematurely. Skip was the first to suggest that the events described in this book may have a wider audience than our family alone. R.I.P dear friend.

I also must recognize my wife Barbara's sacrifice in having me less of a companion to her while sequestering myself in my office during the long hours of writing and re-writing.

I thank them all from the bottom of my heart.

Dan Gielan
Los Angeles, CA.
June, 2018